Reflections from INSPIRED BY TOZER

The first thing by Tozer I ever read was the closing prayer from the first chapter of *The Pursuit of God*. In my memory, it went something like: "God, I have tasted Thee and it has both satisfied me and made me thirsty for more." That changed my life. I've been in pursuit of God ever since.

Britt Merrick
Founding Pastor of the Reality family of churches

What I love most about A. W. Tozer's writing is its heart and authenticity. In a world that celebrates education and ever-growing knowledge, it is refreshing that a man with no more than an elementary education speaks with such wisdom—wisdom that could only be imparted by the Holy Spirit at work in his life. This is why Tozer's writings are so stirring to those who read them.

Scott Smith
Music Director for K-LOVE radio

I never heard Tozer preach. Yet, in a very real sense, this great man of God lives on, influencing my life and many others, for his pen continues to punch holes in our pseudo-sophistication. It prods us awake when we would otherwise nod off into dreamland.

Charles R. Swindoll
Chancellor, Dallas Theological Seminary

If we truly want to reflect the love of God, we must go or destroy mission to uproot every sin, small and great, lurkin We must sniff out every hidden fault and snuff out evei gression that tries to disguise itself as acceptable. I'm seri Reading A. W. Tozer—who wrote prolifically about esche helped me greatly in my understanding of the necessity o lessly with sin.

Joni Eareckson Tada
Founder and CEO of Joni and Friends International Disability Center

As a young man, I had determined to hear as many great preachers of my day as possible. Since these great men knew God, walked with God, and had the influence of God on their ministries, I wanted their God to touch me. That is why I went to hear A. W. Tozer. I wanted to touch God, but more importantly, I wanted God to touch me. To tell you the truth, I don't remember the title of Tozer's message or its content. But I do remember experiencing the presence of God in the building. I remember feeling that Tozer knew God in a way that I didn't. In spite of not remembering what he said, I will forever be glad I braved the wind and rain to hear A. W. Tozer preach that evening. Being in the presence of this godly man strengthened my own longing for God.

Elmer L. Towns
Dean Emeritus of the School of Religion and Theological Seminary at Liberty University

God used A. W. Tozer to turn a directionless, dry Christ-follower into a joy-filled, passionate worshiper, and this is why I am a worship leader to this day! God's anointing in Tozer's writings has played a huge role in giving me this great passion to make people long for God, worship God, and, out of that, serve God!

Tommy Walker
Songwriter and Worship Leader, Christian Assembly, Los Angeles

3-IN-1 EDITION

The ESSENTIAL
Tozer
COLLECTION

THE PURSUIT OF GOD
THE PURPOSE OF MAN
THE CRUCIFIED LIFE

A. W. TOZER

COMPILED AND EDITED BY JAMES L. SNYDER

BETHANYHOUSE

a division of Baker Publishing Group
Minneapolis, Minnesota

Published by Bethany House Publishers
11400 Hampshire Avenue South
Bloomington, Minnesota 55438
www.bethanyhouse.com

Bethany House Publishers is a division of
Baker Publishing Group, Grand Rapids, Michigan

Bethany House 3-in-1 edition published 2017
ISBN 978-0-7642-1891-0

Printed in the United States of America

Library of Congress Control Number: 2016962252

Cover design by Rob Williams, InsideOutCreativeArts

22 23 24 25 26   12 11 10 9 8

THE DEFINITIVE CLASSIC

Edited by James L. Snyder

The Pursuit of
GOD

A.W. TOZER

BETHANYHOUSE

a division of Baker Publishing Group
Minneapolis, Minnesota

Contents

Introduction

I was 15 years old when first introduced to *The Pursuit of God*. A retired missionary in our congregation approached me one Sunday, and I noticed she had a book in hand.

"Young man," she said rather soberly, "here is a book I think you ought to read."

She thrust the book into my hands and disappeared. I looked at the book; it was *The Pursuit of God* by a man I had heard my pastor quote quite often, Dr. A. W. Tozer.

The woman had probably overheard me say I enjoyed reading. What she had *not* heard was that I enjoyed reading novels, not books by preachers. Reading a book by some dead minister was not on my to-do list. I liked preachers, but I just did not think at the time they had much relevance in my life. For the most part, preachers preached over my head. At least, I used that excuse at the time. But I brought the book home and, frankly, forgot about it.

The next Sunday this same missionary was waiting for me as I entered the church.

"Did you read the book? How did you like the book?"

At first I did not know what she was talking about, and then it dawned on me: She had given me a book the previous Sunday. I shook my head and told her I really did not have time to read during the week, what with school and all.

The following Sunday the same scenario took place.

"Did you read the book? How did you like the book?"

My response was the same as the week before. This went on for several weeks until it occurred to me: If I wanted to have to face this retired missionary every Sunday as I walked into the church, I would let things stand as they were and avoid the book. However, if I wanted to get this over with, I needed to at least read the first chapter. I thought that would satisfy her and then I could go on with life.

So I found *The Pursuit of God* and began reading it. That was the end of my life as I knew it. I was amazed by what I read. Up to this point, I had believed that any book written by a preacher would be too theologically sophisticated and full of religious jargon for me to understand. However, much to my delight, Tozer's teaching was simple and clear. Here was a man writing on *my* level, and teaching things about God in such a manner that I understood what he was saying.

The following Sunday, the retired missionary stood waiting at the church door for me. When she saw me, and my smile, she knew. She knew I had read the book, but not only that, the book had read *me*.

I did something then that I do not do as a rule even now: I hugged her and said, "Thanks for the book. I did read it and I do love it." She smiled and told me her prayers had been answered. After that, every time I saw her in church, usually from a distance, she nodded and smiled my way.

Since then I have read *The Pursuit of God* more times than I can remember. The discovery of this book started me on a journey with God I am still pursuing today, and reading works from Tozer became a lifelong habit.

After high school I attended a small Bible institute to train for the ministry; one professor required us to write a biographical essay on an author who had powerfully influenced our lives up to that point. For me there was no question about it: A. W. Tozer.

When I wrote that essay, I discovered that there was very little biographical material written on Tozer. One book, *A. W. Tozer: A Twentieth Century Prophet*, had a biographical profile in the first chapter, and the remainder of the book contained quotes from the ministry and writings of Dr. Tozer.[1] However, no official biography of Tozer existed.

During the course of my pastoral ministry, whenever I met someone who knew anything of Dr. Tozer, I peppered that person with questions. I began taking notes, but not with any idea of writing a biography. After all, I was not a writer at the time, and writing a book is a major undertaking. I just wanted all the material I could find about Dr. Tozer for my own information; and as I began collecting, my file grew delightfully larger.

I also began collecting Tozer's audio sermons. I built an impressive library and listened to these sermons regularly, enjoying them every time.

About this time I met a woman who had devoted her life to collecting the sermons of Tozer. Some of the sermons were on the old reel-to-reel tapes, so together we put them on cassette tapes. Later, of course, they needed to be transferred to a digital format.

Eventually, I had amassed about 600 audio sermons of Dr. Tozer. Rarely a week went by without listening to at least one of these sermons.

It wasn't long before I started thinking about a biography, and I began writing biographical essays. The first magazine to buy an article on A. W. Tozer was the *Fundamentalist Journal*, founded by the late Dr. Jerry Falwell. Several other magazines also bought articles on the life of Tozer. *Alliance Life* magazine published one of my articles, which caught the attention of a publisher.

Soon, the publisher contacted me and said they thought there was a market for an A. W. Tozer biography. This, of course, thrilled me and I began seriously working the material I had collected into a book proposal.

In my research of Dr. Tozer's life, I became acquainted with one of Tozer's friends, Paris Reidhead (1919–1992). I lived about an hour from him and spent quite a bit of time in his study. He became a marvelous and wonderful friend. He even filled my pulpit when I was away. I later learned that he never did this for anybody else.

One day as I was sitting in his study—I am not sure what we were discussing at the time—he paused and I noticed a faraway look in his eye. He stared at me for a long moment. Finally, he said, "Brother, if you really want to understand Tozer and appreciate his passion for God, let me make a suggestion to you. Read the three definitive books of Tozer in the order in which he wrote them."

Of course, he was referring to *The Pursuit of God, The Divine Conquest* (retitled, *The Pursuit of Man*) and *The Knowledge of the Holy*. There are 43 chapters in these three books. I took Reidhead's suggestion seriously and set out to read one chapter per day until I had read all three books in the order in which they were written.

Reidhead cautioned, "Don't read these books like you are reading a novel. Read them slowly, meditatively, and try to enter into the spirit in which these books were written. And, as Tozer did, always seek the face of God as you read."

Reading through these three books was an amazing experience. I had to discipline myself and only read one chapter per day, Monday through Friday. For someone who is a compulsive reader, this was very difficult and yet I managed to do it.

At the end of my reading, I was so encouraged that I decided to read the collection once more. As I began the second reading of these three books, an idea came to me: Why not listen to an audio sermon before I read a chapter? In this way, I believed, I would more fully understand the message Tozer was trying to convey.

I did not know that I was starting a wonderful tradition in my own devotional life. The second time of reading through the three books and listening to the messages of A. W. Tozer, I began to understand him, as Reidhead predicted, and to appreciate the direction in which these books were going.

Since that time, I have made reading and listening to Tozer a spiritual discipline in my own life. Occasionally I will take a week or a month off but soon I am anxious to return to my in-depth study of Tozer's work. In reading these books, I have found that, no matter where I am in my Christian development, there is always something appropriate and nourishing within their pages for my inner life.

In the introduction of *The Pursuit of God*, Tozer writes, "This book is a modest attempt to aid God's hungry children so to find him." This, I believe, is the beginning of our journey as a believer. In *The Divine Conquest*, Dr. Tozer says, "I expect to show that if we would know the power of the Christian message our nature must be invaded by an Object from beyond it; that That which is external must become internal; that the objective Reality which is God must cross the threshold of our personality and take residence within."[2]

In the third book in this devotional trilogy, *The Knowledge of the Holy*, Tozer explains, "It is my hope that this small book may contribute somewhat to the promotion of personal heart religion among us; and should a few persons by reading it be encouraged to begin the practice of reverent meditation on the being of God, that will more than repay the labor required to use it."[3]

How to Read the Pursuit of God

Tozer was an enthusiastic admirer of Francois de Salignac de la Mothe-Fénelon, the seventeenth-century French saint whose eloquent sermons contributed greatly to the spiritual education of his contemporaries and whose generosity did much to mitigate the sufferings caused by the War of the Spanish Succession. Fénelon was a man who knew God, who lived in Him as a bird lives in the air. Providentially, he was endowed with the ability to lead others into the same kind of life. In Fénelon, there was no trace of the morbidity that has marked some of the men and women who have been known as mystics.

When Harper & Row republished Fénelon's *Christian Counsel* under the title *Christian Perfection*, Tozer was delighted. He wrote an article on the subject, urging *Alliance Witness* readers to secure a copy. "Come [to the book]," he said, "with a spirit of longing. Without strong desire, nothing will do you much good. Be determined to know God. Read only after prayer and meditation on the Word itself. The heart must be readied for this book, otherwise it will be like any other and have little effect.

"Come in an attitude of devotion, in silence and humble expectation. If possible, get alone to read it. The presence of even the dearest friend often distracts the heart and prevents complete concentration. Get surrendering and consecrating done before coming to Fénelon; he begins where others leave off. Be in earnest. Fénelon assumes the seriousness of his readers. If anyone should be infected with the strange notion that religion should afford amusement as well as salvation, let him or her pass Fénelon by.

"This book is for the person who thirsts after God . . . Never read more than one chapter a day. It would be a mistake to hurry through the book. It is to be studied, meditated on, marked, prayed over and returned to as often and as long as it continues to minister to the soul."[4]

Tozer's admonition about reading Fénelon can easily be transferred to *The Pursuit of God*. Taking Tozer's advice will go far in meditating upon this book at hand.

A Spiritual Mentor

In the stormy world of Christianity in which we live today, Tozer stands out as a reliable, faithful spiritual mentor. Such mentors are drastically needed yet rarely found.

Tozer once said, "Never honor a man until after he is dead. The last year of his life he may do things that will completely destroy any good he has done up to that point." Of course, he was saying this with tongue-in-cheek humor. But there is a point to it. If a small percentage of that is true, then I suggest Tozer qualifies as an able and valuable spiritual mentor to be respected.

Fifty years ago this year, A. W. Tozer went home to be with the Lord. Although the messenger is gone, the message still rings loud and true. One of the amazing things about working with this Tozer material is just how relevant he is today. At times I have to stop and remind myself that the sermon based on this book was preached in the 1950s. How did Tozer know what it was going to be like 50 years after his death?

Every once in a while somebody will ask me, "What would Tozer say if he were alive today?" My answer is simple: Tozer would say today the same things he said all through his ministry. He did not dabble in the passing trends but instead dealt with the eternal realities of God's truth—and that never changes.

In many ways, the Church today is as dysfunctional as Tozer predicted it would be. And the solution is the same as it was 50 years ago, 100 years ago, 1,000 years ago, all the way back to the early Church.

The solution for today's Church is simply Jesus Christ. To know Him in the fullness of His glory was the great passion of A. W. Tozer. If we are going to overcome the problems we are facing today, it will be because we have entered into the glory of Jesus and the essence of His power through the Holy Spirit.

My prayer for this definitive classic edition of *The Pursuit of God* is that a new generation will discover its message and see it ignite their passion for God.

James L. Snyder

Notes

1. David J. Fant, Jr., *A. W. Tozer: A Twentieth Century Prophet* (Harrisburg, PA: Christian Publications, Inc., 1964).
2. A. W. Tozer, *Divine Conquest* (Harrisburg, PA: Christian Publications, Inc., 1950).
3. A. W. Tozer, *Knowledge of the Holy* (New York, NY: Harper & Row, 1961).
4. James L. Snyder, *The Life of A. W. Tozer: In Pursuit of God* (Ventura, CA: Regal Books, 2009), pp. 155-156.

Preface

In this hour of all-but-universal darkness one cheering gleam appears: within the fold of conservative Christianity there are to be found increasing numbers of persons whose religious lives are marked by a growing hunger after God Himself. They are eager for spiritual realities and will not be put off with words, nor will they be content with correct "interpretations" of truth. They are athirst for God, and they will not be satisfied till they have drunk deep at the Fountain of Living Water.

This is the only real harbinger of revival which I have been able to detect anywhere on the religious horizon. It may be the cloud the size of a man's hand for which a few saints here and there have been looking. It can result in a resurrection of life for many souls and a recapture of that radiant wonder which should accompany faith in Christ, that wonder which has all but fled the Church of God in our day.

But this hunger must be recognized by our religious leaders. Current evangelicalism has (to change the figure) laid the altar and divided the sacrifice into parts, but now seems satisfied to count the stones and rearrange the pieces with never a care that there is not a sign of fire upon the top of lofty Carmel. But God be thanked that there are a few who care. They are those who, while they love the altar and delight in the sacrifice, are yet unable to reconcile themselves to the continued absence of fire. They desire God above all. They are athirst to taste for themselves the "piercing sweetness" of the love of Christ about Whom all the holy prophets did write and the psalmists did sing.

There is today no lack of Bible teachers to set forth correctly the principles of the doctrines of Christ, but too many of these seem satisfied to teach the fundamentals of the faith year after year, strangely unaware that there is in their ministry no manifest Presence, nor anything unusual in their personal lives. They minister constantly to believers who feel within their breasts a longing which their teaching simply does not satisfy.

I trust I speak in charity, but the lack in our pulpits is real. Milton's terrible sentence applies to our day as accurately as it did to his: "The hungry sheep look up, and are not fed." It is a solemn thing, and no small scandal in the Kingdom, to see God's children starving while actually seated at the Father's table. The truth of Wesley's words is established before our eyes: "Orthodoxy, or right opinion, is, at best, a very slender part of religion. Though right tempers cannot subsist without right opinions, yet right opinions may subsist without right tempers. There may be a right opinion of God without either love or one right temper toward Him. Satan is a proof of this."

Thanks to our splendid Bible societies and to other effective agencies for the dissemination of the Word, there are today many millions of people who hold "right opinions," probably more than ever before in the history of the Church. Yet I wonder if there was ever a time when true spiritual worship was at a lower ebb. To great sections of the Church the art of worship has been lost entirely, and in its place has come that strange and foreign thing called the "program." This word has been borrowed from the stage and applied with sad wisdom to the type of public service which now passes for worship among us.

Sound Bible exposition is an imperative must in the Church of the Living God. Without it no church can be a New Testament church in any strict meaning of that term. But exposition may be carried on in such a way as to leave the hearers devoid of any true spiritual nourishment whatever. For it is not mere words that nourish the soul, but God Himself, and unless and until the hearers find God in personal experience they are not the better for having heard the truth. The Bible is not an end in itself, but a means to bring men to an intimate and satisfying knowledge of God, that they may enter into Him, that they may delight in His Presence, may taste and know the inner sweetness of the very God Himself in the core and center of their hearts.

This book is a modest attempt to aid God's hungry children so to find Him. Nothing here is new except in the sense that it is a discovery which my own heart has made of spiritual realities most delightful and wonderful to me. Others before me have gone much farther into these holy mysteries than I have done, but if my fire is not large it is yet real, and there may be those who can light their candle at its flame.

A. W. Tozer
Chicago, Illinois June 16, 1948

1

Following Hard
After God

My soul followeth hard after thee:
thy right hand upholdeth me.
PSALM 63:8

Christian theology teaches the doctrine of prevenient grace, which briefly stated means this: that before a man can seek God, God must first have sought the man.

Before a sinful man can think a right thought of God, there must have been a work of enlightenment done within him; imperfect it may be, but a true work nonetheless, and the secret cause of all desiring and seeking and praying which may follow.

We pursue God because, and only because, He has first put an urge within us that spurs us to the pursuit. "No man can come to me," said our Lord, "except the Father which hath sent me draw him," and it is by this very prevenient drawing that God takes from us every vestige of credit for the act of coming. The impulse to pursue God originates with God, but the outworking of that impulse is our following hard after Him; and all the time we are pursuing Him we are already in His hand: "Thy right hand upholdeth me."

In this divine "upholding" and human "following" there is no contradiction. All is of God, for as von Hügel teaches, God is always previous. In practice, however, (that is, where God's previous working meets man's present response) man must pursue God. On our part there must be positive reciprocation if this secret drawing of God is to eventuate in identifiable experience of the Divine. In the warm language of personal feeling this is stated in the forty-second psalm: "As the hart panteth after the water brooks, so panteth my soul after thee, O God. My soul thirsteth for God, for the living God: when shall I come and appear before God?" This is deep calling unto deep, and the longing heart will understand it.

The doctrine of justification by faith—a biblical truth, and a blessed relief from sterile legalism and unavailing self-effort—has in our time fallen into evil company and been interpreted by many in such manner as actually to bar men from the knowledge of God. The whole transaction of religious conversion has been made mechanical and spiritless. Faith may now be exercised without a jar to the moral life and without embarrassment to the Adamic ego. Christ may be "received" without creating any special love for Him in the soul of the receiver. The man is "saved," but he is not hungry nor thirsty after God. In fact he is specifically taught to be satisfied and encouraged to be content with little.

The modern scientist has lost God amid the wonders of His world; we Christians are in real danger of losing God amid the wonders of His Word. We have almost forgotten that God is a Person and, as such, can be cultivated as any person can. It is inherent in personality to be able to know other personalities, but full knowledge of one personality by another cannot be achieved in one encounter. It is only after long and loving mental intercourse that the full possibilities of both can be explored.

All social intercourse between human beings is a response of personality to personality, grading upward from the most casual brush between man and man to the fullest, most intimate communion of which the human soul is capable. Religion, so far as it is genuine, is in essence the response of created personalities to the Creating Personality, God. "This is life eternal, that they might know thee the only true God, and Jesus Christ, whom thou hast sent."

God is a Person, and in the deep of His mighty nature He thinks, wills, enjoys, feels, loves, desires and suffers as any other person may. In making Himself known to us He stays by the familiar pattern of personality. He communicates with us through the avenues of our minds, our wills and our emotions. The continuous and unembarrassed interchange of love and thought between God and the soul of the redeemed man is the throbbing heart of New Testament religion.

This intercourse between God and the soul is known to us in conscious personal awareness. It is personal: that is, it does not come through the body of believers, as such, but is known to the individual, and to the body through the individuals which compose it. And it is conscious: that is, it does not stay below the threshold of consciousness and work there unknown to the soul (as, for instance, infant baptism is thought by some to do), but comes within the field of awareness where the man can "know" it as he knows any other fact of experience.

You and I are in little (our sins excepted) what God is in large. Being made in His image we have within us the capacity to know Him. In our sins we lack only the power. The moment the Spirit has quickened us to life in regeneration our whole being senses its kinship to God and leaps up in joyous recognition. That is the heavenly birth without which we cannot see the Kingdom of God. It is, however, not an end but an inception, for now begins the glorious pursuit, the heart's happy exploration of the infinite riches of the Godhead. That is where we begin, I say, but where we stop no man has yet discovered, for there is in the awful and mysterious depths of the triune God neither limit nor end.

Shoreless Ocean, who can sound Thee?
Thine own eternity is round Thee,
Majesty divine!

To have found God and still to pursue Him is the soul's paradox of love, scorned indeed by the too-easily-satisfied religionist, but justified in happy experience by the children of the burning heart. St. Bernard stated this holy paradox in a musical quatrain that will be instantly understood by every worshipping soul:

We taste Thee, O Thou Living Bread,
And long to feast upon Thee still:
We drink of Thee, the Fountainhead
And thirst our souls from Thee to fill.

Come near to the holy men and women of the past and you will soon feel the heat of their desire after God. They mourned for Him, they prayed and wrestled and sought for Him day and night, in season and out, and when they had found Him the finding was all the sweeter for the long seeking. Moses used the fact that he knew God as an argument for knowing Him better. "Now, therefore, I pray thee, if I have found grace in thy sight, show me now thy way, that I may know thee, that I may find grace in thy sight"; and from there he rose to make the daring request, "I beseech thee, show me thy glory." God was frankly pleased by this display of ardor, and the next day called Moses into the mount, and there in solemn procession made all His glory pass before him.

David's life was a torrent of spiritual desire, and his psalms ring with the cry of the seeker and the glad shout of the finder. Paul confessed the mainspring of his life to be his burning desire after Christ. "That I may know Him" was the goal of his heart, and to this he sacrificed everything. "Yea doubtless, and I count all things but loss for the excellency of the knowledge of Christ Jesus my Lord: for whom I have suffered the loss of all things, and do count them but refuse, that I may win Christ."

Hymnody is sweet with the longing after God, the God whom, while the singer seeks, he knows he has already found. "His track I see and I'll pursue," sang our fathers only a short generation ago, but that song is heard no more in the great congregation. How tragic that we in this dark day have had our seeking done for us by our teachers. Everything is made to center upon the initial act of "accepting" Christ (a term, incidentally, which is not found in the Bible) and we are not expected thereafter to crave any further revelation of God to our souls. We have been snared in the coils of a spurious logic which insists that if we have found Him we need no more seek Him. This is set before us as the last word in orthodoxy, and it is taken for granted that no Bible-taught Christian ever believed otherwise. Thus the whole testimony of the worshipping, seeking, singing Church on that subject is crisply set aside. The experiential heart-theology of a grand army of fragrant saints is rejected in favor of a smug interpretation of Scripture which would certainly have sounded strange to an Augustine, a Rutherford or a Brainerd.

In the midst of this great chill there are some, I rejoice to acknowledge, who will not be content with shallow logic. They will admit the force of the argument, and then turn away with tears to hunt some lonely place and pray, "O God, show me thy glory." They want to taste, to touch with their hearts, to see with their inner eyes the wonder that is God.

I want deliberately to encourage this mighty longing after God. The lack of it has brought us to our present low estate. The stiff and wooden quality about our religious lives is a result of our lack of holy desire. Complacency is a deadly foe of all spiritual growth. Acute desire must be present or there will be no manifestation of Christ to His people. He waits to be wanted. Too bad that with many of us He waits so long, so very long, in vain.

Every age has its own characteristics. Right now we are in an age of religious complexity. The simplicity which is in Christ is rarely found among us. In its stead are programs, methods, organizations and a world of nervous activities which occupy time and attention but can never satisfy the longing of the heart. The shallowness of our inner experience, the hollowness of our worship, and that servile imitation of the world which marks our promotional methods all testify that we, in this day, know God only imperfectly, and the peace of God scarcely at all.

If we would find God amid all the religious externals we must first determine to find Him, and then proceed in the way of simplicity. Now as always God discovers Himself to "babes" and hides Himself in thick darkness from the wise and the prudent. We must simplify our approach to Him. We must strip down to essentials (and they will be found to be blessedly few). We must put away all effort to impress, and come with the guileless candor of childhood. If we do this, without doubt God will quickly respond.

When religion has said its last word, there is little that we need other than God Himself. The evil habit of seeking God-and effectively prevents us from finding God in full revelation. In the "and" lies our great woe. If we omit the "and" we shall soon find God, and in Him we shall find that for which we have all our lives been secretly longing.

We need not fear that in seeking God only we may narrow our lives or restrict the motions of our expanding hearts. The opposite is true. We can well afford to make God our All, to concentrate, to sacrifice the many for the One.

The author of the quaint old English classic, *The Cloud of Unknowing*, teaches us how to do this. "Lift up thine heart unto God with a meek stirring of love; and mean Himself, and none of His goods. And thereto, look thee loath to think on aught but God Himself. So that nought work in thy wit, nor in thy will, but only God Himself. This is the work of the soul that most pleaseth God."

Again, he recommends that in prayer we practice a further stripping down of everything, even of our theology. "For it sufficeth enough, a naked intent direct unto God without any other cause than Himself." Yet underneath all his thinking lay the broad foundation of New Testament truth, for he explains that by "Himself" he means "God that made thee, and bought thee, and that graciously called thee to thy degree." And he is all for simplicity: If we would have religion "lapped and folden in one word, for that thou shouldst have better hold thereupon, take thee but a little word of one syllable: for so it is better than of two, for even the shorter it is the better it accordeth with the work of the Spirit. And such a word is this word GOD or this word LOVE."

When the Lord divided Canaan among the tribes of Israel, Levi received no share of the land. God said to him simply, "I am thy part and thine inheritance," and by those words made him richer than all his brethren, richer than all the kings and rajas who have ever lived in the world. And there is a spiritual principle here, a principle still valid for every priest of the Most High God.

The man who has God for his treasure has all things in One. Many ordinary treasures may be denied him, or if he is allowed to have them, the enjoyment of them will be so tempered that they will never be necessary to his happiness. Or if he must see them go, one after one, he will scarcely feel a sense of loss, for having the Source of all things he has in One all satisfaction, all pleasure, all delight. Whatever he may lose he has actually lost nothing, for he now has it all in One, and he has it purely, legitimately and forever.

O God, I have tasted Thy goodness, and it has both satisfied me and made me thirsty for more. I am painfully conscious of my need of further grace. I am ashamed of my lack of desire. O God, the Triune God, I want to want Thee; I long to be filled with longing; I thirst to be made more thirsty still. Show me Thy glory, I pray Thee, that so I may know Thee indeed. Begin in mercy a new work of love within me. Say to my soul, "Rise up, my love, my fair one, and come away." Then give me grace to rise and follow Thee up from this misty lowland where I have wandered so long. In Jesus' Name, Amen.

2

The Blessedness of Possessing Nothing

Blessed are the poor in spirit:
for theirs is the kingdom of heaven.
MATTHEW 5:3

Before the Lord God made man upon the earth He first prepared for him by creating a world of useful and pleasant things for his sustenance and delight. In the Genesis account of the creation these are called simply "things." They were made for man's uses, but they were meant always to be external to the man and subservient to him. In the deep heart of the man was a shrine where none but God was worthy to come. Within him was God; without, a thousand gifts which God had showered upon him.

But sin has introduced complications and has made those very gifts of God a potential source of ruin to the soul.

Our woes began when God was forced out of His central shrine and "things" were allowed to enter. Within the human heart "things" have taken over. Men have now by nature no peace within their hearts, for God is crowned there no longer, but there in the moral dusk stubborn and aggressive usurpers fight among themselves for first place on the throne.

This is not a mere metaphor, but an accurate analysis of our real spiritual trouble. There is within the human heart a tough fibrous root of fallen life whose nature is to possess, always to possess. It covets "things" with a deep and fierce passion. The pronouns "my" and "mine" look innocent enough in print, but their constant and universal use is significant. They express the real nature of the old Adamic man better than a thousand volumes of theology could do. They are verbal symptoms of our deep disease. The roots of our hearts have grown down into things, and we dare not pull up one rootlet lest we die. Things have become necessary to us, a development never originally intended. God's gifts now take the place of God, and the whole course of nature is upset by the monstrous substitution.

Our Lord referred to this tyranny of things when He said to His disciples, "If any man will come after me, let him deny himself, and take up his cross, and follow me. For whosoever will save his life shall lose it: and whosoever shall lose his life for my sake shall find it."

Breaking this truth into fragments for our better understanding, it would seem that there is within each of us an enemy which we tolerate at our peril. Jesus called it "life" and "self," or as we would say, the self-life. Its chief characteristic is its possessiveness: the words "gain" and "profit" suggest this. To allow this enemy to live is in the end to lose everything. To repudiate it and give up all for Christ's sake is to lose nothing at last, but to preserve everything unto life eternal. And possibly also a hint is given here as to the only effective way to destroy this foe: it is by the Cross. "Let him take up his cross and follow me."

The way to deeper knowledge of God is through the lonely valleys of soul poverty and abnegation of all things. The blessed ones who possess the Kingdom are they who have repudiated every external thing and have rooted from their hearts all sense of possessing. These are the "poor in spirit." They have reached an inward state paralleling the outward circumstances of the common beggar in the streets of Jerusalem; that is what the word "poor" as Christ used it actually means. These blessed poor are no longer slaves to the tyranny of things. They have broken the yoke of the oppressor; and this they have done not by fighting but by surrendering. Though free from all sense of possessing, they yet possess all things. "Theirs is the kingdom of heaven."

Let me exhort you to take this seriously. It is not to be understood as mere Bible teaching to be stored away in the mind along with an inert mass of other doctrines. It is a marker on the road to greener pastures, a path chiseled against the steep sides of the mount of God. We dare not try to by-pass it if we would follow on in this holy pursuit. We must ascend a step at a time. If we refuse one step we bring our progress to an end.

As is frequently true, this New Testament principle of spiritual life finds its best illustration in the Old Testament. In the story of Abraham and Isaac we have a dramatic picture of the surrendered life as well as an excellent commentary on the first Beatitude.

Abraham was old when Isaac was born, old enough indeed to have been his grandfather, and the child became at once the delight and idol of his heart. From that moment when he first stooped to take the tiny form awkwardly in his arms he was an eager love slave of his son. God went out of His way to comment on the strength of this affection. And it is not hard to understand. The baby represented everything sacred to his father's heart: the promises of God, the covenants, the hopes of the years and the long messianic dream. As he watched him grow from babyhood to young manhood the heart of the old man was knit closer and closer with the life of his son, till at last the relationship bordered upon the perilous. It was then that God stepped in to save both father and son from the consequences of an uncleansed love.

"Take now thy son," said God to Abraham, "thine only son Isaac, whom thou lovest, and get thee into the land of Moriah; and offer him there for a burnt-offering upon one of the mountains which I will tell thee of." The sacred writer spares us a close-up of the agony that night on the slopes near Beersheba when the aged man had it out with his God, but respectful imagination may view in awe the bent form and convulsive wrestling alone under the stars. Possibly not again until a Greater than Abraham wrestled in the Garden of Gethsemane did such mortal pain visit a human soul. If only the man himself might have been allowed to die. That would have been easier a thousand times, for he was old now, and to die would have been no great ordeal for one who had walked so long with God. Besides, it would have been a last sweet pleasure to let his dimming vision rest upon the figure of his stalwart son who would live to carry on the Abrahamic line and fulfill in himself the promises of God made long before in Ur of the Chaldees.

How should he slay the lad! Even if he could get the consent of his wounded and protesting heart, how could he reconcile the act with the promise, "In Isaac shall thy seed be called"? This was Abraham's trial by fire, and he did not fail in the crucible. While the stars still shone like sharp white points above the tent where the sleeping Isaac lay, and long before the gray dawn had begun to lighten the east, the old saint had made up his mind. He would offer his son as God had directed him to do, and then trust God to raise him from the dead. This, says the writer to the Hebrews, was the solution his aching heart found sometime in the dark night, and he rose "early in the morning" to carry out the plan. It is beautiful to see that, while he erred as to God's method, he had correctly sensed the secret of His great heart. And the solution accords well with the New Testament Scripture, "Whosoever will lose for my sake shall find."

God let the suffering old man go through with it up to the point where He knew there would be no retreat, and then forbade him to lay a hand upon the boy. To the wondering patriarch He now says in effect, "It's all right, Abraham. I never intended that you should actually slay the lad. I only wanted to remove him from the temple of your heart that I might reign unchallenged there. I wanted to correct the perversion that existed in your love. Now you may have the boy, sound and well. Take him and go back to your tent. Now I know that thou fearest God, seeing that thou hast not withheld thy son, thine only son, from me."

Then heaven opened and a voice was heard saying to him, "By myself have I sworn, saith the Lord, for because thou hast done this thing, and hast not withheld thy son, thine only son: that in blessing I will bless thee, and in multiplying I will multiply thy seed as the stars of the heaven, and as the sand which is upon the sea shore; and thy seed shall possess the gate of his enemies; and in thy seed shall all the nations of the earth be blessed; because thou hast obeyed my voice."

The old man of God lifted his head to respond to the Voice, and stood there on the mount strong and pure and grand, a man marked out by the Lord for special treatment, a friend and favorite of the Most High. Now he was a man wholly surrendered, a man utterly obedient, a man who possessed nothing. He had concentrated his all in the person of his dear son, and God had taken it from him. God could have begun out on the margin of Abraham's life and worked inward to the center; He chose rather to cut quickly to the heart and have it over in one sharp act of separation. In dealing thus He practiced an economy of means and time. It hurt cruelly, but it was effective.

I have said that Abraham possessed nothing. Yet was not this poor man rich? Everything he had owned before was his still to enjoy: sheep, camels, herds, and goods of every sort. He had also his wife and his friends, and best of all he had his son Isaac safe by his side. He had everything, but he possessed nothing. There is the spiritual secret. There is the sweet theology of the heart which can be learned only in the school of renunciation. The books on systematic theology overlook this, but the wise will understand.

After that bitter and blessed experience I think the words "my" and "mine" never had again the same meaning for Abraham. The sense of possession which they connote was gone from his heart. Things had been cast out forever. They had now become external to the man. His inner heart was free from them. The world said, "Abraham is rich," but the aged patriarch only smiled. He could not explain it to them, but he knew that he owned nothing, that his real treasures were inward and eternal.

There can be no doubt that this possessive clinging to things is one of the most harmful habits in the life. Because it is so natural, it is rarely recognized for the evil that it is; but its outworkings are tragic.

We are often hindered from giving up our treasures to the Lord out of fear for their safety; this is especially true when those treasures are loved relatives and friends. But we need have no such fears. Our Lord came not to destroy but to save. Everything is safe which we commit to Him, and nothing is really safe which is not so committed.

Our gifts and talents should also be turned over to Him. They should be recognized for what they are, God's loan to us, and should never be considered in any sense our own. We have no more right to claim credit for special abilities than for blue eyes or strong muscles. "For who maketh thee to differ from another? and what hast thou that thou didst not receive?"

The Christian who is alive enough to know himself even slightly will recognize the symptoms of this possession malady, and will grieve to find them in his own heart. If the longing after God is strong enough within him, he will want to do something about the matter. Now, what should he do?

First of all he should put away all defense and make no attempt to excuse himself either in his own eyes or before the Lord. Whoever defends himself will have himself for his defense, and he will have no other; but let him come defenseless before the Lord and he will have for his defender no less than God Himself. Let the inquiring Christian trample under foot every slippery trick of his deceitful heart and insist upon frank and open relations with the Lord.

Then he should remember that this is holy business. No careless or casual dealings will suffice. Let him come to God in full determination to be heard. Let him insist that God accept his all, that He take things out of his heart and Himself reign there in power. It may be he will need to become specific, to name things and people by their names one by one. If he will become drastic enough he can shorten the time of his travail from years to minutes and enter the good land long before his slower brethren who coddle their feelings and insist upon caution in their dealings with God.

Let us never forget that such a truth as this cannot be learned by rote as one would learn the facts of physical science. They must be experienced before we can really know them. We must in our hearts live through Abraham's harsh and bitter experiences if we would know the blessedness which follows them. The ancient curse will not go out painlessly; the tough old miser within us will not lie down and die obedient to our command. He must be torn out of our heart like a plant from the soil; he must be extracted in agony and blood like a tooth from the jaw. He must be expelled from our soul by violence as Christ expelled the money changers from the temple. And we shall need to steel ourselves against his piteous begging, and to recognize it as springing out of self-pity, one of the most reprehensible sins of the human heart.

If we would indeed know God in growing intimacy, we must go this way of renunciation. And if we are set upon the pursuit of God, He will sooner or later bring us to this test. Abraham's testing was, at the time, not known to him as such, yet if he had taken some course other than the one he did, the whole history of the Old Testament would have been different. God would have found His man, no doubt, but the loss to Abraham would have been tragic beyond the telling. So we will be brought one by one to the testing place, and we may never know when we are there. At that testing place there will be no dozen possible choices for us; just one and an alternative, but our whole future will be conditioned by the choice we make.

Father, I want to know Thee, but my coward heart fears to give up its toys. I cannot part with them without inward bleeding, and I do not try to hide from Thee the terror of the parting. I come trembling, but I do come. Please root from my heart all those things which I have cherished so long and which have become a very part of my living self, so that Thou mayest enter and dwell there without a rival. Then shalt Thou make the place of Thy feet glorious. Then shall my heart have no need of the sun to shine in it, for Thyself wilt be the light of it, and there shall be no night there.

In Jesus' Name, Amen.

3

Removing the Veil

*Having therefore, brethren, boldness to enter
into the holiest by the blood of Jesus.*
HEBREWS 10:19

Among the famous sayings of the Church fathers none is better known than Augustine's, "Thou hast formed us for Thyself, and our hearts are restless till they find rest in Thee."

The great saint states here in few words the origin and interior history of the human race. God made us for Himself: that is the only explanation that satisfies the heart of a thinking man, whatever his wild reason may say. Should faulty education and perverse reasoning lead a man to conclude otherwise, there is little that any Christian can do for him. For such a man I have no message. My appeal is addressed to those who have been previously taught in secret by the wisdom of God; I speak to thirsty hearts whose longings have been wakened by the touch of God within them, and such as they need no reasoned proof. Their restless hearts furnish all the proof they need.

God formed us for Himself. The shorter catechism, "Agreed upon by the Reverend Assembly of Divines at Westminster," as the old New England Primer has it, asks the ancient questions what and why and answers them in one short sentence hardly matched in any uninspired work. "Question: What is the chief End of Man? Answer: Man's chief End is to glorify God and enjoy Him forever." With this agree the four and twenty elders who fall on their faces to worship Him that liveth for ever and ever, saying, "Thou art worthy, O Lord, to receive glory and honour and power: for thou hast created all things, and for thy pleasure they are and were created."

God formed us for His pleasure, and so formed us that we as well as He can in divine communion enjoy the sweet and mysterious mingling of kindred personalities. He meant us to see Him and live with Him and draw our life from His smile. But we have been guilty of that "foul revolt" of which Milton speaks when describing the rebellion of Satan and his hosts. We have broken with God. We have ceased to obey Him or love Him and in guilt and fear have fled as far as possible from His Presence.

Yet who can flee from His Presence when the heaven and the heaven of heavens cannot contain Him? when as the wisdom of Solomon testifies, "the Spirit of the Lord filleth the world"? The omnipresence of the Lord is one thing, and is a solemn fact necessary to His perfection; the manifest Presence is another thing altogether, and from that Presence we have fled, like Adam, to hide among the trees of the garden, or like Peter to shrink away, crying, "Depart from me, for I am a sinful man, O Lord."

So the life of man upon the earth is a life away from the Presence, wrenched loose from that "blissful center" which is our right and proper dwelling place, our first estate which we kept not, the loss of which is the cause of our unceasing restlessness.

The whole work of God in redemption is to undo the tragic effects of that foul revolt, and to bring us back again into right and eternal relationship with Himself. This required that our sins be disposed of satisfactorily, that a full reconciliation be effected and the way opened for us to return again into conscious communion with God and to live again in the Presence as before. Then by His prevenient working within us He moves us to return. This first comes to our notice when our restless hearts feel a yearning for the Presence of God and we say within ourselves, "I will arise and go to my Father." That is the first step, and as the Chinese sage Lao-tze has said, "The journey of a thousand miles begins with a first step."

The interior journey of the soul from the wilds of sin into the enjoyed Presence of God is beautifully illustrated in the Old Testament tabernacle. The returning sinner first entered the outer court where he offered a blood sacrifice on the brazen altar and washed himself in the laver that stood near it. Then through a veil he passed into the holy place where no natural light could come, but the golden candlestick which spoke of Jesus the Light of the World threw its soft glow over all. There also was the shewbread to tell of Jesus, the Bread of Life, and the altar of incense, a figure of unceasing prayer.

Though the worshipper had enjoyed so much, still he had not yet entered the Presence of God. Another veil separated from the Holy of Holies where above the mercy seat dwelt the very God Himself in awful and glorious manifestation. While the tabernacle stood, only the high priest could enter there, and that but once a year, with blood which he offered for his sins and the sins of the people. It was this last veil which was rent when our Lord gave up the ghost on Calvary, and the sacred writer explains that this rending of the veil opened the way for every worshipper in the world to come by the new and living way straight into the divine Presence.

Everything in the New Testament accords with this Old Testament picture. Ransomed men need no longer pause in fear to enter the Holy of Holies. God wills that we should push on into His Presence and live our whole life there. This is to be known to us in conscious experience. It is more than a doctrine to be held; it is a life to be enjoyed every moment of every day.

This Flame of the Presence was the beating heart of the Levitical order. Without it all the appointments of the tabernacle were characters of some unknown language; they had no meaning for Israel or for us. The greatest fact of the tabernacle was that Jehovah was there; a Presence was waiting within the veil. Similarly the Presence of God is the central fact of Christianity. At the heart of the Christian message is God Himself waiting for His redeemed children to push in to conscious awareness of His Presence. That type of Christianity which happens now to be the vogue knows this Presence only in theory. It fails to stress the Christian's privilege of present realization. According to its teachings we are in the Presence of God positionally, and nothing is said about the need to experience that Presence actually. The fiery urge that drove men like McCheyne is wholly missing. And the present generation of Christians measures itself by this imperfect rule. Ignoble contentment takes the place of burning zeal. We are satisfied to rest in our judicial possessions and for the most part we bother ourselves very little about the absence of personal experience.

Who is this within the veil who dwells in fiery manifestations? It is none other than God Himself, "One God the Father Almighty, Maker of heaven and earth, and of all things visible and invisible," and "One Lord Jesus Christ, the only begotten Son of God; begotten of His Father before all worlds, God of God, Light of Light, Very God of Very God; begotten, not made; being of one substance with the Father," and "the Holy Ghost, the Lord and Giver of life, Who proceedeth from the Father and the Son, Who with the Father and the Son together is worshipped and glorified." Yet this holy Trinity is One God, for "we worship one God in Trinity, and Trinity in Unity; neither confounding the Persons, nor dividing the Substance. For there is one Person of the Father, another of the Son, and another of the Holy Ghost. But the Godhead of the Father, of the Son, and of the Holy Ghost, is all one: the glory equal and the majesty co-eternal." So in part run the ancient creeds, and so the inspired Word declares.

Behind the veil is God, that God after Whom the world, with strange inconsistency, has felt, "if haply they might find Him." He has discovered Himself to some extent in nature, but more perfectly in the Incarnation; now He waits to show Himself in ravishing fullness to the humble of soul and the pure in heart.

The world is perishing for lack of the knowledge of God and the Church is famishing for want of His Presence. The instant cure of most of our religious ills would be to enter the Presence in spiritual experience, to become suddenly aware that we are in God and that God is in us. This would lift us out of our pitiful narrowness and cause our hearts to be enlarged. This would burn away the impurities from our lives as the bugs and fungi were burned away by the fire that dwelt in the bush.

What a broad world to roam in, what a sea to swim in is this God and Father of our Lord Jesus Christ. He is eternal, which means that He antedates time and is wholly independent of it. Time began in Him and will end in Him. To it He pays no tribute and from it He suffers no change. He is immutable, which means that He has never changed and can never change in any smallest measure. To change He would need to go from better to worse or from worse to better. He cannot do either, for being perfect He cannot become more perfect, and if He were to become less perfect He would be less than God. He is omniscient, which means that He knows in one free and effortless act all matter, all spirit, all relationships, all events. He has no past and He has no future. He is, and none of the limiting and qualifying terms used of creatures can apply to Him. Love and mercy and righteousness are His, and holiness so ineffable that no comparisons or figures will avail to express it. Only fire can give even a remote conception of it. In fire He appeared at the burning bush; in the pillar of fire He dwelt through all the long wilderness journey. The fire that glowed between the wings of the cherubim in the holy place was called the "shekinah," the Presence, through the years of Israel's glory, and when the Old had given place to the New, He came at Pentecost as a fiery flame and rested upon each disciple.

Spinoza wrote of the intellectual love of God, and he had a measure of truth there; but the highest love of God is not intellectual, it is spiritual. God is spirit and only the spirit of man can know Him really. In the deep spirit of a man the fire must glow or his love is not the true love of God. The great of the Kingdom have been those who loved God more than others did. We all know who they have been and gladly pay tribute to the depths and sincerity of their devotion. We have but to pause for a moment and their names come trooping past us smelling of myrrh and aloes and cassia out of the ivory palaces.

Frederick Faber was one whose soul panted after God as the roe pants after the water brook, and the measure in which God revealed Himself to his seeking heart set the good man's whole life afire with a burning adoration rivaling that of the seraphim before the throne. His love for God extended to the three Persons of the Godhead equally, yet he seemed to feel for each One a special kind of love reserved for Him alone. Of God the Father he sings:

Only to sit and think of God,
Oh what a joy it is!
To think the thought, to breathe the Name;
Earth has no higher bliss.

Father of Jesus, love's reward!
What rapture will it be,
Prostrate before Thy throne to lie,
And gaze and gaze on Thee!

His love for the Person of Christ was so intense that it threatened to consume him; it burned within him as a sweet and holy madness and flowed from his lips like molten gold. In one of his sermons he says, "Wherever we turn in the church of God, there is Jesus. He is the beginning, middle and end of everything to us. . . . There is nothing good, nothing holy, nothing beautiful, nothing joyous which He is not to His servants. No one need be poor, because, if he chooses, he can have Jesus for his own property and possession. No one need be downcast, for Jesus is the joy of heaven, and it is His joy to enter into sorrowful hearts. We can exaggerate about many things; but we can never exaggerate our obligation to Jesus, or the compassionate abundance of the love of Jesus to us. All our lives long we might talk of Jesus, and yet we should never come to an end of the sweet things that might be said of Him. Eternity will not be long enough to learn all He is, or to praise Him for all He has done, but then, that matters not; for we shall be always with Him, and we desire nothing more." And addressing our Lord directly he says to Him:

> I love Thee so, I know not how
> My transports to control;
> Thy love is like a burning fire
> Within my very soul.

Faber's blazing love extended also to the Holy Spirit. Not only in his theology did he acknowledge His deity and full equality with the Father and the Son, but he celebrated it constantly in his songs and in his prayers. He literally pressed his forehead to the ground in his eager fervid worship of the Third Person of the Godhead. In one of his great hymns to the Holy Spirit he sums up his burning devotion thus:

> O Spirit, beautiful and dread!
> My heart is fit to break
> With love of all Thy tenderness
> For us poor sinners' sake.

I have risked the tedium of quotation that I might show by pointed example what I have set out to say, viz., that God is so vastly wonderful, so utterly and completely delightful that He can, without anything other than Himself, meet and overflow the deepest demands of our total nature, mysterious and deep as that nature is. Such worship as Faber knew (and he is but one of a great company which no man can number) can never come from a mere doctrinal knowledge of God. Hearts that are "fit to break" with love for the Godhead are those who have been in the Presence and have looked with opened eye upon the majesty of Deity. Men of the breaking hearts had a quality about them not known to or understood by common men. They habitually spoke with spiritual authority. They had been in the Presence of God and they reported what they saw there. They were prophets, not scribes, for the scribe tells us what he has read, and the prophet tells what he has seen.

The distinction is not an imaginary one. Between the scribe who has read and the prophet who has seen there is a difference as wide as the sea. We are today overrun with orthodox scribes, but the prophets, where are they? The hard voice of the scribe sounds over evangelicalism, but the Church waits for the tender voice of the saint who has penetrated the veil and has gazed with inward eye upon the Wonder that is God. And yet, thus to penetrate, to push in sensitive living experience into the holy Presence, is a privilege open to every child of God.

With the veil removed by the rending of Jesus' flesh, with nothing on God's side to prevent us from entering, why do we tarry without? Why do we consent to abide all our days just outside the Holy of Holies and never enter at all to look upon God? We hear the Bridegroom say, "Let me see thy countenance, let me hear thy voice; for sweet is thy voice and thy countenance is comely." We sense that the call is for us, but still we fail to draw near, and the years pass and we grow old and tired in the outer courts of the tabernacle. What doth hinder us?

The answer usually given, simply that we are "cold," will not explain all the facts. There is something more serious than coldness of heart, something that may be back of that coldness and be the cause of its existence. What is it? What but the presence of a veil in our hearts? a veil not taken away as the first veil was, but which remains there still shutting out the light and hiding the face of God from us. It is the veil of our fleshly fallen nature living on, unjudged within us, uncrucified and unrepudiated. It is the close-woven veil of the self-life which we have never truly acknowledged, of which we have been secretly ashamed, and which for these reasons we have never brought to the judgment of the cross. It is not too mysterious, this opaque veil, nor is it hard to identify. We have but to look in our own hearts and we shall see it there, sewn and patched and repaired it may be, but there nevertheless, an enemy to our lives and an effective block to our spiritual progress.

This veil is not a beautiful thing and it is not a thing about which we commonly care to talk, but I am addressing the thirsting souls who are determined to follow God, and I know they will not turn back because the way leads temporarily through the blackened hills. The urge of God within them will assure their continuing the pursuit. They will face the facts however unpleasant and endure the cross for the joy set before them. So I am bold to name the threads out of which this inner veil is woven.

It is woven of the fine threads of the self-life, the hyphenated sins of the human spirit. They are not something we do, they are something we are, and therein lies both their subtlety and their power.

To be specific, the self-sins are these: self-righteousness, self-pity, self-confidence, self-sufficiency, self-admiration, self-love and a host of others like them. They dwell too deep within us and are too much a part of our natures to come to our attention till the light of God is focused upon them. The grosser manifestations of these sins, egotism, exhibitionism, self-promotion, are strangely tolerated in Christian leaders even in circles of impeccable orthodoxy. They are so much in evidence as actually, for many people, to become identified with the gospel. I trust it is not a cynical observation to say that they appear these days to be a requisite for popularity in some sections of the Church visible. Promoting self under the guise of promoting Christ is currently so common as to excite little notice.

One should suppose that proper instruction in the doctrines of man's depravity and the necessity for justification through the righteousness of Christ alone would deliver us from the power of the self-sins; but it does not work out that way. Self can live unrebuked at the very altar. It can watch the bleeding Victim die and not be in the least affected by what it sees. It can fight for the faith of the Reformers and preach eloquently the creed of salvation by grace, and gain strength by its efforts. To tell all the truth, it seems actually to feed upon orthodoxy and is more at home in a Bible Conference than in a tavern. Our very state of longing after God may afford it an excellent condition under which to thrive and grow.

Self is the opaque veil that hides the Face of God from us. It can be removed only in spiritual experience, never by mere instruction. As well try to instruct leprosy out of our system. There must be a work of God in destruction before we are free. We must invite the cross to do its deadly work within us. We must bring our self-sins to the cross for judgment. We must prepare ourselves for an ordeal of suffering in some measure like that through which our Saviour passed when He suffered under Pontius Pilate.

Let us remember: When we talk of the rending of the veil, we are speaking in a figure, and the thought of it is poetical, almost pleasant; but in actuality there is nothing pleasant about it. In human experience that veil is made of living spiritual tissue; it is composed of the sentient, quivering stuff of which our whole beings consist, and to touch it is to touch us where we feel pain. To tear it away is to injure us, to hurt us and make us bleed. To say otherwise is to make the cross no cross and death no death at all. It is never fun to die. To rip through the dear and tender stuff of which life is made can never be anything but deeply painful. Yet that is what the cross did to Jesus and it is what the cross would do to every man to set him free.

Let us beware of tinkering with our inner life in hope ourselves to rend the veil. God must do everything for us. Our part is to yield and trust. We must confess, forsake, repudiate the self-life, and then reckon it crucified. But we must be careful to distinguish lazy "acceptance" from the real work of God. We must insist upon the work being done. We dare not rest content with a neat doctrine of self-crucifixion. That is to imitate Saul and spare the best of the sheep and the oxen. Insist that the work be done in very truth and it will be done. The cross is rough, and it is deadly, but it is effective. It does not keep its victim hanging there forever. There comes a moment when its work is finished and the suffering victim dies. After that is resurrection glory and power, and the pain is forgotten for joy that the veil is taken away and we have entered in actual spiritual experience the Presence of the living God.

Lord, how excellent are Thy ways, and how devious and dark are the ways of man. Show us how to die, that we may rise again to newness of life. Rend the veil of our self-life from the top down as Thou didst rend the veil of the Temple. We would draw near in full assurance of faith. We would dwell with Thee in daily experience here on this earth so that we may be accustomed to the glory when we enter Thy heaven to dwell with Thee there. In Jesus' name, Amen.

4

Apprehending God

O taste and see.
PSALM 34:8

It was Canon Holmes, of India, who more than twenty-five years ago called attention to the inferential character of the average man's faith in God. To most people God is an inference, not a reality. He is a deduction from evidence which they consider adequate; but He remains personally unknown to the individual. "He must be," they say, "therefore we believe He is." Others do not go even so far as this; they know of Him only by hearsay. They have never bothered to think the matter out for themselves, but have heard about Him from others, and have put belief in Him into the back of their minds along with the various odds and ends that make up their total creed. To many others God is but an ideal, another name for goodness, or beauty, or truth; or He is law, or life, or the creative impulse back of the phenomena of existence.

These notions about God are many and varied, but they who hold them have one thing in common: they do not know God in personal experience. The possibility of intimate acquaintance with Him has not entered their minds. While admitting His existence they do not think of Him as knowable in the sense that we know things or people.

Christians, to be sure, go further than this, at least in theory. Their creed requires them to believe in the personality of God, and they have been taught to pray, "Our Father, which art in heaven." Now personality and fatherhood carry with them the idea of the possibility of personal acquaintance. This is admitted, I say, in theory, but for millions of Christians, nevertheless, God is no more real than He is to the non-Christian. They go through life trying to love an ideal and be loyal to a mere principle.

Over against all this cloudy vagueness stands the clear scriptural doctrine that God can be known in personal experience. A loving Personality dominates the Bible, walking among the trees of the garden and breathing fragrance over every scene. Always a living Person is present, speaking, pleading, loving, working, and manifesting

Himself whenever and wherever His people have the receptivity necessary to receive the manifestation.

The Bible assumes as a self-evident fact that men can know God with at least the same degree of immediacy as they know any other person or thing that comes within the field of their experience. The same terms are used to express the knowledge of God as are used to express knowledge of physical things. "O taste and see that the Lord is good." "All thy garments smell of myrrh, and aloes, and cassia, out of the ivory palaces." "My sheep hear my voice." "Blessed are the pure in heart, for they shall see God." These are but four of countless such passages from the Word of God. And more important than any proof text is the fact that the whole import of the Scripture is toward this belief.

What can all this mean except that we have in our hearts organs by means of which we can know God as certainly as we know material things through our familiar five senses? We apprehend the physical world by exercising the faculties given us for the purpose, and we possess spiritual faculties by means of which we can know God and the spiritual world if we will obey the Spirit's urge and begin to use them.

That a saving work must first be done in the heart is taken for granted here. The spiritual faculties of the unregenerate man lie asleep in his nature, unused and for every purpose dead; that is the stroke which has fallen upon us by sin. They may be quickened to active life again by the operation of the Holy Spirit in regeneration; that is one of the immeasurable benefits which come to us through Christ's atoning work on the cross.

But the very ransomed children of God themselves: why do they know so little of that habitual conscious communion with God which the Scriptures seem to offer? The answer is our chronic unbelief. Faith enables our spiritual sense to function. Where faith is defective the result will be inward insensibility and numbness toward spiritual things. This is the condition of vast numbers of Christians today. No proof is necessary to support that statement. We have but to converse with the first Christian we meet or enter the first church we find open to acquire all the proof we need.

A spiritual kingdom lies all about us, enclosing us, embracing us, altogether within reach of our inner selves, waiting for us to recognize it. God Himself is here waiting our response to His Presence. This eternal world will come alive to us the moment we begin to reckon upon its reality.

I have just now used two words which demand definition; or if definition is impossible, I must at least make clear what I mean when I use them. They are "reckon" and "reality."

What do I mean by reality? I mean that which has existence apart from any idea any mind may have of it, and which would exist if there were no mind anywhere to entertain a thought of it. That which is real has being in itself. It does not depend upon the observer for its validity.

I am aware that there are those who love to poke fun at the plain man's idea of reality. They are the idealists who spin endless proofs that nothing is real outside of the mind. They are the relativists who like to show that there are no fixed points in the universe from which we can measure anything. They smile down upon us from their lofty intellectual peaks and settle us to their own satisfaction by fastening upon us the reproachful term "absolutist." The Christian is not put out of countenance by this show of contempt. He can smile right back at them, for he knows that there is only One who is Absolute, that is God. But he knows also that the Absolute One has made this world for man's uses, and, while there is nothing fixed or real in the last meaning of the words (the meaning as applied to God), for every purpose of human life we are permitted to act as if there were. And every man does act thus except the mentally sick. These unfortunates also have trouble with reality, but they are consistent;

they insist upon living in accordance with their ideas of things. They are honest, and it is their very honesty that constitutes them a social problem.

The idealists and relativists are not mentally sick. They prove their soundness by living their lives according to the very notions of reality which they in theory repudiate and by counting upon the very fixed points which they prove are not there. They could earn a lot more respect for their notions if they were willing to live by them; but this they are careful not to do. Their ideas are brain-deep, not life-deep. Wherever life touches them they repudiate their theories and live like other men.

The Christian is too sincere to play with ideas for their own sake. He takes no pleasure in the mere spinning of gossamer webs for display. All his beliefs are practical. They are geared into his life. By them he lives or dies, stands or falls for this world and for all time to come. From the insincere man he turns away.

The sincere plain man knows that the world is real. He finds it here when he wakes to consciousness, and he knows that he did not think it into being. It was here waiting for him when he came, and he knows that when he prepares to leave this earthly scene it will be here still to bid him good-bye as he departs. By the deep wisdom of life he is wiser than a thousand men who doubt. He stands upon the earth and feels the wind and rain in his face and he knows that they are real. He sees the sun by day and the stars by night. He sees the hot lightning play out of the dark thundercloud. He hears the sounds of nature and the cries of human joy and pain. These he knows are real. He lies down on the cool earth at night and has no fear that it will prove illusory or fail him while he sleeps. In the morning the firm ground will be under him, the blue sky above him and the rocks and trees around him as when he closed his eyes the night before. So he lives and rejoices in a world of reality.

With his five senses he engages this real world. All things necessary to his physical existence he apprehends by the faculties with which he has been equipped by the God who created him and placed him in such a world as this.

Now, by our definition also God is real. He is real in the absolute and final sense that nothing else is. All other reality is contingent upon His. The great Reality is God who is the Author of that lower and dependent reality which makes up the sum of created things, including ourselves. God has objective existence independent of and apart from any notions which we may have concerning Him. The worshipping heart does not create its Object. It finds Him here when it wakes from its moral slumber in the morning of its regeneration.

Another word that must be cleared up is the word "reckon." This does not mean to visualize or imagine. Imagination is not faith. The two are not only different from, but stand in sharp opposition to, each other. Imagination projects unreal images out of the mind and seeks to attach reality to them. Faith creates nothing; it simply reckons upon that which is already there.

God and the spiritual world are real. We can reckon upon them with as much assurance as we reckon upon the familiar world around us. Spiritual things are there (or rather we should say here) inviting our attention and challenging our trust.

Our trouble is that we have established bad thought habits. We habitually think of the visible world as real and doubt the reality of any other. We do not deny the existence of the spiritual world but we doubt that it is real in the accepted meaning of the word.

The world of sense intrudes upon our attention day and night for the whole of our lifetime. It is clamorous, insistent and self-demonstrating. It does not appeal to our faith; it is here, assaulting our five senses, demanding to be accepted as real and final. But sin has so clouded the lenses of our hearts that we cannot see that other reality, the City of God, shining around us. The world of sense triumphs. The visible becomes the enemy of the invisible; the temporal, of the eternal. That is the curse inherited by every member of Adam's tragic race.

At the root of the Christian life lies belief in the invisible. The object of the Christian's faith is unseen reality.

Our uncorrected thinking, influenced by the blindness of our natural hearts and the intrusive ubiquity of visible things, tends to draw a contrast between the spiritual and the real; but actually no such contrast exists. The antithesis lies elsewhere: between the real and the imaginary, between the spiritual and the material, between the temporal and the eternal; but between the spiritual and the real, never. The spiritual is real.

If we would rise into that region of light and power plainly beckoning us through the Scriptures of truth, we must break the evil habit of ignoring the spiritual. We must shift our interest from the seen to the unseen. For the great unseen Reality is God. "He that cometh to God must believe that he is, and that he is a rewarder of them that diligently seek him." This is basic in the life of faith. From there we can rise to unlimited heights. "Ye believe in God," said our Lord Jesus Christ, "believe also in me." Without the first there can be no second.

If we truly want to follow God, we must seek to be other-worldly. This I say knowing well that that word has been used with scorn by the sons of this world and applied to the Christian as a badge of reproach. So be it. Every man must choose his world. If we who follow Christ, with all the facts before us and knowing what we are about, deliberately choose the Kingdom of God as our sphere of interest, I see no reason why anyone should object. If we lose by it, the loss is our own; if we gain, we rob no one by so doing. The "other world," which is the object of this world's disdain and the subject of the drunkard's mocking song, is our carefully chosen goal and the object of our holiest longing.

But we must avoid the common fault of pushing the "other world" into the future. It is not future, but present. It parallels our familiar physical world, and the doors between the two worlds are open. "Ye are come," says the writer to the Hebrews (and the tense is plainly present), "unto Mount Zion, and unto the city of the living God, the heavenly Jerusalem, and to an innumerable company of angels, to the general assembly and church of the firstborn, which are written in heaven, and to God the Judge of all, and to the spirits of just men made perfect, and to Jesus the mediator of the new covenant, and to the blood of sprinkling, that speaketh better things than that of Abel." All these things are contrasted with "the mount that might be touched" and "the sound of a trumpet and the voice of words" that might be heard. May we not safely conclude that, as the realities of Mount Sinai were apprehended by the senses, so the realities of Mount Zion are to be grasped by the soul? And this not by any trick of the imagination, but in downright actuality. The soul has eyes with which to see and ears with which to hear. Feeble they may be from long disuse, but by the life-giving touch of Christ alive now and capable of sharpest sight and most sensitive hearing.

As we begin to focus upon God, the things of the spirit will take shape before our inner eyes. Obedience to the word of Christ will bring an inward revelation of the Godhead (John 14:21-23). It will give acute perception, enabling us to see God even as is promised to the pure in heart. A new God consciousness will seize upon us and we shall begin to taste and hear and inwardly feel the God who is our life and our all. There will be seen the constant shining of the light that lighteth every man that cometh into the world. More and more, as our faculties grow sharper and more sure, God will become to us the great All, and His Presence the glory and wonder of our lives.

O God, quicken to life every power within me, that I may lay hold on eternal things. Open my eyes that I may see; give me acute spiritual perception; enable me to taste Thee and know that Thou art good. Make heaven more real to me than any earthly thing has ever been. Amen.

5

The Universal Presence

Whither shall I go from thy spirit?
or whither shall I flee from thy presence?
PSALM 139:7

In all Christian teaching certain basic truths are found, hidden at times, and rather assumed than asserted, but necessary to all truth as the primary colors are found in and necessary to the finished painting. Such a truth is the divine immanence.

God dwells in His creation and is everywhere indivisibly present in all His works. This is boldly taught by prophet and apostle and is accepted by Christian theology generally. That is, it appears in the books, but for some reason it has not sunk into the average Christian's heart so as to become a part of his believing self. Christian teachers shy away from its full implications, and, if they mention it at all, mute it down till it has little meaning. I would guess the reason for this to be the fear of being charged with pantheism; but the doctrine of the divine Presence is definitely not pantheism.

Pantheism's error is too palpable to deceive anyone. It is that God is the sum of all created things. Nature and God are one, so that whoever touches a leaf or a stone touches God. That is of course to degrade the glory of the incorruptible Deity and, in an effort to make all things divine, banish all divinity from the world entirely.

The truth is that while God dwells in His world, He is separated from it by a gulf forever impassable. However closely He may be identified with the work of His hands, they are and must eternally be other than He, and He is and must be antecedent to and independent of them. He is transcendent above all His works even while He is immanent within them.

What now does the divine immanence mean in direct Christian experience? It means simply that God is here. Wherever we are, God is here. There is no place, there can be no place, where He is not. Ten million intelligences standing at as many points in space and separated by incomprehensible distances can each one say with equal truth, God is here. No point is nearer to God than any other point. It is exactly as near to God from any place as it is from any other place. No one is in mere distance any further from or any nearer to God than any other person is.

These are truths believed by every instructed Christian. It remains for us to think on them and pray over them until they begin to glow within us.

"In the beginning God." Not matter, for matter is not self-causing. It requires an antecedent cause, and God is that Cause. Not law, for law is but a name for the course which all creation follows. That course had to be planned, and the Planner is God. Not mind, for mind also is a created thing and must have a Creator back of it. In the beginning God, the uncaused Cause of matter, mind and law. There we must begin.

Adam sinned and, in his panic, frantically tried to do the impossible: he tried to hide from the Presence of God. David also must have had wild thoughts of trying to escape from the Presence, for he wrote, "Whither shall I go from thy spirit? or whither shall I flee from thy presence?" Then he proceeded through one of his most beautiful psalms to celebrate the glory of the divine immanence. "If I ascend up into heaven, thou art there: if I make my bed in hell, behold, thou art there. If I take the wings of the morning, and dwell in the uttermost parts of the sea; even there shall thy hand lead me, and thy right hand shall hold me." And he knew that God's being and God's seeing are the same, that the seeing Presence had been with him even before he was born, watching the mystery of unfolding life. Solomon exclaimed, "But will God indeed dwell on the earth? behold the heaven and the heaven of heavens cannot contain thee: how much less this house which I have builded." Paul assured the Athenians that "God is not far from any one of us: for in him we live, and move, and have our being."

If God is present at every point in space, if we cannot go where He is not, cannot even conceive of a place where He is not, why then has not that Presence become the one universally celebrated fact of the world? The patriarch Jacob, "in the waste howling wilderness," gave the answer to that question. He saw a vision of God and cried out in wonder, "Surely the Lord is in this place; and I knew it not." Jacob had never been for one small division of a moment outside the circle of that all-pervading Presence. But he knew it not. That was his trouble, and it is ours. Men do not know that God is here. What a difference it would make if they knew.

The Presence and the manifestation of the Presence are not the same. There can be the one without the other. God is here when we are wholly unaware of it. He is manifest only when and as we are aware of His Presence. On our part there must be surrender to the Spirit of God, for His work it is to show us the Father and the Son. If we cooperate with Him in loving obedience, God will manifest Himself to us, and that manifestation will be the difference between a nominal Christian life and a life radiant with the light of His face.

Always, everywhere God is present, and always He seeks to discover Himself. To each one He would reveal not only that He is, but what He is as well. He did not have to be persuaded to discover Himself to Moses. "And the Lord descended in the cloud, and stood with him there, and proclaimed the name of the Lord." He not only made a verbal proclamation of His nature but He revealed His very Self to Moses so that the skin of Moses' face shone with the supernatural light. It will be a great moment for some of us when we begin to believe that God's promise of self-revelation is literally true: that He promised much, but promised no more than He intends to fulfill.

Our pursuit of God is successful just because He is forever seeking to manifest Himself to us. The revelation of God to any man is not God coming from a distance upon a time to pay a brief and momentous visit to the man's soul. Thus to think of it is to misunderstand it all. The approach of God to the soul or of the soul to God is not to be thought of in spatial terms at all. There is no idea of physical distance involved in the concept. It is not a matter of miles but of experience.

To speak of being near to or far from God is to use language in a sense always understood when applied to our ordinary human relationships. A man may say, "I feel that my son is coming nearer to me as he gets older," and yet that son has lived by his father's side since he was born and has never been away from home more than a day or so in his entire life. What then can the father mean? Obviously he is speaking of experience. He means that the boy is coming to know him more intimately and with deeper understanding, that the barriers of thought and feeling between the two are disappearing, that father and son are becoming more closely united in mind and heart.

So when we sing, "Draw me nearer, nearer, blessed Lord," we are not thinking of the nearness of place, but of the nearness of relationship. It is for increasing degrees of awareness that we pray, for a more perfect consciousness of the divine Presence. We need never shout across the spaces to an absent God. He is nearer than our own soul, closer than our most secret thoughts.

Why do some persons "find" God in a way that others do not? Why does God manifest His Presence to some and let multitudes of others struggle along in the half-light of imperfect Christian experience? Of course the will of God is the same for all. He has no favorites within His household. All He has ever done for any of His children He will do for all of His children. The difference lies not with God but with us.

Pick at random a score of great saints whose lives and testimonies are widely known. Let them be Bible characters or well-known Christians of post-biblical times. You will be struck instantly with the fact that the saints were not alike. Sometimes the unlikenesses were so great as to be positively glaring. How different for example was Moses from Isaiah; how different was Elijah from David; how unlike each other were John and Paul, St. Francis and Luther, Finney and Thomas à Kempis. The differences are as wide as human life itself: differences of race, nationality, education, temperament, habit and personal qualities. Yet they all walked, each in his day, upon a high road of spiritual living far above the common way.

Their differences must have been incidental and in the eyes of God of no significance. In some vital quality they must have been alike. What was it?

I venture to suggest that the one vital quality which they had in common was spiritual receptivity. Something in them was open to heaven, something which urged them Godward. Without attempting anything like a profound analysis, I shall say simply that they had spiritual awareness and that they went on to cultivate it until it became the biggest thing in their lives. They differed from the average person in that when they felt the inward longing they did something about it. They acquired the lifelong habit of spiritual response. They were not disobedient to the heavenly vision. As David put it neatly, "When thou saidst, Seek ye my face; my heart said unto thee, Thy face, Lord, will I seek."

As with everything good in human life, back of this receptivity is God. The sovereignty of God is here, and is felt even by those who have not placed particular stress upon it theologically. The pious Michael Angelo confessed this in a sonnet:

My unassisted heart is barren clay,
That of its native self can nothing feed:
Of good and pious works Thou art the seed,
That quickens only where Thou sayest it may:
Unless Thou show to us Thine own true way
No man can find it: Father! Thou must lead.

These words will repay study as the deep and serious testimony of a great Christian.

Important as it is that we recognize God working in us, I would yet warn against a too great preoccupation with the thought. It is a sure road to sterile passivity. God will not hold us responsible to understand the mysteries of election, predestination and the divine sovereignty. The best and safest way to deal with these truths is to raise our eyes to God and in deepest reverence say, "O Lord, Thou knowest." Those things belong to the deep and mysterious Profound of God's omniscience. Prying into them may make theologians, but it will never make saints.

Receptivity is not a single thing; it is a compound rather, a blending of several elements within the soul. It is an affinity for, a bent toward, a sympathetic response to, a desire to have. From this it may be gathered that it can be present in degrees, that we may have little or more or less, depending upon the individual. It may be increased by exercise or destroyed by neglect. It is not a sovereign and irresistible force which comes upon us as a seizure from above. It is a gift of God, indeed, but one which must be recognized and cultivated as any other gift if it is to realize the purpose for which it was given.

Failure to see this is the cause of a very serious breakdown in modern evangelicalism. The idea of cultivation and exercise, so dear to the saints of old, has now no place in our total religious picture. It is too slow, too common. We now demand glamour and fast flowing dramatic action. A generation of Christians reared among push buttons and automatic machines is impatient of slower and less direct methods of reaching their goals. We have been trying to apply machine-age methods to our relations with God. We read our chapter, have our short devotions and rush away, hoping to make up for our deep inward bankruptcy by attending another gospel meeting or listening to another thrilling story told by a religious adventurer lately returned from afar.

The tragic results of this spirit are all about us. Shallow lives, hollow religious philosophies, the preponderance of the element of fun in gospel meetings, the glorification of men, trust in religious externalities, quasi-religious fellowships, salesmanship methods, the mistaking of dynamic personality for the power of the Spirit: these and such as these are the symptoms of an evil disease, a deep and serious malady of the soul.

For this great sickness that is upon us no one person is responsible, and no Christian is wholly free from blame. We have all contributed, directly or indirectly, to this sad state of affairs. We have been too blind to see, or too timid to speak out, or too self-satisfied to desire anything better than the poor average diet with which others appear satisfied. To put it differently, we have accepted one another's notions, copied one another's lives and made one another's experiences the model for our own. And for a generation the trend has been downward. Now we have reached a low place of sand and burnt wire grass and, worst of all, we have made the Word of Truth conform to our experience and accepted this low plane as the very pasture of the blessed.

It will require a determined heart and more than a little courage to wrench ourselves loose from the grip of our times and return to biblical ways. But it can be done. Every now and then in the past Christians have had to do it. History has recorded several large-scale returns led by such men as St. Francis, Martin Luther and George Fox. Unfortunately there seems to be no Luther or Fox on the horizon at present. Whether or not another such return may be expected before the coming of Christ is a question upon which Christians are not fully agreed, but that is not of too great importance to us now.

What God in His sovereignty may yet do on a world-scale I do not claim to know: but what He will do for the plain man or woman who seeks His face I believe I do know and can tell others. Let any man turn to God in earnest, let him begin to exercise himself unto godliness, let him seek to develop his powers of spiritual receptivity by trust and obedience and humility, and the results will exceed anything he may have hoped in his leaner and weaker days.

Any man who by repentance and a sincere return to God will break himself out of the mold in which he has been held, and will go to the Bible itself for his spiritual standards, will be delighted with what he finds there.

Let us say it again: The Universal Presence is a fact. God is here. The whole universe is alive with His life. And He is no strange or foreign God, but the familiar Father of our Lord Jesus Christ whose love has for these thousands of years enfolded the sinful race of men. And always He is trying to get our attention, to reveal Himself to us, to communicate with us. We have within us the ability to know Him if we will but respond to His overtures. (And this we call pursuing God!) We will know Him in increasing degree as our receptivity becomes more perfect by faith and love and practice.

O God and Father, I repent of my sinful preoccupation
with visible things. The world has been too much with me.
Thou hast been here and I knew it not. I have been blind to
Thy Presence. Open my eyes that I may behold Thee
in and around me. For Christ's sake, Amen.

6

The Speaking Voice

In the beginning was the Word,
and the Word was with God,
and the Word was God.
JOHN 1:1

An intelligent plain man, untaught in the truths of Christianity, coming upon this text, would likely conclude that John meant to teach that it is the nature of God to speak, to communicate His thoughts to others. And he would be right. A word is a medium by which thoughts are expressed, and the application of term to the Eternal Son leads us to believe that self-expression is inherent in the Godhead, that God is forever seeking to speak Himself out to His creation. The whole Bible supports the idea. God is speaking. Not God spoke, but God is speaking. He is by His nature continuously articulate. He fills the world with His speaking Voice.

One of the great realities with which we have to deal is the Voice of God in His world. The briefest and only satisfying cosmogony is this: "He spake and it was done." The why of natural law is the living Voice of God immanent in His creation. And this word of God which brought all worlds into being cannot be understood to mean the Bible, for it is not a written or printed word at all, but the expression of the will of God spoken into the structure of all things. This word of God is the breath of God filling the world with living potentiality. The Voice of God is the most powerful force in nature, indeed the only force in nature, for all energy is here only because the power-filled Word is being spoken.

The Bible is the written word of God, and because it is written it is confined and limited by the necessities of ink and paper and leather. The Voice of God, however, is alive and free as the sovereign God is free. "The words that I speak unto you, they are spirit, and they are life." The life is in the speaking words. God's word in the Bible can have power only because it corresponds to God's word in the universe. It is the present Voice which makes the written Word all-powerful. Otherwise it would lie locked in slumber within the covers of a book.

We take a low and primitive view of things when we conceive of God at the creation coming into physical contact with things, shaping and fitting and building like a carpenter. The Bible teaches otherwise: "By the word of the Lord were the heavens made; and all the host of them by the breath of his mouth. . . . For he spake, and it was done; he commanded, and it stood fast." "Through faith we understand that the worlds were framed by the word of God." Again we must remember that God is referring here not to His written Word, but to His speaking Voice. His world-filling Voice is meant, that Voice which antedates the Bible by uncounted centuries, that Voice which has not been silent since the dawn of creation, but is sounding still throughout the full far reaches of the universe.

The Word of God is quick and powerful. In the beginning He spoke to nothing, and it became something. Chaos heard it and became order; darkness heard it and became light. "And God said—and it was so." These twin phrases, as cause and effect, occur throughout the Genesis story of the creation. The said accounts for the so. The so is the said put into the continuous present.

That God is here and that He is speaking—these truths are back of all other Bible truths; without them there could be no revelation at all. God did not write a book and send it by messenger to be read at a distance by unaided minds. He spoke a Book and lives in His spoken words, constantly speaking His words and causing the power of them to persist across the years. God breathed on clay and it became a man; He breathes on men and they become clay. "Return ye children of men" was the word spoken at the Fall by which God decreed the death of every man, and no added word has He needed to speak. The sad procession of mankind across the face of the earth from birth to the grave is proof that His original Word was enough.

We have not given sufficient attention to that deep utterance in the Book of John, "That was the true Light, which lighteth every man that cometh into the world." Shift the punctuation around as we will and the truth is still there: the Word of God affects the hearts of all men as light in the soul. In the hearts of all men the light shines, the Word sounds, and there is no escaping them. Something like this would of necessity be so if God is alive and in His world. And John says that it is so. Even those persons who have never heard of the Bible have still been preached to with sufficient clarity to remove every excuse from their hearts forever. "Which show the work of the law written in their hearts, their conscience also bearing witness, and their thoughts the mean while either accusing or else excusing one another." "For the invisible things of him from the creation of the world are clearly seen, being understood by the things that are made, even his eternal power and Godhead; so that they are without excuse."

This universal Voice of God was by the ancient Hebrews often called Wisdom, and was said to be everywhere sounding and searching throughout the earth, seeking some response from the sons of men. The eighth chapter of the Book of Proverbs begins, "Doth not wisdom cry? and understanding put forth her voice?" The writer then pictures wisdom as a beautiful woman standing "in the top of the high places, by the way in the places of the paths." She sounds her voice from every quarter so that no one may miss hearing it. "Unto you, O men, I call; and my voice is to the sons of men." Then she pleads for the simple and the foolish to give ear to her words. It is spiritual response for which this Wisdom of God is pleading, a response which she has always sought and is but rarely able to secure. The tragedy is that our eternal welfare depends upon our hearing, and we have trained our ears not to hear.

This universal Voice has ever sounded, and it has often troubled men even when they did not understand the source of their fears. Could it be that this Voice distilling like a living mist upon the hearts of men has been the undiscovered cause of the troubled conscience and the longing for immortality confessed by millions since the dawn of recorded history? We need not fear to face up to this. The speaking Voice is a fact. How men have reacted to it is for any observer to note.

When God spoke out of heaven to our Lord, self-centered men who heard it explained it by natural causes: they said, "It thundered." This habit of explaining the Voice by appeals to natural law is at the very root of modern science. In the living, breathing cosmos there is a mysterious Something, too wonderful, too awful for any mind to understand. The believing man does not claim to understand. He falls to his knees and whispers, "God." The man of earth kneels also, but not to worship. He kneels to examine, to search, to find the cause and the how of things. Just now we happen to be living in a secular age. Our thought habits are those of the scientist, not those of the worshipper. We are more likely to explain than to adore. "It thundered," we exclaim, and go our earthly way. But still the Voice sounds and searches. The order and life of the world depend upon that Voice, but men are mostly too busy or too stubborn to give attention.

Every one of us has had experiences which we have not been able to explain: a sudden sense of loneliness, or a feeling of wonder or awe in the face of the universal vastness. Or we have had a fleeting visitation of light like an illumination from some other sun, giving us in a quick flash an assurance that we are from another world, that our origins are divine. What we saw there, or felt, or heard, may have been contrary to all that we had been taught in the schools and at wide variance with all our former beliefs and opinions. We were forced to suspend our acquired doubts while, for a moment, the clouds were rolled back and we saw and heard for ourselves. Explain such things as we will, I think we have not been fair to the facts until we allow at least the possibility that such experiences may arise from the Presence of God in the world and His persistent effort to communicate with mankind. Let us not dismiss such an hypothesis too flippantly.

It is my own belief (and here I shall not feel bad if no one follows me) that every good and beautiful thing which man has produced in the world has been the result of his faulty and sin-blocked response to the creative Voice sounding over the earth. The moral philosophers who dreamed their high dreams of virtue, the religious thinkers who speculated about God and immortality, the poets and artists who created out of common stuff pure and lasting beauty: how can we explain them? It is not enough to say simply, "It was genius." What then is genius? Could it be that a genius is a man haunted by the speaking Voice, laboring and striving like one possessed to achieve ends which he only vaguely understands? That the great man may have missed God in his labors, that he may even have spoken or written against God does not destroy the idea I am advancing. God's redemptive revelation in the Holy Scriptures is necessary to saving faith and peace with God. Faith in a risen Saviour is necessary if the vague stirrings toward immortality are to bring us to restful and satisfying communion with God. To me this is a plausible explanation of all that is best out of Christ. But you can be a good Christian and not accept my thesis.

The Voice of God is a friendly Voice. No one need fear to listen to it unless he has already made up his mind to resist it. The blood of Jesus has covered not only the human race but all creation as well. "And having made peace through the blood of his cross, by him to reconcile all things unto himself; by him, I say, whether they be things in earth, or things in heaven." We may safely preach a friendly Heaven. The heavens as well as the earth are filled with the good will of Him that dwelt in the bush. The perfect blood of atonement secures this forever.

Whoever will listen will hear the speaking Heaven. This is definitely not the hour when men take kindly to an exhortation to listen, for listening is not today a part of popular religion. We are at the opposite end of the pole from there. Religion has accepted the monstrous heresy that noise, size, activity and bluster make a man dear to God. But we may take heart. To a people caught in the tempest of the last great conflict, God says, "Be still, and know that I am God," and still He says it, as if He means to tell us that our strength and safety lie not in noise but in silence.

It is important that we get still to wait on God. And it is best that we get alone, preferably with our Bible outspread before us. Then if we will we may draw near to God and begin to hear Him speak to us in our hearts. I think for the average person the progression will be something like this: First, a sound as of a Presence walking in the garden. Then a voice, more intelligible, but still far from clear. Then the happy moment when the Spirit begins to illuminate the Scriptures, and that which had been only a sound, or at best a voice, now becomes an intelligible word, warm and intimate and clear as the word of a dear friend. Then will come life and light, and best of all, ability to see and rest in and embrace Jesus Christ as Saviour and Lord and All.

The Bible will never be a living Book to us until we are convinced that God is articulate in His universe. To jump from a dead, impersonal world to a dogmatic Bible is too much for most people. They may admit that they should accept the Bible as the Word of God, and they may try to think of it as such, but they find it impossible to believe that the words there on the page are actually for them. A man may say, "These words are addressed to me," and yet in his heart not feel and know that they are. He is the victim of a divided psychology. He tries to think of God as mute everywhere else and vocal only in a book.

I believe that much of our religious unbelief is due to a wrong conception of and a wrong feeling for the Scriptures of Truth. A silent God suddenly began to speak in a book and when the book was finished lapsed back into silence again forever. Now we read the book as the record of what God said when He was for a brief time in a speaking mood. With notions like that in our heads, how can we believe? The facts are that God is not silent, has never been silent. It is the nature of God to speak. The second Person of the

Holy Trinity is called the Word. The Bible is the inevitable outcome of God's continuous speech. It is the infallible declaration of His mind for us put into our familiar human words.

I think a new world will arise out of the religious mists when we approach our Bible with the idea that it is not only a book which was once spoken, but a book which is now speaking. The prophets habitually said, "Thus saith the Lord." They meant their hearers to understand that God's speaking is in the continuous present. We may use the past tense properly to indicate that at a certain time a certain word of God was spoken, but a word of God once spoken continues to be spoken, as a child once born continues to be alive, or a world once created continues to exist. And those are but imperfect illustrations, for children die and worlds burn out, but the Word of our God endureth forever.

If you would follow on to know the Lord, come at once to the open Bible, expecting it to speak to you. Do not come with the notion that it is a thing which you may push around at your convenience. It is more than a thing; it is a voice, a word, the very Word of the living God.

Lord, teach me to listen. The times are noisy and my ears are weary with the thousand raucous sounds which continuously assault them. Give me the spirit of the boy Samuel when he said to Thee, "Speak, for thy servant heareth." Let me hear Thee speaking in my heart. Let me get used to the sound of Thy Voice, that its tones may be familiar when the sounds of earth die away and the only sound will be the music of Thy speaking Voice. Amen.

7

The Gaze of the Soul

Looking unto Jesus the author and finisher of our faith.
HEBREWS 12:2

Let us think of our intelligent plain man mentioned in chapter six coming for the first time to the reading of the Scriptures. He approaches the Bible without any previous knowledge of what it contains. He is wholly without prejudice; he has nothing to prove and nothing to defend.

Such a man will not have read long until his mind begins to observe certain truths standing out from the page. They are the spiritual principles behind the record of God's dealings with men, and woven into the writings of holy men as they "were moved by the Holy Ghost." As he reads on he might want to number these truths as they become clear to him and make a brief summary under each number. These summaries will be the tenets of his biblical creed. Further reading will not affect these points except to enlarge and strengthen them. Our man is finding out what the Bible actually teaches.

High up on the list of things which the Bible teaches will be the doctrine of faith. The place of weighty importance which the Bible gives to faith will be too plain for him to miss. He will very likely conclude: Faith is all-important in the life of the soul. Without faith it is impossible to please God. Faith will get me anything, take me anywhere in the Kingdom of God, but without faith there can be no approach to God, no forgiveness, no deliverance, no salvation, no communion, no spiritual life at all.

By the time our friend has reached the eleventh chapter of Hebrews, the eloquent encomium which is there pronounced upon faith will not seem strange to him. He will have read Paul's powerful defense of faith in his Roman and Galatian epistles. Later if he goes on to study church history he will understand the amazing power in the teachings of the Reformers as they showed the central place of faith in the Christian religion.

Now if faith is so vitally important, if it is an indispensable must in our pursuit of God, it is perfectly natural that we should be deeply concerned over whether or not we possess this most precious gift. And our minds being what they are, it is inevitable that sooner or later we should get around to inquiring after the nature of faith. "What is faith?" would lie close to the question "Do I have faith?" and would demand an answer if it were anywhere to be found.

Almost all who preach or write on the subject of faith have much the same things to say concerning it. They tell us that it is believing a promise, that it is taking God at His word, that it is reckoning the Bible to be true and stepping out upon it. The rest of the book or sermon is usually taken up with stories of persons who have had their prayers answered as a result of their faith. These answers are mostly direct gifts of a practical and temporal nature such as health, money, physical protection or success in business. Or if the teacher is of a philosophic turn of mind he may take another course and lose us in a welter of metaphysics or snow us under with psychological jargon as he defines and re-defines, paring the slender hair of faith thinner and thinner till it disappears in gossamer shavings at last. When he is finished we get up disappointed and go out "by that same door where in we went." Surely there must be something better than this.

In the Scriptures there is practically no effort made to define faith. Outside of a brief fourteen-word definition in Hebrews 11:1, I know of no biblical definition, and even there faith is defined functionally, not philosophically; that is, it is a statement of what faith is in operation, not what it is in essence. It assumes the presence of faith and shows what it results in, rather than what it is. We will be wise to go just that far and attempt to go no further. We are told from whence it comes and by what means: "Faith is a gift of God," and "Faith cometh by hearing, and hearing by the word of God." This much is clear, and, to paraphrase Thomas à Kempis, "I had rather exercise faith than know the definition thereof."

From here on, when the words "faith is" or their equivalent occur in this chapter, I ask that they be understood to refer to what faith is in operation as exercised by a believing man. Right here we drop the notion of definition and think about faith as it may be experienced in action. The complexion of our thoughts will be practical, not theoretical.

In a dramatic story in the Book of Numbers faith is seen in action. Israel became discouraged and spoke against God, and the Lord sent fiery serpents among them. "And they bit the people; and much people of Israel died." Then Moses sought the Lord for them and He heard and gave them a remedy against the bite of the serpents. He commanded Moses to make a serpent of brass and put it upon a pole in sight of all the people, "and it shall come to pass, that everyone that is bitten, when he looketh upon it, shall live." Moses obeyed, "and it came to pass, that if a serpent had bitten any man, when he beheld the serpent of brass, he lived" (Num. 21:4-9).

In the New Testament this important bit of history is interpreted for us by no less an authority than our Lord Jesus Christ Himself. He is explaining to His hearers how they may be saved. He tells them that it is by believing. Then to make it clear He refers to this incident in the Book of Numbers: "As Moses lifted up the serpent in the wilderness, even so must the Son of man be lifted up: that whosoever believeth in him should not perish, but have eternal life" (John 3:14-15).

Our plain man in reading this would make an important discovery. He would notice that "look" and "believe" were synonymous terms. "Looking" on the Old Testament serpent is identical with "believing" on the New Testament Christ. That is, the looking and the believing are the same thing. And he would understand that while Israel looked with their external eyes, believing is done with the heart. I think he would conclude that faith is the gaze of a soul upon a saving God.

When he had seen this he would remember passages he had read before, and their meaning would come flooding over him. "They looked unto him, and were lightened: and their faces were not ashamed" (Ps. 34:5). "Unto thee lift I up mine eyes, O thou that dwellest in the heavens. Behold, as the eyes of servants look unto the hand of their masters, and as the eyes of a maiden unto the hand of her mistress; so our eyes wait upon the Lord our God, until that he have mercy upon us" (Ps. 123:1-2). Here the man seeking mercy looks straight at the God of mercy and never takes his eyes away from Him till mercy is granted. And our Lord Himself looked always at God. "Looking up to heaven, he blessed, and brake, and gave the bread to his disciples" (Matt. 14:19). Indeed Jesus taught that He wrought His works by always keeping His inward eyes upon His Father. His power lay in His continuous look at God (John 5:19-21).

In full accord with the few texts we have quoted is the whole tenor of the inspired Word. It is summed up for us in the Hebrew epistle when we are instructed to run life's race "looking unto Jesus the author and finisher of our faith." From all this we learn that faith is not a once-done act, but a continuous gaze of the heart at the Triune God.

Believing, then, is directing the heart's attention to Jesus. It is lifting the mind to "behold the Lamb of God," and never ceasing that beholding for the rest of our lives. At first this may be difficult, but it becomes easier as we look steadily at His wondrous Person, quietly and without strain. Distractions may hinder, but once the heart is committed to Him, after each brief excursion away from Him the attention will return again and rest upon Him like a wandering bird coming back to its window.

I would emphasize this one committal, this one great volitional act which establishes the heart's intention to gaze forever upon Jesus. God takes this intention for our choice and makes what allowances He must for the thousand distractions which beset us in this evil world. He knows that we have set the direction of our hearts toward Jesus, and we can know it too, and comfort ourselves with the knowledge that a habit of soul is forming which will become after a while a sort of spiritual reflex requiring no more conscious effort on our part.

Faith is the least self-regarding of the virtues. It is by its very nature scarcely conscious of its own existence. Like the eye which sees everything in front of it and never sees itself, faith is occupied with the Object upon which it rests and pays no attention to itself at all. While we are looking at God we do not see ourselves—blessed riddance. The man who has struggled to purify himself and has had nothing but repeated failures will experience real relief when he stops tinkering with his soul and looks away to the perfect One. While he looks at Christ the very things he has so long been trying to do will be getting done within him. It will be God working in him to will and to do.

Faith is not in itself a meritorious act; the merit is in the One toward Whom it is directed. Faith is a redirecting of our sight, a getting out of the focus of our own vision and getting God into focus. Sin has twisted our vision inward and made it self-regarding. Unbelief has put self where God should be, and is perilously close to the sin of Lucifer who said, "I will set my throne above the throne of God." Faith looks out instead of in and the whole life falls into line.

All this may seem too simple. But we have no apology to make. To those who would seek to climb into heaven after help or descend into hell, God says, "The word is nigh thee, even the word of faith." The word induces us to lift up our eyes unto the Lord and the blessed work of faith begins.

When we lift our inward eyes to gaze upon God, we are sure to meet friendly eyes gazing back at us, for it is written that the eyes of the Lord run to and fro throughout all the earth. The sweet language of experience is "Thou God seest me." When the eyes of the soul looking out meet the eyes of God looking in, heaven has begun right here on this earth.

"When all my endeavour is turned toward Thee because all Thy endeavour is turned toward me; when I look unto Thee alone with all my attention, nor ever turn aside the eyes of my mind, because Thou dost enfold me with Thy constant regard; when I direct my love toward Thee alone because Thou, who art Love's self hast turned Thee toward me alone. And what, Lord, is my life, save that embrace wherein Thy delightsome sweetness doth so lovingly enfold me?"[1] So wrote Nicholas of Cusa four hundred years ago.

I should like to say more about this old man of God. He is not much known today anywhere among Christian believers, and among current Fundamentalists he is known not at all. I feel that we could gain much from a little acquaintance with men of his spiritual flavor and the school of Christian thought which they represent. Christian literature, to be accepted and approved by the evangelical leaders of our times, must follow very closely the same train of thought, a kind of "party line" from which it is scarcely safe to depart. A half-century of this in America has made us smug and content. We imitate each other with slavish devotion and our most strenuous efforts are put forth to try to say the same thing that everyone around us is saying—and yet to find an excuse for saying it, some little safe variation on the approved theme or, if no more, at least a new illustration.

Nicholas was a true follower of Christ, a lover of the Lord, radiant and shining in his devotion to the Person of Jesus. His theology was orthodox, but fragrant and sweet as everything about Jesus might properly be expected to be. His conception of eternal life, for instance, is beautiful in itself and, if I mistake not, is nearer in spirit to John 17:3 than that which is current among us today. Life eternal, says Nicholas, is "nought other than that blessed regard wherewith Thou never ceasest to behold me, yea, even the secret places of my soul. With Thee, to behold is to give life; 'tis unceasingly to impart sweetest love of Thee; 'tis to inflame me to love of Thee by love's imparting, and to feed me by inflaming, and by feeding to kindle my yearning, and by kindling to make me drink of the dew of gladness, and by drinking to infuse in me a fountain of life, and by infusing to make it increase and endure."[2]

Now, if faith is the gaze of the heart at God, and if this gaze is but the raising of the inward eyes to meet the all-seeing eyes of God, then it follows that it is one of the easiest things possible to do. It would be like God to make the most vital thing easy and place it within the range of possibility for the weakest and poorest of us.

Several conclusions may fairly be drawn from all this. The simplicity of it, for instance. Since believing is looking, it can be done without special equipment or religious paraphernalia. God has seen to it that the one life-and-death essential can never be subject to the caprice of accident. Equipment can break down or get lost, water can leak away, records can be destroyed by fire, the minister can be delayed or the church burn down. All these are external to the soul and are subject to accident or mechanical failure: but looking is of the heart and can be done successfully by any man standing up or kneeling down or lying in his last agony a thousand miles from any church.

Since believing is looking, it can be done any time. No season is superior to another season for this sweetest of all acts. God never made salvation depend upon new moons or holy days or sabbaths. A man is not nearer to Christ on Easter Sunday than he is, say, on Saturday, August 3, or Monday, October 4. As long as Christ sits on the mediatorial throne, every day is a good day and all days are days of salvation.

Neither does place matter in this blessed work of believing God. Lift your heart and let it rest upon Jesus and you are instantly in a sanctuary though it be a Pullman berth or a factory or a kitchen. You can see God from anywhere if your mind is set to love and obey Him.

Now, someone may ask, "Is not this of which you speak for special persons such as monks or ministers who have by the nature of their calling more time to devote to quiet meditation? I am a busy worker and have little time to spend alone." I am happy to say that the life I describe is for every one of God's children regardless of calling. It is, in fact, happily practiced every day by many hard working persons and is beyond the reach of none.

Many have found the secret of which I speak and, without giving much thought to what is going on within them, constantly practice this habit of inwardly gazing upon God. They know that something inside their hearts sees God. Even when they are compelled to withdraw their conscious attention in order to engage in earthly affairs, there is within them a secret communion always going on. Let their attention but be released for a moment from necessary business and it flies at once to God again. This has been the testimony of many Christians, so many that even as I state it thus I have a feeling that I am quoting, though from whom or from how many I cannot possibly know.

I do not want to leave the impression that the ordinary means of grace have no value. They most assuredly have. Private prayer should be practiced by every Christian. Long periods of Bible meditation will purify our gaze and direct it; church attendance will enlarge our outlook and increase our love for others. Service and work and activity; all are good and should be engaged in by every Christian. But at the bottom of all these things, giving meaning to them, will be the inward habit of beholding God. A new set of eyes (so to speak) will develop within us enabling us to be looking at God while our outward eyes are seeing the scenes of this passing world.

Someone may fear that we are magnifying private religion out of all proportion, that the "us" of the New Testament is being displaced by a selfish "I." Has it ever occurred to you that one hundred pianos all tuned to the same fork are automatically tuned to each other? They are of one accord by being tuned, not to each other, but to another standard to which each one must individually bow. So one hundred worshippers met together, each one looking away to Christ, are in heart nearer to each other than they could possibly be were they to become "unity" conscious and turn their eyes away from God to strive for closer fellowship. Social religion is perfected when private religion is purified. The body becomes stronger as its members become healthier. The whole Church of God gains when the members that compose it begin to seek a better and a higher life.

All the foregoing presupposes true repentance and a full committal of the life to God. It is hardly necessary to mention this, for only persons who have made such a committal will have read this far.

When the habit of inwardly gazing Godward becomes fixed within us, we shall be ushered onto a new level of spiritual life more in keeping with the promises of God and the mood of the New Testament. The Triune God will be our dwelling place even while our feet walk the low road of simple duty here among men. We will have found life's *summum bonum* indeed. "There is the source of all delights that can be desired; not only can nought better be thought out by men and angels, but nought better can exist in mode of being! For it is the absolute maximum of every rational desire, than which a greater cannot be."[3]

The Vision of God

O Lord, I have heard a good word inviting me to look away to Thee and be satisfied. My heart longs to respond, but sin has clouded my vision till I see Thee but dimly. Be pleased to cleanse me in Thine own precious blood, and make me inwardly pure, so that I may with unveiled eyes gaze upon Thee all the days of my earthly pilgrimage. Then shall I be prepared to behold Thee in full splendor in the day when Thou shalt appear to be glorified in Thy saints and admired in all them that believe. Amen.

Notes
1. Nicholas of Cusa, *The Vision of God* (New York: E. P. Dutton & Co., Inc., 1928).
2. Ibid.
3. Ibid.

8

Restoring the Creator-Creature Relation

Be thou exalted, O God, above the heavens;
let thy glory be above all the earth.
PSALM 57:5

It is a truism to say that order in nature depends upon right relationships; to achieve harmony each thing must be in its proper position relative to each other thing. In human life it is not otherwise.

I have hinted before in these chapters that the cause of all our human miseries is a radical moral dislocation, an upset in our relation to God and to each other. For whatever else the Fall may have been, it was most certainly a sharp change in man's relation to his Creator. He adopted toward God an altered attitude, and by so doing destroyed the proper Creator-Creature relation in which, unknown to him, his true happiness lay. Essentially, salvation is the restoration of a right relation between man and his Creator, a bringing back to normal of the Creator-Creature relation.

A satisfactory spiritual life will begin with a complete change in relation between God and the sinner; not a judicial change merely, but a conscious and experienced change affecting the sinner's whole nature. The atonement in Jesus' blood makes such a change judicially possible and the working of the Holy Spirit makes it emotionally satisfying. The story of the prodigal son perfectly illustrates this latter phase. He had brought a world of trouble upon himself by forsaking the position which he had properly held as son of his father. At bottom his restoration was nothing more than a re-establishing of the father-son relation which had existed from his birth and had been altered temporarily by his act of sinful rebellion. This story overlooks the legal aspects of redemption, but it makes beautifully clear the experiential aspects of salvation.

In determining relationships we must begin somewhere. There must be somewhere a fixed center against which everything else is measured, where the law of relativity does not enter and we can say "IS" and make no allowances. Such a center is God. When God would make His Name known to mankind He could find no better word than "I AM." When He speaks in the first person He says,

"I AM"; when we speak of Him we say, "He is"; when we speak to Him we say, "Thou art." Everyone and everything else measures from that fixed point. "I am that I am," says God. "I change not."

As the sailor locates his position on the sea by "shooting" the sun, so we may get our moral bearings by looking at God. We must begin with God. We are right when and only when we stand in a right position relative to God, and we are wrong so far and so long as we stand in any other position.

Much of our difficulty as seeking Christians stems from our unwillingness to take God as He is and adjust our lives accordingly. We insist upon trying to modify Him and to bring Him nearer to our own image. The flesh whimpers against the rigor of God's inexorable sentence and begs like Agag for a little mercy, a little indulgence of its carnal ways. It is no use. We can get a right start only by accepting God as He is and learning to love Him for what He is. As we go on to know Him better, we shall find it a source of unspeakable joy that God is just what He is. Some of the most rapturous moments we know will be those we spend in reverent admiration of the Godhead. In those holy moments the very thought of change in Him will be too painful to endure.

So let us begin with God. Back of all, above all, before all is God; first in sequential order, above in rank and station, exalted in dignity and honor. As the self-existent One He gave being to all things, and all things exist out of Him and for Him. "Thou art worthy, O Lord, to receive glory and honour and power: for thou hast created all things, and for thy pleasure they are and were created."

Every soul belongs to God and exists by His pleasure. God being Who and What He is, and we being who and what we are, the only thinkable relation between us is one of full lordship on His part and complete submission on ours. We owe Him every honor that it is in our power to give Him. Our everlasting grief lies in giving Him anything less.

The pursuit of God will embrace the labor of bringing our total personality into conformity to His. And this not judicially, but actually. I do not here refer to the act of justification by faith in Christ. I speak of a voluntary exalting of God to His proper station over us and a willing surrender of our whole being to the place of worshipful submission which the Creator-Creature circumstance makes proper.

The moment we make up our minds that we are going on with this determination to exalt God over all, we step out of the world's parade. We shall find ourselves out of adjustment to the ways of the world, and increasingly so as we make progress in the holy way. We shall acquire a new viewpoint; a new and different psychology will be formed within us; a new power will begin to surprise us by its upsurgings and its outgoings.

Our break with the world will be the direct outcome of our changed relation to God. For the world of fallen men does not honor God. Millions call themselves by His Name, it is true, and pay some token respect to Him, but a simple test will show how little He is really honored among them. Let the average man be put to the proof on the question of who is above, and his true position will be exposed. Let him be forced into making a choice between God and money, between God and men, between God and personal ambition, God and self, God and human love, and God will take second place every time. Those other things will be exalted above. However the man may protest, the proof is in the choices he makes day after day throughout his life.

"Be thou exalted" is the language of victorious spiritual experience. It is a little key to unlock the door to great treasures of grace. It is central in the life of God in the soul. Let the seeking man reach a place where life and lips join to say continually "Be thou exalted," and a thousand minor problems will be solved at once. His Christian life ceases to be the complicated thing it had been before and becomes the very essence of simplicity. By the exercise of his will he has set his course, and on that course he will stay as if guided by an automatic pilot. If blown off course for a moment by some adverse wind he will surely return again as by a secret bent of the soul. The hidden motions of the Spirit are working in his favor, and "the stars in their courses" fight for him. He has met his life problem at its center, and everything else must follow along.

Let no one imagine that he will lose anything of human dignity by this voluntary sell-out of his all to his God. He does not by this degrade himself as a man; rather he finds his right place of high honor as one made in the image of his Creator. His deep disgrace lay in his moral derangement, his unnatural usurpation of the place of God. His honor will be proved by restoring again that stolen throne. In exalting God over all he finds his own highest honor upheld.

Anyone who might feel reluctant to surrender his will to the will of another should remember Jesus' words, "Whosoever committeth sin is the servant of sin." We must of necessity be servant to someone, either to God or to sin. The sinner prides himself on his independence, completely overlooking the fact that he is the weak slave of the sins that rule his members. The man who surrenders to Christ exchanges a cruel slave driver for a kind and gentle Master whose yoke is easy and whose burden is light.

Made as we were in the image of God we scarcely find it strange to take again our God as our All. God was our original habitat and our hearts cannot but feel at home when they enter again that ancient and beautiful abode.

I hope it is clear that there is a logic behind God's claim to pre-eminence. That place is His by every right in earth or heaven. While we take to ourselves the place that is His, the whole course of our lives is out of joint. Nothing will or can restore order till our hearts make the great decision: God shall be exalted above.

"Them that honour me I will honour," said God once to a priest of Israel, and that ancient law of the Kingdom stands today unchanged by the passing of time or the changes of dispensation. The whole Bible and every page of history proclaim the perpetuation of that law. "If any man serve me, him will my Father honour," said our Lord Jesus, tying in the old with the new and revealing the essential unity of His ways with men.

Sometimes the best way to see a thing is to look at its opposite. Eli and his sons are placed in the priesthood with the stipulation that they honor God in their lives and ministrations. This they fail to do, and God sends Samuel to announce the consequences. Unknown to Eli this law of reciprocal honor has been all the while secretly working, and now the time has come for judgment to fall. Hophni and Phineas, the degenerate priests, fall in battle, the wife of Hophni dies in childbirth, Israel flees before her enemies, the ark of God is captured by the Philistines, and the old man Eli falls backward and dies of a broken neck. Thus stark utter tragedy followed upon Eli's failure to honor God.

Now set over against this almost any Bible character who honestly tried to glorify God in his earthly walk. See how God winked at weaknesses and overlooked failures as He poured upon His servants grace and blessing untold. Let it be Abraham, Jacob, David, Daniel, Elijah or whom you will; honor followed honor as harvest the seed. The man of God set his heart to exalt God above all; God accepted his intention as fact and acted accordingly. Not perfection, but holy intention made the difference.

In our Lord Jesus Christ this law was seen in simple perfection. In His lowly manhood He humbled Himself and gladly gave all glory to His Father in heaven. He sought not His own honor, but the honor of God who sent Him. "If I honour myself," He said on one occasion, "my honour is nothing; it is my Father that honoureth me." So far had the proud Pharisees departed from this law that they could not understand one who honored God at his own expense. "I honour my Father," said Jesus to them, "and ye do dishonour me."

Another saying of Jesus, and a most disturbing one, was put in the form of a question, "How can ye believe, which receive honour one of another, and seek not the honour that cometh from God alone?" If I understand this correctly Christ taught here the alarming doctrine that the desire for honor among men made belief impossible. Is this sin at the root of religious unbelief? Could it be that those "intellectual difficulties" which men blame for their inability to believe are but smoke screens to conceal the real cause that lies behind them? Was it this greedy desire for honor from man that made men into Pharisees and Pharisees into Deicides? Is this the secret back of religious self-righteousness and empty worship? I believe it may be. The whole course of the life is upset by failure to put God where He belongs. We exalt ourselves instead of God and the curse follows.

In our desire after God, let us keep always in mind that God also hath desire, and His desire is toward the sons of men, and more particularly toward those sons of men who will make the once-for-all decision to exalt Him over all. Such as these are precious to God above all treasures of earth or sea. In them God finds a theater where He can display His exceeding kindness toward us in Christ Jesus. With them God can walk unhindered, toward them He can act like the God He is.

In speaking thus I have one fear; it is that I may convince the mind before God can win the heart. For this God-above-all position is one not easy to take. The mind may approve it while not having the consent of the will to put it into effect. While the imagination races ahead to honor God, the will may lag behind and the man never guess how divided his heart is. The whole man must make the decision before the heart can know any real satisfaction. God wants us all, and He will not rest till He gets us all. No part of the man will do.

Let us pray over this in detail, throwing ourselves at God's feet and meaning everything we say. No one who prays thus in sincerity need wait long for tokens of divine acceptance. God will unveil His glory before His servant's eyes, and He will place all His treasures at the disposal of such a one, for He knows that His honor is safe in such consecrated hands.

O God, be Thou exalted over my possessions. Nothing of earth's treasures shall seem dear unto me if only Thou art glorified in my life. Be Thou exalted over my friendships. I am determined that Thou shalt be above all, though I must stand deserted and alone in the midst of the earth. Be Thou exalted above my comforts. Though it mean the loss of bodily comforts and the carrying of heavy crosses, I shall keep my vow made this day before Thee. Be Thou exalted over my reputation. Make me ambitious to please Thee even if as a result I must sink into obscurity and my name be forgotten as a dream. Rise, O Lord, into Thy proper place of honor, above my ambitions, above my likes and dislikes, above my family, my health and even my life itself. Let me decrease that Thou mayest increase; let me sink that Thou mayest rise above. Ride forth upon me as Thou didst ride into Jerusalem mounted upon the humble little beast, a colt, the foal of an ass, and let me hear the children cry to Thee, "Hosanna in the highest."

9

Meekness and Rest

Blessed are the meek: for they shall inherit the earth.
MATTHEW 5:5

A fairly accurate description of the human race might be furnished one unacquainted with it by taking the Beatitudes, turning them wrong side out and saying, "Here is your human race." For the exact opposite of the virtues in the Beatitudes are the very qualities which distinguish human life and conduct.

In the world of men we find nothing approaching the virtues of which Jesus spoke in the opening words of the famous Sermon on the Mount. Instead of poverty of spirit we find the rankest kind of pride; instead of mourners we find pleasure seekers; instead of meekness, arrogance; instead of hunger after righteousness we hear men saying, "I am rich and increased with goods and have need of nothing"; instead of mercy we find cruelty; instead of purity of heart, corrupt imaginings; instead of peacemakers we find men quarrelsome and resentful; instead of rejoicing in mistreatment we find them fighting back with every weapon at their command.

Of this kind of moral stuff civilized society is composed. The atmosphere is charged with it; we breathe it with every breath and drink it with our mother's milk. Culture and education refine these things slightly but leave them basically untouched. A whole world of literature has been created to justify this kind of life as the only normal one. And this is the more to be wondered at seeing that these are the evils which make life the bitter struggle it is for all of us. All our heartaches and a great many of our physical ills spring directly out of our sins. Pride, arrogance, resentfulness, evil imaginings, malice, greed: these are the sources of more human pain than all the diseases that ever afflicted mortal flesh.

Into a world like this the sound of Jesus' words comes wonderful and strange, a visitation from above. It is well that He spoke, for no one else could have done it as well; and it is good that we listen. His words are the essence of truth. He is not offering an opinion; Jesus never uttered opinions. He never guessed; He knew, and He knows.

His words are not as Solomon's were, the sum of sound wisdom or the results of keen observation. He spoke out of the fullness of His Godhead, and His words are very Truth itself. He is the only one who could say "blessed" with complete authority, for He is the Blessed One come from the world above to confer blessedness upon mankind. And His words were supported by deeds mightier than any performed on this earth by any other man. It is wisdom for us to listen.

As was often so with Jesus, He used this word "meek" in a brief crisp sentence, and not till some time later did He go on to explain it. In the same book of Matthew, He tells us more about it and applies it to our lives. "Come unto me, all ye that labour and are heavy laden, and I will give you rest. Take my yoke upon you, and learn of me; for I am meek and lowly in heart: and ye shall find rest unto your souls. For my yoke is easy, and my burden is light." Here we have two things standing in contrast to each other, a burden and a rest. The burden is not a local one, peculiar to those first hearers, but one which is borne by the whole human race. It consists not of political oppression or poverty or hard work. It is far deeper than that. It is felt by the rich as well as the poor for it is something from which wealth and idleness can never deliver us.

The burden borne by mankind is a heavy and a crushing thing. The word Jesus used means a load carried or toil borne to the point of exhaustion. Rest is simply release from that burden. It is not something we do; it is what comes to us when we cease to do. His own meekness, that is the rest.

Let us examine our burden. It is altogether an interior one. It attacks the heart and the mind and reaches the body only from within. First, there is the burden of pride. The labor of self-love is a heavy one indeed. Think for yourself whether much of your sorrow has not arisen from someone speaking slightingly of you. As long as you set yourself up as a little god to which you must be loyal, there will be those who will delight to offer affront to your idol. How then can you hope to have inward peace? The heart's fierce effort to protect itself from every slight, to shield its touchy honor from the bad opinion of friend and enemy, will never let the mind have rest. Continue this fight through the years and the burden will become intolerable. Yet the sons of earth are carrying this burden continually, challenging every word spoken against them, cringing under every criticism, smarting under each fancied slight, tossing sleepless if another is preferred before them.

Such a burden as this is not necessary to bear. Jesus calls us to His rest, and meekness is His method. The meek man cares not at all who is greater than he, for he has long ago decided that the esteem of the world is not worth the effort. He develops toward himself a kindly sense of humor and learns to say, "Oh, so you have been overlooked? They have placed someone else before you? They have whispered that you are pretty small stuff after all? And now you feel hurt because the world is saying about you the very things you have been saying about yourself? Only yesterday you were telling God that you were nothing, a mere worm of the dust. Where is your consistency? Come on, humble yourself, and cease to care what men think."

The meek man is not a human mouse afflicted with a sense of his own inferiority. Rather he may be in his moral life as bold as a lion and as strong as Samson; but he has stopped being fooled about himself. He has accepted God's estimate of his own life. He knows he is as weak and helpless as God has declared him to be, but paradoxically, he knows at the same time that he is in the sight of God of more importance than angels. In himself, nothing; in God, everything. That is his motto. He knows well that the world will never see him as God sees him and he has stopped caring. He rests perfectly content to allow God to place His own values. He will be patient to wait for the day when everything will get its own price tag and real worth will come into its own. Then the righteous shall shine forth in the Kingdom of their Father. He is willing to wait for that day.

In the meantime he will have attained a place of soul rest. As he walks on in meekness he will be happy to let God defend him. The old struggle to defend himself is over. He has found the peace which meekness brings.

Then also he will get deliverance from the burden of pretense. By this I mean not hypocrisy, but the common human desire to put the best foot forward and hide from the world our real inward poverty. For sin has played many evil tricks upon us, and one has been the infusing into us a false sense of shame. There is hardly a man or woman who dares to be just what he or she is without doctoring up the impression. The fear of being found out gnaws like rodents within their hearts. The man of culture is haunted by the fear that he will some day come upon a man more cultured than himself. The learned man fears to meet a man more learned than he. The rich man sweats under the fear that his clothes or his car or his house will sometime be made to look cheap by comparison with those of another rich man. So-called "society" runs by a motivation not higher than this, and the poorer classes on their level are little better.

Let no one smile this off. These burdens are real, and little by little they kill the victims of this evil and unnatural way of life. And the psychology created by years of this kind of thing makes true meekness seem as unreal as a dream, as aloof as a star. To all the victims of the gnawing disease, Jesus says, "Ye must become as little children." For little children do not compare; they receive direct enjoyment from what they have without relating it to something else or someone else. Only as they get older and sin begins to stir within their hearts do jealousy and envy appear. Then they are unable to enjoy what they have if someone else has something larger or better. At that early age does the galling burden come down upon their tender souls, and it never leaves them till Jesus sets them free.

Another source of burden is artificiality. I am sure that most people live in secret fear that some day they will be careless and by chance an enemy or friend will be allowed to peep into their poor empty souls. So they are never relaxed. Bright people are tense and alert in fear that they may be trapped into saying something common or stupid. Traveled people are afraid that they may meet some Marco Polo who is able to describe some remote place where they have never been.

This unnatural condition is part of our sad heritage of sin, but in our day it is aggravated by our whole way of life. Advertising is largely based upon this habit of pretense. "Courses" are offered in this or that field of human learning frankly appealing to the victim's desire to shine at a party. Books are sold, clothes and cosmetics are peddled, by playing continually upon this desire to appear what we are not. Artificiality is one curse that will drop away the moment we kneel at Jesus' feet and surrender ourselves to His meekness. Then we will not care what people think of us so long as God is pleased. Then what we are will be everything; what we appear will take its place far down the scale of interest for us. Apart from sin we have nothing of which to be ashamed. Only an evil desire to shine makes us want to appear other than we are.

The heart of the world is breaking under this load of pride and pretense. There is no release from our burden apart from the meekness of Christ. Good keen reasoning may help slightly, but so strong is this vice that if we push it down one place it will come up somewhere else. To men and women everywhere Jesus says, "Come unto me, and I will give you rest." The rest He offers is the rest of meekness, the blessed relief which comes when we accept ourselves for what we are and cease to pretend. It will take some courage at first, but the needed grace will come as we learn that we are sharing this new and easy yoke with the strong Son of God Himself. He calls it "my yoke," and He walks at one end while we walk at the other.

Lord, make me childlike. Deliver me from the urge to compete with another for place or prestige or position. I would be simple and artless as a little child. Deliver me from pose and pretense. Forgive me for thinking of myself. Help me to forget myself and find my true peace in beholding Thee. That Thou mayest answer this prayer I humble myself before Thee. Lay upon me Thy easy yoke of self-forgetfulness that through it I may find rest. Amen.

10

The Sacrament of Living

Whether therefore ye eat, or drink,
or whatsoever ye do, do all to the glory of God.
1 CORINTHIANS 10:31

One of the greatest hindrances to internal peace which the Christian encounters is the common habit of dividing our lives into two areas, the sacred and the secular. As these areas are conceived to exist apart from each other and to be morally and spiritually incompatible, and as we are compelled by the necessities of living to be always crossing back and forth from the one to the other, our inner lives tend to break up so that we live a divided instead of a unified life.

Our trouble springs from the fact that we who follow Christ inhabit at once two worlds, the spiritual and the natural. As children of Adam we live our lives on earth subject to the limitations of the flesh and the weaknesses and ills to which human nature is heir. Merely to live among men requires of us years of hard toil and much care and attention to the things of this world. In sharp contrast to this is our life in the Spirit. There we enjoy another and higher kind of life; we are children of God; we possess heavenly status and enjoy intimate fellowship with Christ.

This tends to divide our total life into two departments. We come unconsciously to recognize two sets of actions. The first are performed with a feeling of satisfaction and a firm assurance that they are pleasing to God. These are the sacred acts and they are usually thought to be prayer, Bible reading, hymn singing, church attendance and such other acts as spring directly from faith. They may be known by the fact that they have no direct relation to this world, and would have no meaning whatever except as faith shows us another world, "an house not made with hands, eternal in the heavens."

Over against these sacred acts are the secular ones. They include all of the ordinary activities of life which we share with the sons and daughters of Adam: eating, sleeping, working, looking after the needs of the body and performing our dull and prosaic duties here on earth. These we often do reluctantly and with many misgivings, often apologizing to God for what we consider a waste of time and strength. The upshot of this is that we are uneasy most of the time.

We go about our common tasks with a feeling of deep frustration, telling ourselves pensively that there's a better day coming when we shall slough off this earthly shell and be bothered no more with the affairs of this world.

This is the old sacred-secular antithesis. Most Christians are caught in its trap. They cannot get a satisfactory adjustment between the claims of the two worlds. They try to walk the tight rope between two kingdoms and they find no peace in either. Their strength is reduced, their outlook confused and their joy taken from them.

I believe this state of affairs to be wholly unnecessary. We have gotten ourselves on the horns of a dilemma, true enough, but the dilemma is not real. It is a creature of misunderstanding. The sacred-secular antithesis has no foundation in the New Testament. Without doubt a more perfect understanding of Christian truth will deliver us from it.

The Lord Jesus Christ Himself is our perfect example, and He knew no divided life. In the Presence of His Father He lived on earth without strain from babyhood to His death on the cross. God accepted the offering of His total life, and made no distinction between act and act. "I do always the things that please him," was His brief summary of His own life as it related to the Father. As He moved among men He was poised and restful. What pressure and suffering He endured grew out of His position as the world's sin bearer; they were never the result of moral uncertainty or spiritual maladjustment.

Paul's exhortation to "do all to the glory of God" is more than pious idealism. It is an integral part of the sacred revelation and is to be accepted as the very Word of Truth. It opens before us the possibility of making every act of our lives contribute to the glory of God. Lest we should be too timid to include everything, Paul mentions specifically eating and drinking. This humble privilege we share with the beasts that perish. If these lowly animal acts can be so performed as to honor God, then it becomes difficult to conceive of one that cannot.

That monkish hatred of the body which figures so prominently in the works of certain early devotional writers is wholly without support in the Word of God. Common modesty is found in the Sacred Scriptures, it is true, but never prudery or a false sense of shame. The New Testament accepts as a matter of course that in His incarnation our Lord took upon Him a real human body, and no effort is made to steer around the downright implications of such a fact. He lived in that body here among men and never once performed a non-sacred act. His presence in human flesh sweeps away forever the evil notion that there is about the human body something innately offensive to the Deity. God created our bodies, and we do not offend Him by placing the responsibility where it belongs. He is not ashamed of the work of His own hands. Perversion, misuse and abuse of our human powers should give us cause enough to be ashamed. Bodily acts done in sin and contrary to nature can never honor God. Wherever the human will introduces moral evil, we have no longer our innocent and harmless powers as God made them; we have instead an abused and twisted thing which can never bring glory to its Creator.

Let us, however, assume that perversion and abuse are not present. Let us think of a Christian believer in whose life the twin wonders of repentance and the new birth have been wrought. He is now living according to the will of God as he understands it from the written Word. Of such a one it may be said that every act of his life is or can be as truly sacred as prayer or baptism or the Lord's Supper. To say this is not to bring all acts down to one dead level; it is rather to lift every act up into a living kingdom and turn the whole life into a sacrament.

If a sacrament is an external expression of an inward grace, then we need not hesitate to accept the above thesis. By one act of consecration of our total selves to God we can make every subsequent act express that consecration. We need no more be ashamed of our body—the fleshly servant that carries us through life—than Jesus was of the humble beast upon which He rode into Jerusalem. "The Lord hath need of him" may well apply to our mortal bodies. If Christ dwells in us we may bear about the Lord of glory as the little beast did of old and give occasion to the multitudes to cry, "Hosanna in the highest."

That we see this truth is not enough. If we would escape from the toils of the sacred-secular dilemma, the truth must "run in our blood" and condition the complexion of our thoughts. We must practice living to the glory of God, actually and determinedly. By meditating upon this truth, by talking it over with God often in our prayers, by recalling it to our minds frequently as we move about among men, a sense of its wondrous meaning will begin to take hold of us. The old painful duality will go down before a restful unity of life. The knowledge that we are all God's, that He has received all and rejected nothing, will unify our inner lives and make everything sacred to us.

This is not quite all. Long-held habits do not die easily. It will take intelligent thought and a great deal of reverent prayer to escape completely from the sacred-secular psychology. For instance, it may be difficult for the average Christian to get hold of the idea that his daily labors can be performed as acts of worship acceptable to God by Jesus Christ. The old antithesis will crop up in the back of his head sometimes to disturb his peace of mind. Nor will that old serpent the devil take all this lying down. He will be there in the cab or at the desk or in the field to remind the Christian that he is giving the better part of his day to the things of this world and allotting to his religious duties only a trifling portion of his time. And unless great care is taken, this will create confusion and bring discouragement and heaviness of heart.

We can meet this successfully only by the exercise of an aggressive faith. We must offer all our acts to God and believe that He accepts them. Then hold firmly to that position and keep insisting that every act of every hour of the day and night be included in the transaction. Keep reminding God in our times of private prayer that we mean every act for His glory; then supplement those times by a thousand thought-prayers as we go about the job of living. Let us practice the fine art of making every work a priestly ministration. Let us believe that God is in all our simple deeds and learn to find Him there.

A concomitant of the error which we have been discussing is the sacred-secular antithesis as applied to places. It is little short of astonishing that we can read the New Testament and still believe in the inherent sacredness of places as distinguished from other places. This error is so widespread that one feels all alone when he tries to combat it. It has acted as a kind of dye to color the thinking of religious persons and has colored the eyes as well so that it is all but impossible to detect its fallacy. In the face of every New Testament teaching to the contrary, it has been said and sung throughout the centuries and accepted as a part of the Christian message, the which it most surely is not. Only the Quakers, so far as my knowledge goes, have had the perception to see the error and the courage to expose it.

Here are the facts as I see them. For four hundred years Israel had dwelt in Egypt, surrounded by the crassest idolatry. By the hand of Moses they were brought out at last and started toward the land of promise. The very idea of holiness had been lost to them. To correct this, God began at the bottom. He localized Himself in the cloud and fire and later when the tabernacle had been built He dwelt in fiery manifestation in the Holy of Holies. By innumerable distinctions God taught Israel the difference between holy and unholy. There were holy days, holy vessels, holy garments. There were washings, sacrifices, offerings of many kinds. By these means Israel learned that God is holy. It was this that He was teaching them. Not the holiness of things or places, but the holiness of Jehovah was the lesson they must learn.

Then came the great day when Christ appeared. Immediately He began to say, "Ye have heard that it was said by them of old time. . . . but I say unto you" (Matt. 5:21-22). The Old Testament schooling was over. When Christ died on the cross the veil of the temple was rent from top to bottom. The Holy of Holies was opened to everyone who would enter in faith. Christ's words were remembered, "The hour cometh, when ye shall neither in this mountain, nor yet at Jerusalem, worship the Father. . . . But the hour cometh, and now is, when the true worshippers shall worship the Father in spirit and in truth: for the Father seeketh such to worship Him. God is Spirit, and they that worship him must worship him in spirit and in truth" (John 4:21-23).

Shortly after, Paul took up the cry of liberty and declared all meats clean, every day holy, all places sacred and every act acceptable to God. The sacredness of times and places, a half-light necessary to the education of the race, passed away before the full sun of spiritual worship.

The essential spirituality of worship remained the possession of the Church until it was slowly lost with the passing of the years. Then the natural legality of the fallen hearts of men began to introduce the old distinctions. The Church came to observe again days and seasons and times. Certain places were chosen and marked out as holy in a special sense. Differences were observed between one and another day or place or person. "The sacraments" were first two, then three, then four until with the triumph of Romanism they were fixed at seven.

In all charity, and with no desire to reflect unkindly upon any Christian, however misled, I would point out that the Roman Catholic church represents today the sacred-secular heresy carried to its logical conclusion. Its deadliest effect is the complete cleavage it introduces between religion and life. Its teachers attempt to avoid this snare by many footnotes and multitudinous explanations, but the mind's instinct for logic is too strong. In practical living the cleavage is a fact.

From this bondage reformers and puritans and mystics have labored to free us. Today the trend in conservative circles is back toward that bondage again. It is said that a horse after it has been led out of a burning building will sometimes by a strange obstinacy break loose from its rescuer and dash back into the building again to perish in the flame. By some such stubborn tendency toward error Fundamentalism in our day is moving back toward spiritual slavery. The observation of days and times is becoming more and more prominent among us. "Lent" and "holy week" and "good" Friday are words heard more and more frequently upon the lips of gospel Christians. We do not know when we are well off.

In order that I may be understood and not be misunderstood, I would throw into relief the practical implications of the teaching for which I have been arguing, i.e., the sacramental quality of everyday living. Over against its positive meanings I should like to point out a few things it does not mean.

It does not mean, for instance, that everything we do is of equal importance with everything else we do or may do. One act of a good man's life may differ widely from another in importance. Paul's sewing of tents was not equal to his writing of an Epistle to the Romans, but both were accepted of God and both were true acts of worship. Certainly it is more important to lead a soul to Christ than to plant a garden, but the planting of the garden can be as holy an act as the winning of a soul.

Again, it does not mean that every man is as useful as every other man. Gifts differ in the body of Christ. A Billy Bray is not to be compared with a Luther or a Wesley for sheer usefulness to the

Church and to the world; but the service of the less gifted brother is as pure as that of the more gifted, and God accepts both with equal pleasure.

The "layman" need never think of his humbler task as being inferior to that of his minister. Let every man abide in the calling wherein he is called and his work will be as sacred as the work of the ministry. It is not what a man does that determines whether his work is sacred or secular; it is why he does it. The motive is everything. Let a man sanctify the Lord God in his heart and he can thereafter do no common act. All he does is good and acceptable to God through Jesus Christ. For such a man, living itself will be sacramental and the whole world a sanctuary. His entire life will be a priestly ministration. As he performs his never so simple task, he will hear the voice of the seraphim saying, "Holy, Holy, Holy, is the Lord of hosts: the whole earth is full of his glory." Lord, I would trust Thee completely; I would be altogether Thine; I would exalt Thee above all. I desire that I may feel no sense of possessing anything outside of Thee. I want constantly to be aware of Thy overshadowing Presence and to hear Thy speaking Voice. I long to live in restful sincerity of heart. I want to live so fully in the Spirit that all my thought may be as sweet incense ascending to Thee and every act of my life may be an act of worship. Therefore I pray in the words of Thy great servant of old,

> *"I beseech Thee so for to cleanse the intent of mine heart with the unspeakable gift of Thy grace, that I may perfectly love Thee and worthily praise Thee." And all this I confidently believe Thou wilt grant me through the merits of Jesus Christ Thy Son. Amen.*

The Life of A. W. Tozer

Tozer's Conversion to Christ

Aiden Wilson Tozer was born on April 21, 1897, in La Jose, a tiny farming community in a mountainous region of western Pennsylvania. From early on he preferred using his initials "A. W." rather than his given names.

Life on the Tozer farm was typical of farm life at that time in that area. The Tozers were a close-knit farm family. They worked together, played together and knew each other well.

For a young man ambitious to see what was beyond the fences and hills of Western Pennsylvania, farm life was drudgery and more humdrum than exciting. Often Tozer and his older sister Essie would sit on a fallen log out behind the barn and plan how they could get away—not that they did anything about it then; but talking and planning seemed to ease their minds.

As a teenager, Tozer's family moved from the farm to the city of Akron, Ohio. Tozer was not overly thrilled about farm life and so looked forward to living in the city area.

Tozer's first job, selling candy, peanuts and books as a "butcher boy" on the Vicksburg and Pacific Railroad, was not an auspicious beginning. He worked on commission, and because he preferred to sit and read the books he was supposed to be selling, his earnings were negligible. He had an insatiable passion for reading and a hearty disinclination for peddling. Selling definitely was not his calling.

He and Essie eventually found jobs at Goodyear. Tozer's job was to hand cut chunks of crude rubber into tiny pieces. Tozer worked nights, and as he did very monotonous work with his hands, he would put up a book of poetry in front of him and memorize it as he went. If the work was boring, it was less so than farm work in La Jose. Memories of the farm were a strong motivation for Tozer to make good at Goodyear.

One day as he was walking home from his work at the rubber factory, he noticed a small gathering of people along the way. An old man was talking to them. Young Tozer went over to investigate because he was curious about what the gentleman was saying.

The speaker had a strong German accent, but it did not take Tozer long to realize he was preaching. Tozer began to wonder about him. *Doesn't this man have a church to preach in? It isn't even Sunday! Why is this old man so excited?*

Tozer was startled by these words from the preacher: "If you don't know how to be saved, just call on God, saying, 'God, be merciful to me—a sinner,' and God will hear you."

Those words burned their way into Tozer's heart, and he could not get the preacher's voice out of his head. As he walked home, he gave serious thought to what the preacher said. He had never heard such a message before. The man's words deeply troubled him.

"Saved," he muttered to himself. "'If you don't know how to be saved.' That's what the preacher said." At home, young Tozer headed straight to the attic to be alone so he could think these things through.

Tozer entered the attic a convicted sinner and emerged as a new creation in Christ Jesus. His was a radical conversion experience, and the beginning of a new life, a new world and a new outlook. This change set him firmly in his pursuit of God and from this moment on nothing else mattered. He was utterly committed to following the Lord Jesus Christ.

The Beginning of His Pursuit

The Tozer home was crowded with siblings and several boarders, but he managed to find a regular time and place for prayer and Bible study—a small corner of the basement behind the furnace. He cleaned up that spot and designated it a place to regularly meet with God, his heavenly Father. Here he was able to get alone with God, to pray, meditate and study the Word. This was the foundation for his upcoming ministry.

Essie would often hear her brother groaning in prayer behind the furnace. The first time she heard him, she was frightened; then realized it was her brother praying and "wrestling" with God.

This began a pattern in Tozer's life. He would withdraw from others and seek a quiet spot where he could be alone with God. He began a habit of carrying a little notebook with him in order to keep a journal of his prayers and God's answers to them. Quietness and solitude became very important to him.

The nearby Grace Methodist Episcopal Church, where he soon became an active member, helped Tozer's spiritual pilgrimage along, although he was baptized by immersion in a local Church of the Brethren. The decision to attend Grace Methodist proved fortuitous: There he met his future wife, Ada.

Ada Cecelia Pfautz, a young girl of 15, fresh from the country, was among several being received into church membership. It was Tozer's assignment to usher her to the front at the proper time for the membership ceremony. Ada was embarrassed to learn her escort would be a handsome, clean-cut young man still in his teens.

"This is worse than a wedding," Ada whispered to a girlfriend as Tozer reached her pew. He could not help but overhear her remark, which further embarrassed the young woman.

Following the morning service, the church youth planned a picnic lunch followed by a Bible study and an afternoon social time in the church parlor. Tozer, never one to pass up an opportunity, invited Ada to attend the gathering with him.

"Oh, no," objected Ada. "I couldn't do that. I have to hurry home; my mother is expecting me."

"Well," persisted Tozer, "there's a telephone over there. Why don't you call your mother and tell her that a very nice young man will be bringing you home later this afternoon?"

Ada laughed. Tozer's arguments prevailed. Ada did stay and he did take her home that afternoon. In fact, Tozer soon became a regular caller at the Pfautz home.

It was Kate Pfautz, Ada's mother, who, a year and a half after Tozer's conversion to Christ, prayed with him to be filled with the Holy Spirit.

"Young man," Mrs. Pfautz said, "you must get down on your knees and die to yourself before the Holy Spirit will fill you." She backed up the statement with detailed instruction and patient persistence. One evening in her home, Tozer knelt by the sofa, and Kate prayed with him. He was instantly filled with the Holy Spirit.

"I was 19 years old," Tozer recalled, "earnestly in prayer, when I was baptized with a mighty infusion of the Holy Spirit." In a later sermon, he told his congregation about the experience.

"I know with assurance what God did for me and within me. At that point, nothing on the outside held any important meaning for me. In desperation and in faith, I took a leap away from everything that was unimportant to that which was most important: to be possessed by the Spirit of the living God.

"Any tiny work that God has ever done through me and through my ministry for Him dates back to that hour when I was filled with the Spirit. That is why I plead for the spiritual life of the body of Christ and the eternal ministries of the eternal Spirit through God's children, His instruments."

Tozer would later write extensively on the subject of the filling of the Holy Spirit.

"Neither in the Old Testament nor in the New, nor in Christian testimony as found in the writings of the saints, as far as my knowledge goes, was any believer ever filled with the Holy Spirit who did not know he had been filled. Neither was anyone filled who did not know when he was filled. And no one was ever filled gradually.

"Behind these three trees, many half-hearted souls have tried to hide like Adam from the presence of the Lord, but they are not good enough hiding places: The man who does not know when he was filled was never filled (though, of course, it is possible to forget the date). And the man who hopes to be filled gradually will never be filled at all."

What mother would not be happy to welcome such a son-in-law into the household? On April 26, 1918, three years after Tozer and Ada first met, and five days after his twenty-first birthday, Aiden Wilson Tozer and Ada Cecelia Pfautz became husband and wife.

By this time, Tozer was an active street preacher as well. Nearly every evening found him involved in street meetings. If his sermons were not models of good spoken English, at least he was beginning his ministry and gaining valuable experience.

However, not according to the thinking of Grace Methodist Episcopal Church. They were not particularly pleased with the direction Tozer was setting for himself. Not that the church was opposed to evangelism or to one of its members entering the ministry; but the street was hardly the place for evangelism, he was told, and those aspiring to gospel ministry should go the route of college and seminary.

Meanwhile, Tozer had encountered some street evangelists who said they were members of the nearby Christian and Missionary Alliance Church. The name was a tongue twister, he decided, but the members were extremely interested in evangelism—just as he was.

Several teams from the church were regularly out on street corners doing what he and some of his friends were doing. Tozer and his wife decided to visit the church, and while there met the pastor, Reverend Samuel M. Gerow, who organized the church youth into evangelistic teams that conducted street meetings throughout the city.

On the way home, Tozer announced to Ada, "That's the church we'll be going to from now on. I like it." That settled the matter. Soon both Tozer and his wife were active participants in the life and ministry of the Christian and Missionary Alliance.

Called to the Ministry

In 1919, Tozer, with no formal theological education, was called to the pastorate of a small, storefront church in Nutter Fort, a little village situated in the rolling hills of central West Virginia. From these humble beginnings, Tozer and his young bride launched a ministry that continues to influence people to the present day. He later served churches in Indiana and Ohio. The Tozers lived a simple lifestyle with their seven children—six boys and one girl.

In the early days of his ministry, money was hard to come by. Nonetheless, the Tozers made a pact to trust God for all their needs. He said, "We are convinced that God can send money to His believing children—but it becomes a pretty cheap thing to get excited about the money and fail to give the glory to Him who is the Giver!"

After several years of ministry in West Virginia, the ordination council of the Christian and Missionary Alliance examined young Tozer for ordination. At this point Tozer had no formal education let alone any college degree. After the committee interviewed him, they sent him out and discussed his merits. One pastor said, "I don't think anything will ever come of this man's ministry." Most were in agreement but one convinced them to accept him for ordination despite his lack of qualifications.

After serving churches in West Virginia, Ohio and Indiana, Tozer's next charge proved to be a long-term one. For thirty-one of his forty-four years of ministry he gained prominence as the pastor of Southside Alliance Church in Chicago, Illinois. He served there from 1928 to 1959 as pastor, author, editor, Bible conference speaker and denominational leader. To many people, he was a reliable spiritual mentor.

Going to Chicago was not an easy matter. Tozer was enjoying a wonderful ministry in Indianapolis and was reluctant to leave. The Chicago church was a very small church worshiping in a converted garage. In all regards, it would have been a step down.

Finally, they convinced him to go and preach for one Sunday. Whatever happened that week, Tozer changed his mind about going to Chicago. Little did he know the ministry that awaited him there.

A commercial illustrator, Francis Chase, attended Tozer's first service in the Chicago church and said, "He [Tozer] said very little and I didn't expect much. He was slight with plenty of black hair, and certainly not a fashion plate, as we say. He wore a black tie around one and a half inches in width. His shoes were even then outmoded: high tops with hooks part way up. I introduced him and exited the platform. He said nothing about being pleased to be there or any other pat phrases usually given on such occasions, but simply introduced his sermon topic, which was, 'God's Westminster Abbey,' based on the eleventh chapter of Hebrews." Francis Chase became a close friend to Tozer through the years.

During his Chicago years, Tozer had a very busy schedule. In order to get away and have some time with God, he would often board a westbound train from Chicago and ride for four hours. He would get a Pullman car, which guaranteed him privacy during his travel. During those four hours of privacy, he would kneel before God with an outspread Bible. Those were precious times of drawing near to God. Nobody could interrupt him nor could anybody find him.

After a four-hour trip, he caught another train back to Chicago for another four hours of time alone with God. During these times of prayer and meditation, he often wrote essays, editorials and sermons. They proved to be some of his most productive times.

Tozer stayed in Chicago until 1959. The neighborhood had drastically changed and the church needed to move out into the suburbs. Tozer did not feel that with his work schedule, his writing and speaking, he had the time to do it justice. In 1959, he resigned from the Chicago church and planned to go to New York City and spend the rest of his days writing, editing and speaking at conferences.

Such was not to be the case. The leadership at a Toronto church convinced him to go there and lead. He agreed to go, but only on a temporary basis and only to preach; others would have to run the church. They agreed and that temporary assignment turned into four of his most productive years of ministry.

Tozer's last pastorate was at the Avenue Road Church in Toronto, Canada (1959-1963).

Pen of a Ready Writer

Tozer always searched for and ministered to those who were hungry for God. In *The Pursuit of God*, Tozer wrote, "My appeal is addressed to those who have been previously taught in secret by the wisdom of God; I speak to thirsty hearts whose longings have been wakened by the touch of God within them, and such as they need no reasoned proof. Their restless hearts furnish all the proof they need."

For 13 years (1950-1963) Tozer was the editor of *The Alliance Weekly*, the official publication of the Christian and Missionary Alliance. This periodical received a new title in 1958 when it became *The Alliance Witness*, which then became *Alliance Life* in 1987. Under Tozer's leadership, the magazine flourished, and its circulation doubled.

His first editorial set the tone for the rest of his editorship. "It will cost something to walk slow in the parade of the ages, while excited men of time rush about confusing motion with progress. But it will pay in the long run and the true Christian is not much interested in anything short of that."

The Alliance Witness, more than anything else, helped establish Tozer as a spokesman to the evangelical church at large. Many subscribed to the magazine mainly to read Tozer's prophetic editorials, which were also published in Great Britain in *The Life of Faith* magazine. H. F. Stevenson, editor of *The Life of Faith*, said, "His [Tozer's] survey of the contemporary scene was as relevant to Britain as to his own country, so that his articles and books were read avidly here also."

Dr. Nathan Bailey, former President of the Christian and Missionary Alliance, was likewise amazed at the freshness of Tozer's writings. He stated, "In his writings he gave the superficial and the obvious and the trivial for others to thrash around, applying himself to the field of study and prayer that resulted in articles and books that reached deep into the hearts of men."

Tozer wrote many books, as well, all springing from a deeply burdened heart. He had a message from God he knew he had to give. In his preface to *The Divine Conquest* (now entitled *The Pursuit of Man*), he explained, "The sight of the languishing church around me and the operation of a new spiritual power within me have set up a pressure impossible to resist. Whether or not the book ever reaches a wide public, still it has to be written if for no other reason than to relieve an unbearable burden on the heart."

His last literary work was completed just before his death and published posthumously several months later. It was entitled *The Christian Book of Mystical Verse*, and was a compilation of a wealth of mystic poetry that had blessed Tozer's heart throughout the years.

In the introduction to *The Christian Book of Mystical Verse*, Tozer wrote, "The word 'mystic' as it occurs in the title of this book refers to that personal spiritual experience common to the saints of Bible times and well known to multitudes of persons in the post-biblical era. I refer to the evangelical mystic who has been brought by the gospel into intimate fellowship with the Godhead. His theology is no less and no more than is taught in the Christian Scriptures. He walks the high road of truth where walked of old prophets and apostles, and where down the centuries walked martyrs, reformers, Puritans, evangelists and missionaries of the cross. He differs from the ordinary orthodox Christian only because he experiences his faith down in the depths of his sentient being while the other does not. He exists in a world of spiritual reality. He is quietly, deeply, and sometimes almost ecstatically aware of the Presence of God in his own nature and in the world around him. His religious experience is something elemental, as old as time and the creation. It is immediate acquaintance with God by union with the Eternal Son. It is to recognize that which transcends knowledge."[1]

Tozer lived in a profound sense of God enveloping him in reverence and adoration. His one daily exercise was the practice of the presence of God, pursuing Him with all his strength and energy. To him, Jesus Christ was a daily wonder, a recurring astonishment and a continual amazement of love and grace.

On occasions while Raymond McAfee, a longtime associate of Tozer's, was praying, he would hear Tozer rustling about. After opening an eye to see what was going on, he would discover Tozer, pencil in hand, writing. While McAfee was praying, Tozer had a thought he wanted to capture.

Tozer met with his church staff regularly for prayer. Once, during a staff prayer meeting, Tozer was prone on the floor in deep conversation with God. The telephone rang. Tozer broke off his prayer to answer the phone. He carried on about a 20-minute conversation with a pastor, giving him all sorts of instructions and advice that he himself never followed—taking time off, going on a vacation, and so on. The staff just sat there listening and chuckling to themselves because Tozer never took a vacation in his life. Hanging up the telephone, Tozer resumed his position on the floor and picked up where he left off by saying, "Now, God, as I was saying . . ."

Tozer was a man of prayer and often commented, "As a man prays, so is he." His entire ministry flowed out of fervent prayer.

Voice of a Prophet

His sermons were powerful, and his outstanding books established him as a classic devotional writer. In addition, Tozer had a weekly radio broadcast aired on WMBI—the radio station of the Moody Bible Institute in Chicago. His program was called "Talks from a Pastor's Study," and those programs emanated from Tozer's study at Southside Alliance Church. Because of those broadcasts, he received frequent invitations to minister at Chicago-area Bible colleges, which he greatly enjoyed.

To understand Tozer, one must focus on his devotional life. For him, correct doctrine was not enough. He observed, "You can be straight as a gun barrel theologically and as empty as one spiritually." When he preached and taught, he did not stress systematic theology; rather, he stressed the importance of a personal relationship with God—a relationship so personal and so overpowering as to entirely captivate a person's attention. He longed for what he called a "God-conscious soul"—a heart aflame for God.

Faithfully, Tozer called evangelicals to return to the authentic biblical positions that had characterized the Church when it was most faithful to Christ and His Word. While his messages were profound and sober, Tozer often spiced them with his wonderful sense of humor. However, he carefully kept humor out of his books.

Tozer loved to have fellowship with God. He once wrote, "I have found God to be cordial and generous and in every way easy to live with." In a similar vein he wrote, "Labor that does not spring out of worship is futile and can only be wood, hay, and stubble in the day that shall try every man's work."

Tozer loved hymns and acquired an extensive collection of old hymnals. He often used these hymnals as means for meditation and devotional reading. Oftentimes, he would counsel people to get a hymnbook—"but don't find one that is less than a hundred years old." In one article for *The Alliance Witness* he wrote, "After the Bible the next most valuable book for the Christian is a good hymnal. Let any young Christian spend a year prayerfully meditating on the hymns of [Isaac] Watts and [Charles] Wesley alone, and he will become a fine theologian. Then let him read a balanced diet of the Puritans and the Christian mystics. The results will be more wonderful than he could have dreamed."

Tozer criticized entertainment in churches, which made him somewhat infamous and less popular with some Christians. This attitude stemmed from his high regard for worship, which he felt was violated oftentimes by attempts to bring entertainment to God's people. To him, worship was to be pure and unsullied by worldly affairs.

Tozer was greatly concerned about the ways in which worldliness was making inroads into the Church and how it was affecting Christians. He was particularly critical of some forms of evangelism, which he felt lowered the standards that the Church should be upholding.

To Preach the Word

Tozer's goal in preaching was to lead the listener straight into the presence of God. Therefore, everything that would distract from the message, and particularly from God, he ruthlessly cut out.

In prayer, God would lay a burden on Tozer's heart. Then, as time passed, he would preach a series of sermons related to this burden.

When he was away from his own pulpit, he would preach the same sermons. Sometimes the weight of the burden would increase and weigh him down to the point that even in preaching he could find no release. This would then lead him to writing and the fruit would eventually take the shape of a book.

Tozer's method of preaching included the strong declaration of biblical principles, never merely an involvement in word studies, clever outlines or statistics. Listening to his recorded sermons or reading any of his many books, the observer will notice the absence of alliteration common to many preachers. His style was the simple unfolding of truth as naturally as a flower unfolds in the sunlight.

According to Tozer, every preacher must develop the habit of "reading good writing." He urged people to go back to the classics and said, "Read some of the great Puritan authors and some of the mystics. Read and memorize good poetry. Observe how these writers express themselves. Become word conscious. Pay attention to words and the effect they have. Get a good dictionary and use it often. Whenever I come across a word I'm not familiar with, I look it up immediately and study it. With a large vocabulary, you are able to be precise in what you are saying. Nothing takes the place of using the right word. [Gustave] Flaubert (1821–1880) used to say there are no synonyms. Find the right word, and use it."

One trademark in Tozer's preaching was that he always seemed to have the right word at his disposal. Psalm 104, a meditation upon the majesty and providence of God, thrilled Tozer's heart, and he often preached from it. At the close of one such sermon, a member of the congregation stated, "He out-Davided David!"

Regarding his preaching, he said, "I like to compare the preacher to an artist. An artist works in water, oil, sand, stone, gold, glass. On the other hand, the preacher works in the stuff called mankind. The artist has an idea of abstract beauty and he seeks to reproduce it in visible, concrete things. The preacher has Christ and attempts to make Him visible in human lives. The artist has genius while the preacher has the Holy Spirit. The artist draws his inspiration from other artists while the preacher draws his inspiration in prayer alone with God.

"The tools of the artist are brushes, chisels, paint. But the tools of the preacher are words. Ninety-nine percent of your public service will be using words. A preacher, like the artist, must master his tools. He must toil and labor and strive for mastery in this area. At first he will make awkward attempts, but if he keeps at it, he will become an expert."

Regarding his preparation for preaching, Tozer said, "Many times I come here to my study as uninspired as a burnt shingle. I have editorials due, the preaching ministry here, plus outside preaching engagements. Often when I come here, I kneel by that old sofa over there with my Bible and a hymnbook. I'll read some Scripture, softly sing a few hymns and in a short time my heart is worshiping God. God begins to manifest Himself to me and pour matter into my soul. Before long I take up my pencil and start jotting down sketches and outlines for editorials and sermons."

Clearly, he was a defender of the faith once delivered unto the saints. He once made this statement: "I believe everything is wrong until God sets it right."

The Importance of Worship

Tozer wrote, "Worship is to feel in your heart and express in some appropriate manner a humbling but delightful sense of admiring awe, astonished wonder, and overpowering love in the presence of that most ancient Mystery, that Majesty which philosophers call the First Cause, but which we call Our Father in Heaven."

Tozer's hunger for God led him to consider the Christian mystics, and in them he found a deep knowledge of God and an absorbing love for Him, which propelled him to go deeper with God. He said, "These people know God, and I want to know what they know about God and how they came to know it."

Raymond McAfee was Tozer's associate pastor, choir director and song leader in Chicago for fifteen years. They often met together for prayer and conversation. McAfee wrote, "On a day that I shall never forget, Tozer knelt down by his chair, took off his glasses and laid them on the chair, rested back on his bent ankles. He clasped his hands together, raised his face with his eyes closed and began, 'O God, we are before Thee.' With that there came a rush of God's presence that literally filled the room, and we both worshiped God in silent ecstasy, wonder and adoration."

McAfee went on, "I've never forgotten that moment and I don't want to forget it. The memory lingers in my mind, almost with the same freshness and vivacity as that morning. That, to me, was Dr. Tozer."

Once at a special conference where Tozer was the keynote speaker, he was not on hand when the service started. The song leader thought that perhaps he was running a little late and he would eventually get to the service in time to preach. However, when the time came for the sermon, Tozer was nowhere to be found and a substitute had to fill in for him.

The next day the song leader ran across Tozer and in a rather kidding fashion said, "I guess you missed your appointment last night?"

Without smiling, Tozer merely said, "I had a more important appointment last night."

Later the leader discovered Tozer had spent the whole day and night in prayer on his knees before God. Such was his commitment to his fellowship with God.

Tozer, of course, was not a perfect human being. Who is? A disposition of a recluse at times and a very heavy schedule left little time for his wife, Ada, and their children.

Many, even members of his own house, did not truly understand him, especially when he insisted on being alone so often. Some people even regarded him as being a bit odd, but what others thought of him did not bother Tozer in the least. His main concern was the worship of God, and nothing else mattered all that much to him.

Tozer certainly marched to the beat of a different drummer, but not in the same way a rebel might do. It was simply that he was totally sold out to Jesus Christ. His family, friends and even the ministry had to take a back seat to his pursuit of God. He entitled one of his essays "The Saint Must Walk Alone," thus providing us with significant insights into his perspective and priorities.

Occasionally he would come to the family dinner table, especially after the children had left, and not utter a word—not because he was mad at anyone, but because he was so focused on God, and refused to violate that focus even for fellowship around the table with family and friends. In light of this, Tozer did not spend much time perfecting his social graces.

Tozer loved to be shut in alone with God. He cultivated his ability to focus on Him every day. In so doing, he would quiet his heart and adore and worship his heavenly Father.

At conferences, Tozer often seemed preoccupied with something, which he was; he was musing about some aspect of the God he loved so much. He told others that he had dreams of God, as well, so his focus on God continued even after he went to sleep!

Tozer generously shared the lessons he had learned through worship with all who seemed interested. He firmly believed ministry had to flow from worship and that any work that does not flow from worship is unacceptable to God.

He never entangled himself in social or political issues, even though he was highly opinionated regarding many of them. As a minister of the gospel, however, he understood his task was to preach the good news and to lead people to Jesus. Because of this,

his writings are as fresh today as they were when he first wrote them; they appeal to the essential needs of human beings, regardless of the age in which they live.

The Pursuit of God

In 1945, Dr. Tozer was preaching along a particular line of Bible truth. Shortly before this, he had had a fresh encounter with God and was sharing this meaningful experience with his congregation. The sermons were richly blessed of God, and the people in the Chicago church were deeply affected by them.

As he preached to other audiences, he continued to share his experience with each one. In preaching these sermons, he sensed a strange pressure building inside himself. At first, this phenomenon confused him, but after long hours of prayer and meditation, he began to see how God was leading him.

Tozer was struggling under the increasing pressure of the first of these burdens when he received an invitation to preach in McAllen, Texas—far down toward the Mexican border. He saw in it an opportunity. The long train ride from Chicago would afford him ample time to think and to write.

Boarding the Pullman at the old LaSalle Street Station, Tozer requested of the porter a small writing table for his roomette. There, with only his Bible before him, he began to write. About 9:00 PM, the porter knocked on the door. "This is the last call for dinner," he announced. "Would you want me to bring you something to eat?"

"Yes," Tozer responded. "Please bring me some toast and tea." With only toast and tea to fortify him physically, Tozer continued to write. He wrote all night long, the words coming to him as fast as he could jot them down. The manuscript was almost writing itself, he was so full of his subject. Early the next morning when the train pulled into McAllen, a rough draft of *The Pursuit of God* was complete.

The main thesis of *The Pursuit of God* is achieving the heart's true goal in God. Although Tozer approached his subject from various angles, he never departed from his central theme—God, and man's relation to Him, and how to maintain that relationship. One reviewer said, "The style is natural, free and easy, abounding in the pithy sentences that characterize Tozer's writing. In some of the chapters, the movement is more stately, the tone rather philosophical. It awakens thought and expectancy, and while never heavy, it is profound."

The Pursuit of God catapulted Tozer into the forefront of what was still, in 1948, a relatively small group of evangelical writers. Readers rushed out to buy copies. Here was a penetrating message for the twentieth century, written in a style refreshingly different.

Rev. H. M. Shuman, who was the president of the Christian and Missionary Alliance and also the editor of the *Alliance Weekly*, said, "This book is mystical—in the best sense. Certainly is not the pale, negative, gloomy type of much of the religious mysticism of earlier times. It is a vigorous, mid-twentieth-century model of true Christian mysticism, if we are to apply that word to it at all. Its language, approach, and spirit bespeak a virile type of spiritual Christianity in the midst of materialism and sensuality."

The book's success was a pleasant surprise for Tozer. In reply to an especially appreciative letter, Tozer wrote, "After reading your letter I am left with few words. I am both gratified and awestruck. 'This is the Lord's doing; it is marvelous in our eyes.' The blessing that has rested on this little book is so much greater than I had dared to hope that I cannot say God is blessing it because of my prayers."

After more than 65 years, *The Pursuit of God* is still in demand and has been published in many different languages. It still is doing what Tozer set out for it to do in a marvelous and wonderful way: point the reader toward achieving the heart's true goal in God.

Tozer's Legacy

The legacy left by Tozer is found in the majesty of God. His supreme desire was to exalt the Lord Jesus Christ. "If you major on knowing God," Tozer once wrote, "and cultivate a sense of His presence in your daily life, and do what Brother Lawrence advises, 'Practice the presence of God' daily and try to know the Holy Spirit in the Scriptures, you will go a long way in serving your generation for God. No man has any right to die until he has served his generation."

Many people, including Dr. Louis L. King (president of the Christian and Missionary Alliance), Leonard Ravenhill and Dr. Stephen F. Olford, considered Tozer a prophet to the Body of Christ. Because he was such a respected man of God, many would come to him for advice and counsel, including students from nearby Wheaton College.

During the next few years, Tozer's reputation and ministry enjoyed a steady growth. Many invited him to conference platforms, summer Bible camps, and Christian gatherings of all descriptions. People came to his study for counsel—people like the young evangelist Billy Graham and politician Mark O. Hatfield—because they knew he was a man well acquainted with God.

Tozer said, "Years ago I prayed that God would sharpen my mind and enable me to receive everything He wanted to say to me. I then prayed that God would anoint my head with the oil of the prophet so I could say it back to the people. That one prayer has cost me plenty since, I can tell you that. Don't ever pray such a prayer if you don't mean it, and if you want to be happy, don't pray it, either."

Toward the end of his ministry, Tozer asked for prayer from his congregation. He said, "Pray for me in the light of the pressures of our times. Pray that I will not just come to a wearied end—an exhausted, tired old preacher interested only in hunting a place to roost. Pray that I will be willing to let my Christian experience and Christian standards cost me something right down to the last gasp!"

The rest of his life and ministry proved how wondrously God answered that prayer.

On May 12, 1963, A. W. Tozer's earthly labors ended. His faith in God's majesty became sight as he entered into His presence. At the funeral, his daughter Becky said, "I can't feel sad. I know Dad's happy; he's lived for this all his life."

Although his physical presence has been removed from us, Tozer will continue to minister to those who are thirsty for the things of God. Some have referred to him as the "conscience of evangelicalism." As such, he recognized modern Christianity sailing through a dense spiritual fog and pointed out the rocks on which it could flounder if it persisted in its course. His spiritual intention enabled him to sense error, name it for what it was and reject it—all in one decisive act.

Tozer was buried in Ellet Cemetery in Akron, Ohio, his epitaph offering an accurate description of his life: "A. W. Tozer—a Man of God."

This biography is adapted from
The Life of A. W. Tozer: In Pursuit of God
by James L. Snyder.

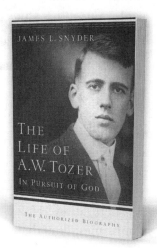

Note

1. A. W. Tozer, *The Christian Book of Mystical Verse* (Harrisburg, PA: Christian Publications, Inc., 1963).

A.W. TOZER

Compiled and Edited by JAMES L. SNYDER

THE
PURPOSE
OF
MAN

DESIGNED TO WORSHIP

BETHANYHOUSE
a division of Baker Publishing Group
Minneapolis, Minnesota

CONTENTS

A. W. TOZER:
A HEART TO WORSHIP

For more than 44 years, Aiden Wilson Tozer served as a minister in the Christian and Missionary Alliance. His most prominent ministry was 31 years at the Southside Alliance Church in Chicago, often referred to as that citadel of Fundamentalism. His ministry, however, went beyond the confines of a denomination. He served as a voice to the entire Body of Christ. His books and articles were eagerly read, and his conference ministry attended with great expectation. Rarely did he disappoint those who knew him. If you were looking for formulaic Christianity, you were disappointed with him. If you were interested in what he referred to as "feel good Christianity," you were greatly disappointed.

During his life, Tozer earned a reputation for many things: an outspoken critic of the religious scene, an outstanding preacher, editor of a leading Christian periodical and author of several devotional classics. The real focus, however, of his daily life centered on the worship of God. Nothing else so occupied his mind and life. This worship of God was not something tacked on to a busy schedule. It became the one great passion of his life. Everything revolved around his personal worship of God.

Worship as a Lifestyle

Tozer paid the price for this lifestyle of worship. Many, even of his own family, did not understand him and his insistence on being alone. Some even regarded him as a bit odd; but what others thought of him did not trouble him in the least. His primary business was the worship of God. Nothing else mattered more than that.

To appreciate the ministry of Tozer, you must comprehend his passion for worship. If not, you will likely misunderstand not only his words, but his actions as well. He was completely committed to this one solemn activity and pursued it with all the passion he had. Tozer's ideas regarding worship were hammered into conviction that governed his life and ministry. "Worship," Tozer explained, "is to feel in your heart and express in some appropriate manner a humbling but delightful sense of admiring awe and astonished wonder and overpowering love in the presence of that most ancient Mystery, that majesty which philosophers call the First Cause but which we call Our Father Which Art in Heaven."

Tozer walked to the beat of a different drummer, but it was not simply because he was a rebel. That may have been a small part of it, but the main factor was his complete sellout to Jesus Christ. Family, friends and even the ministry had to take a back seat to this yearning of his. Perhaps his essay "The Saint Must Walk Alone" explains to a certain degree his idea of true spirituality. His focus in life was on the person of Jesus Christ, and he would do everything within his power to sharpen that focus. All his spiritual energies and disciplines were directed in that singular path. Consequently, in a certain degree, he was difficult to live with, not because he was demanding or irascible, but because he was simply focused on God.

At times, he would come to the family dinner table, especially after the children had left home, and not speak a word. He wasn't mad at anyone; he was focused on God, and would not break the focus even for fellowship around the table with friends and family. Tozer did not spend too much time working on his social graces, probably one glaring weakness in his character. Yet, to do the work he believed God called him to demanded much time away from people and shut up alone with God.

Tozer daily cultivated the ability to focus on God. He would quiet his heart, and out of that quietness would come adoration and worship for the triune Godhead.

Often at conferences, Tozer seemed preoccupied. He was always musing on some aspect of God. He once claimed that he had dreams of God, so much were his thoughts directed toward the Godhead. Although quite knowledgeable on a variety of subjects, and with strong opinions on many of them, in later life, Tozer's focus on God got sharper and he disengaged from most other subjects to the exclusion of worship.

The lessons Tozer learned in worship he generously shared with all who would listen. His preaching and writing were simply the clear declarations of what he had experienced in his private sessions with God. Emerging from his prayer closet, dripping with the fragrance of the Presence, he was eager to report all he had witnessed. After such a sermon during his Chicago ministry, one in the congregation observed, "He out-Davided David."

A Message for the Generations

Few writers get to the heart of a subject as quickly as Tozer. He bypassed the trivia and concentrated on those essential ingredients important to the believer's walk with God. In this book, he bares his soul on worship—the one great obsession of his life. Though many have written about worship, I believe that Tozer surpasses them all in simple passion and supreme purpose. A reader coming away from this book will not only understand worship but will also experience it in his or her own heart.

You may not always agree with him, but you will always know what he believes and why. He says, "This will be the best teaching in my ministry, comparing myself with myself." The ensuing messages prove Tozer to be the prophet his reputation suggests. "I want to deliver my soul as a prophet of God to the people, and to explain why we were created and why we are here, not to the satisfaction of the immediate appetite only but to something bigger, grander and more eternal, that we might worship God and enjoy Him forever."

Throughout this book, Dr. Tozer systematically presents his teaching on a subject close to his heart. Nowhere will anyone find a more fully developed thesis on worship with such sanctified passion. Tozer was one of the first in evangelical circles to call attention to this neglected Bible doctrine. He issued a clarion call for Christians to return to their first love. Now that the pendulum has swung to the other extreme in the evangelical church, these teachings are as needed today as when Tozer first preached them.

Many people are interested in the subject of worship, and most books focus on technology and performance. Here is a book deeply rooted in Bible doctrine and historic writings that focus on the Presence of God. One of the great aspects of this book is how Tozer blends Scripture with some of the great devotional writers throughout history. Many refer to these as Mystics, and Tozer is responsible for introducing these great saints to Protestants and evangelicals. The book is well seasoned with the thoughts of these great saints of the past and their Spirit-inspired writings.

A close study of Tozer's ministry will warrant the simple conclusion that his ministry was not just cranking out sermons, articles and editorials. He always had something significant to report. His entire ministry was marked with this distinction. He firmly believed that his labor must flow from a life of worship. Any work that does not flow from worship is unacceptable to God. And, after all, it is God we are trying to please, not man.

Throughout his long ministry, Tozer never became entangled in social or political issues. Not that he did not have an opinion on these subjects, for he did. His conviction was that he was responsible to stick to the great essentials of life. That is why his writings today are just as fresh and relevant as when first published. He believed that certain things never change, whatever the generation. He kept to those fundamentals, and you either loved what Tozer said or hated it. While other ministers were becoming involved in political issues, Tozer contented himself with preaching about God.

In this book on worship, Tozer's purpose is twofold: to deliver his soul on a subject close to his heart and to inspire others to cultivate a spirit of worship in daily living. Tozer lays a solid foundation here, and once a person has read this book, he can go on to develop a lifestyle of worship that dominates his life. No one who reads this book all the way through will be the same as before, especially when it comes to his or her personal worship of God.

Often, when in a thoughtful mood, Tozer confided to a friend, "My ambition is to love God more than any one of my generation." Whatever he meant by that, it is evident that he possessed a passion for God that controlled everything in his life. Some evidence exists suggesting he achieved his goal more than he imagined.

The first book he wrote that brought him to the attention of the Christian public was *The Pursuit of God*. The last book was *The Knowledge of the Holy*. Tozer lived between these two books. Tozer *lived* a lifestyle of worship, and nothing else truly mattered to him. He sacrificed family, friends and reputation in his pursuit of God.

Tozer's criticism of entertainment within the church made him quite infamous during his lifetime. At times, his high view of worship caused him to lash out mercilessly. Worship was to be pure and untainted by worldly things. In his mind, the two were opposed to each other. When someone suggested that singing a hymn was a form of entertainment, it riled Tozer's fury. Some of his most eloquent denunciations were in this direction. He was justly concerned about the inroads worldliness was making in the Church, and its effect on Christians. Especially was he adamant about contemporary evangelism methods that many were advocating. He felt it lowered the standards of the Church, and he was dead set against it.

His comments at times are sharp because of his deep love for the Church and the fellowship of God's people. He did not relish the idea of any compromise with the message or the spirit of New Testament Christianity. He truly believed that the Church of Jesus Christ had a viable message for the world and he was anxious that the message not be mixed or diluted. Desperate times require strong medicine, and Tozer felt that the Church was backing away from her strong medicine and becoming adjusted to the world around.

He aptly described his philosophy when he said, "I believe everything is wrong until God sets it right." This is where he began; and from that position, he proclaimed freedom through the Lord Jesus Christ.

Entertainment in the Church

Tozer once wrote a booklet, "The Menace of the Religious Movie," in which he set forth in irresistible logic his conviction on the matter of entertainment in the church. The opinions are strong yet backed by biblical principles. Not only must the message please God but the methods of getting that message out must please God and be compatible with the character and nature of God. He continually ridiculed the idea that "new days demand new ways."

To appreciate fully Tozer's criticism of entertainment, his idea of worship must be examined. He firmly believed that entertainment would undermine Christian worship and put the Church in jeopardy, a thought abhorrent to Tozer. The integrity of the church, as Tozer saw it, was in danger of being compromised by the introduction of "things" into the sanctuary. His ideas of music, prayer, evangelism and missions sprang from the imperative of worship within the Christian community.

Tozer's Spiritual Legacy

The legacy of Tozer is in the area of *the majesty of God*. Whatever else Tozer did, his supreme desire was to exalt the Lord Jesus Christ as simply as possible. He tried to set before his generation the importance of certain virtues, such as simplicity and solitude, and to turn the attention of the young preachers, for he had a great influence among them, away from sham and pretense and all kinds of flesh that could creep into church politics. Getting alone with your Bible and a hymnal was highly recommended by Tozer. It was this intimacy with God that made his ministry what it became and is remembered now.

Another significant aspect of his legacy is *spiritual insight*. Tozer saw into the nature of things so deeply that it burdened him. He once made the remark that if you want to be happy, do not pray for discernment. Tozer had the gift of spiritual discernment. He could see beyond the present action to the impending result in the years to come. He could see that the way the evangelical church of his day was going, it soon would be in serious spiritual trouble. His message was always to turn back to God despite the inconvenience or cost. He urged churches to forget the Madison Avenue techniques, the strategies of the world and their programs and priorities. He advocated a life of sacrifice, self-denial and service for Christ.

During his lifetime, Tozer was widely recognized as a spokesman for God. His insight into spiritual matters was penetratingly accurate. He was widely read, but rarely followed. Those who did have the courage to follow discovered, to their delight, spiritual realities surpassing anything this world has to offer. And once experienced, it is difficult to go back to the religious boredom of the average Christian.

Tozer usually directed his ministry toward the common Christian. His message could be understood by the common person in the pew, but the average Christian, delighting in mediocrity, took no delight in his pronouncements and spiritual ardor. It was once said of St. Augustine, Bishop of Hippo, that he was a radical Christian. Such could be said of A. W. Tozer.

In his prayers, Tozer never feigned a sanctimonious posture but maintained a continuous sense of God that enveloped him in reverence and adoration. His one daily exercise was the practice of the presence of God, pursuing Him with all his time and energy. To him, Jesus Christ was a daily wonder, a recurring astonishment, a continual amazement of love and grace.

"If you major on knowing God," Tozer once wrote, "and cultivate a sense of His presence in your daily life, and do what Brother Lawrence advises, 'Practice the presence of God' daily and seek to know the Holy Spirit in the Scriptures, you will go a long way in serving your generation for God. No man has any right to die until he has served his generation."

Correct doctrine was not enough for Tozer. "You can be," Tozer delighted in saying, "straight as a gun barrel theologically and as empty as one spiritually." His emphasis was always on a personal relationship with God; a relationship so real, so personal and so overpowering as to utterly captivate a person's full attention. He longed for what he termed a God-conscious soul, a heart aflame for God.

The lack of spirituality among men and women today is embarrassingly evident. Tozer zeroed in on one of the primary causes. "I am convinced," Tozer said, "that the dearth of great saints in these times even among those who truly believe in Christ is due at least in part to our unwillingness to give sufficient time to the cultivation of the knowledge of God." He went on to develop this further. "Our religious activities should be ordered in such a way as to leave plenty of time for the cultivation of the fruits of solitude and silence."

There were times when Tozer stood alone on certain issues, which never intimidated him in the least. He never concerned himself about who stood with him on any issue. His concern was always with the truth. He was fearless in his denunciation, which made enemies rather quickly. He once criticized a popular new Bible translation. "Reading that new translation," opined Tozer, "gave me the same feeling a man might have if he tried to shave with a banana."

People waited upon Tozer's ministry with expectancy, knowing that they would hear old truths robed in fresh and sparkling, sometimes startling expressions. Tozer once said, "Years ago, I prayed that God would sharpen my mind and enable me to receive everything He wanted to say to me. I then prayed that God would anoint my head with the oil of the prophet so I could say it back to the people. That one prayer has cost me plenty since, I can tell you that."

Raymond McAfee, Tozer's assistant for more than 15 years, regularly met in Tozer's study each Tuesday, Thursday and Saturday morning for a half hour of prayer. Often when McAfee would enter, Tozer would read aloud something he recently had been reading—it might be from the Bible, a hymnal, a devotional writer or a book of poetry. Then he would kneel by his chair and begin to pray. At times, he prayed with his face lifted upward. Other times he would pray prostrate on the floor, a piece of paper under his face to keep him from breathing carpet dust.

McAfee recalls one especially memorable day. "Tozer knelt by his chair, took off his glasses and laid them on the chair. Resting on his bent ankles, he clasped his hands together, raised his face with his eyes closed and began: 'O God, we are before Thee.' With that, there came a rush of God's presence that filled the room. We both worshiped in silent ecstasy and wonder and adoration. I've never forgotten that moment, and I don't want to forget it."

In prayer, Tozer would shut out everything and everyone and focus on God. His Mystic mentors taught him that. They showed him how to practice daily the presence of God. He learned the lesson well.

The primary emphasis of Tozer's ministry in preaching and writing was in this area of worship. To him, worship is the Christian's full-time occupation. Nothing should be allowed to interfere or diminish this sacred duty of the believer. According to Tozer, whatever did not flow naturally, if not spontaneously, out of our worship was not authentic and was at best contrived. Only cunning works of silver and gold should be offered to God.

Almost as a lone voice in his generation, Tozer stressed the need for a drastic reform of worship, both personally and congregationally, and that our ideas of worship must be in complete harmony with the revealed Word of God.

During the 1950s, Tozer found a kindred spirit in a plumber from Ireland, Tom Haire, a lay preacher. Haire became the subject of seven articles Tozer wrote for *Alliance Life* entitled "The Praying Plumber from Lisburn," later reissued as a booklet. Two men could hardly have been more different, yet their love for God and their sense of His worth drew them together.

Once, while Haire was visiting Chicago, Tozer's church was engaged in a night of fasting and prayer. Haire joined them. In the middle of the night, he got thirsty and went out for a cup of tea. Some church members felt that Tom, by so doing, had "yielded to the flesh." Tozer disagreed. He saw in that act the beautiful liberty Tom enjoyed in the Lord.

Just before Haire was to return to his homeland, he stopped by Chicago to say good-bye.

"Well, Tom," Tozer remarked, "I guess you'll be going back to Ireland to preach."

"No," Tom replied in his thick Irish brogue. "I intend to cancel all appointments for the next six months and spend that time preparing for the judgment seat of Christ while I can still do something about it."

It was an attitude not uncharacteristic of Tozer himself.

If this book drives you to your knees in penitential worship before God and encourages you to withdraw from the rat race of religious life and focus on your birthright of worship, it will be well worth the pains of publication.

—James Snyder

DESIGNED TO WORSHIP

THE TRAGEDY OF
HUMAN DEPRAVITY

My heart is inditing a good matter: I speak of the things which I
have made touching the king: my tongue is the pen of a ready writer.
Thou art fairer than the children of men: grace is poured into thy lips:
therefore God hath blessed thee for ever. Gird thy sword upon thy thigh,
O most mighty, with thy glory and thy majesty. And in thy majesty ride
prosperously because of truth and meekness and righteousness; and thy
right hand shall teach thee terrible things. Thine arrows are sharp in the
heart of the king's enemies; whereby the people fall under thee.

PSALM 45:1-5

In the beginning, God created Adam and Eve, placing them in
the beautiful garden east of Eden. We have only a little glimpse
into the beauty of that mysterious and wondrous world. All we
know is that God created it and afterwards said, "It is good,"
meaning that all creation was in absolute harmony with God
and fulfilling its ordained purpose.

Perhaps it would be correct to suggest that many people in
their frantic pursuit of life have forgotten the purpose of their
creation, from God's point of view. Keep in mind that whatever

God created, He created for His purpose and pleasure (see Rev. 4:11). To entertain the idea that God would do anything capriciously or without purpose is to misunderstand completely the nature of God.

After God had created everything else, He said with a smile on His face, "I'll make me a man." Stooping down, He took up the clay from the bed of the river, shaped it and worked on it like a nanny bending over her baby. He shaped and formed man and blew into his nostrils the breath of life, and man became a living soul. God stood man upon his feet and said, "Look around, this is all yours; and look at Me, I am yours; and I'll look at you and I'll see in your face the reflection of My own glory. That is your end, that is why you were created, that you might worship Me and enjoy Me and glorify Me and have Me as yours forever."

God then put Adam into a deep sleep, and out of his ribs formed woman, whom Adam called Eve. Together they were created with one purpose.

God's purpose in creating Adam and Eve is summed up in what they could do for God that nothing else in the whole creation could do. They had an exclusive on God shared by no other of God's creation. Unlike everything else in this mystic and marvelous world of God's creation, Adam and Eve could worship God, and God anticipated that worship. In the cool of the day, God came down and walked with Adam and Eve in the Garden of Eden where they joyously offered their reverence and adoration. Nowhere do we read that God came down and hugged a tree or walked with any animal or plant He created, nor did He talk to any of the animals. Only Adam and Eve were able to provide the fellowship God desired. It was their unique purpose shared by nothing else in all of God's creation.

Thinking of those occasions of God walking with them in the cool of the day in the garden, I wonder what they talked about. The weather was ideal; Adam and Eve enjoyed perfect health; and sports had not been invented. Obviously, it was a fellowship based upon compatibility between both parties. Something in man responded to the presence of God like nothing else in all God's creation. God created man in His own image, and out of that flowed the marvelous dynamic of worship. Adam and Eve's unique purpose in the garden was to bring pleasure, joy and fellowship to God, which is the foundation of all genuine worship.

Everything in the garden was in perfect harmony and symmetry. Then God withdrew for a moment and, while gone, that old, evil one, the dragon who is called Satan, came and sowed poisonous seed in the mind of Adam and Eve. Consequently, they rebelled against God and His purpose for them. When Adam and Eve crossed the line, immediately God knew the fellowship was broken, for God knows all things.

Fig-Leaf Religion

Also, for Adam and Eve, there was a terrific sense of disorientation resulting in spiritual amnesia. They looked at themselves for the first time and saw themselves in a different light. They saw their nakedness and, in a state of spiritual disorientation, gathered fig leaves to hide their nakedness. Thus was born religion: Fig-Leaf Religion. Religion always focuses on the externals, and Adam and Eve were consumed with their outward condition. They had lost the focus of their inward beauty and purpose, and no longer satisfied the criteria of fellowship with their Creator.

When God came as usual for His fellowship, Adam and Eve were nowhere to be found; and God sought them among the trees in the garden, and called out to Adam, "Where art thou?"

God called out to the man who had fled from Him and hid out among the trees of the garden. Adam heard the voice of the Lord in the cool of the day as before, but Adam was confused. Why was God coming to Eden eastward? What was He doing there? He was coming for His customary time with Adam when Adam should worship, admire and adore the God who made him.

Adam, shamefaced, came crawling out from behind some tree.

God asked, "What did you do?"

Adam regretfully replied, "We ate of the forbidden fruit." Then to justify his actions, he said, "But it was the woman you gave me."

God turned to the woman. "What did you do?" Immediately she put the blame on the serpent.

Already they had learned to blame somebody else for the condition of their soul. This blaming someone else for all our iniquities is one of the great evidences of sin and is the forerunner of religion.

Something happened, changing the whole scenario, hijacking and barring humanity from the knowledge of God. Adam and Eve, in that perfect environment and with their one supreme purpose of worshiping God, rebelled against their purpose, resulting in what theologians call the Fall of man, or Depravity.

Our world is full of tragedy because of this great, overwhelming cosmic tragedy back in the Garden. Repercussions still vibrate in contemporary society.

The burning question needing an answer is what was the tragic consequence of this Fall? Why does this matter for us today, and why should we inquire into it?

Some say the Fall is the source of all the problems plaguing humanity down through the years. Some point to the proliferation of disease as a direct outcome. Others point to all of the hatred infecting humanity throughout the centuries: nation rising against nation, kingdom against kingdom and holocausts that have happened periodically throughout history. No generation has escaped such hatred and anger. However, these are short-term effects and simply a consequence not representing the real tragedy of the Fall.

Purpose Lost

What was the real tragedy of that dreadful cosmic rupture forever affecting mankind? The real tragedy in the Garden of Eden was that Adam and Eve lost their purpose. They forgot who they were. They did not know where they were; they did not understand where they came from or what they were here for. They forgot the purpose of their existence. Trying their best to shake off this moral fog, they could not; for no matter what they did, it would not shake. Therefore, hand in hand, they made their way out into the world, not knowing where they were going. Humanity still wanders in this moral and spiritual wilderness.

They suffered from what I will refer to as spiritual amnesia. This spiritual morass is illustrated, as is often the case, in the physical world. A man wakes up in the hospital only to discover that he has been in a coma for about a week. He does not know how he got there or why he is there. He does not know where he is; in fact, he cannot even remember his name. He is told that over a week ago he encountered muggers who beat him severely, robbing him of everything, including his identity. Anything to tell who he was or why he was in the city was stripped from him. The doctors diagnosed him with amnesia. It is a real problem, because the man has no memory of what happened to him. He has lost all perspective of his life, not even knowing his own name, making him vulnerable to people he does not know.

This identity crisis is a serious condition and, thankfully, for many people it is only temporary. With the diligent work and patient help of the medical staff, memory can be restored. But until he regains his memory, he has lost all purpose in life and must rely on others to help him define his purpose.

This is the way that it is spiritually. Because the enemy of man's soul has mugged humanity, robbing them of their identity, men and women wander around in a spiritual and moral fog, not knowing who they are, what they are or where they are going.

This is exactly where humanity is today. We have a strange spiritual amnesia and cannot remember who we are or why we are here, and we look around for some explanation of our existence. Unfortunately, men and women suffering from this seek answers from anyone offering some hope. Too often, they get the wrong answers from those with less credible integrity, not to mention personal agenda.

Ask a young university graduate, "Bob, why are you here?"

"I want to get married; I'd like to make money; and I'd like to travel."

"But listen, Bob, those are shortsighted things. You will do them and then you will get old and die. What is the big overriding purpose of your life?"

Looking rather strangely, Bob might say, "I don't know whether I have any purpose in life."

This is the condition of the world today, everywhere and in every culture. From the universities to the coal mines, people do not know why they are here. People have a strange moral and spiritual amnesia and do not know their purpose in life, why they were created or what they are sent to do. Consequently, lives are filled with confusion, reaching out for any explanation; hence the proliferation of religions in our world. Religion only addresses man's external condition, not his internal confusion.

In spite of this confusion, we try to get around somehow. We travel, play golf, drive cars, eat, sleep, look at beautiful things; but they are all shortsighted aspects of our life.

The enemy of man's soul has successfully sabotaged this search for moral and spiritual identity. He does everything within his extensive power to prevent us from discovering who and what we are. Defiantly, knowing our purpose, he stands between us and dares us to cross his line. He offers everything and anything to keep us from finding the right solution. Unfortunately, he has many takers.

Where in the world can we find any answer to this dilemma? What authority in this world can bring us to an understanding of why we are here?

Fortunately for us, the Bible is such an authority and explains to us why we are here.

Purpose Regained

I desire to deliver my soul as a prophet of God and explain from the Bible why we were created and why we are here. It may not satisfy the temporary needs at the time, but it will satisfy something bigger, grander and more eternal. *That biblically defined purpose is that we might worship God and enjoy Him forever.* Apart from that, man has no other purpose; and short of that, man wanders in a spiritual disorientation taking him further from finding his created purpose.

God never does anything without a good purpose behind it. God is intelligent because intellect is an attribute of deity. This intellect is seen in every aspect of creation. Nothing in creation is without meaning, even if we do not see or understand the meaning at the time.

Deep within the heart of every person is an insatiable longing to know this purpose of life, which I contend, is indication of the residue of memory prior to the Fall in the Garden of Eden. Men and women strive to know the "why" of everything. They express a legitimate concern and pose an important question demanding a satisfactory answer. The problem is, most people get the wrong answer to their inquiry.

But there is a good and legitimate answer to this query, summed up in the following Scripture: "My heart is inditing a good matter; I speak of the things . . . touching the king. . . . So shall the king greatly desire thy beauty: for he is thy Lord; and worship thou him" (Ps. 45:1,11).

And I could go farther over into the psalms: "O come, let us worship and bow down: let us kneel before the LORD our maker" (Ps. 95:6) and Psalm 96.

Additionally, I could turn to many more passages of sacred Scripture offering to all mankind a call to worship. It is the echo of the voice of worship telling us why we were born: that we might worship God and enjoy Him forever. It is informing us that we are to glorify Him forever and, above all other creatures, know, admire, love and adore the triune God. We are to give to God that which He desires.

In our Bibles, we read of those who worship God day and night in the temple and never cease chanting, "Holy, holy, holy, is the LORD of hosts, the whole earth is full of his glory" (Isa. 6:3).

Compare this with the average run-of-the-mill church, even today's evangelical church, where there seems to be a great love of everything but this. What passes for worship in many churches today is anything and everything but what reflects the holy mind and nature of God or even pleases God. Worship in many cases is stiff and artificial, with no semblance of life in it. I am afraid that many have truly forgotten what it means to worship God in the sacred assembly. There is ritual and routine aplenty but lacking the overwhelming passion of being in the holy presence of God.

Some say the answer to all our problems in the church today is revival, as though that is a panacea for all our spiritual ills and shortcomings. Most people's idea of revival, however, runs the gamut of a week of meetings to a high-energy display of emotionalism. What is real revival? It's the kind that has changed the course of human history. Throughout church history, every revival resulted in a sudden intensification of the presence of God, resulting in the spontaneous worship of God. Anything less is superficial, artificial and even detrimental to true spiritual health.

When the Holy Ghost came on the Day of Pentecost, why did the believers break out into ecstatic language? Simply, it was because they were rightly worshiping God for the first time. Intensive worship unexpectedly leaped out of their hearts. It was nothing planned or perpetrated by some "worship leader." God was in their midst. Whenever there is a move of the Holy Spirit, it is always a call for God's people to be worshipers of the Most High God above everything else. Whatever else revival does, it must restore the purpose and meaning of being a worshiper.

In the world created by God, nothing exists without meaning and purpose. Science seeks to discover the meaning of things and their relationship to each other, their interaction and effect upon each other. That is science; I have nothing against science. However, science and scientists only deal with short-term affairs, never with the overarching purpose with man created in the image of God.

Admittedly, science has made great strides in eliminating some diseases that in a former generation took the lives of thousands. And for this, we all stand with head bowed and utter profuse thanks.

I grant you that science, especially medical science, has made great improvements in the quality of our life. But even that has limitations. Science can save a baby from diphtheria, save a teen from smallpox, save a person in his twenties from polio, save a man in his fifties from a heart attack and keep him right on going with good health until he is 90. But the question I pose is this: If he still does not know why he is here, what does he gain?

If he does not know why he is here and does not know his purpose, all you are doing is simply perpetuating the life without direction or purpose. If a person is living just because it is the best alternative to dying, what good is it?

Somebody observed about Christopher Columbus, "Columbus went out not knowing where he was going; and when he got there he did not know where he was; and when he got back he did not know where he had been, and he did it all on other people's money."

This is the way of religion today. People do not know where they are, they do not know where they have been, they do not know why they are here, they do not know where they are going; and they do the whole thing on borrowed time, borrowed money, borrowed thinking, and then die. Science may be able to help keep you, but it cannot help you here. Science can keep you alive so that you have longer to think it over, but it will never give you any answer for the purpose of your life.

When I was 17 years old, I associated with a certain group of people. They were not educated people and certainly not scientists. They were plain, simple Christians, the saints and mystics, and the Brethren of the Common Life. They were the people of God and had a simple and more beautiful view of the world than many scientists. They did not know much, certainly not as much as a scientist, but they did know why they were here and where they were going. They celebrated their purpose of life by worshiping God enthusiastically and unashamedly.

Suppose I would visit some university and encounter a celebrated doctor of philosophy. I would not know nearly as much as he would know. However, if I met him downtown, wandering around, and he did not know where he was, I would know more than he would on that one thing.

He might stop me and ask, in a very cultured manner, "Where am I?"

I could say to him, "You're between Hamilton and Vineland."

"Thank you," he would say. I would smile to myself and think, *I have not studied in Germany, and I do not have all his degrees, but I know more than he did about one thing. I knew where he was, and he did not.*

I have read Albert Einstein's work on the fourth dimension and have never been able to understand it. I quit trying, but I take pleasure in knowing something Einstein did not know. I know why I am here. I belong to that company of plain Christians who believe a book called the Bible that says, "In the beginning God created the heaven and the earth" (Gen. 1:1).

God made man in His own image and blew in him the breath of life to live in His presence and worship Him. God then sent man out into the world to increase, multiply and fill the earth with men and women who would worship God in the beauty of holiness. That is our supreme purpose.

I do not walk around with my head down, looking sad, because somebody has written more books than I have or knows more than I know or has been to school longer than I have. Because I have a little secret: I can tell you why I was born, why I am here and my everlasting duties while the ages roll.

The plain people I admire so much say that God created the flowers to bloom so that man might enjoy them. God created the birds to sing for man's pleasure. However, no scientist would be caught dead admitting something that simple. The scientist has to come up with some complicated reasons of what this all means. The problem is, he never begins with God.

The scientist would object and say, "God did not create the birds to sing. Only the male bird sings, and he only sings to attract a female so he can have a nest of little ones. That is just simply a biological fact, that is all."

I think to myself, *Why couldn't the bird just warble or something? Why does the bird have to sing like a harp? Why do these birds sing so beautifully?* Because the God who made them is the composer of the cosmos. He made them, put a harp in their little throats, surrounded them with feathers and said, "Now, go sing." And they have been singing ever since, much to my delight.

I believe God that made the trees to bear fruit; but the scientist shrugs his shoulders and objects, "There you go again, you Christians. What a hopeless bunch you are. The trees bear fruit not for you but so there are seeds so that there will be more fruit."

God made the fruit, blessed it and told us to help ourselves. God also made the beast of the field to clothe mankind and the sheep to give us wool so that we can make a nice sweater to keep us warm in the winter. God made the humble little Japanese silk worm in the mulberry trees in order that we might spin their cocoon and make silk.

Throughout the Bible, the prophets and apostles all testify that God made us for a purpose and, according to them, that purpose is to sing His praises before the hushed audience of all creation. God created the silkworm to make silk; the bird was created to sing; the sheep for their wool. Everything in God's creation has its purpose.

Looking at the man He created, God said, "I am making man in my image and man is to be above all other creatures." Man's supreme purpose is to be above the beast of the earth and the birds of the air and the fish of the sea, even above the angels in the heaven. Ultimately, this man is to enter God's presence and unashamedly worship God, looking upon his face while the ages roll. That is why man was created; that is man's chief end.

Apart from that, we have no more idea why we are here. God gave you a harp and placed it in your own heart. God made you in order that you might stand up and charm the rest of the universe as you sing praises to the Lord Jesus Christ. That is why we were made in His image.

With Isaac Watts we can sing:

I'll praise my Maker while I've breath,
And when my voice is lost in death,
Praise shall employ my nobler powers.
My days of praise shall ne'er be past,
While life, and thought, and being last,
Or immortality endures.

Prayer

Lord God, for years we have wandered in the state of spiritual amnesia not knowing who we are, where we came from or what our purpose in life is. We knew not that we were made in Thy image for the single purpose of worshiping and adoring Thee. Our plight has been empty and futile. Then Christ, through the work of the Holy Spirit, awakened us to our true purpose in life. Now our days are filled with praise. And we praise Thee with our whole being, honoring Thee, adoring Thee in the beauty of Thy Holiness. Amen.

2

Searching for Man's Lost Identity

Thou art worthy, O Lord, to receive glory and honour
and power: for thou hast created all things, and for thy
pleasure they are and were created.

Revelation 4:11

Christian ministry is based on the assumption that there are
some serious-minded people who want to know who they are,
what they are, why they are here and where they are going. Maybe
not many compared to the great masses of the world's popula-
tion, but enough to form a nice congregation almost everywhere you go. If I am wrong about this, I might as well leave my
Bible closed.

Searching for Purpose

But I firmly believe there are some who are serious and want to
know the answer to the question, "What is my purpose in life?"
Unfortunately, the masses have been given the wrong answer,
leading them farther away from the knowledge of God. This includes all the religions and philosophies of our world. This has
been a neat and successful trick of the enemy of man's soul.

Many people have tried to answer that question and consequently have led many people astray. Let me take several of them now and point out how empty and futile they really are; and may God deliver us from such utter foolishness.

Identity Through Work

Some would insist that our chief purpose in life is to work. No other place in the world, since the days of Adam to this present time, has given more honor to work than on the North American continent. Not that we like to work, we just like to talk about what an honorable thing it is.

Have you ever stopped to consider what work is?

Let me put work in its simplest form. Work is moving things and rearranging them. We have something over here and we work to put it over there. Something is in the pail and we put it on the side of the house, which we call painting. Something is in the cupboard, we work to put that into a skillet and then on the table to put it into your husband, and that is called cooking.

Smile at this simplification, but you will find this definition of work a very good and sound one. Work is taking something that is somewhere, putting it somewhere else and rearranging it. To the observer of humanity, the obvious thing about work is the fact that it has a short-range focus; it never has long-range purpose.

The farmer has some corn in his barn, puts it in the field and covers it up. After nature has worked on it for three or four months, he takes it from there and puts it back where he got it, only there is more of it. The next year the corn is gone;

the cattle ate the corn. Therefore, work always has a short-range purpose.

But what is the result of all this? Why do all this? Why put that green, red or white paint in that pail and put it on your house? You say, in order that the house might not be affected by the weather, that it might stay nice and look nice.

That is very good, but there never was a house built yet but it will rot and get rundown and finally be replaced with something newer. Nobody can convince me that I am merely made to work like a farm horse without having any future or any reason except that work. A man can work all his life, be identified by that work and then retire. Shortly after retirement, he dies because he has lost his purpose in life. The end result of work is utter futility.

Identity Through Education

Somebody else insists that we are here for a higher purpose than merely work. Our purpose is to educate ourselves, develop ourselves and perfect our intellectual nature. The process of this cultivation of the human mind is extensive.

A young person will go through school and be taught all the important things of life. He then might continue through college and learn science, art, literature and history. If he is ambitious, he will go on to do postgraduate work and get a degree.

I only see one little catch in this scenario. That young man, educated and well cultivated, is going to die and take all that education with him down into the grave. All that culture, that love of Bach, of Brahms and everything else will go right down with him into the grave.

Everything we do for a man is going to go right down into the grave with him when he dies. If he earns 40 degrees, they can put that on his tombstone, but he does not know anything about it. He is dead. Education alone is not the reason we were born. Our purpose is not for the perfecting of our intellectual nature, the education or development of our mind. I am not against education, because the alternative is simple ignorance. Education, however, does not answer the eternal purpose of why I am here.

Identity Through Pleasure

Others have a simpler viewpoint and tell us that we are here merely to enjoy ourselves. Epicurus, the father of Epicureanism, taught that pleasure is the chief end of man. Unfortunately, he earned a terrible reputation, but his idea was not as bad as it sounds. Epicurus did not teach that our purpose was to go out on a three-week binge or smoke opium or engage every physical and carnal pleasure known to man. He taught something quite the contrary.

Epicurus taught that pleasure is the end of all things: the pleasures of friendship and the beauty of literature and poetry and music and art. "The noble pleasures of a good conscience," he said, "is what we were born for in order that we might enjoy life."

Although he had good intentions and tried taking the high road, he had it all wrong. Joys and pleasures all pass away.

An old man who used to sit and listen enraptured to the music of the classics, now sits and nods in the corner and does not know Brahms from Frank Sinatra, because his mind is gone and his ability to enjoy pleasures is gone as well. What does a man do when life offers him no more pleasure? Some have answered this emptiness by suicide, a tragic end of a life that never found the real purpose of existence.

Identity Through Thrills

The younger and more energetic among us have the idea that the thrills of life are all that matter. Experiencing all the thrills of life is the ultimate point of living. It is a philosophy and is widely practiced and held by a good number of people who are not Christians. It is the philosophy that sex, food, sports, excitement and the gathering of goods is the chief end of man and our purpose in life. Our purpose in life is whatever produces a thrill.

Those who dedicate their time and the purpose of their life to getting a thrill out of life are going to have one of two things happen to them. Either they are going to run down physically or they are going to run down mentally until they lose all ability to experience any thrill anymore.

Nothing is quite as pathetic as an old rogue who has no thrill left anymore. A bored, weary, defeated, burned-out old man who has spent his life seeking physical thrills wherever he could find them and at any cost now is old, tired and burned out. Nothing thrills him anymore. Trying to get through to him is like sticking an ice pick into a wooden leg. There is no response, no reaction, no life or feeling left.

If that is all life is for, I think God made a terrible mistake when he created this whole world. If that is all, with my hand over my face, I cry to God Almighty, complain and say, "Why did You make me thus?"

Restored Identity

But, the exciting news is, that is not the reason or purpose of our life. I bring you to the Scriptures themselves, not to man's philosophy but to what God says about our purpose in life. The Scripture teaches us a number of things about the purpose of our life. It teaches us that God created all things out of His own pleasure. "Thou art worthy, O Lord, to receive glory and honour and power: for thou hast created all things, and for thy pleasure they are and were created" (Rev. 4:11).

When God decided to create mankind, it was a high day in heaven accompanied with a big celebration "when the morning stars sang together, and all the sons of God shouted for joy" (Job 38:7). Here was the heavenly host celebrating when God decided to create the heaven and the earth and, in particular, man to worship Him.

This is taught throughout the entire Bible, that God created man to worship Him. Man is the darling of the universe, the centerpiece of God's affection; however, many unbelievers denied this.

A very intelligent man once commented when asked what he thought to be the biggest mistake or error made by people: "I consider the biggest mistake to be the belief that we are special objects of Almighty God and that we are more than other things in the world, and God has a special fondness for people."

Regardless of that man's opinion, I base my whole life on the belief of God creating man with a special, unique, divine purpose. I do not care how brilliant this man is, he cannot jar me from my conviction. It would be as useless as throwing cooked peas at a 10-story building to destroy any of my beliefs or doctrines or commitment to this faith.

When a little baby is born into the world, the father searches intensely to see if the baby looks like him. He may be too tough to say it, but every father looks earnestly into the little wrinkled face to see whether it looks like him or not. We want things to look like us, and if they are not born to us, we go out and make them. We paint pictures; we write music; we do something, because we want to create. Everything we create is a reflection of our personality. In the world of art, a Monet is easily distinguished from a Rembrandt. Each painting reflects the personality of the artist.

God made man to be like Him so that man could give more pleasure to God than all the other creatures. Only in man, as created by God, can God admire Himself. Man is the mirror image in which God looks to see Himself. Man is the reflection of the glory of God, which was the purpose and intention of God originally. Man's supreme function through all eternity is to reflect God's highest glory, and that God might look into the mirror called man and see His own glory shining there. Through man, God could reflect His glory to all creation.

You are a mirror of the Almighty, and this is the reason you were created in the first place. This is your purpose. You are not created so that you might only take something over here and put it over there—*work*. You were not created only that you might develop your brain so that you can speak with a cultured accent—*education*. Neither are we here to enjoy ourselves, even the pure *pleasures* of life. Nor are we here for the *thrills* life brings.

All the holy prophets and apostles teach that man fell from his first estate and destroyed the glory of God, and the mirror was broken. God could no longer look at sinful man and see

His glory reflected. Man failed to fulfill the created purpose of worship to his Creator in the beauty of holiness. He forgot this, forfeited it by sin and is busy now finding other things to fill that emptiness. It is terrible what people will look to if they lose God. If there is no God in their eyes, then they get something else in their eyes; and if they do not enjoy worshiping the great God Almighty that made them, they find something else to worship.

If a person does not have God, he has to have something else. Maybe it is boats, or maybe it is money, amounting to idolatry, or going to parties or just simply raising the devil. They have lost God, and they do not know what to do, so they find something to do, which is why all the pleasures in life have been invented.

God made man to reflect His glory; but unfortunately, man does not. The flowers are still as beautiful as God meant them to be. The sun still shines yonder with spacious firmament on high. Evening shadows fall and the moon takes up the wonders and tells us whether the hand that made us is divine. Bees still gather their honey from flower to flower, and the birds sing a thousand songs and the seraphim still chant "holy, holy, holy" before the throne of God. Yet man alone sulks in his cave. Man, made more like God than any creature, has become less like God than any creature.

Man, made to be a mirror—to reflect the deity—now reflects only his own sinfulness. Sulking in his cave while the silent stars tell their story, man, except for his swearing, boasting, threatening, cursing and all the nervous and ill-conceived laughter and songs without joy, is silent before the universe.

Change the figure now from a mirror to a harp. God has put in man a harp bigger than anything else, and He meant that harp to be tuned to Himself. However, when man sinned and fell in this tragic and terrible thing we call the Fall of man, man threw that harp down into the mud; it is full of silt and sand, and the strings are broken.

The mightiest disaster ever known in the world was the soul of man, more like God than anything, and more fitted to God's sweet music than all other creatures, with the light gone from his mind and the love gone from his heart, stumbling through a dark world to find himself a grave. From God's point of view, man needed redemption. What is the purpose of redemption? Redemption is to restore us back to God again; to restring that harp; to purge it, cleanse it and refurbish it by the grace of God and the blood of the Lamb.

I have wonderful news for you. God, who made us like that, did not give up on us. He did not say to the angels, "Write them off and block them from my memory." Rather, He said, "I still want that mirror to shine in which I can look and see My glory. I still want to be admired in My people; I still want a people to enjoy Me and to love Me forever." Out of this insatiable passion, God sent His only begotten Son, and He became incarnated in the form of a man; and when He walked the earth, He was the reflected glory of God. God, finally, had His man.

The New Testament says, "Who being the brightness of his glory, and the express image of his person . . ." (Heb. 1:3). When God looked at Mary's son, He saw Himself reflected. Jesus said, "Believe me that I am in the Father, and the Father in me: or else believe me for the very works' sake" (John 14:11).

45

What did Jesus mean, "When you see me, you see the Father's glory reflected"? "I have glorified thee on the earth," said Jesus. "I have finished the work thou gavest Me to do," and there God glorified Himself in His son, and that Son went out to die, and all that glory was marred more than any man, and His features more than the son of man. They pulled out His beard, bruised His face, tore out His hair and made lumps on His forehead. Then they nailed Him on that cross where for six hours He sweated, twisted and groaned and finally gave up the ghost. The bells rang in heaven because man had been redeemed now. On the third day, He arose from the dead and now He is at God's right hand, and God now is busy redeeming the people back to Him again, back to the original purpose, to be mirrors reflecting God's glory.

I hope to explain what worship is and point out how tragically low this worship is among the churches. I hope to define worship and explain how we can recapture this worship for our generation and the generations to come.

Worship is man's full reason for existence. Worship is why we are born and why we are born again. Worship is the reason for our genesis in the first place and our regenesis that we call regeneration. Worship is why there is church, the assembly of the Redeemed, in the first place. Every Christian church in every country across the world in every generation exists to worship God first, not second; not tacking worship at the end of our service as an afterthought, but rather to worship God primarily, with everything else coming in second, at best. Worshiping God is our first call.

John Keats wrote of a tongueless nightingale ("The Eve of St. Agnes"). "As though a tongueless nightingale should swell Her throat in vain, and die, heart-stifled, in her dell." I have often thought that this great figure of speech was a beautiful thing. The tongueless nightingale died of suffocation because it had so much song in it that it could not get it out. We are the other way around. We have such a tremendous tongue and such little use for it. We have a harp such as no other creature in God's universe, but we play it so infrequently and so poorly.

When the saintly Brother Lawrence was dying, somebody asked him what he was doing. Without hesitation Brother Lawrence simply said, "I'm just doing what I've been doing for 40 years and expect to be doing throughout eternity."

"What's that?" the person inquired.

"Worshiping God."

As far as Brother Lawrence was concerned, dying was secondary, just an item on his agenda. His occupation was worshiping God above and before all other things. He had been worshiping God for 40 years, and facing death did not change that. When he felt his thoughts getting low, he was still worshiping God. He died, and they buried his body somewhere, but Brother Lawrence is still worshiping God in that coveted place we call the Presence of God.

You will be worshiping God long after everything else has ceased to exist. Too bad if you do not learn to worship Him now so that you do not have to cram for the last examination. For my part, I want to worship God in my own private life so fully and satisfyingly to the end so that I will not have to cram for the final exams. I can nearly stop breathing with quietness and say, "I worship Him; I am still worshiping Him; and I expect to worship Him for all eternity."

That is what you are here for, to glorify God and enjoy Him thoroughly and forever, telling the universe how great God is.

The Way of Perfection
by Frederick William Faber (1814-1863)

Oh how the thought of God attracts
And draws the heart from earth,
And sickens it of passing shows
And dissipating mirth!

'Tis not enough to save our souls,
To shun the eternal fires;
The thought of God will rouse the heart
To more sublime desires.

God only is the creature's home,
Though rough and straight the road;
Yet nothing less can satisfy
The love that longs for God.

Prayer

*Oh, Thou God of the universe! The God that created all things
that are, and created them for Thy pleasure, I humbly acknowledge Thee as my Creator. Restore to me the joy of Thy
salvation. Restore the harp within that has been broken.
Restring that harp in order that I might sing Thy praises
throughout the universe and unto all the angels populating
Thy heavens. In Jesus' name, amen.*

3

DISCOVERING THE HEART OF MAN'S NATURE

So shall the king greatly desire thy beauty: for he is thy Lord;
and worship thou him.

PSALM 45:11

To the diligent student, the Bible is amazing in its consistency. The whole import and substance of the Bible is unswerving in what it teaches: that God created man to worship Him. That God, who does not need anything and who is complete in Himself, nevertheless desires worshipers. God in His uncreated nature is self-sufficient and possesses no lack whatsoever, yet He looks to man created in His image for worship. This represents a spiritual oxymoron. The Creator needs the creature.

This is the truth upon which I want to build; that God made everything for a purpose. His supreme purpose in making man was to have somebody capable to properly and sufficiently worship Him and satisfy His own heart. Man fell by sin and now is failing to carry out that created purpose. He is like a cloud without water; it gives no rain. Like a sun that gives no heat or a star that gives no light or a tree that no longer yields fruit, a bird that no longer sings or a harp that is silent and no longer gives off music.

This is the longing of God's heart; deep calling unto deep. The Bible insists that when our Lord shall come, He shall be admired; He shall be glorified first in the saints and admired in all who believe. There is glorification and admiration, and our Lord is coming for that. "When he shall come to be glorified in his saints, and to be admired in all them that believe (because our testimony among you was believed) in that day" (2 Thess. 1:10).

The devil would like to tell us, for our own unbelieving minds, that God does not particularly desire our worship, as we owe it to Him. Satan would have us believe that God is not concerned or interested in our worship. But the truth is quite the contrary. God wants man to worship Him, and only redeemed man can worship Him acceptably. We are not unwanted children; God greatly desires our fellowship.

Why else would it be when Adam sinned and broke his fellowship with God that God came in the cool of the day, and when He could not find Adam called out, "Adam, where art thou?" It was God seeking worship from Adam who had sinned and in rebellion broke his fellowship. The harp within Adam had become unstrung and the voice of Adam choked in his throat.

God has commanded us to worship Him; and if you notice in Psalm 45:11, "So shall the king greatly desire thy beauty," God finds something in us that He put there for His personal pleasure. That "beauty" belongs to God.

This is quite contrary to what is usually heard in the average evangelical pulpit. Not only does God want man to worship Him, but man, even in his fallen state, has something within trying to respond, but not succeeding. Usually, we are told that men do not want to worship God. However, there is not a tribe in the world but practices some kind of religion and form of worship. The apostle Paul talked about the whole world stretching out its hands if perchance they might feel after God, so men desire to worship God.

Hymn writer Isaac Watts (1674-1748) expressed this for us in marvelous language:

Eternal Power
Eternal Power, Whose high abode
Becomes the grandeur of a God,
Infinite lengths beyond the bounds
Where stars resolve their little rounds!
The lowest step around Thy seat,
Rises too high for Gabriel's feet;
In vain the favored angel tries
To reach Thine height with wond'ring eyes.
There while the first archangel sings,
He hides his face behind his wings,
And ranks of shining thrones around
Fall worshiping, and spread the ground.
Lord, what shall earth and ashes do?
We would adore our Maker, too;
From sin and dust to Thee we cry,
The Great, the Holy, and the High.

Earth from afar has heard Thy fame,
And worms have learned to lisp Thy Name;
But, O! the glories of Thy mind
Leave all our soaring thoughts behind.
God is in Heaven, and men below;
Be short our tunes, our words be few;
A solemn reverence checks our songs,
And praise sits silent on our tongues.

When a man falls on his knees and stretches his hands heavenward, he is doing the most natural thing in the world. Something deep within compels him to seek someone or something outside of himself to worship and adore. In his unredeemed condition, man has lost the way and cannot clearly define the object of his wistful adoration, and so his search takes him far from God. When he does not find God, man will fill the void in his heart with anything he can find. That which is not God can never satiate the heart exclusively created for God's presence.

There is another facet of faith for our consideration. That is, we do not believe we are as dear to God as He says we are. We do not believe we are as precious or that He desires us as much as He says He does. The enemy of man's soul has sold this lie to us to not only beat us down, but to also keep us from the loving fellowship of God's presence. He cares not a whit for us, but his hatred of God drives him to do all in his power to deny God that which rightfully belongs to Him. If everybody could suddenly have a baptism of pure cheerful belief that God wants and desires us to worship, admire and praise Him, it could transform us overnight into the most radiantly happy people in the world. We would finally discover our purpose: that God delights in us, and longs for our fellowship.

If man had not fallen, worship would continue to be the most natural thing because God specifically designed man to worship Him. God created man as His special instrument of music—offering to Him natural sweet praise. However, when man rebelled and fell away from this purpose, when sin came into his life, sin has become natural. Man's nature is fallen, but this was not God's original intention for us. If everybody had cancer, then we could say cancer was natural and accept it as so. However, it is not natural, because when God made the human body, He did not have in mind wild cells forming called cancer and destroying man.

When God made the human soul in His own image, He did so that we might act according to that Divine nature. He never intended the virus of sin to infect that sacred place within man. Sin, therefore, is the unnatural thing. It is a foreign substance defiling man's heart and life, repelling God's gaze. Because of this condition in man, sin is natural, worship is unnatural; and so few people really do it.

Because of this, it is important to understand that nobody can devise their own pattern of worship or worship God any way they please. The pleasure here belongs to God alone. The One who created us to worship Him also has decreed how we shall worship Him. We cannot worship God as we will; our worship must always conform to God's pleasure. God does not accept just any kind of worship. He accepts worship only when it is pure and when it flows from a heart under the afflatus of the

Holy Spirit. Only such worship, compatible with His holy nature, can possibly be accepted by Him.

This deception destroys the lives of multitudes of people in every generation. It is a favorite ploy of the devil and a favorite pet of unconverted poets to suggest that we just worship God any way we want to worship and at our whim, and all will be well, as long as we are sincere.

The fallacy in this is the fact that religious experience is altogether possible apart from Christ and apart from redemption. It is entirely feasible to have an authentic religious experience and not be a Christian and to be on your way to an eternal hell. It happens all the time all over the world.

It might be hard to conceive, but it is entirely possible to have an experience with God and yet not have a saving experience with God. So not only is it possible to have a religious experience apart from Christ, and apart from salvation, but it is also possible to have worship apart from Christ and apart from salvation. This is chilling to think it is possible to go through the motions of worship and not worship right. "They worshiped they know not what," said Jesus of a certain group. It is possible to have elements of worship: adoration, self-abasement, surrender and man still not be redeemed at all.

Thomas Carlyle in his "Heroes and Hero Worship" warned us not to make the mistake of thinking that the great pagan religions of the world were all counterfeit. He said, "It's not true they were phony, they were real and the terror of them was that they were real."

I once visited an old church in Mexico with a dirt floor. I walked in and took off my hat and observed all the statues and candles. While there, I saw an old Mexican woman come in and walk straight down to the front as if she knew the way and could go in the dark with her eyes closed; she had been there so often. She walked straight to a statue, I think it was the Virgin, knelt and looked up into the face of that statue with a longing and devotion that I would like to see turned to the Lord Himself. She was having an experience of worship, and it was real to her. She was no phony, she was a real worshiper; but look what she was worshiping. Her worship was not directed in the right direction. The sad part about this whole thing is that she did not know it.

The American Indian would stand on the bank of the river, stretch his red arms up to the sky and say to the Manito, "Praises be, praises be to the Manito, praises be." He was experiencing real worship when he cried to his Great Manito.

It is entirely possible to have a religious experience without God, and even reject the God of the Bible. It is possible to have an experience of worship, but not according to the will of God and, consequently, unacceptable with God, because God hates idolatry. Idolatry is simply worship directed in any direction but God's, which is the epitome of blasphemy.

The apostle Paul understood this: "But I say, that the things which the Gentiles sacrifice, they sacrifice to devils, and not to God: and I would not that ye should have fellowship with devils. Ye cannot drink the cup of the Lord, and the cup of devils: ye cannot be partakers of the Lord's table, and of the table of devils" (1 Cor. 10:20-21).

Our Lord said that there would be a day when people would say, "Lord, Lord, have we not prophesied in thy name? and in thy name have cast out devils? and in thy name done many wonderful works? And then will I profess unto them, I never knew you: depart from me, ye that work iniquity" (Matt. 7:22-23). He did not accept their worship. He could not accept their worship because it was not according to the holy nature of God. God cannot accept any worship apart from Himself and incompatible with His holiness.

The One who made us to worship Him also has decreed how we should go about the worship of Him. We cannot worship God as we will, according to our pleasure or mood. God does not accept just any kind of worship. He accepts worship only when it is pure and directed by the Holy Spirit. God has rejected almost all the worship of humanity in our present condition. However, God wants us to worship Him, commands us to and asks us to. Obviously, He was anxious and hurt when Adam failed to worship Him. Nevertheless, God condemns and rejects almost all the worship of humanity.

A worshiper must submit to God's truth or he cannot worship God. He can write poems and get elevations of thought when he sees a sunrise. But he cannot worship God except in faith and according to God's revealed truth. To worship as God can accept means submitting to the truth about God, admitting who God says He is and to admit that Christ is who and what He says He is.

Furthermore, he has to admit the truth about himself that he is as bad a sinner as God says he is. This is the last barrier to repentance. Man in his lost condition refuses to own up to his sinfulness. "God made me this way," so he boasts to alleviate any personal guilt. If I am not responsible for my condition,

I do not need to make any changes. God has to accept me as I am.

Then, he has to admit to the truth of the atonement, the blood of Jesus Christ that cleanses and delivers us from sin, and come God's way. When someone finally owns up to his sinful condition, he is often tempted to make his own atonement. But this has a major flaw. It does not meet God's standard.

For worship to be acceptable to God, you must be renewed after the image of Him that created you. That "image" must be restored. Only the renewed man can worship God in a way worthy of and acceptable to Him.

If the Holy Spirit does not do these things, it would only be wood, hay and stubble. My worship will never reach higher than the top of my own head, and God in heaven will refuse it as He refused the worship of Cain. I have a book, the Bible, which enlightened me. Here is the "light that lighteth every man" that will read it. Jesus Christ is the "light that lighteth every man that cometh into the world." The light of the human heart and the light of this book harmonize; and when the eyes of the soul look to the living Word of God, then we know the truth and we can worship God with truth and in spirit.

In the Old Testament, a priest could not offer a sacrifice until he had been anointed with oil, symbolic of the Spirit of God. No man can worship out of his own heart. Let him search among the flowers, let him search among the bird nests and tombs and wherever he chooses to worship God. Such a search will be futile and lead to spiritual frustration.

He cannot worship out of his own heart. Only the Holy Spirit can worship God acceptably, and He must in us reflect back to God His own glory. If it does not reach our hearts, there is no reflecting back and no worship.

O how big and broad and comprehensive and wonderful is the work of Christ! That is why I cannot have too much sympathy for the kind of Christianity that makes out that the gospel is to save a person from smoking or drinking. Is that all Christianity does, keep me from some bad habit, so I will not play the ponies, beat my wife or lie to my mother-in-law? Of course, regeneration will clean that up, and the new birth will make a man right. Those are the effects of a nature redeemed by the blood of Christ.

The primary purpose of God in redemption is to restore us again to the divine imperative of worship so that we can hear God say again, "So shall the king greatly desire thy beauty: for he is thy Lord; and worship thou him" (Ps. 45:11). The Church Militant conquered the world with their joyous religion because and only because they were worshipers. When the Christian church in any generation ceases to be a company of worshipers, their religion succumbs to mere outer effects, empty works and meaningless rituals.

When you begin to talk about the Lamb that was slain, and the blood that was shed, and God the Father, God the Son and God the Holy Ghost, then you are living and worshiping in truth. When the Spirit of God takes over, we worship in spirit and in truth; and that worship exceeds mere external rituals.

God created you to worship Him. When fundamentalism lost her power to worship, she invented religious claptrap to make her happy. That is why I have hated it, preached against it, condemned it all these years. Claiming to serve the Lord, the only joy they have is the joy that is of the flesh. Elvis Presley was a happier man after he got through with his sensuous music than many Christians are after they have worked themselves up in an emotional frenzy for half an hour.

For the redeemed, the well of the Holy Spirit is an effervescing artesian well, and you do not have to prime the pump. The silver waters of the Holy Spirit flooding up and out of the redeemed and cleansed heart of a worshiping man are as sweet and beautiful to God as the loveliest diamond. We need to learn how to worship to please the God who deserves it.

"So shall the king greatly desire thy beauty: for he is thy Lord; and worship thou him."

Prayer

God our Father, we seek Thee in ways that will bring us to Thee. We turn to the Holy Spirit, to our guide and teacher. May our hearts yield to His work and may He so flood our hearts with joy unspeakable and full of glory that we rise above the din of the world into the Light Unapproachable.

4

THE VARIOUS PATHS
TO WORSHIP

My heart was hot within me, while I was musing the fire burned:
then spake I with my tongue.

PSALM 39:3

Deep within every human is the impulse to worship, and it is the
most natural thing about us. Not all paths, however, lead to the
worship God accepts and delights in. Certain kinds of worship
are abhorrent to God and He cannot accept it, even though it is
directed toward Him and is meant to be given to Him. The God
who desires worship insists the worship be on His terms, and He
allows no exception.

In every generation and culture, there have been primarily
four pathways men and women have taken in their pursuit of
worship. Let me name them for you. These four categories are
true in every generation and culture and have withstood the
passing of time.

The Path of Human Excellence

This path to worship comes so close but falls so far short of
God's requirement. This worship is beautiful in many regards

and represents man's effort at his best. It is giving God what we delight in, disregarding God's command.

The Old Testament is a beautiful illustration of this in the life of Cain. Abel offered unto God the sacrifice of blood while Cain offered a sacrifice without blood. Abel brought to God according to His delight, while Cain brought to God what delighted him without any regard to God. God condemned and rejected the worship of Cain, because it lacked atonement.

Cain came to worship without a blood sacrifice, which is atonement; he came to God with a gift of his choosing for his Creator. He plucked a nice bunch of flowers and some nice delicious fruit and took it to God. God inquired after the blood and Cain said, "What blood?" Cain did not understand that he could not come to God without blood atonement. Cain objected, "I don't care about sin, I'll just bring a gift." He came before God with a bloodless sacrifice and offered flowers and fruit and the growth of the earth to the Lord.

This path of human excellence is not acceptable to God for a variety of reasons. Its basic premise is that God is unnecessary and that by human effort and devotion, we can reach the standard God wants for us. This kind of worship rests upon a mistaken assumption regarding the nature of God. Cain was born of Adam and Eve, fallen parents, and had never heard the voice of God in the Garden himself. When Cain came to worship God, he came to a God of his own imagination, thinking he was acceptable to God in his present condition.

Abel, on the other hand, brought a lamb, and God accepted it. When God refused Cain's worship it infuriated him, and he went out and in a jealous rage committed the first murder. Cain did not comprehend the difference God made between the two offerings. He took it upon himself to assume what would please God and completely disregarded the nature of God.

This kind of worship is all about us even today, even within the confines of what is called the Christian Church. A man can be well educated and even graduate from a seminary and can be taught how to use hand gestures and how to open his mouth and sound learned. He can be a ready-made preacher with all the culture the world of religion can offer. But if he follows the path of human excellence to worship, no matter how beautiful it might be, it will not be acceptable in God's eyes.

Worship acceptable to God is based upon knowing the nature of God. Cain did not know the kind of God he was, and therefore thought that sin was nothing to God. This represented a gross misunderstanding of God's nature.

This path to worship assumes a relationship to God that does not exist. Cain believed he belonged to God and assumed that he could talk to God without an intermediary. Cain failed to understand that he was alienated from God by his sin. Therefore, he never dealt with this sin element that was separating him from God. He acted as though there was no such separation and ignored the implications of such a separation.

Many religious people mistakenly assume a relationship to God that does not exist. They think and teach that we are all God's children, and they talk about the God and Father of mankind. However, the Bible does not teach that God is the Father of mankind; in fact, it teaches the exact opposite. To assume a relationship that does not exist prohibits a person from really knowing God.

Another thing about the path of human excellence is in the area of sin. For example, Cain viewed sin as being less severe than God viewed it. Sin is dismissed as inconsequential to our worship of God. Sin, however, is serious, and God never smiles upon it and never looks at any heart with sin upon it. He hates sin because it has filled the world with pain and sorrow but, more importantly, because it has robbed man of his purpose in life of worshiping God.

Cain represents the excellence of human accomplishment in this area of worship. He thought God was a different kind of God from what He is. He thought he was a different kind of man than what he was and thought sin was less vicious and serious than God said it was. So he came cheerfully, bringing his best, and offered to God worship without atonement.

While God says, "He is thy Lord, worship thou Him," and while He calls "where art thou" and commands us to worship Him in "spirit and in truth," He bluntly and severely rejects worship not founded on redeeming blood.

Apart from the blood atonement on the cross, no church holds any attraction for me. Without the redemption by the blood of Jesus Christ, there is no salvation. This path to worship, no matter how gentle and tender it is or how it may be adorned with beautiful flowers plucked from all parts of the world, is still false, and God frowns upon it because it is false in itself. God simply rejects the path of human excellence to worship.

The Path of Heathen Darkness

If Cain represents man at his best, then heathen worship is man at his worst. Completely disregarding all dignity, man subjects himself to the basest elements of his nature and worships the creation instead of the Creator. It would take a five-foot shelf of books for me to write, even if I were able to do it, to put forth adequately the tenants of this. I could go back if I wanted to and search in to the worship of the early Egyptians, the Egyptian book of the dead and the writings of Zoroaster and Buddha. We could make a case and talk about the worship of the pagans.

Paul talks about this and does not have a kind thing to say about it. He condemns it outright and says, "Because that, when they knew God, they glorified him not as God, neither were thankful; but became vain in their imaginations, and their foolish heart was darkened" (Rom. 1:21).

Down they ascended from God to man and from man to bird and from bird to beast and from beast to fish and from fish to creeping things that wiggled on the earth. That was man's terrible trip downward in his worship. This is man trying his best to be his worst and succeeding beyond expectation. God rejects and completely disowns this kind of worship and any worshipers involved in it.

I believe that if the Christian Church has not crossed the line already, it is perilously close to slipping into heathen oriented worship, rendering to the creature what rightfully belongs to the Creator. Let me explain what I mean. Never has there been a time in Christian history where the Church has been more plagued with celebrities than today, especially in the music department.

On a Saturday night, a "praise and worship band" will hold a concert in a hall downtown. After one song, the audience explodes in applause accompanied with cheers and a standing ovation. To cover his track, the lead singer will say, "Let's give a clap offering to God."

If you do not think this is crowding the line, do this. Take the lyrics of the song that caused such uproar and give it to one of the dear old saints at church on Sunday. Make sure it is one of those saints with an impeccable reputation of holiness and unimpeachable Christian character. Usually this will be one of the saintly prayer warriors of the church. Have this person take these lyrics to the pulpit and quietly read them to the audience. If it does not create the same effect as the night before, maybe it was not the truth in those lyrics the people the night before were applauding but the performers.

The path of heathen darkness to worship always mirrors the culture around it rather than the Christ within.

The Path of Heretical Confusion

This is heretical worship in the correct meaning of the term. A heretic is not a man who denies all the truth; he is just a very fastidious man who picks out what he likes while rejecting what he does not like. Certain aspects of theology appeal to him, but others are rejected because they do not suit him at the time. I refer to these as inconvenient aspects of theology.

A man once addressed a large group of Christian young people offering this advice: "Don't believe anything in the Bible that doesn't square with your own experience." This man had the infinite effrontery to tell young people searching for truth to take the Word of God and judge it by their little wicked hearts. How can you get any worse than that? It is heretical confusion at its best. Heresy means I take what I like and I reject what I do not like. The very word "heretic" means one who picks and chooses. But the Bible says, "And if any man shall take away from the words of the book of this prophecy, God shall take away his part out of the book of life, and out of the holy city, and from the things which are written in this book" (Rev. 22:19).

The Samaritans of Jesus' day represented this kind of worship. The Samaritans were heretics in the right sense of the word, because being heretical does not always mean that we are false. A man can be a heretic and not teach anything particularly false. A heretic does not necessarily teach that there is no Trinity, or that God did not create the earth, or that there is no judgment. Heresy is the selecting and rejecting aspects of truth and applying psychology, humanism and the various religions of all sorts. Every religion is based upon this.

The Lord rejects this path to worship because of its selective nature, picking what it likes and what does not inconvenience its lifestyle. If it does not like something, it explains it away and goes on as if it were a small matter or if it even did not exist.

The Samaritans were heretics in that they chose certain parts of the Bible, the Old Testament. They had a Pentateuch and accepted it but rejected certain parts of David, Isaiah, Jeremiah, Ezekiel and Daniel, 1 and 2 Kings, the Song of Solomon and other parts of Scripture. They believed them and did some translating.

You can translate anything and prove anything. All a person has to say is, "I know Greek" or "I know Hebrew," and after that, that person is on his or her own. He or she is a self-appointed expert on the subject. Every false religion or cult is built on the selecting of favorite Scripture passages to the neglect of other passages. They do not compare Scripture with Scripture, which allows heretical doctrine to come in.

The Samaritans translated the old Pentateuch in such a way as to make Samaria the place of worship. And, of course, they were hostile to the Jews who insisted Jerusalem was the only place to worship Jehovah. The Samaritans used their translation of the Pentateuch to prove their position.

God gave Israel Mount Mariah, and here David took Zion and Solomon built the Temple, and that was the place where the people should worship. It was there Christ came and became the sacrificial Lamb for the sins of mankind. However, the Samaritans refused Jerusalem in favor of Samaria. They did so by selecting certain parts of the Pentateuch to support that position.

I do not think I will have to spell it out and mark it in red ink for you to see how much heresy there is these days. Believing what we want to believe. Emphasizing what we want to emphasize. Following along in one path while rejecting another. Doing one thing but refusing another. We become heretics by picking and choosing among the Word of God what suits us at the time. That is the path of heretical confusion.

The Path of Existential Sublimity

I admit that I have more sympathy with this category than I do with liberalism, which is the enemy of true biblical Christianity (of which Samaritan worship is one). At the same time, I reject this path to worship, which is but the poetry of religion. Religion does have a lot of poetry in it; it is proper, and it should have. Personally, I melt like honey on a hot day when I get to this existential. Poetry is the high enjoyment and contemplation of the sublime.

By nature, we are all poets, and religion brings poetry out more than any other occupation the mind can be engaged in. Moreover, there is a lot that is very beautiful about religion. You will discover a high enjoyment in the contemplation of the divine and sublime. The concentration of the mind upon beauty always brings a high sense of enjoyment.

Some mistake this sublimity, this rapt feeling for true worship, and it is an understandable mistake. God warned Israel that when they arrived in the Promised Land and looked up and saw the sun and the stars, they were not to get on their knees and worship them because if they did, Jehovah would destroy them from out of the land. The world is full of these worshipers. It is a high enjoyment, a concentrating of the mind upon beauty as distinct from the eye and the ear. If your ear hears beauty that is music, or your eye sees beauty that is art, but if you think beautiful thoughts without music or art, that is poetry. We write what we feel inside, and that is poetry.

Some people understandably mistake such rapturous feelings for worship. Ralph Waldo Emerson said, "I have crossed the meadow after a rain on a moonlight night when the moon had come out and the rain and the puddles were still lying in the meadow and the moon shining on the little puddles of water in the grass and I have been glad to the point of fear." He was so happy that he was afraid. I have felt it myself. Emerson did not believe in the deity of Christ or the blood of Christ, and he resigned his church rather than serve communion. He eventually denied the faith. Yet he was glad to the point of fear, because he was a good man. He was a great man, a poet and an artist. A mighty man indeed, but I do not think God accepted his worship at all because it led along the path of existential sublimity, and that was all.

It is easy to confuse the music of religion as true worship because music elevates the mind and raises the heart to near rapture. Music can lift our feelings to a sense of ecstasy. Music has a purifying effect upon us so that it is possible to fall into a happy and elevated state of mind with only a vague notion about God and imagine we are worshiping God when we are doing nothing of the sort. We are simply enjoying an ecstatic moment God put in us that even sin has not yet been able to kill.

I reject the idea of any poetry in hell; I cannot believe that among the terrible sewage of the moral world there is going to be anybody breaking into similes and metaphors. I cannot conceive of anyone breaking into song in that terrible place called hell. We read about music and poetry in heaven because it belongs there. As far as I know in my Bible, we never hear about poetry in hell. We hear about conversations in hell, but we do not hear about song because there is no song there. There is no poetry there, no music there, but plenty of it on earth, even among the unsaved because they were once made in the image of God. While they have lost God from their mind, they still appreciate the sublime and carry within their innermost part a residue of spiritual desire.

Certain men have written books on the importance of sublimity and how to cultivate it. And there is much that is inspirational and beautiful in the world. Sublimity is beauty of the mind in contradistinction (to use a long word), beauty of the eye and ear. Music is the beauty that the ear recognizes. And certain other beautiful things the eye recognizes, but when the heart hears nothing and sees nothing but only feels, then it is the music of the heart. It is beauty within the spirit.

The Scripture tells us that "God is a Spirit: and they that worship him must worship him in spirit and in truth" (John 4:24). The Word must clear away all the mists of obscurity. It takes worship out of the hands of men and puts it in the hands of the Holy Spirit. Therefore, we can have all that and still not worship God at all or even be accepted of God.

We may take whatever path to worship we choose, but not all paths will end at the feet of the Lord Jesus Christ, nor will God accept them. God Almighty sternly rejects it all and says, "I will have nothing to do with it." Jesus our Lord said, "God is Spirit: and they that worship him must . . ." I want you to see the imperative; the word "must" clears away all mists of obscurity and takes worship out of the hands of man.

It is impossible to worship God acceptably apart from the Holy Spirit. The operation of the Spirit of God within us enables us to worship God acceptably through that person we call Jesus Christ, who is Himself God. Therefore, worship originates with God, comes back to us and is reflected from us. That is the worship God accepts, and He accepts no other kind.

Prayer

Oh, God, we ask Thee that as we speak, heaven might be open and there might be a sense of Thy presence and the feeling that there is impending upon this world another world above, an eternal world touching Thee. As the kingdom of heaven touches the kingdom of man, we believe God has heard our prayers. Oh, God, we pray, speak Thou and let us not take anything for granted, let us not believe that something is true when it is not true or assume we are all right when we are not or think that our worship is acceptable when it is not. May we one and all, each and every one of us come humbly, looking to the sacrifice, the mighty sacrifice, and hear the words of love and see the mighty sacrifice and have peace with Thee. Grant this we pray in Christ's holy name. Amen.

The Fervor of Holy Desire
by Madame Guyon

Still, still, without ceasing.
I feel it increasing,
This fervor of holy desire;
And often exclaim,
Let me die in a flame that can never expire!

RELIGION VERSUS WORSHIP

God is a Spirit: and they that worship him must
worship him in spirit and in truth.

JOHN 4:24

Since man's expulsion from the Garden, religion has been an intolerable burden on the back of all mankind. In spite of the drudgery, it is a bondage most are unable or unwilling to break. The word "religion" itself means to bind back; religious people, as a rule, have laid off one set of chains only to take up another. Whatever it takes, man will exercise this inward impulse to worship.

Then along comes our Lord and issues a long-awaited spiritual emancipation proclamation and signs it in blood. Now the people of the world, bearing the heavy yoke of religion, can know the true freedom of genuine worship. Our Lord Jesus spoke words allowing the light to shine upon us so that there is light in our spirits, elevating us and lifting us up out of the mud of depraved society.

God never called man to walk knee-deep in the sludge of the world, nor did He intend for man to be mired down in the traditions of men. Therefore, the Lord sets us free and opens a fountain of healing water for the wounds of the world.

In spite of all this, man deliberately chooses the bondage of religion over the liberating freedom in Christ.

In India, they believe that the goddess Ganga that is the Ganges River has power to cleanse people. Certain saints make pilgrimages to bathe in goddess Ganga, one of the dirtiest rivers in the world. They will fall down full length and then mark with their finger where their forehead was, step forward and put their foot where the mark is and then fall full length again. Literally, they fall across scores of miles to the goddess Ganga, the River Ganges, and bathe themselves, go away and are no cleaner than they were before. In fact, they are not as clean as they were before. Certainly they are wounded and bruised bitterly in their soul.

Our Lord puts into one sentence the words of worship: "God is a Spirit: and they that worship him must worship him in spirit and in truth," forever settling this matter and emphasizing that you cannot please God by bruising your body or by bathing in this or that river. However, they that worship the Father worship Him in spirit and in truth. This is the true healing water for the wounded souls of religious men.

Our Lord explains here that worship is natural to man. There has never been a tribe of people discovered anywhere but what religion was a part of its society. It was perfectly natural for Adam to walk with God in the garden in the cool of the day. The years of Adam were blessed by the velvet-soft, healing voice of God. When Adam sinned, he hid from the presence of God among the trees of the garden. He was conscious of God, but he was not free to worship God, because sin had come in between and tore the strings off the harp. Nothing remained but the outline; the music of the soul was muted; now there was cacophony and discord where there had been harmony before. So he lost the proper object of his worship and was looking about now for something to worship.

Man worships by the necessity of his being. Looking around for something to worship, he recognizes mystery and wonder. The result is, whatever man cannot explain, he will worship. Whatever evokes wonder becomes the object of man's worship. Because the human mind is fallen, he is amazed at external things and objects that impress.

The human mind is enlarged, lifted and filled with wonder, and this very wonder leads to worship and opens mystery. Men used to stand on the seashore and hear the moaning of the sea and watch the gulls turn and see the white clouds float, and cry, "What is all of this, what is all of this?" And they called that something out there Neptune, and said, "This is our God," and got on their knees and made sacrifices to Neptune. The splendor of nature called to mind a need to worship not the Creator but the creation. When they saw the sun rising in the morning and making its journey across the sky, and setting in the sea of blood, they said, "What is this shining thing that always rises in the same place and goes down and never fails?" They called it Phoebus Apollo—a great beautiful god they made with silver wings on his feet so that he went fast across the sky. They worshiped and said this is wonderful. They did not know what it was, but it was wonderful and inspired a need to worship. The Parsis got on their knees before the sun; they called it Mazda, and the light that shines down is Mazda light named after the god of the Zoroastrians, the fire worshipers.

If we do not know how to worship through Jesus Christ our Lord, the human heart will break out somehow like a flood that goes over its banks and will worship. If it does not get going in the right direction, it will go in the wrong direction; but it will worship.

Not only in nature did man find reason to worship but also within the heart and emotions of man. They said, "Look at love, look at this powerful, tremendous thing for which men and women die and think nothing of it. Look at this that binds a man and woman together, binds family together, binds men to the love of their country until they will give and sacrifice themselves freely." They called it Venus; we have named one of the planets after that goddess. We could go on; there is Ceres, the goddess of life, and many others—the list is as endless as the imagination of man. Every emotion, every thought, every imagination of man became the object of mystery and adoration—all leading away from the One behind all this, the Creator.

Another indication of this need to worship can be seen in the artistic and creative work of man. What makes a man want to create something beautiful? Why does he want to write a poem, paint a picture, compose a piece of music? I believe that fallen man has within him somewhere, in the deep of his soul, that which calls out after mystery. Deep calls unto deep at the noise of God's waterspout; the deep voice of God calls and the deep of man struggles to answer back.

Every time a Greek got on his knees at the seashore and offered his sacrifice to Neptune, it was the little blind deep within him answering back to the deep of God. Every time an American Indian stood on the shore of the river and reverently put the bones of the fish back into the sea and apologized to God for killing it and eating it; every time he looked up and said "Manito," and "Praises be," he was giving up to the mystery within him. And every time that great genius Beethoven turned out a page of immortal music, he was feeling something deep within. He was saying, "I know God. He is nearer to me than He is to others; I know this God," and then he wrote his imperishable music. What was he doing? Flinging out wildly, looking to worship something, anything. This great man who hovered back and forth between suicide and life until he gave up and went the way of all flesh was only a sample.

Man has it in him to do this—to admire, to fear—and consequently, many religions have developed because of this. In India, there is a god for everyone, to answer to the compulsion within to worship. By nature man has to admire something. Within his very being he has to adore, and if he loses his ability to adore in his spirit and soar in his heart, he will find some other way to do it. He will get out there somehow. Because of how he was created, man is drawn to mystery wherever he finds it. Some mystery creates within a sense of awe, and when he finds it, he will worship.

This is the impulse behind exploring other worlds and riding out into the vast spaces in the heavens. No other of God's creatures do it, and no other creature thinks of doing it. Man, who has lost the mystery of God within his heart, looks for that mystery elsewhere.

The Samaritan woman in John 4 revealed what is wrong with the entire religious world: "Sir, I understand from what you say that you are a prophet. You know more than the average person would know; you must be a prophet. I've got a question for you." This question was not simply a frivolous one; it was one that separated Jew from Samaritan even though they were related by blood. The question was, "Here in Samaria, in our holy mountain, we worship. Across there a little way in Jerusalem the holy mountain of the Jews, they worship. And we say this is the place to worship and you say Jerusalem is the place to worship. Now, you are a prophet; tell me, where is the right place to worship?"

This woman falls into her own little trap and reveals that chief woe of the religious world. Do I worship here or do I worship there? Do I worship in this church or do I worship in that church? What church is the right church and what denomination is the right one? That is the difficulty and the problem. The whole problem then was externality of worship. Externalism is our problem even today—the biggest problem the church faces.

Jesus our Lord said this beautiful thing: "The time is fast approaching, in fact it is already here where worship won't be tied down to any location, for the Father seeketh such to worship Him in spirit for God is spirit and therefore you must be spiritual worshippers" (see John 4:21-23). If God were a local deity confined to a hill, you would have to go to the hill to worship Him. If God were a river deity confined to the river, you would have to go down to the bank of the river to worship Him. If God were a mountain deity, or if God were a plains deity, you would have to go where He was. Jesus gave us the marvelous liberating news that God is Spirit; therefore, God is everywhere, and we do not worship in places anymore.

The purpose of nature is to lead us to the Creator and to worship Him. The purpose of man's feelings and emotions is to lead to the One who implanted those within the heart of man, to the Creator. Everything in all of creation is to point to the Creator and evoke within adoring wonder and admiration and worship. Wherever we go, we can worship.

Jesus taught essentially that we are portable sanctuaries, and if we are worshiping in spirit and in truth, we can take our sanctuary around with us. Jesus said, "Don't you see that if God is Spirit, worship is spiritual, and anything spiritual has no location in space and it has no location in time?" You do not get up in the morning, look at your calendar and say this is the time to worship. You do not get up, go out, look around and say this is the place to worship. You worship God now, anywhere, any place, any time, because worship is spiritual.

People have made a comedy of religion, because men have enslaved themselves to externals and objects to the point of the ridiculous. These religious pilgrims travel to their holy shrines in order to worship. Many will take a pilgrimage to the Holy Land and believe they are closer to God there than anywhere else on the planet. In God's kingdom, as He has intended it, no place is holier than another. If you cannot worship here, you cannot worship there.

It does not stop here, this bondage of religion. Some make their religion to consist in foods. Some things they do not eat and some things they do eat. The result is that if they do eat it, they are holy; and if they do not eat it, they are not holy. At certain times of the year, you can eat "this," but not at other times of the year. Paul explained that what you ate did not make you better and it did not make you any worse. It might make you sick, but it will not make you holy and it will not hurt you nor help you. If it is decent and good, and you can digest it, help yourself. Holiness does not reside in the food we eat, and worship is not dependent upon that food either. God is a Spirit: and they that worship Him must worship Him in spirit and in truth.

Then, some are enslaved to times. Worship is not in times. I respect our brethren of the church calendar year that begins with one thing and ends with another; but I do not follow it at all. Can you imagine that six weeks out of the year I repent; then after that the lid is off? I could not imagine myself being tied down to times. "Behold now is the accepted time." This is the time; so any time is all right. You can say, "Good morning, God," in the morning. You can say, "Goodnight, God," at night. You can wake in the night and think of God; you can even dream of God—I have. You can have God any time, any place.

There are times of the year when we think of religion a little more. I personally like Easter. If I were going to have a special time of the year, it would be Easter, because that is when birds are returning from Florida and the people of God are looking up and we are hearing, "Christ the Lord Is Risen Today, Hallelujah, Hallelujah." I like Easter, and I think it is a beautiful time of the year. I have a tough time preaching Easter sermons because all of my sermons are based upon His resurrection; and if you take away the resurrection of Jesus Christ, my sermons collapse.

Christ's resurrection is not truer at Easter than any other time of the year. Apart from the resurrection of Christ, all of

Christianity falls to the ground. Our worship cannot be confined to time.

Foods are not holy; times are not holy; and places are not holy. If they do not point to Christ, they become a snare enslaving us to mere religious bondage.

The Jews made the mistake of thinking the Temple was holy; and because the Temple was holy, nothing could happen to the Temple. Jesus pointed out their error. "See this Temple? See these stones? Every bit of it will lie in the dust before very long." It came down to the ground in the year A.D. 70. He said Israel is like a tree. "See that ax, either it will bear fruit or it will be cast down into the fire."

I am talking about worship now and saying worship is a spiritual thing. It is internal; and external things are unnecessary. For instance, we could not sit on the street corner and preach, sing and pray. We need walls to protect us, or heat to keep us warm. Buildings have a place and purpose, so I am not against buildings. You have to have books, and I am for books. God has blessed external things, but the trouble is that we become slaves to them instead of making them our servants.

So, with times and foods and everything else, they are our servants. Therefore, we rise above all the little things of religion and look down on them from our place in the heavenlies. It is wonderful how small things look when you are up high enough. You always know that you are losing altitude when things begin to get big. When fields get the size of postage stamps, you are really up there. When they begin to get a little bit bigger, you are losing altitude; you look at your watch, and say, "We're going to land." The further down, the bigger things look; and the higher up, the smaller. I recommend to you concerning a big problem facing you, rise above it, take off and get up there above it.

True worship elevates us above all the accoutrements of religion into that rarified atmosphere of God's holy and delightful presence. Seventeenth-century French mystic Madame Guyon put these thoughts into a hymn we often sing in church.

Content
by Madame Guyon

My Lord, how full of sweet content,
I pass my years of banishment!
Where'er I dwell, I dwell with Thee,
In heav'n, in earth, or on the sea;
Where'er I dwell, I dwell with Thee,
In heav'n, in earth, or on the sea;

Prayer

We praise thee, O God, that our religion lies not in what we do or eat or where we go. Thou hast set us free from all externals so that we can elevate ourselves above all these and find Thy heart and worship Thee. Amen.

SEEKERS AFTER TRUTH

Jesus saith unto him, I am the way, the truth, and the life:
no man cometh unto the Father, but by me.

JOHN 14:6

In this mixed-up world in which we live there is a group of people claiming to be seekers after truth. "We are seekers after truth," they boast, as if that qualifies them as acceptable worshipers, no matter what their beliefs might be or the truth they are seeking. Some churches actually accommodate this idea and invite people to "come to our church, you do not have to believe anything just be a seeker after truth." This infers a certain openness of mind that accepts anything and everything. In this frame of mind, truth is not absolute but whatever you think of it at the time, or whatever you have determined to be truth.

On the surface, these "seekers after truth" seem to be genuine in their belief or at least heading in the right direction. However, in this day of relativism, truth means different things to different people. What is true to one person may not necessarily be true to another. And what was true yesterday may not be true today. The only thing these "seekers after truth" accomplish is to keep people from seeking the absolute Truth, which is Jesus Christ, "the same yesterday, and today and forever" (Heb. 13:8).

Then there are those who inform us that there is truth in every religion. This is like saying there is water in most poisons, and so it is all right to drink. It is not the water that kills; it is the poison. The more ambiguous the poison, the more dangerous it is. The closer it is to the real thing, the more damage it does. And the enemy of man's soul knows this all too well.

When you study the religions of the world, you will find much in them that is true. However, partial truth is more dangerous than trickery. When I know something is an outright lie, I can stay away from it.

Going back to the Garden of Eden, we see this: The Serpent did not outright lie to Eve; he simply told her partial truth. He only told her what he wanted to tell her in order to mislead her for his advantage. It is what he did not tell her that created all the problems following the Fall in the Garden.

You can tell someone something and not actually lie to him or her, but so present the truth that it keeps this person from the truth.

I can go down to the local zoo and look at a tiger. There it is lying before me, licking itself like a big kitten. Perhaps it is in a playful mood and I can say to myself that this tiger is not dangerous. Why, it is just a big kitty. The tiger can be declawed and all those dangerous teeth extracted. But the partial truth does not change the nature of the tiger. By nature, it is the most efficient killing machine on God's green earth. Its playfulness is only partial truth.

Now, if I approach that tiger accepting only partial truth, I am putting myself in mortal danger. It is what you do not know that can hurt you.

Those who boast that they are seekers after truth are putting themselves and others at greater risk than I would face in the tiger's pen. The tiger can only harm the body; but these partial religious truths can effectively lead me into everlasting spiritual darkness and final damnation.

Every false religion in the world has a base of truth about it. It starts with some truth and then moves away from it subtly and maliciously, though maybe not intentionally. Eve did not intentionally disobey God or knowingly move away from ultimate truth.

When it comes to the worship of God, we must be quite careful that we are not basing it on partial truth, but on the entire revealed truth such as can be found in the Bible.

Man wants to worship God, but he wants to worship God after his own comprehension of truth. So did Cain, so did the Samaritans and so have men and women down the years; but God has rejected it all. Now, there is an imperative to worship deep within the heart of mankind, but with God, there is no tolerance, there is no broad spirit. There is the sharp pinpointing of fact so that every man in his own fallacy is completely rejected.

I have piles of religious poetry, and I have read most of it. People who have not found God, and have not experienced the new birth and the Holy Spirit on them, still have the ancient impulse to worship something. If they come from a third-world country where there is little education, they might kill a chicken, put a feather on their head and dance around a fire, calling for a witch doctor. However, if they have some education, they write poetry.

Edwin Markham (1852-1940) was an American poet who wrote two or three good things. He wrote "Lincoln" and "The Man with the Hoe," and that is good poetry. However, I quote him because this is an example of the way the human mind goes. The world is full of bushel baskets of poetry like this that you can throw out; the kind of poetry and religion that has no anchor, no God, no High Priest, no blood, no altar, but floats around like a drunken butterfly, floating and flopping about not knowing quite where he wants to go, and they all say about the same thing.

> I made a pilgrimage to find the God;
> I listened for His voice at holy tombs,
> Searched for the prints of His immortal feet
> In the dust of broken altars; yet turned back
> With empty heart. But on the homeward road
> A great light came upon me and I heard
> The God's voice ringing in a nesting lark;
> Felt His sweet wonder in a growing rose;
> Received His blessing from a wayside well;
> Looked on His beauty in a lover's face;
> Saw His bright hand send signal from the sun.

He was a good poet in many regards, but his ornithology was not very sound. In the first place, nesting larks do not sing. In the second place, he said that he heard God singing like a bird. Then he said, "I felt his sweet wonder in a swaying rose and received his blessing from a wayside well. Looked on his beauty in a lover's face. Saw His bright hand send signals from the sun."

There you have it: not a crazy man and not a medicine man from the jungles of New Guinea. Here is a man whose poetry is in every anthology. He writes among the poets of the world and goes out looking for God. And he searched for Him in the first place, a graveyard, and did not find Him. He looked at broken altars and could not find Him there; then on the way back, he hears a bird singing and says that it is God. And he sees a happy lover holding hands with his girlfriend and says that's God. And he sees a rose waving in the wind and he says that's God. So he comes home and writes himself a poem.

Now, I want to know, how could he get this bad? How could this man, in a land of Bibles, with the gospel being preached, write that he went looking for God in altars and tombs and in all dark, dusty places, yet didn't find Him? And started home and saw him and heard him singing in a nesting lark; saw him in a rose and saw him in the face of a young lover? Then he looked up and, lo and behold, God was signaling from the sun. I never had any signals from the sun myself, and I do not know of anybody except Edwin Markham who wrote about this.

This kind of thing, it seems to me, needs to be exposed. We need to tell the world that God is Spirit, and they that worship Him must worship Him in spirit and in truth. It must be the Holy Spirit and truth. You cannot worship Him in Spirit alone, for the Spirit without truth is helpless. It cannot be in truth alone, for that would be theology without fire. It must be the truth of God and the Spirit of God.

When a man, yielding and believing the truth of God, is full with the Spirit of God, then his warmest and smallest whisper will be worship. So, we can find that we will worship God by any means if we are full of the Spirit and yielded to the truth. However, when we are yielded to neither the truth nor full of the Spirit, there is no worship at all. God cannot receive into His holy heart just any kind of worship.

Jesus said, "they that worship Him must worship in spirit and in truth" and settled forever how we should worship God. God formed the living flame, and He gave the reasoning mind that only He may claim the worship of mankind. But instead of our worshiping God, every man worships after his own fashion.

Keep in mind, there is only one way to worship God: "I am the way, the truth, and the life: no man cometh unto the Father, but by me" (John 14:6). Instead of being kindly and charitable by allowing an idea to stand that God accepts worship from anybody, anywhere, we are actually injuring and jeopardizing the future of the man or woman we allow to get away with that. Anything incompatible with the holy nature of God only damages a man's soul and ultimately damns that soul forever.

I would do as seventeenth-century hymn writer Isaac Watts did when he tried to put the psalms in meter. He just could not leave a psalm if there was nothing about Jesus in it. He would always put in a stanza about Jesus before he was through. Personally, I am glad he did.

It is an either/or situation. Either a worshiper must submit to God's truth or he cannot worship God at all. A person can write poems and he can get elevations of thought when he sees a sunrise. He can hear the fledgling lark sing, but fledgling larks do not sing. And he can do all sorts of things, but he cannot worship God except in faith. To do so would mean that he has to surrender to the revealed truth about God. He has to confess that God is who He says He is and He is what He says He is. And he has to declare that Christ is who He says He is and what He says He is. He has to own up to the truth about himself and admit that he is as bad a sinner as God says he is. Then he must acknowledge the truth of the atonement, the blood of Jesus Christ that cleanses and delivers from sin. Finally, he has to come God's way. He must be renewed after the image of He that created him.

Only the redeemed man can worship God acceptably. Only the renewed man can worship God acceptably and embrace the truth as God has revealed it in His Word.

So these people who have churches and pray in the name of the "all good" and the "all Father" have no idea of what true worship that is acceptable in the eyes of God is, and they stumble in spiritual darkness. I would rather go out in the park and walk with my New Testament. I can find my God, not the god in a rose but the God who sits on the throne on high and by His side sits the one whose name is Jesus, having all power in heaven and in earth. And I could commune with God walking out on the street rather than worship Him at an altar of Baal.

Man must be renewed. He must have an infusion of the Spirit of truth. Without an infusion of the Holy Ghost, there can be no true worship.

How big God is and how comprehensive is the work of Christ! How imperative is repentance and regeneration in the Holy Spirit! By rejecting the Holy Spirit, we put out our eyes and blunder on in darkness, sightless and lost. Let us not be guilty of that in this day of open Bibles and plenty of truth.

Bernard of Clairvaux (1091–1153), in his great hymn, expresses the heart of all those who are truly seeking after truth.

> Jesus, Thou Joy of loving hearts,
> Thou Fount of life, Thou Light of men,
> From the best bliss that earth imparts,
> We turn unfilled to Thee again.
> Thy truth unchanged hath ever stood;
> Thou savest those that on Thee call;
> To them that seek Thee Thou art good,
> To them that find Thee all in all.
> We taste Thee, O Thou living Bread,
> And long to feast upon Thee still;
> We drink of Thee, the Fountainhead,
> And thirst our souls from Thee to fill.
> Our restless spirits yearn for Thee,
> Where'er our changeful lot is cast;
> Glad when Thy gracious smile we see,
> Blessed when our faith can hold Thee fast.
> O Jesus, ever with us stay,
> Make all our moments calm and bright;
> Chase the dark night of sin away,
> Shed over the world Thy holy light.

Prayer

*O God, how wonderful is the work of Thy Son. It fills the
whole universe with wonder and awe and admiration.
My heart is overwhelmed with the intensity of that work
within me. I seek Thee, but I only find Thee when I have sought
Thee with my whole heart and mind. My wonderment at
Thee has all but exhausted my expressions of praise and worship.
Thy presence is my comfort day and night. Amen.*

WHAT CAME FIRST:
WORKERS OR
WORSHIPERS?

I believe in one God, the Father Almighty, Maker of heaven and earth, and of all things visible and invisible. And in one Lord Jesus Christ, the only-begotten Son of God, begotten of the Father before all worlds; God of God, Light of Light, very God of very God; begotten, not made. . . .

NICENE CREED

Thou art the King of Glory, O Christ, thou art the everlasting Son of the Father. When thou tookest upon thee to deliver man, thou didst humble thyself to be born of a Virgin. When thou hadst overcome the sharpness of death, thou didst open the Kingdom of Heaven to all believers.

TE DEUM LAUDAMUS

These ancient assertions or creeds, as they are sometimes called, were made by the church down the centuries, declaring herself with great joy and a sense of deep unworthiness. I join my voice with theirs and say that I believe these things and I believe that He, the King of Glory, everlasting Son of the Father took upon

Him to deliver man and overcame the sharpness of death and the resurrection and is now opened the Kingdom of heaven to all believers.

In light of this, the human mind must give answer to some questions. One of those questions is why did all of this take place? God of gods and Light of light, He was born of a virgin, suffered under Pontius Pilate, overcame the sharpness of death and opened the Kingdom of heaven to all believers. Back of this must be a purpose, for God has intellect. Intellect is one of the attributes of deity and, therefore, God must have a reasonable purpose that can stand up under the scrutiny of sanctified human reason. Why did God do all of this?

As an evangelical, I am deeply worried and concerned to the point of some degree of suffering over the state of evangelicals these days. By evangelicals, I mean the free churches generally—the churches that have order, those that do not have order and the ones that have disorder. The churches that have beautiful services and plain services, hit-and-miss and off-the-cuff services, and churches whose ministers feel they must be a cross between the apostle Paul, Moses and Bob Hope.

The supreme reason the Lord was born of the Virgin Mary to suffer under Pontius Pilate to be crucified, die and be buried; the reason He overcame death and rose again from the grave is that He might make worshipers out of rebels. We are the recipients of a grace meant to save us from self-centeredness and make worshipers out of us.

Thomas Boston said the difference between man and beast is that a beast looks down and a man is made to look up. A man can engage the God above while the beast goes about and only sees the ground underneath its short legs. But man can see into the heavens above. A beast bows under his burden, but a man lifts his heart in praise to his Burden bearer, Jesus Christ.

God is infinitely more concerned that He has worshipers than that He has workers. Unfortunately, most evangelicals do not share this concern. For the most part, evangelicals have been reduced to the position where God is a supervisor desperately seeking help. Standing at the wayside, He tries to find how many helpers will come to His rescue and bail Him out of a tight spot. We mistakenly believe that God needs workers, and so we cheerfully say, "I'll go to work for the Lord." If we could only remember that as far as His plans are concerned, God does not need us.

I think we should work for the Lord, but it is a matter of grace on God's part. However, I do not think we should ever work until we learn to worship. A worshiper can work with eternal quality in his work but a worker who does not worship is only piling up wood, hay and stubble for the time when God sets the world on fire. God wants worshipers before He wants workers. He calls us back to that for which we were created—to worship the Lord God and to enjoy Him forever. And then out of our deep worship flows our work for Him. Our work is only acceptable to God if our worship is acceptable.

Many of the great hymns of the church came out of revival of some kind. They can be traced through the Lutheran Reformation, the Wesleyan Revival and the Moravian Revival. These hymns were born out of the times when the church of God labored. The Spirit fell upon it, heaven was opened and she saw visions of God; radiance beamed from the throne above reflected from the hearts of His people.

If the devil has a sense of humor, I think he must laugh and hold his sooty sides when he sees a church of dead Christians singing a hymn written by a spiritually awakened and worshiping composer. Many great hymns I didn't like in my early days, because I heard them sung in some dead prayer meeting with a dead song leader who did not expect anything, and a dead congregation in front of him who did not expect anything. Both would have been shocked if anything happened. They had a spirit of no expectation. True worship that is pleasing to God creates within the human heart a spirit of expectation and insatiable longing.

We must understand that the Holy Spirit only descends on a heart engaged in worship. Out of your fiery worship, God will call you to work for Him. But He is not interested in you jumping up and starting some slapdash religious project. This is where the contemporary church is today. Any untrained, unprepared, spiritually empty rattletrap of a fellow who is a bit ambitious can start something religious, like The Fig-Leaf Gospel Tabernacle. People listen to him and work to try to help this man who never heard from God in the first place. Many confuse this wild amateurism as spiritually dynamic worship and offer it to God. From my point of view, nobody who worships God is likely to do anything offbeat or out of place. Nobody who is a true worshiper is likely to give himself up to carnal and worldly religious projects.

Every glimpse we have of worshiping creatures or of heaven show people worshiping. I read Ezekiel 1:1-28, and think about these strange, beautiful creatures with wings, high and lifted up; creatures that put down their wings and drop quietly by the throne of God in reverent worship. At the voice of the Lord, they raised their wings, and their faces stayed straight forward and did not turn where they went (see v. 12). I love that too. This is a glorious picture of the creatures and God's people worshiping in ecstatic wonder and adoration.

Then you find in Isaiah, the sixth chapter, an account of rapturous worship. "In the year that King Uzziah died, I saw the Lord sitting upon a throne, high and lifted up, and His train filled the temple. Above it stood the seraphims: each one had six wings; with twain he covered his face; and with twain he covered his feet . . ." (Isa. 6:1-2). They answered each other antiphonally, and they said, "Holy, holy, holy is the LORD of Hosts: the whole earth is full of his glory" and the temple was filled with the incense, and the temple doors shook, or pillars shook (vv. 3-4). They were worshiping God in joyous and awesome wonder. Not irreverent, emotional outbursts that serve only to stroke the flesh.

Worship is also found in the book of Revelation (4:9-11): "And when those beasts give glory and honour and thanks to him that sat on the throne, who liveth for ever and ever, the four and twenty elders fall down before him that sat on the throne and worship him that liveth for ever and ever, and cast their crowns before the throne, saying, 'Thou art worthy, O Lord, to receive glory and honour and power: for thou hast created all things, and for thy pleasure they are and were created.'"

A little further on, "Every creature which is in heaven, and on earth, and under the earth, and such as are in the sea, and all that are in them, heard I them saying, Blessing, and honor, and glory, and power, be unto him that sitteth upon the throne, and unto the Lamb forever and ever. And the four beasts said, Amen. And the four and twenty elders fell down and worshipped him that liveth forever and ever" (Rev. 5:13-14).

I see a wonderful picture of some class of being called elders. I do not know whether they are elders such as we elect in our churches or not. Then there are beasts, which otherwise are called living creatures. They are all worshiping the Lord God, and wherever you look in heaven, you will find them engaged in worship. If worship bores you, you are not ready for heaven. Worship is the very atmosphere of heaven focusing on the person of Jesus Christ.

I believe in justification by faith as strongly as Martin Luther ever did. I believe that we are only saved by faith in the Son of God as Lord and Savior. But what concerns me is an automatic quality about being saved nowadays. It works something like this: simply put a nickel of faith in the slot, pull down a lever and take out the little coin of salvation, tuck it in your pocket and off you go. It is that simple. After that, you say you are saved. When questioned, you simply say, "I put the nickel in; I accepted Jesus and I signed the card." Very good, there is nothing wrong with signing a card so that we can know who they are. It is the only way we know that some people are Christians. How tragic.

Christianity is not a result of coming to God and becoming an automatic cookie-cutter Christian, stamped out with a die: "One size fits all"; "What God has done for others He'll do for you." These are marvelous mottos with a grain of truth in them, but they lead us far from the absolute truth. We come to Christ so that we might be individually redeemed and made in the image of Christ—vibrant, personal Christians who love God with all our heart and worship Him in the beauty of holiness.

Not only is worship the normal employment for moral beings, but worship is also the moral imperative. The book of Luke tells us that when they came nigh the mount of Olives, the whole multitude of the disciples began to rejoice and praise God with a loud voice for all the mighty works that they had seen (see Luke 19:37).

Some people believe they are worshiping when they are making a lot of noise and chatter and racket. They can never worship without noise and commotion. Religious noise and worship do not necessarily mean the same thing.

On the other side, I want to warn you cultured, quiet, self-possessed, poised, sophisticated people so sure of yourself that it embarrasses you if anybody says "Amen" out loud in a church meeting. Throughout history, the people of God have always been a little bit noisy.

I often think of that dear English saint going back 600 years—Lady Julian of Norwich. She was meditating on how high and lofty Jesus was and yet how He "meeked" Himself down to the lowest part of our human desire, and she just could not control herself. She let go with a shout and prayed aloud in Latin, which translated into English meant, "Well, glory to God! Isn't this a marvelous thing?!"

If that bothers you, something is wrong.

Our Lord was faced with such criticism: "And when he was come nigh, even now at the descent of the mount of Olives, the whole multitude of the disciples began to rejoice and praise God with a loud voice for all the mighty works that they had seen" (Luke 19:37). I am quite sure they were not in tune. When you get a crowd of people whom the Lord has blessed, and when they go out of themselves with worship and joy, they are just as likely as not to praise God a little bit off key.

"Saying, Blessed be the King that cometh in the name of the Lord: peace in heaven, and glory in the highest. And some of the Pharisees from among the multitude said unto him, Master, rebuke thy disciples" (vv. 38-39). It offended the Pharisees to hear anybody sing glory to God aloud. So they said to Jesus, "Master, rebuke thy disciples."

"And he answered and said unto them, I tell you that, if these should hold their peace, the stones would immediately cry out" (v. 40). Jesus said, in effect, that He was to be worshiped. Those Pharisees would have died in their tracks if they had heard a rock praising the Lord. These poor people were praising God at the top of their voices.

Worship is a moral imperative, and yet I believe that it is the missing jewel in evangelical circles. The crown is here but the jewels are missing. The church has decked herself with every ornament, but one shining gem is missing—the jewel of worship.

This has practical implications in the local church. For example, a man who will never attend a prayer meeting finds himself on the church board, making decisions for the entire church. He would never go to a prayer meeting because he is not a worshiper; he is just a fellow who runs the church; and in his mind, he can separate the two. My brother, you cannot separate the two.

I do not believe that any man has a right to debate a church issue or vote on it unless he is a praying, worshiping man. Only a worshiping man has the ability to make spiritual decisions within the context of the local church. If we are not worshipers, we are wasting other people's money and only piling up wood, hay and stubble to be burned at the last day. It might be business as usual, but it is not glorious worship.

Worship is an awesome thing, and I would rather worship God than any other thing I know of in the entire world.

If you were to go to my study, you would discover piles of hymnbooks. As a singer, I leave a lot to be desired; but that is nobody's business. My singing is an expression of my worship of the Almighty God above. God listens while I sing to Him old French hymns and translations of the old Latin hymns and old Greek hymns from the Eastern Church; and of course, the beautiful songs done in meter as well as some of the simpler songs of Watts and Wesley and the rest. The Christian hymnal is a beautiful place to begin a daily regimen of worshiping God.

Some might point out that it is a waste of time to spend your time worshiping God. "There is work to be done for the Master," we are told. There is no time for loafing, as though worship was in the category of loafing. The beautiful part about this is, if you worship God, you will be an active person.

People ablaze with the radiant worship of God did every deed done in the church of Christ. The great mystics, the great hymn writers and the great saints were the ones doing all the work. The saints who wrote the great hymns that we sing were active to the point where you wondered how they ever did it. George Whitefield, John and Charles Wesley, Bernard of Clairvaux, Gerhard Tersteegen and others wrote our hymns of faith. The more intense their worship the more extended their work. Hospitals grew out of the hearts of worshiping men. Insane asylums grew out of the heart of worshiping men. Worshiping men and women learned to be compassionate to those whose minds had failed them.

Look at some of the great advances in civilizations and you will discover they were made by worshiping men and women. Whenever the church came out of her lethargy and rose from her spiritual slumber and into a renaissance and revival, worshipers were always back of it all.

We are called to worship, and we are failing God when we are not worshiping to the fullness of our redeemed potential. When we substitute worship with work, we are failing God in ways that we can hardly imagine. When the glory of God came down on the Temple in olden days, the priest could not stand and minister, such was the awesome presence of God.

When a traveling salesman got to the town where Charles Finney's revival was going on in New England, he sensed that something was happening. The first man he met he inquired about it. He was told, "There's a revival in this town; God is here and people are being converted, saloons are being closed up, halfway houses are being nailed shut. Men and women are cleaning up. Evil men are quitting their daily habits and getting right with God. God's in this place."

This is what we lack in evangelical churches. We do not have it in our Bible conferences, in our camp meetings or in our churches. Most churches today are run the way you would run a club or business, and it grieves my heart. I wish we might get back again to worship so that when people entered church, they would find God's people worshiping and fall on their faces and say, "Truly God is in this place."

The presence of the Lord is the most wonderful thing in the entire world. I once prayed under a tree with some preachers and a Salvation Army captain. I prayed and the others prayed. Then the Salvation Army man began to pray. I cannot remember a word he said, but I knew that here was a man engaging God in an awesome, marvelous, elevated feeling in the holy act of worship.

As a lad, I belonged to a very liberal church. At the time, I did not know any better. One Sunday night, a little girl got up to sing. She was a hunchback and had a face that looked as if she had suffered a lot. Her appearance did not generate much expectation, at least from me. However, when she began to sing, something changed. What a beautiful little face she had. She stood there and sang with a child's voice. She was worshiping God.

This is missing in the churches. We used to sing an old hymn written by Isaac Watts.

Bless, O my soul, the living God,
Call home thy thoughts that rove abroad:
Let all the powers within me join
In work and worship so divine,
In work and worship so divine.

Bless, O my soul, the God of grace;
His favors claim thy highest praise;
Why should the wonders He hath wrought
Be lost in silence and forgot,
Be lost in silence and forgot?

"Why should the wonders He hath wrought be lost in silence and forgot?" Why should we be silent about the wonders of God? "Why should the wonders that He hath wrought be lost in silence and forgot?" Let the whole earth His power confess; let the whole earth adore His grace. The Gentiles with the Jews shall join in worship and work so divine.

That is what a church is supposed to be, not a big ecclesiastical machine with someone turning the crank with a big smile you could not wipe off, who loves everybody and everybody loves him. He has the building to pay for, and he turns the crank and the machine runs. Oh, this kind of thing grieves my heart. I want to be among worshipers. I want to be among a people who know the presence of God in their midst, resulting in radiant and sometimes ecstatic worship.

Prayer

Dear Lord Jesus, we love Thee and we love Thy Holy Father.
We love the blessed Holy Ghost, the Comforter, the Lord and
giver of life who with the Father and Son together is
worshiped and glorified; we love Thee, O God. We expect to
spend eternity with Thee, not standing in behind,
worshiping the altar, but like the creatures out of the
fire worshiping with trembling joy and then rising to go and
do Thy service somewhere in the far reaches of the Creation
and hurrying back to the Throne to report, O God.

We look forward to this; we used to feel that death is
a terrible, dark, ugly, cruel river; but in another way it's a

door into a new light, and we love to look upon Thy face and see Thy people, see Abraham and Isaac and Jacob, and sit down in the kingdom of God with thy people and every tongue and tribe and nation around the world. O Lord, prepare us now for that hour. Teach us the protocol of heaven; teach us the etiquette of the kingdom. Teach us now so that we will not be doing anything strange when we pick up our harp and join the company innumerable or sing in the choir invisible. Bless this people, Lord. Holy Ghost with light divine, shine upon this heart of mine. Holy Ghost with power divine, come we pray Thee, and give power and grace and strength to these hearts of ours, for Christ's sake.

8

THE COMPONENTS OF
TRUE WORSHIP

And the glory which thou gavest me I have given them;
that they may be one, even as we are one.

JOHN 17:22

Worship is not confined to emotion and feelings but is an inward attitude and a state of mind subject to degrees of perfection and intensity. It is not possible to always worship with the same degree of wonder and love as at other times, but wonder and love always has to be there.

A father may not always love his family with the same intensity when he is tired and his business is having trouble. Although he may not have a feeling of love toward his family, still it is there because it is not a feeling only; it is an attitude and a state of mind and a sustained act subject to varying degrees of intensity and perfection.

With this in mind, I want to give you a definition of worship as it ought to be found in the church. It embodies a number of factors or ingredients, both spiritual and emotional.

A Definition of Worship

First, worship is to feel in the heart. I use that word "feel" boldly and without apology. I do not believe that we are to be a feeling-less people. I came into the kingdom of God the old-fashioned way. I believe that I know something of the emotional life that goes with being converted; so I believe in feeling. I do not think we should follow feeling, but I believe that if there is no feeling in our heart, then we are dead. If you woke up in the morning and suddenly had no feeling in your right arm, you would call a doctor. You would dial with the left hand because your right hand was dead. Anything that has no feeling in it, you can be quite sure is dead. Real worship, among other things, is a feeling in the heart.

Worship is to feel in the heart and express in some appro-priate manner a humbling but delightful sense of admiring awe. Worship will humble a person as nothing else can. The egotisti-cal, self-important man cannot worship God any more than the arrogant devil can worship God. There must be humility in the heart before there can be worship.

When the Holy Spirit comes and opens heaven until people stand astonished at what they see, and in astonished wonder-ment confess His uncreated loveliness in the presence of that most ancient mystery, then you have worship. If it is not mys-terious, there can be no worship; if I can understand God, then I cannot worship God.

I will never get on my knees and say, "Holy, holy, holy" to that which I can figure out. That which I can explain will never overawe me, never fill me with astonishment, wonder or ad-miration. But in the presence of that most ancient mystery, that unspeakable majesty, which the philosophers have called a *mysterium tremendum*, which we who are God's children call "our Father which art in heaven," I will bow in humble worship. This attitude ought to be present in every church today.

Blaise Pascal (1623–1662) was one of the greatest minds that ever lived. When he was only in his teens, he wrote advanced books on mathematics, astonishing people. He became a great philosopher, mathematician and thinker.

One night, he met God, and his whole world was changed. He wrote down his experience on a piece of paper while it was still fresh in his mind. According to his testimony, from 10:30 P.M. to about 12:30 A.M., he was overwhelmed by the presence of God. To express what he was experiencing, he wrote one word, "fire."

Pascal was neither a fanatic nor an ignorant farmer with hayseeds back of his ears. He was a great intellectual. God broke through all that and for two solid hours, he experienced something he could only characterize later as fire.

Following his experience, he prayed; and to keep as a reminder of that experience, he wrote it out: "God of Abraham, God of Isaac, God of Jacob, not of the philosophers and of the learned." This was not a prayer for somebody who reads his prayers; this was not formal religious ritual. This was the ecstatic utterance of a man who had two wonderful, awesome hours in the presence of his God. "God of Abraham, God of Isaac, God of Jacob not of the philosophers and of the learned. God of Jesus Christ. . . . Thy God shall be my God. Forgetfulness of the world and of everything, except God. . . . He is only found by the ways taught in the Gospel. . . . Righteous Father, the world has not known Thee, but I have known Thee. Joy, joy, joy, tears of joy. . . ." And he put an "Amen" after that, folded it up, put it in his shirt pocket and kept it there.

That man could explain many mysteries in the world, but he was awestruck before the wonder of wonders, even Jesus Christ. His worship flowed out of his encounter with that "fire" and not out of his understanding of who and what God is.

Four Ingredients of Worship

I have given a running definition of worship; now I want to define four major factors or ingredients in worship.

Confidence

Many cannot rightly worship these days because they do not have a high enough opinion of God. In our mind, God has been reduced, modified, edited, changed, amended until He does not resemble the God Isaiah saw high and lifted up, but something else again. And because He has been reduced in the minds of the people, they do not have that boundless confidence in his character that marked a former generation of Christians.

Confidence is necessary to respect. Without confidence in a man, it is difficult to respect him. Extend that upward to God. If we cannot respect Him, it becomes impossible to worship Him. In the church today, our worship rises and falls altogether depending upon whether the idea of God is low or high. We must always begin with God where everything begins. Everywhere and always God has to be antecedent; God is always there first, always previous, always prior. The God who is there is not the homemade cheap god you can buy these days marked down because He's shelf-worn. However, the God and Father, the awesome God, the mysterious God, the God who watches over the world and holds the universe in His great hands, this God we must worship.

One thing needed in this time is a reformation of worship. Our concepts of God must be rescued from the deplorable depths they have sunk. God needs no rescue, but we must rescue our concepts from their fallen and frightfully inadequate condition that hinders pure and delightful worship.

Boundless confidence is one thing. Without absolute confidence in God, I cannot worship Him. It is impossible to sit down with a man and have fellowship with him if you have reason to fear that he is out to get you or is tricking or deceiving or cheating you. You have to respect Him before you can sit down quietly and enjoy mutual fellowship, which is the core of pure worship.

When we go to God, we must raise our affections and our confidence to God. And in the presence of God, we must be without doubt or nervousness or worry or fear that God will cheat us or deceive us or let us down or break His covenant or lie or do something wrong. We have to be convinced to the point where we can go into the presence of God in absolute confidence and say, "Let God be true though every man be a liar." The God of the whole earth cannot do wrong; and when we can do this in the presence of God, it is the beginning of worship.

Admiration

The second component in our worship is admiration.

It is possible to respect a man and not especially admire him. The same would apply to God. Someone may have a theological respect for God that is purely academic while, at the same time, not admire God, or even be unable to admire. But when God made man in His own image, He gave him a capability of appreciation, the ability to appreciate and admire his Creator.

One of the greatest Bible teachers of his generation, Dr. D. Watson, talked often about the love we have for God. He taught two kinds of love: the love of gratitude and the love of excellence. We could love God because we are grateful to Him or we could go on past that and love God because of what He is. It is possible for a child to love his father or mother out of gratitude, which is proper and right; he should, of course. Years later, when he gets to know his parents, or maybe after they are gone, he will remember that he loved them also out of the love of excellence.

Some people we are supposed to love but there is no excellence there. You have to love them with infused love; you cannot love them with a love called out by their excellence. God Almighty is excellent, beyond all other beings. He is excellent; and so this love of excellence surpasses the love of gratitude. God's children rarely get beyond the love they have for Him because He has been good to them. You rarely hear anybody praying in admiration of God and worshiping the excellence of God and talking to God about His own excellence. The psalms do this; Christ did this; and the apostles did, but we do not hear it much now. This generation has produced Christians that are primarily Santa Claus Christians. They eagerly look for God to put up a Christmas tree with all their gifts under it. They are grateful to God, and it is right and proper to be thankful for all things that He does for us and all the good, large and small, that He gives us. That is, however, only the lower, elementary kind of love.

Going beyond that comes the love of excellence where you can go into the presence of God and not want to rush out again, but stay in the presence of God, because you are in the presence of utter, infinite excellence. Naturally, you admire this, and this knowledge can grow until your heart has been lifted into the excellency of love and admiration.

Fascination

The third component I find in worship is fascination.

Fascination is to be full of moral excitement. You cannot read your Bible very long until you find that God fascinated some people. They were fascinated by Him and were filled with a high moral excitement. It would be difficult to find much of this today in the average church in America.

Wherever God is known indeed by the Holy Spirit illumination, there is a fascination and a high moral excitement. There is a fascination captured, charmed, and entranced by the presence and person of God. To be fascinated is to be struck with astonished wonder at the inconceivable elevation and magnitude and splendor of God.

For me it is either God or agnosticism. I do not know many churches I would want to join and get into the rat race. I do not want to be part of any religious group where each person is merely a cog in the wheel: the pastor turns the crank, and if it comes out all right in the end of the year and there is no deficit, he is a good man. I am not interested in that at all. I want to begin with God and end with God. Of course, I can never end with God, because there is no end in Him.

Many of the hymns of the church came out of this sense of admiration and fascination in the hearts of men.

"Oh, Jesus, Jesus, dearest Lord, forgive me if I say for very love Thy precious name a thousand times a day." That came out of a man, Fredrick W. Faber (1814–1863), fascinated by what he saw. He admired God until he was charmed and struck with wonder at the inconceivable elevation and magnitude and moral splendor of this being we call God.

Adoration

The fourth component of worship is adoration.

Adoration is white heat made incandescent with the fire of the Holy Spirit, and it is to love with all the powers within us. It is to feel, to love with fear, wonder, yearning and awe. I shudder when I think of how many are doing things today in regards to worship in the church completely counter to this spirit of adoration. Adoration cannot be conjured up by the manipulation of some worship leader.

Sure, they preach about Jesus dying for us, and say, "Now, if you believe that and accept Him, everything will be all right." But there is no fascination, no admiration, no adoration, no love, no fear, no wonder, no yearning, no awe, no longing, no hunger and no thirst. I wonder if they really have met God at all. How could they and not be elevated into the holy atmosphere of adoration?

A young couple has their first baby, and lays its little warm, pitching, kicking form in the cradle. They love their baby and continue to love it. They love it because it is alive. There never was a doll made anywhere by the most skillful artist, the most beautifully and human looking thing that could bring out the shining-eyed wonder in a couple's face that a newborn baby can bring out. It does not have to be pretty; it just has to be their baby, alive, warm and breathing. There is no difference between this mechanical "nickel-in-the-slot" Christianity passing for Christianity now and that Christianity of our fathers, where men worshiped God in awful wonder and adoration.

Bishop James Usher would go down by the bank of the river on a Saturday and spend the afternoon on his knees in the presence of God, in awesome worship. Jonathan Edwards' son-in-law, David Brainerd, would kneel in the snow and be so lost in worship, prayer and intercession that when he was through the snow would be melted around him in a wide circle. John Fletcher, the saint of Methodism, used to kneel in his little bare room on the floor. When he lived out his life and had gone to be with God, they found that he had made a concave place in the floor where his knees actually wore out the boards. The walls in his room were stained with his breath where he had waited on God and where he had worshiped his God in the beauty of holiness.

I am very careful when I use the word "adore." I refuse to say about any person, "Oh, I adore him," or "I adore her." I love babies, I love people; but I never adore them. Personally, I use the word "adoration" for the only One who deserves it. In no other presence and before no other being can I kneel in fear, wonder and yearning and feel the sense of possessiveness that cries "mine, mine." There are those who are so theologically stilted that they feel it is not right to say "mine."

I have gone through hymnbooks and in some I have seen where the editors had edited the hymns of Wesley and Watts. They replaced the "I's" and the "me's" and the "mine's" and put "ours." "I love thee, Oh God," is changed to, "We love thee, Oh God."

Because they are so modest, they cannot imagine saying "I," but you will find in worship they cry out, "Oh, God, thou art my God, early will I seek thee," and so it becomes a love experience between God and the person so that it's "I" and "Thee."

Paul was like that and David and Isaiah and Moses and the rest. I desire to possess God; "God is my God"; "the Lord is my shepherd, I shall not want; He maketh me to lie down in green pastures."

Can you imagine what an editor would have done with that: "the Lord is our shepherd, we shall not want, He maketh us to lie down in green pastures." That is togetherness, all right. Therefore, we will all lie down together, but nobody has anything that means "I." You can say "God and I," but you cannot say "us" and mean anything.

Unless you have been able to meet God in loneliness of soul, you and God, as if there is nobody else in the world, you will never know what it is to love other people in the world.

This adoration is the desire to be poured out at God's feet; we desire it; we want to be poured out at God's feet. When trying to elude King Saul, David got a touch of homesickness and said, "Oh that I might have a drink out of the good ole well of Bethlehem, as in my day of my boyhood." One of his men, looking for a promotion, started for the well, risking his life, got some water and brought it back to David. David picked up the cup and said,

"I can't drink this; this is blood. This cost you the rest of your life." So he poured it out as a drink offering unto God.

David knew God enough, had a boundless confidence in God's character and came to admire Him and love Him for His excellence. Consecration is not hard for the person that has met God. This person insists on giving himself entirely to God.

The list I have described—confidence, admiration, fascination, adoration—have these factors in varying degrees of intensity, of course. They condition our thoughts, our words and our deeds. They hallow every place, time and setting, and give back the glory that Christ had before the world. To the Christian, "we in Him and He in us and the glory He had, I have given unto them" (see John 17:22ff).

I read of a creature that God created, who sealed up the sun, and which was filled with wisdom and physical beauty (see Ezek. 28:14-16).

The Old Testament tells us that somewhere out there beyond where the farthest rocket can go, God had a cherub created for that purpose. He was a creature created without embarrassment or fear, burning in the presence of God, covering the stones of fire before the throne. He fell in love with his own beauty, and God said, "Thou art profane." Most Bible teachers believe that this is the devil. The creature was created to worship God, but he turned his worship on himself, and God cast him down.

My concern is that unless we have a real spiritual awakening, and Jesus tarries a while longer, we need missionaries from Africa or China to reintroduce North America to Christianity. God has no particular fondness for nations or buildings or denominations. He longs to be worshiped. When the Church loses her love, she becomes sick.

We are born to worship, and if we are not worshiping God in the beauty of His holiness, we have missed the reason for being born. Worship is a delightful, awesome, humbling, wonderful experience, which we can have in varying degrees, but if you have all those, you can live in the middle of it. You never need to leave church if you are worshipers. You can lock the building and be driven away from the place, but you have not left church at all, because we carry our sanctuary with us; we never leave it.

If you know that your heart is cold, then it is not yet a hard heart; God has not rejected it. Therefore, if there is a yearning within, God put that yearning there. He did not put it there to mock you; He put it there that you might rise to it. God puts the bait of yearning in your heart. He does not turn His back on you; He puts it there because He is there to meet you. Decide now that you are going to get ahead of a spiritually cold way of living.

A wonderful hymn, translated by John Wesley, expresses this thought better than anything I can think of.

Jesus, Thy Boundless Love to Me
by Paul Gerhardt (1607–1676)
Translated by John Wesley

Jesus, Thy boundless love to me
No thought can reach, no tongue declare;
O knit my thankful heart to Thee
And reign without a rival there.
Thine wholly, thine alone I am:
Be thou alone my constant Flame.

Prayer

Our Father, we praise Thee that Thy love indeed is boundless.
Our wretchedness thankfully has great bounds established by
Thy grace and is overcome by the boundlessness of Thy love.
Grant to my heart a true sense of Thy presence.
I pray in Jesus' name. Amen.

9

THE MYSTERY OF
TRUE WORSHIP

And in thy majesty ride prosperously because of truth and meekness and
righteousness; and thy right hand shall teach thee terrible things.

PSALM 45:4

In examining the subject of worship, I cannot emphasize enough that mystery surrounds it, and happy the Christian who penetrates and breaks through this mystery. True Christian worship does not rise or fall on the will of man, for there is only one object of worship worthy of man, and that is God.

I wish I could adequately set forth the glory of the object we are to worship. If we could set forth these thousand attributes dwelling in unapproachable light where no man can see Him and live—fully eternal, omniscient, omnipotent and sovereign—we would be greatly humbled. God's people are not as humble as they ought to be, and I believe this is why we do not truly see God in His sovereignty.

We are instructed to worship God, and I wonder how it could be that we Christians would fall on our knees before a man and say, "Thy throne, O God, is forever and ever." That man does not exist before whom I will kneel and say, "God," with one lone supreme exception of the man Christ Jesus—the man whom the prophets saw in the vision and addressed him and said, "Thy throne, O God."

All mystery has about it an ambience of confusion. How can we get out of this state of confusion if there is one God and none other? And how can we say that Jesus Christ is a man and we are taught never to worship man? How can we get down on our knees before Him and worship? Here is the great mystery. I stand bareheaded before it, kneel, take my shoes off my feet before this burning bush and confess I do not understand it. This mystery envelopes my heart, and I bow down in reverence and submission.

Simply put, the mystery is that God and man are united in one person, not two persons. All that is God and all that is man are fused eternally, inexplicably and inseparably in the man, Jesus Christ. When we kneel before the man, Christ Jesus, we are in fact kneeling before God.

The Old Testament illustrates this with Moses before the burning bush. The fire burned in the bush, and the bush was not consumed. Moses instinctively knelt before the bush and worshiped God. Moses understood that God was in the bush. The bush was ordinary until God's presence permeated it and set it aflame. Some could have charged Moses with idolatry— those that could not see the fire in the bush. They could not know the fire he was worshiping was none other than Jehovah.

Suppose there had been some Israelites who knew the teaching from Abraham that one God alone is to be worshiped. Suppose they had seen this man kneeling before a bush with his face in his hands, hiding his face, but they had not been able to see the fire. They would say, and rightly so, "What do you mean worshiping a bush? You are an idolater. Don't you know the Scripture?"

Of course, Moses would have known better. He knew the Scripture, but he knew what the others did not know. He knew that the bush and the fire were united and infused there before him. They were essentially one. There was the nature of the bush and then there was the nature of Jehovah fused into one object. The bush was not consumed and Moses worshiped not the bush but the God who dwells in the bush. Therefore, he knelt before that bush.

I admit that this is an imperfect and inadequate illustration; for as soon as the fire departed from the bush, it was but a bush again and no man could kneel and worship that bush ever again.

This was a picture of the coming of Christ. Christ Jesus was indeed God with all of the full implications of deity. Although Jesus was man in the perfect sense of the word, he was also God in the perfect sense of the word. Jesus Christ in the New Testament is the equivalent of the Old Testament burning bush. The striking difference is, the burning bush was a temporary experience, but Jesus Christ is both God and man for all eternity.

There was never any departure except for that awful moment on the cross when He said, "My God, My God why hast thou forsaken me?" He took all of the putrefying terrible mass of our sin on His holy self and died there. God turned His back on Him but the deity and the humanity never parted, and they remain today united in that one man. When we kneel before that man and say, "My Lord and My God, thy throne O God is for ever and ever," we are talking to God, for by the mystery of the theanthropic union man has become God and God has become man in the person of the Son, Jesus Christ.

We worship this One in mystery and wonder. We worship not man but God in the flesh.

Fusing Meekness and Majesty

If I did not believe the Bible for any other reason, I would believe it for Psalm 45 and Isaiah 53. I would see how the prophets foresaw down the centuries and proclaimed the great mystery of the one called Christ. These men of God described Him as radiantly beautiful and romantic, and as a winsome deity. They said of Him that He was fair, He was royal, He was gracious, He was majestic, He was true, He was meek, righteous, loving, glad and fragrant. Human language was exhausted in trying to set forth the opulence of this One we call Christ; and after a while, even the prophets gave up trying to describe Him.

If I were searching the dictionary to find words to describe something or somebody, I would be glad to kneel before this: He is fair and He is kingly, and yet He is gracious. He is not a king who stands in His dignity and looks down his nose at the world, but He is a gracious king. His graciousness does not take away from His majesty; He is true and He is meek. *Meekness and majesty.* I would like to write a hymn or a book about it or maybe paint a picture or compose music about it—the meekness and majesty of Jesus. You do not find meekness and majesty united very much. The meekness was His humanity, and the majesty was His deity. He was a human being like any other human being, but He was God, and in His majesty He stood before Herod and before Pilate. And when He comes down from the sky, it will be in His majesty, the majesty of God; and yet it will be the majesty of the man who is God.

Our Lord Jesus Christ is majestic and meek. Before His foes, He stands in majesty; and before His friends, He bows in meekness. You can experience either side you want. If you choose not the meek side of Jesus, you will experience the majestic side of Jesus. The harlots came to Him, and the babies, and the publicans, and the sick, and the bleeding woman, and the devil-possessed man. They came from everywhere, touched Him and found Him so meek that His power went out to them and healed them.

I do not think you have to be very fanciful or poetic when you talk about worshiping the Lord in the beauty of holiness if you know that you are talking about something that will please the heavenly host.

Fused in the person of Christ is all the beauty and wonderment of God, enabling us to worship God in the beauty of holiness. The tremendous aspect of this worship is that we can worship God wherever Jesus is. Wherever we find Him is the perfect place to worship. I cannot explain this mystery; I only can revel in it and kneel before this eternal burning bush.

Portable Worship

Why is it that when we think of worship, we think of something we do when we go to church? God's poor stumbling, bumbling people; how confused we can get, and stay confused for a lifetime and die confused. Books are written confusing us further, and we write songs to confirm the books and confuse ourselves and others even further; and we do it all as if the only place one can worship God is in a church building we call the house of God. We enter the house dedicated to God, made out of bricks, linoleum and other stuff, and we say, "The Lord is in His holy temple; let all kneel before Him."

I personally enjoy starting a service that way occasionally. But it does not stop there. Come 9:00 A.M. Monday morning, if you do not walk into your office and say, "The Lord is in my office and all the world is silent before Him," then you were not worshiping the Lord on Sunday. If you cannot worship Him on Monday, then you did not worship Him on Sunday. If you do not worship Him on Saturday, your worship on Sunday is not authentic. Some people put God in a box we call the church building. God is not present in church any more than He is present in your home. God is not here any more than He is in your factory or office.

As a young Christian, I worked for the BF Goodrich Company in Akron, Ohio, helping to make rubber tires. I worshiped God at my assembly line station until I had tears in my eyes. Nobody ever saw the tears or asked me about them, but I would not have hesitated to tell them why.

As I went along and worked a while at something, it became automatically converted to thinking about something else. Some daydream; I worshiped. I got to where I could do my work with passing skill and worship God at the same time. God was at my work just as much as He was at my church. As far as I was concerned, there was no difference. If God is not in your factory, if God is not in your store, if God is not in your office, then God is not in your church when you go there. When we worship our God, the breath of songs on Earth starts the organs playing in heaven above.

The total life, the whole man and woman, must worship God. Faith, love, obedience, loyalty, conduct and life—all of these are to worship God. If there is anything in you that does not worship God, then there is not anything in you that does worship God very well. If you departmentalize your life and let certain parts worship God, but other parts do not worship God, then you are not worshiping God as you should. It is a great delusion we fall into, the idea that in church or in the presence of death or in the midst of sublimity is the only setting for worship.

You carry worship inside your heart. You can have your worship with you. I have been with people who became very spiritual when standing on a mountain looking down. I remember being caught in a storm one time in the mountains in Pennsylvania, and I could see it out there. I don't remember how many miles away they told us it was—I think it was 50 miles from where we were—but you could see it out there. We huddled up against a rock while the storm and the hailstones hit us. They came rattling and roaring down on us, and we huddled against the car against the rock of that great storm in its white fury over the mountain.

I do not have to see a storm on a mountain to make me know how jealous God is. The stars and their courses tell about it, and the babe that cries yonder tells about it; the flower that blooms by the way tells about it and the fine snow that drifts down tells about it. We do not have to have it dramatically brought home to us for it to be true. It is a great delusion to think that because we feel a sense of the poetic in the presence of a storm or the stars or a mountain that we are spiritual. That is not necessarily true at all, because murderers, tyrants and drunkards also can feel like that.

There never was a drunkard that when he came to himself did not have such feelings, and there never was a tyrant after giving the command to slay a dozen men, on his way home might see something that would raise poetic worship in him. That is not imagined; that is worship, my brethren.

Worship pleasing to God saturates our whole being. There is no worship pleasing to God until there is nothing in me displeasing to God. I cannot departmentalize my life, worship God on Sunday and not worship Him on Monday. I cannot worship Him in my songs and displease Him in my business engagements. I cannot worship God in silence in the church on Sunday, to the sound of hymns, then go out on the next day and be displeasing to Him in my activities. No worship is wholly pleasing to God until there is nothing in us that is displeasing to God.

Without Jesus Christ, there is no goodness, and so I do not apologize at all when I say that your worship has to be all-inclusive and take you all in. If you are not worshiping God in all your life, then you are not worshiping Him acceptably in any area of your life.

Worship Disciplines

Although worship is a natural desire of Christians, there are disciplines we must employ. I believe that personal preparation is essential in our worship of God. That preparation is not always a pleasant thing and must include some revolutionary changes. Some things must be destroyed in your life. The gospel of Jesus Christ is not only constructive, but it is also destructive, destroying certain elements in you that should not be there, impeding worship. The fire in the burning bush only consumed those elements that should not be there. And so, as we yield ourselves to the operations of the Holy Spirit, He will begin routing out those elements in our life that impede worship; and that is both satisfying to us and acceptable to God.

Pray in the Nature of Jesus

For example, many are hampered in their worship by the inclusion of magic. Certain words and phrases carry some magical essence for some people. There is no magic in faith and no magic in the name of Jesus. Reciting certain phrases or even certain special verses of Scripture has no miraculous effect in our life. This is what the Bible refers to as vain repetition.

Some may think they are worshiping in the name of Jesus, but they are not necessarily worshiping in the nature of Jesus. *Name* and *nature* are one in the Bible. It is impossible to divide Jesus between name and nature. When we ask anything in the name of Jesus, it does not mean pronouncing the name "Jesus." It means that we are in conformity to His nature. To chant the name "Jesus" has no power in it. Whoever asks after His nature and asks in accordance to His Word, that man can get what he wants.

I cannot live contrary to the nature of Jesus on Monday and then Monday night when I face a crisis and I get on my knees and call on the name of Jesus and think that there is some magic in that name. I would be disappointed and disillusioned; for if I am not living in that name, I cannot pray properly in that name. If I am not living in that nature, I cannot pray rightfully in that nature. We cannot live after our nature and worship after His. When His nature and ours begin to harmonize under the influence of the Holy Spirit, the power of His name begins to be felt.

The Bible clearly teaches, "But we have the mind of Christ" (1 Cor. 2:16). Then Paul says, "To whom God would make known what is the riches of the glory of this mystery among the Gentiles; which is Christ in you, the hope of glory" (Col. 1:27).

The same mystery that united Jesus with God also unites us with Jesus.

Worship in Whatever You Do

I know that the name of Jesus is far above all the names of all kings and queens and archangels and presidents and prime ministers. Above Moses, Aaron and all that have ever had honor in the entire world. I know that at the "name of Jesus every knee should bow, . . . and that every tongue confess that Jesus Christ is Lord, to the glory of God the Father" (Phil. 2:10-11). And that He will ride down the sky and He will call to the nations of the earth, and they will come before Him and He will be their judge supreme. I also know that we cannot take advantage of that name by any twisted religious magic. We have to live in that name; and you cannot rest until every area in your life rests in God, and everything honors God.

Does your business honor God? Are you living it yourself? If it does not honor God, then I cannot see you living for God and honoring Him. If your business does not honor God, you cannot honor God. You are buying and selling. You cut corners, you push and scream, and you cannot possibly please God.

What about your relation to the opposite sex? How can we worship God if our relation to the opposite sex is such that God is displeased? I am not a prude, but I believe that our relation with each other ought to be right and pure in every way.

I wonder about the relationships in your home life and your school life and your use of money and time. Is all this pleasing to God? Some imagine their time is their own and they can do with it as they please. Your time is not your own; it belongs to the God who created time.

If God gives you a few more years, remember, it is not yours. Your time must honor God, your home must honor God, your activity must honor God, and everything about you must honor God.

If you want to die right, then you have to live right; and if you want to be right when you are old, then you have to be right when you are young.

You are not worshiping right in any place until you are worshiping God right in every place. If you cannot worship Him in the kitchen, then you cannot worship Him audibly in the church.

How utterly terrible is the current idea that Christians can serve God at their own convenience. Do we seem to be the follower of the One who had nowhere to lay His head until He laid it back against the cross and died? So we need that time for preparation, testing and choosing. Thank God, there is time; I do not know when time will be called on us one of these days, but there is time now.

Worship is not a spotlight focusing on one area of life. True worship, worship that is pleasing to God, radiates throughout a person's entire life.

Prayer

Oh, God, we humble ourselves before that Mystery uniting us with Thee. We worship Thee not according to our understanding, which is inadequate, but we worship Thee in Spirit and truth. We honor Thee within our hearts, bow before that sacred burning bush and hide our faces in reverential fear.

In Jesus' name, amen.

10

THE NATURAL DWELLING PLACE OF GOD

But the hour cometh, and now is, when the true worshippers
shall worship the Father in spirit and in truth: for the
Father seeketh such to worship him.

JOHN 4:23

True worship accords with the nature of God. By that I mean we worship God according to what God is, and not according to what He is not. The frightful error of idolatry, and the reason God hates it so, is because it is worship according to what God is not. He said about the Samaritans, "You do not know what you worship; you worship according to what God is not. We Jews know what we worship" (see John 4:22). Salvation was of the Jews not because they were better than other people, because they were not. Their prophets said distinctly that they were worse than some people were, but God chose to reveal the truth to them and gave them the oracles. By such revelation, God made it possible for Israel to worship according to the nature of God. And Jesus Christ our Lord says that God is Spirit, and we worship according to that nature of God.

In light of this, we must keep in mind that God is not affected by the attributes of matter—He is not affected by weight, size or space. A well-taught Christian knows that the great God is not affected by space and that He contains space in His bosom. The well-instructed Christian knows that God is not affected by speed. God gets around all points. God is Spirit; God is not affected by location, and He is not in some place to which you come and recede; but God is all about us and contains space, and so He is not nearer to one place than He is to another. It is a great comfort to know that God is as near to one place as He is to another place.

Because God made us in His image, there is a part of us that is like God. The human soul is most like God of anything that has ever been created, and uniquely corresponds to God.

How can this be? There is so much sin in the world and so much that seems so ungodly. The simple answer is sin. Because man has fallen does not mean that which is fallen doesn't have about it yet the luminance of the likeness of God. It is easy for God to restore us and redeem us, because God has material to work with once made in His image.

Let us bring in an Old Testament illustration. Suppose a potter is making a beautiful clay pot. While spinning on the wheel, it runs into some sand or grit and falls apart. There it is now, broken and no longer useful. But the material out of which it is made, while it doesn't look like a teapot anymore, and there is no artistry there, and while the soul of the artist is not in it and cannot be in it because it has been broken on the wheel, still it is a simple matter for the potter to take up that material again, take out the offending parts and make it into another vessel. He could not do that if he had iron; he could not do it if he had rock; but he could do it with clay, because clay is the material with which he works. It was broken the first time, but he can restore it using the same material.

God made us in His image; and while we are not altogether clear about what that image of God is, we do know that the human soul relates to and responds to God. In the temptation in the Garden, man fell apart and lost the artistry, the beauty, the holiness of God. But he did not lose the potential to become godlike again if he got into the hands of the Divine Artist.

This is the purpose in redemption: taking on the material of fallen man and by the mystery of regeneration and sanctification, restoring it again so that he is like God and like Christ. This is why we preach redemption. That is what redemption is; it is not saving us from hell, although it does save us from hell; but more importantly, it is making it so that we can be like God again.

How does this take place?

Pray in the Spirit

First, nobody can worship without the Holy Ghost. God is Spirit; the Holy Spirit is the Spirit of God and, therefore, the Holy Spirit is the only one properly to lead the heart to worship God acceptably. The fallen human mind does not know how to worship God acceptably, so the Holy Spirit takes the fallen human mind, points it up, corrects it, purges it, aims it and directs it so that it is worshiping God. That is why it is so vastly and vitally important that we should know the Holy Spirit.

I have often felt like getting on my knees and apologizing to the Holy Spirit for the way the Church has treated Him. We have treated Him shoddily. We have treated Him in such a manner that if you were to treat a guest that way, the guest would slip away grief stricken and never return. We have treated the Holy Spirit wretchedly. He is God Himself, the link binding the Father and the Son, and is the substance uncreated, which is deity. Yet the Holy Spirit is typically ignored in the average church, even in the average gospel church.

If we have a doxology to begin the service, we sing, "Praise God from whom all blessings flow; Praise Him all creatures here below; Praise Him above ye heavenly host; Praise Father, Son and Holy Ghost." That is a mention of the Holy Spirit. And if we have a benediction at the close, we say, "The love of God the Father and the communion of the Holy Ghost." So we have the Holy Spirit again. We have Him at the opening of the service and at the closing of the service. Outside of that, we do not count on His presence. Talking about the Holy Spirit is not the same as honoring Him in our worship.

How many go to church on a Sunday, counting on the Holy Spirit being present? How many really count on the Holy Spirit speaking to them? How many trust the Holy Spirit to take on a human voice and speak through it? That He is going to take a human ear and listen through it?

The idea that anybody can offer worship is all wrong. The view that we can worship ignoring the Spirit is all wrong. To crowd the Spirit into a corner and ignore Him, quench Him, resist Him and yet worship God acceptably is a great heresy, which needs correcting. Only the Holy Spirit knows how to worship God acceptably.

In the book of Romans (8:26), you will find that only the Holy Spirit knows how to pray. "Likewise the Spirit also helpeth our infirmities: for we know not what we should pray for as we ought: but the Spirit itself maketh intercession for us with groanings which cannot be uttered. And he that searcheth the hearts knoweth what is the mind of the Spirit, because he maketh intercession for the saints according to the will of God" (vv. 26-27). In our prayers, there will be mutterings and repetition until the Holy Spirit takes them, purges them, cleanses them and makes them acceptable to God through Jesus Christ our Mediator.

Therefore, it is impossible to pray without the Spirit. The most powerful prayers are prayed in the Spirit, and we cannot worship without the Holy Spirit. Either we ignore Him or we exploit Him for our personal pleasure and entertainment. I think it is time we rethink this whole matter of the place of the Holy Spirit in the church of our Lord Jesus Christ. We should rethink it in the light of the Scriptures, because without the Holy Spirit, we are as Israel when she continued worshiping God after the fire left the holy place and there was no Shekinah, no glory, no fire, no light and no Presence there. Yet Israel continued to worship vainly and futilely. Pitifully, she continued to worship, forgetting that the Spirit of worship had left her long ago.

Spirituality is one of the ingredients of worship, and without spirituality, I cannot worship God in a way that is acceptable to Him, no matter how much I worship. If it is not acceptable worship, then it is vain worship and better not attempted.

Pray with Sincerity

The second ingredient in worship is sincerity as distinct from formality or duplicity. We have extreme and heinous examples of the latter from our missionaries. The missionaries tell us about the heathen who worshiped their god, and they liked to cheat him.

You do not have to go to some pagan society to see this. Some of us have become quite brazen in this. We make promises to God that we do not intend to keep, thinking we can get from God what we want. We think that we can cheat the Lord, and by crossing our fingers, the Lord will not hear, will not notice us.

We have to be absolutely sincere if we are going to worship God, which is distinct from formality. I do not know whether anything merely done formally has any meaning at all. It is possible to go to religious ritual and not even know what we are doing or why we are doing it; we're just going through meaningless motions and repeating empty words and phrases.

The Lord pointed to a little child and said that the little child was an example. I believe that one thing about a little child is complete sincerity. No matter how many embarrassing things he may be saying, a child is nevertheless absolutely sincere. And it is this sincerity that we must cultivate prayerfully if our worship is to be accepted of almighty God.

What a terrible thing to spend a lifetime making offerings to the Almighty, all of which are rejected. Cain made his offering to the Almighty, but God did not answer and would not accept it, and Cain's countenance fell.

Pray with Honesty

Honesty is the third ingredient. It must be in all our prayers distinct from mere propriety. I suppose honesty and sincerity are twin brothers and cannot be separated, although they are separate and not identical. But there must be complete honesty before God. If I get on my knees and pray, "Oh, Lord, meet our missionary budget," and then the Lord knows that I am not going to give anything toward it, He knows that I am praying dishonestly.

If I pray, "Oh, Lord, save this man," but I have never done anything toward winning him, I'm dishonest. If I ask God to do things that I could do for myself, I am dishonest in my praying. But we have glossed this over until it sounds shocking to hear it said. It is true nevertheless.

Pray with Simplicity

Fourth, we must have simplicity in worship as distinct from sophistry and sophistication.

I have heard a few people pray that were utterly simple, almost embarrassingly simple. They were so simple-hearted that you tended to feel perhaps that they were not intellectually strong. But there is no incompatibility between intellectual power and simplicity of heart. Jesus Christ our Lord was simple to the point of being direct in His relationships. To our old Quaker friends who lived generations ago, simplicity was everything to them.

When the old English Quakers went before the king, they would not take off their broad-rimmed hats because they thought that was giving too much honor to a man. They would do anything before God, but insisted on wearing those hats and looked out many a set of bars in many a prison just for that reason. Personally, I do not think there would be any harm in it; I would take my hat off. There is nothing wrong with uncovering your head. You are certainly not worshiping anybody; but the point is, they did what they believed and God honored them for living according to their faith. Simplicity, utter simplicity. They said "thee" and "thou" and they called each other Mary and John, whatever the name was, and they taught the church of Christ to be simple.

If we would ever break ourselves down and suddenly be faced with death or some other tragedy or terror, we would be forced to see how unnatural we are and how unlike ourselves. We have lived like zoo lions, utterly unlike the lions that roam the wilds of Africa; and so we are in this civilization of ours pressed on every side.

There must be simplicity before going to pray or worship God. You must worship God simply; and I do not care who you are or what you are, it must be simple.

It takes simplicity and humility to worship God acceptably. Most of us are a half dozen people. I have four or five reputations. To some people I am this; to some people I am that; and I suppose everyone else is the same. When we try to live up to our reputations, it is always difficult, and we always get into trouble.

Pray from the Heart

Then, true worship must be internal—internality as distinct from externalism. We ought to thank God from the depths of our heart that we do not need any machinery to worship God.

You can worship God in spirit and in truth through the depths of your own heart as well as the angels in glory can worship God. You do not have to have anything; you do not have to die with a crucifix in your hand, or any other religious artifact.

Anything may mean something to a worshiping heart, and it can mean nothing if the heart is not worshiping. A wedding ring may mean a great deal to a woman, but only because she believes it tells her something about a man, not because it has any intrinsic value. If she loses it down the sink, she will sorrow a little, but she will not lose her husband, she will not lose his love and she will not lose that for which it stood. She can get another ring. Therefore, worship is an internal thing.

My personal worship tells something about God and me. I can worship truly, because something is true between God and me. If after years of going to the same church, I come to associate that church with worshiping God, that is natural, that is psychological, that is a conditional reflex; I think they call it that in psychology. But it does not mean that if I do not go to that church again, or the church burns down, that I cannot worship God.

I believe it is time that illuminating persons begin the arduous task of reforming Christian worship. And as we begin to understand it again in the church of Christ, I believe it will bring revival to us.

Back to our basic text: "Who is thy Lord, worship thou Him, so that He shall greatly desire thy beauty."

The soul is a God-shaped void. If I would carry it further, I would say your soul is a God-shaped garment, like a glove shaped to fit your hand. God cannot enter, because it is full of rubbish. Try putting a lot of junk in the glove sometime and then try placing your hand into it; you cannot do it. That glove must be empty before a hand can go into it.

The heart must be empty before God can enter. That is why at the altars, in times of evangelism and prayer and the pressure to get people right with God, we insist on an emptying out of ourselves. Your soul is a God-shaped garment, and God wants to clothe Himself with it. But He cannot enter because there is rubbish in it. Search your heart and find out how much rubbish you have collected over the past years. How much moral rubbish, how much intellectual rubbish, how much rubbish of habit, of custom, of things you do and do not do, think and do not think. We must empty it all out.

I would like to say that I have found some new way, but there is no new way. Empty the rubbish out of your soul, turn yourself up to God in the name of the Lord Jesus Christ and He will fill you, come in and clothe Himself with you. God will not wear an unclean garment. God wants to wear a pure garment.

Once we have emptied ourselves of everything, we must be cleansed. Only through the blood of the Lamb can that emptied soul be cleansed so that God can enter. An emptied and cleansed soul is the natural dwelling place of God. So let us ask God to cleanse us. We can empty ourselves but we can never cleanse ourselves.

If you have something in you preventing God from entering, you can empty that out. But if after you empty, you are still unclean, you can never cleanse yourself. Only God can do that by the blood of the everlasting covenant, by the fire of the Holy Ghost and by the discipline of obedience. God cleanses

His people and makes them white and pure in the blood of the Lamb.

Everyone who knows about birds knows there is what is called natural habitats. You do not go to the swamp to find a wood thrush. If you want to hear a wood thrush, you go to the cool woods when the shadows fall. Go there and wait for the evening to come and then the wood thrush will come. Quietly at first, and then louder and bolder, and as the shadows grow deeper, she will play her lovely flute in the darkness. But she will never go to the swamp.

If you want to hear a red-winged blackbird make its clumping sound, you do not go to the cool woods in the evening; you go to the swampy land where the cattails slip their brown flowers up. There you will find the red-winged blackbird. If you want to hear a wren sing, you do not go to the woods, and you do not go to the swamp; you go to your own backyard and there she will be with delight. It is what they call natural habitat.

I believe that the Holy Spirit has a natural habitat. By habitat, I mean He makes Himself at home, heard or felt; it is where He can speak and where He can live. That natural habitat is nothing else but the soul of a man or woman.

You ask how such a thing can be. Because God made that soul in the image of God, and God can dwell in His own image without embarrassment. And just as the blackbird can sing among the cattails, and just as the rabbit can hop among the briars, and just as the wood thrush can sing unseen at the edge of the woods at night, so the Holy Spirit wants to come into your soul and live in it. Not weekending there, not a houseguest for a while, but making your soul a permanent habitation.

Only sin can prevent that, which is why worship and sin are incompatible. That is why you cannot deal with the matter of true worship and omit the question of sin. Sin can prevent worship. You cannot worship God with unconfessed sin reigning in your heart. "Behold, I stand at the door, and knock: if any man hear my voice, and open the door, I will come in to him, and will sup with him, and he with me" (Rev. 3:20). Here is the picture of Jesus in your house, dwelling with you. "I will come in, unto you. I will take you unto me, but I will come in unto you." Jesus desires to be in the house of His friend—in your house.

Your soul is a God-shaped glove. God wants to enter into it, but it is full of rubbish. Get rid of the rubbish and you will not have to beg God to come in.

The old-fashioned light bulb was made in such a way that at the end of it was a little projection. When pumped empty, it became a vacuum. As a kid, I used to take a pair of pliers and break that little projection off, and there was a popping sound as 14 pounds per square inch of atmospheric pressure rushed into that bulb. You did not have to get in the bulb and get on your knees, beg and say, "Please come, atmosphere, please come in." All you had to do was take away the obstruction and the atmosphere rushed in. Nature abhors a vacuum.

The human soul is a vacuum, and we have filled it with trash. As far as God is concerned, we only have to empty it and God rushes in, cleanses it and fills it. Not for us, but for Himself; and He does not have to be begged. The most natural thing in the universe is for the Creator to indwell the soul of man.

The Home
by Gerhard Tersteegen (1697-1769)

Thou who givest of Thy gladness
Till the cup runs o'er—
Cup whereof the pilgrim weary
Drinks to thirst no more
Not a-nigh me, but within me
Is Thy joy divine;
Thou, O Lord, hast made Thy dwelling
In this heart of mine.

Prayer

*Eternal God, who dwells in the heavens above us, we humbly
bow before Thee with anxious thoughts of fellowship with
Thee. We thank Thee that Thou hast been enough for us. Our
thirsty hearts have been satiated in Thee. Amen.*

11

THE ABSOLUTE WORTH-SHIP OF CHRIST

I charge you, O daughters of Jerusalem, if ye find my beloved, that ye tell him, that I am sick of love. What is thy beloved more than another beloved, O thou fairest among women? what is thy beloved more than another beloved, that thou dost so charge us? My beloved is white and ruddy, the chiefest among ten thousand. His head is as the most fine gold, his locks are bushy, and black as a raven. His eyes are as the eyes of doves by the rivers of waters, washed with milk, and fitly set. His cheeks are as a bed of spices, as sweet flowers: his lips like lilies, dropping sweet smelling myrrh. His hands are as gold rings set with the beryl: his belly is as bright ivory overlaid with sapphires. His legs are as pillars of marble, set upon sockets of fine gold: his countenance is as Lebanon, excellent as the cedars. His mouth is most sweet: yea, he is altogether lovely. This is my beloved, and this is my friend, O daughters of Jerusalem.

SONG OF SONGS 5:8-16

This passage in Song of Songs is a parable of our relationship with this one called the Shepherd. It details the marvelous details of that relationship. Our Lord is the Shepherd; the Redeemed Church is the fair bride. In an hour of distress, this

Bride tells the daughters of Jerusalem among whom she lives, "If you find my beloved tell him that I am sick with love." Naturally, they inquire, "What is your beloved more than another beloved that thou doest so charge us?"

It is a legitimate question, and the world has a perfect right to ask it of the Church. If the Church insists that the Lord is worthy and a worthy lover, then the world has a right to ask what kind of lover He is. Why should we be promoting Him, "what is thy beloved more than another beloved?"

Others are offered up for the world's admiration and worship, so why this One? What qualities recommend him to them?

Lord of All

In the book of Psalms, David talks about this. "My heart is indicting a good matter: I speak of the things, which I have made touching the king: my tongue is the pen of a ready writer. Thou art fairer than the children of men: grace is poured forth by thy lips . . . all thy garments smell of myrrh, and aloes, and cassia, out of the ivory palaces, whereby they have made thee glad" (Ps. 45:1-2,8). This psalm is a rapt description of this shepherd king wooing the young bride to himself. Ask Peter that question and he would say, "He is Lord of all."

The entire purpose and focus of our worship is none other than the Lord Himself, our righteousness, the Lord Jesus Christ. He is the Lord of all, and in order that we might get it before us, we need to know what He is Lord of and why we should love Him.

This is a fair consideration. Why is He more than any other man? Furthermore, why should we worship him? We can worship Jesus Christ the man without idolatry because He is also God. By the mystery of the theanthropic union, He has united humanity to deity. Jesus Christ is both divine and human in nature and has taken humanity up into God so that He Himself is God. He has joined in the beauty and wonder of the theanthropic union of God and man in one so that whatever God is, Christ is as well. Therefore, Jesus could truthfully say, "He that hath seen me has seen the Father" (John 14:9).

Our confidence is that when we worship the Lord Jesus, we are not displeasing the Father, for we are worshiping the Father in Him. This is the mystery of the hypostatic union, joining us forever to God through the Lord Jesus Christ.

I will divide it a little bit so that we can understand it better. Let me begin with a marvelous hymn by Oliver Wendell Holmes (1809–1894):

Lord of all being, throned afar,
Thy glory flames from sun and star;
Centre and soul of every sphere,
Yet to each loving heart how near!

The hymn writer did not say "He is the Lord of all beings" but that He is the "Lord of all being," which is something else, and something more. He is the Lord of all actual existence. He is the Lord of all kinds of beings—the Lord of all spiritual being and all natural being and all physical being. He is the Lord of all being, and when we worship Him, we encompass all being.

Some give themselves up to the disciplines of science, technology, philosophy, art and music. When we worship the Lord

Jesus Christ, we embrace and encompass all disciplines, because He is the Lord of them all. Therefore, He is the Lord of all being, and the enemy of all not being. He is the Lord of all life.

These are fundamental to any right understanding that Jesus Christ is the Lord of all life: "For the life was manifested, and we have seen it, and bear witness, and show unto you that eternal life, which was with the Father, and was manifested unto us" (1 John 1:2).

Charles Wesley understood this and put it in his immortal hymn, "Jesus, Lover of My Soul."

> Plenteous grace with thee is found,
> grace to cover all my sin;
> let the healing streams abound,
> make and keep me pure within.
> Thou of life the fountain art,
> freely let me take of thee;
> spring thou up within my heart . . .

Lord of Creation

He is the Lord of all kinds of life, so He is the Lord of all essential possibilities of life.

All of creation is populated with many kinds of life. In the spring, the buds will come out, promising floral life all over. He is the Lord of that kind of life. Spring will bring back the birds, the rabbits will be out, and you will see the animals. That is another kind of life, and He is the Lord of that kind as well.

Then we have intellectual life: the life of imagination and reason. He is the Lord of that kind of life.

And we have the spiritual life, and He is the Lord of that kind of life. He is the Lord of angels, and He is the Lord of the cherubim and seraphim. So He is the Lord of all life, and He is the Lord of all sorts of life.

So, in response to the inquiry, "What is thy beloved more than another beloved?" We can say with confidence, "He is Lord of all."

Lord of Wisdom

Further, the Holy Spirit says, "He is the Lord of all wisdom." All eternal wisdom lies in Jesus Christ as a treasure hidden away, and no wisdom exists outside of Him. All the eternal purposes of God are in Him, because His perfect wisdom enables Him to plan ahead. All history is the slow development of His purposes.

This is difficult to justify in light of the world around us. Today all we see are the laborers in creation at work. We see the laborers working on the external scaffoldings, and things do not look very beautiful now. Any building in the stage of construction will not possess the beauty of its finished state.

Whether they know it or not, these laborers are doing the will of God and are bringing things about. The individual workers may not have the finished picture in mind, only the small area they are working on at the time; however, they are moving the project to its final state of completion, fulfilling the will of the general contractor. Even the devil unwittingly fulfills God's will. God is making all evil men as well as all good men; and all adverse things as well as all favorable things work for a bringing forth of His glory in the day when all shall be fulfilled in Him (see Rom. 8:28).

Lord of Righteousness

Then, He is the Lord of all righteousness and all concepts of righteousness and all possibilities of righteousness. He is wisdom and righteousness, and there is no getting around Him. No book you can read on Christian ethics or any other kind of ethics can tell you anything He does not already know and that He is not already Lord of. It is written, "But unto the Son He said, 'Thy throne, O God, is for ever and ever, a sceptre of thy kingdom is a right sceptre. Thou lovest righteousness and hatest wickedness: therefore God, thy God, hath anointed thee with the oil of gladness above thy fellows'" (Ps. 445:6-7).

When the Old Testament High Priest went into the holy of holies to offer sacrifices once a year, he wore a miter on his forehead. On that miter were engraved in Hebrew the words "holiness unto the Lord." This Jesus Christ our Lord and High Priest is righteous, and He is the Lord of Righteousness.

He is also the Lord of all mercy, for He establishes His kingdom upon rebels.

First, He has to redeem them, win them and renew a right spirit within them; and all this He does. He is the Lord of all mercy, He is the Lord of all power and He transforms these rebels according to His righteousness.

Lord of Moral Beauty

God put something in the human breast making it capable of understanding and appreciating beauty. He put in us the love of harmonious forms, the love of and appreciation for color and beautiful sounds. It is in everyone. He put in us also the love of moral forms of line and color. All things that are beautiful to the eye and the ear are only the external counterparts of that internal beauty, which is moral beauty.

It was said of Jesus Christ our Lord that there was no beauty in Him that we should desire Him. Artists have painted Jesus with a tender feminine face and clear beautiful eyes and an open delightful countenance, and with curly hair streaming down His shoulders. They have completely forgotten that the Bible declares that there was no beauty in Him that we should desire Him.

They had forgotten that when the high priest would crucify Jesus, they had to make an arrangement to identify Him. Judas Iscariot did not say, "When we get there, pick out that beautiful one with a feminine face, curls down His back and the light on His face; He is the one." They were standing there with their typical Jewish haircuts and Hebrew garments, all looking alike, so Judas had to give the soldiers a signal. "The one I kiss, that will be the one." They did not recognize Jesus. When Jesus came, Judas passed by Peter, John, Philip and the rich man, kissed Jesus, and said, "That's the man there."

If Jesus had looked as beautiful physically as they paint Him, why would it be necessary that He had to be betrayed with a kiss? He simply did not look like that; there was no beauty in Him that we should desire Him.

The beauty of Jesus that has charmed the centuries is this moral beauty of which even His enemies acknowledge. Friedrich Nietzsche, the great German philosopher, perhaps the greatest nihilist and one of the greatest antichrists that ever lived in the world, died beating his forehead on the floor of his cell. He once said, "That man Jesus I love, but I don't like

Paul." He did not like theology, and he did not like to hear how you have to be saved and about the necessity of the new birth. In particular, he objected to justification by faith. However, there was something attractive about Jesus that he could not help but love.

So there is moral beauty in the Lord Jesus Christ, and He is the Lord of all beauty of moral form and moral texture. He is the Lord of it all.

Halfway Between Heaven and Hell

Sin has scarred the world and made it inharmonious, unsymmetrical and has filled hell with ugliness. If you love beautiful things, you had better stay out of hell, for hell will be the quintessence of all that is morally ugly. The spirit of things determines the external manifestation of that spirit, and I believe hell will be the ugliest place in all God's creation. When rough men say something is as "ugly as hell," they are using a proper and valid comparison.

Heaven is the place of harmonious numbers. Heaven is the place of loveliness; the place of beauty, because the One who is all beautiful is there. He is the Lord of all beauty, and earth lies between all that is ugly in hell and all that is beautiful in heaven. Earth lies between it, and you see the ugliness set over against the beauty.

Why is it like that? Why is there light and shadows? Why is there ugliness and beauty? Why are there so much good and so much bad? Why is there that which is pleasant and that which is tragic and hard to live with? It is because the earth lies halfway between heaven's beauty and hell's ugliness.

You say, "Why are people capable of doing what they do?" The answer is because they lie halfway between heaven and hell.

The Lord of All and His Bride

Is there any Christian who has not been hurt by some other Christian, and maybe a real Christian too? Why is it that a man will be on his knees praying earnestly one day and another day he will hurt another Christian? Because we stand halfway between heaven and hell. You and I must be pulled out of all this. The Lord of beauty is saving His people from the ugliness of sin.

Our Lord Jesus Christ came into the world that He might save us from the ugliness of sin to a beautiful heaven.

The Old Testament gives us the story of a man named Isaac. His father, Abraham, called for his servant to go find an acceptable bride for his son (see Gen. 24). With the help of the Holy Spirit, that old servant went down into the town Abraham indicated and found a young woman there. The Bible pictures her as being very beautiful. Her name was Rebekkah and she must have been beautiful, because the servant was instructed to find a bride that was beautiful to look upon.

Isaac is a type of our Lord Jesus Christ. God the Father sent the Holy Spirit out among the people of the world to win a bride for Christ, one that was worthy of Him. The bride's significance was to rest in the groom. She has no worth of her own, but her worth lies in her relationship to the groom. Jesus Christ is the groom and is worthy of our love, adoration and joyful worship.

Rebekkah was merely the daughter of her father. But, when she was taken to Isaac, she took on a new identity—the identify of her groom. Our identity is now in our Groom. The past identity is forgotten, with all its obligations. Our Groom is now our identity, and nothing in our past matters anymore. The bride not only takes on the identity of the groom but also his name as well. She is now forever known by that name.

This Groom Shepherd is worthy of our affection and is deserving of us leaving everything behind and embracing Him as our own.

Prayer

Oh God, in great humility we bow before Thee and take upon ourselves Thy name and Thy nature. Everything in our past is lost in glorious oblivion, and all our future is wrapped up in Thee. We accept Thee as our Groom Shepherd and are eternally grateful that the gracious Spirit of God sought us out and brought us unto Thee. We long for nothing else but Thee. Amen.

12

THE AUTHENTICITY OF OWNERSHIP

But unto the Son he saith, Thy throne, O God, is for ever and ever:
a sceptre of righteousness is the sceptre of thy kingdom. Thou hast loved
righteousness, and hated iniquity; therefore God, even thy God, hath
anointed thee with the oil of gladness above thy fellows.

HEBREWS 1:8-9

During the first few years of my ministry, if I could not have prayed and asked God for things, I would have starved to death, dragging my wife and family down with me. So I believe in praying for things. I believe that we can claim the promises of God to supply our daily needs. But that is not all there is to Christianity, and it certainly represents the lowest section of it. Too many people are all possessed with the idea of getting things from God to the extent of obscuring everything else.

There is so much more in the Christian life than getting things from God. Our personal relationship to Jesus Christ is the most important thing about us, which is defined for us in the worship we offer to God. The important thing is the object of our worship; and for the Christian, that is none other than

God, the Father of our Lord Jesus Christ. Because of the crucial aspect of this, we must know who it is we worship.

The Scriptures teach us that He is the Lord of all wisdom and He is the Lord of the Father of the everlasting ages. Not the "everlasting Father" as it says in our *King James Version*, but the "Father of the everlasting ages." This Father lays out the ages as an architect would lay out his blueprint or as a real estate developer lays out a small town and then builds hundreds of houses on it. But God is not dealing with buildings and local developments. He is dealing with the ages and is the Lord of all wisdom. Because He is perfect in wisdom, He is able to do this, and history is but the slow development of His purposes.

A Plan for the Ages

Take a house that is being built; the architect has drawn it down to the last tiny dot and X. He knows everything about it, has studied it thoroughly and writes his name at the bottom. The plans are now complete, and he turns it over to the contractor who farms it out to the electrician and plumber and all the rest. The building process begins. In the beginning, it does not look too encouraging. Visit the site and you will wonder what it is going to be. It doesn't look like anything at the moment. It is a mess now, with a steam shovel's great ugly nose digging out a hole and throwing it up on the bank or into trucks to haul away. In another place trucks are unloading bricks, and everything seems to be a confused conglomeration of this and that.

Come back six, eight, ten months later, and you see a charming house there with no signs of the construction confusion. The landscapers have been in, and the evergreen trees are standing there with their little green spikes by the windows, and it is a beautiful thing.

Order Out of the Chaos

We now are to believe that the Father of the everlasting ages, the Lord of all wisdom, has laid out His plan and is working toward a predetermined goal. All we see now is a church all mixed up and sore, distressed by schisms, and rent asunder by heresies. We see her backslidden in one part of the world, in confusion in another part, and we shrug our shoulders and wonder, What is all this, and who is behind all this? The answer is, He is the Lord of the ages; He is laying it all out, and what you are seeing now is only the steam shovel working, the truck backed up with bricks, that is all. You can only see workers in overalls going about killing time. You are just seeing people, and people make you sick because of the way we do, the way we are. To the uninitiated, everything looks like confusion and turmoil, as though no one was in charge.

We backslide and tumble around and are mixed up and run after will-o'-the-wisp and think it is the Shekinah glory. We hear an owl hoot and think it is the silver trumpet, and we take off in the wrong direction and spend a century catching up on ourselves. Return in another millennium or so and see what the Lord of all wisdom has done with it. No matter how much of a mess it appears, God has a way of working everything out for His glory. He is the Lord of all wisdom, and history is but the slow development of His purposes.

I am glad I am attached to something good, that there is something good somewhere in the universe. Despite appearances, behind all the mess of our world is the Lord of all wisdom sorting it out in His way and in His time.

I could not possibly be a Pollyanna optimist. I was born wrong. I would have to have had a different father and mother and a different ancestral line back at least 10 generations for me to have been a Pollyanna plum-pudding philosopher believing that everything was good. I cannot believe that. I do not think it is true. There is so much that is not right—everywhere. We might as well admit it. Wickedness prevails on so many fronts that it would be impossible to ignore it.

Some religious people try to black out all the negative and concentrate on the positive. If you want to get ahead in life, so they advise, ignore the negatives in your life and focus on the positive; and in the end, the positive will override all negative.

But, if you take the Bible as your guide, righteousness is not found among us. If you think it is, get on a bus somewhere when there's a crowd and you'll find that no matter how old and feeble you are, you will get the rib or two, or at least badly dinged by the elbow of some housewife on her way home. It is hard to concentrate on the positive with a sharp elbow in your side. And people are just not good. Among the first things we learn to do is something bad and something mean. The first word a baby learns to say is "no." Sin is everywhere.

Turn on the radio and try to get something educational or cultural and all you hear are songs about automobiles and cigarettes and sex. If it were not for the bad news on radio, the airwaves would be gloriously silent. It is not a good world we live in. You can become a Protestant, but that does not help much. You can be an American boasting in all your Bill of Rights guaranteed in the Constitution, and that does not help too much either.

Righting All That Is Wrong

However, when you attach yourself to the Lord of Glory, you are connected with something righteous. He is righteousness itself, and all of the possibility of righteousness is summed up in Him. "But unto the Son he saith, Thy throne, O God, is for ever and ever: a sceptre of righteousness is the sceptre of thy kingdom. Thou hast loved righteousness, and hated iniquity; therefore God, even thy God, hath anointed thee with the oil of gladness above thy fellows" (Heb. 1:8-9).

In this mixed-up, confused world, we need not despair, for we have a perfectly righteous Savior. He proved Himself with life among the people of His day. During His earthly life and ministry, His enemies spied on Him, sending people to search into His life to trip Him in something. Can you imagine if Jesus had made a mistake anywhere or lost His temper even once? All the sharp beady eyes of hell were following Him, trying to catch something out of His mouth. When the end of His days had almost come, He turned on them and said, "Which one of you convicts me of sin?" Nobody answered.

Sometime, I want to preach a sermon on mercy; I do not think I ever have. Of course, I have woven it into all of my preaching, but never just on the mercy of the Lord Jesus Christ. Our Lord sees how bad we are, but He is the Lord of all mercy and He does not care. In His great kindness, He takes rebels and unrighteous persons, sinners, and makes them His own and establishes them in righteousness and renews a right spirit within them. His righteousness becomes their righteousness, and out of chaos comes the divine order. This is the church, a company of believers, and together He is their Lord. He is the Lord of all power.

In the New Testament, we have a counterpart to the Song of Songs:

> And after these things I heard a great voice of much people in heaven, saying, Alleluia; Salvation, and glory, and honour, and power, unto the Lord our God: For true and righteous are his judgments: for he hath judged the great whore, which did corrupt the earth with her fornication, and hath avenged the blood of his servants at her hand. Again, they said, Alleluia. And her smoke rose up for ever and ever. And the four and twenty elders and the four beasts fell down and worshipped God that sat on the throne, saying, Amen; Alleluia. And a voice came out of the throne, saying, Praise our God, all ye his servants, and ye that fear him, both small and great (Rev. 19:1-5).

This is not hysteria, but ecstasy; there is a difference. Hysteria is based on emotion manipulated by exterior stimulus; but ecstasy is based upon mystery illuminating in the interior part of man's nature. This was ecstasy. It would be worthwhile to be put in a salt mine on the Isle of Patmos to have a vision like that.

Redeeming All That Is Lost

Years ago, I read one of the greatest books ever written of its kind, *Les Misérables* by Victor Hugo. In it, there was one of the tenderest and pathetic passages I think I have ever read in all literature.

You would have to go to the Bible to find things as deeply moving. Here was the story of a young man, one of the upper class of nobles, and the noble woman he was in love with. Then there was a pale face, a little urchin girl from the streets of Paris, dressed in poor rags, with a pale, tubercular face. She also loved the nobleman but did not dare say so. The young nobleman used the young girl to carry notes back and forth to his fiancée and never dreamed this poor sallow-faced girl dressed in rags had lost her heart to him and his nobility. When he discovered this, he went to find her and see what he could do to help her and found her lying on the bed of rags in the tenement house in the low section of Paris.

This time she cannot get up to greet him or carry a note to his fiancée. He says to her, "What can I do for you?"

She tells him, "I'm dying; I'll be gone in a moment."

"What can I do? Tell me, anything."

And she said, "Would you do one thing for me before I close my eyes for the last time? Would you, when I am dead, kiss my forehead?"

I know it was only Victor Hugo's brilliant imagination, but he had seen that in Paris. He had gone through the sewers, had seen this and knew about it. Hugo knew that you could beat a girl down, clothe her in rags, fill her with tuberculosis and make her so thin that the wind would blow her off course when she walked down a dirty street. But you could not take out of her heart that thing that makes her want to love a man.

God told Adam, "And the LORD God said, It is not good that the man should be alone; I will make him an help meet for him" (Gen. 2:18). And God made a woman to be a helpmeet for man;

you cannot take that out of human nature. Victor Hugo knew it when he wrote his classic novel. In human nature is planted the desire and need to love.

Our Lord Jesus Christ came down and found the human race like that: consumptive, wan, pale-faced and dying, and He took on Himself all her death and rose the third day and took all the pathos out and all of the pity out. Now she comes leaning on the arm of her beloved. She comes walking into the presence of God, and He presents her not as a poor pitiful wretch whose forehead He kissed when she was dead, but as His happy bright-eyed bride, to be partaker with all the saints, worthy to stand beside Him and be His bride in the glory. What is her authority, what is her right and by what authority does she walk into the presence of God?

We have an Old Testament illustration of this. Abraham sent his trusted servant to go and bring back a bride for his son Isaac. This servant was authorized to bestow upon her jewelry as a token from her groom. It was a symbol of his acceptance of the bride. Now, how was Isaac going to know his bride? What would set her apart from all others? He was going to know her by the jewelry that she had on. He had sent it, and when she came back with it, he would recognize her by his jewelry she wore. And so Scripture says that Isaac took Rebekkah and she became his bride.

The Lord of Glory sent the Holy Ghost at Pentecost to get a bride, and He will know her by the jewelry she wears.

And what is that jewelry?

For one, it is the fruit of the Spirit. Love, joy, peace, temperance, kindness, and all that. He will know her by what

He has bestowed upon her. Each of the fruit of the Spirit responds to the nature of Christ. He looks into our life, sees what He recognizes as coming from Him and accepts it.

Perhaps the biggest jewel will be that of worship—the bright, shiny, glorious spirit of worship that rests upon the bride of Christ. It is something that is implanted deep into the nature of man. Not all the depravity of human wickedness can destroy that impulse to reach out and up in worship. When God sees that worship, purified by the Spirit and the Blood, He responds and recognizes it as His.

Our Lord Jesus Christ will know His bride. He knows who you are, and He knows you by the jewelry He has given you. "He is thy Lord and he shall greatly desire thy beauty, worship thou Him."

The Irish hymn writer Jean Sophia Pigott (1845–1882) understood this and gave the world the essence of her joy in Christ.

Jesus, I am resting, resting,
In the joy of what Thou art;
I am finding out the greatness
Of thy loving heart.
Thou hast bid me gaze upon Thee,
And Thy beauty fills my soul,
For by Thy Transforming power
Thou hast made me whole.

These are the marks on us that authenticate our belonging to this "Lord of the Father of the everlasting ages."

Prayer

O God our Father, we thank Thee for Jesus Christ
Thy Son. We have not done anything that we can
think of but what we are ashamed. We have not done
anything but of what we ought to be ashamed. We have not
got anything—our brains, our bodies, our souls, our spirits,
we have not done anything ourselves—except what Thou
hast given us. What Thou hast given us we are not ashamed of.
We are glad for and deeply appreciative of Thy jewels that
adorn our life; these jewels that show the world whose we are.
In Jesus' name, amen.

13

THE LORD OF OUR WORSHIP

But ye are a chosen generation, a royal priesthood, an holy nation, a peculiar people; that ye should shew forth the praises of him who hath called you out of darkness into his marvellous light.

1 PETER 2:9

What is the purpose of the local church? And why is the church necessary?

According to the Bible, a local church exists to do corporately what each Christian should do individually all week: namely, worship God and show forth the excellencies of Him who has called us out of darkness into His marvelous light; reflect back the glory of Him who shined down on us, even God, even Christ, even the Holy Ghost. All that Christ has done for us in the past and all that He is doing now leads to this one end. This is not being taught very much today—that we are saved to worship God. We have it that we are saved for a number of reasons.

If you were to ask the average Christian why he was saved, he might respond by referring to peace of mind or being delivered from smoking. If he is a businessman, he might say he took the Lord Jesus as his helper because he was failing in business and wanted Him to be his business partner. We have many other reasons, and I am not going to be too hard on people. In the New Testament, people came to the Lord for many reasons. One man came because his boy was sick. A woman came because her daughter was sick. Another woman came because she had had a chronic disease for 12 years. A politician climbed a tree and looked down because his heart ached; and Nicodemus came by night to the Lord because his religion was not adequate and his heart was empty. Therefore, the Lord received them all, and the Lord receives everyone who comes to Him in faith today, even if their motives may not be the highest.

The point is, why should we always stay where we began? Why should the church be a spiritual school composed of first-graders who never go beyond the first grade? Nobody wants to get any further than this, and I do not mind saying that I am somewhat sick about it all. It seems to be an awful, mixed-up concept of Christianity.

The Lord Jesus Christ died on the cross that He might make His people worshipers of God. That is why we were born, that we might show forth the excellencies of Him who has called us out of darkness into His marvelous light. "He is thy Lord, worship thou Him." And we see that purpose—worship—when it is all over and the consummation has taken place and been fulfilled. The beasts, the elders and the creatures under the sea, above the earth, in the earth, and in the heavens are all crying aloud, "Holy, holy, holy to the Lord God Almighty, which was, and is, and is to come." The purpose of God is that He might redeem us, put us all in the heavenly choir and keep us there singing His praises and showing forth His excellencies while the ages roll. This is the purpose of God in redemption.

He has done it for us and is still doing now what He has done; everything leads to one end, and all we do should lead to one end. We must bring our ideas into harmony with the Lord of the Church. That means bringing your whole thought, your whole philosophy of Christianity, your whole conception of what the church is into harmony with the Lord of the Church and His teachings.

The Church's High Design

Religious people are a very noisy, wordy and active people. But activity for activity's sake is not of God. We might first clear away the idea that church is a social club. A church must have certain social commitments and certain fellowship, but we are not a social club. And we are not a current events forum. We often tend to read some magazine and then take off like an airplane off a ramp from what we've just read. So, we are not a current events forum and we are not a religious theater to provide a place for amateur entertainers to display their talent. We are none of these things.

We are a holy people, a royal priesthood, a holy generation called out of darkness to show forth the glory of the One who called us out. We should take whatever steps are needed to fulfill our high design as a New Testament church. To do less than this is to fail utterly, to fail God and to fail our Lord Jesus Christ who redeemed us. It is to fail ourselves and it is to fail our children. It is to fail the Holy Ghost who is come from the heart of Jesus to do in us a work. This work is to be done to make us a holy people, a sanctified people that are mirrors of the Almighty to reflect the glory of the most high God.

Why is this important? For the simple reason that if a local church in one generation fails of its high design of worship, the next generation in that church will depart from the faith altogether. That is how liberalism comes about. Many churches stand as a monument that the generation before failed God, and as a result the present generation succumbs to liberalism and does not preach the Word of God at all. With no Spirit of God upon them and no fire-baptized leaders, they need to compensate. Therefore, they keep it up by social activities and by tying into whatever is going on in the world. But as a church, it has failed and is not a church anymore. The glory has departed.

If we could see the visible cloud hanging over churches, the cloud that once hung over the camp of Israel in the wilderness, we could easily identify those churches acting in accord with their spiritual nature. If we were permitted to see the fire by night and the cloud by day, visibly hanging as a plume over the churches in which God is pleased, I wonder how many churches we would see testifying to all the world that this is God's dwelling place? Instead of that, we would see only monuments out in the country.

The church must not be accepted as it is or as we find it. We must check it with the Word of God and see if this is the way it should be. Then reverently and quietly, slowly but surely, patiently and lovingly bring the church into line with the New Testament to see if this is the way it would be done if the Holy Ghost were pleased. And when that takes place, the Holy Ghost begins to glow like lights in the church, and that is what my heart longs to see.

Live for the Purpose You Were Created

For individual professed Christians, if we fail the purpose for which God created us, then we had better never have been born.

How utterly and unspeakably tragic to be forever a broken vase. How utterly tragic that God should make me to be a vase in which He would place the flowers of paradise, the lily of the valley and the rose of Sharon, and out from that simple earthly vessel there would go forth a fragrance that would fill the universe of God. Then I allow that vase to be shattered on the floor, and it cannot be used for the purpose God had intended.

How utterly tragic to be a stringless harp and to have all the shape, outline and form of a Christian but have no strings that the Holy Ghost could play over.

How utterly terrible to be a barren fig tree, with nothing but leaves and no fruit!

Jesus walked out from Jerusalem with His people and saw a fig tree; it had leaves on it, and He went to that tree and found that it had no figs. The way a fig tree grows is the fruit comes first and then the leaves. When the leaves appear on the landscape, they tell everybody, "Come, there's fruit here"; and according to the nature of the tree, the fruit should have been there before the leaves. But in this case, the leaves were there and the order had been reversed; and when Jesus came, parted the leaves and reached in for figs, and there were no figs, He turned to His disciples and told them to look at that tree. There would be no more fruit forever, and He cursed it, and it withered from the top down.

What could be more terrible then a barren fig tree, to have the form and delineation of the Christian, but have no fruit. To be a star that shines not. To be those solemn, awful men in 2 Peter and Jude in his little epistle. Think about the dark stars that shine not and clouds without rain. How terrible to be a shattered mirror of the Almighty, meant of God to catch and reflect the beautiful light of God back to the entire universe. But instead is a cracked and shattered mirror that can reflect nothing, and thus is disapproved of God and banished from the garden; how terrible to be eternally aware of all this.

The frightful thing about human beings is our consciousness—that we are aware of things. If it was not for our awareness, nothing could harm us.

The rich man who died and found himself in hell was conscious he was there and knew his brothers were not there but would be coming soon. Hell would not be hell if it were not for the consciousness of it. If men slept comatose in hell, it could never be hell.

In the realm of psychology and psychiatry these days the devil is very busy, and has many men who can use phrases they have borrowed from Freud and the rest of them, telling us that we ought not to allow the consciousness of guilt to get us down because that is a guilt complex. We ought not to be too much bothered by religion.

One of the great heads of a great mental institution, after he had been long years head of that institution, was told, "Well, doctor, I suppose an awful lot of your patients in here have gone crazy over religion." He said, "To the best of my knowledge, in all the years that I have been head of this institution, I have never known one patient that came here because of religion; but I have known hundreds that came here that could have been saved from here by religion."

You ought to thank God if you have a care. I would not take that care away from you at all.

You have to be a purified people if you are going to be a worshiper of God, reflecting the image of Him that created you. But broken vessels, stringless harps, barren fig trees, clouds without water, cracked mirrors—how tragic and terrible it is.

You must be a purified people and be born into the world, unable to go back and cancel out your being, and yet before God be a broken vase. Before God be a life that does not shine. Before God be a harp that does not play, a tongue that does not bear fruit, failing God.

If you had teeth that were desperately in need of attention, the first thing you ought to do when you could afford to take a day off from work is attend to them. How much more important it is that I should find the blood that cleanses me from sin. Nothing should be permitted to hinder me. Friendships, they mean nothing. Business, better to sell peanuts on the corner than to be caught in a business that grieves the Holy Ghost, breaks the vase and shatters the mirror. Pleasures are for a pleasure mad people. Rome perished from bread and circuses.

Rome, that has given us a language and laws and literature and standards, believed it would never die, yet went down like a great rotten tree. Before whom did Rome go down? Rome went down by the pagan hordes from the North, the Huns, the Longbards and the rest of the vandals. People unworthy to carry their shoes, or black them. Rome did not die by military conquest from without; Rome died from bread and circuses and pleasure and divorce and fun and too much of everything. She got fat and weak; and when she was fat and weak, she died.

It is the way with churches and the way with you if you do not look out. It is also the way with countries. I say that nothing should permit us or hinder us, not fear itself, because is there anything more fearful than failure before God?

What shall we do then? We ought to amend our ways. "Thus saith the Lord of hosts, the God of Israel, amend your ways and your doings, and I will cause you to dwell in this place. But if ye trust not in lying words, saying The temple of the Lord, The temple of the Lord, The temple of the Lord, are these." This is our Christian religion. If you thoroughly amend your ways and your doings, then God will cause you to dwell in this place in the land that He gave your fathers forever and ever. So let us amend our giving and our praying, our relationships to others, our personal discipline, our prayer lives. Let us amend our ways before God that we might be a pure people completely acceptable to God; for no pure man can ever be defeated. No pure church can ever perish.

Prayer

O Lord Jesus, we remember Thy words back there where one of Thy churches allowed her love to cool off, Thou didst reach down and remove her candlestick, and not a trace was left of that church in that city. O Christ, we would seek before Thee tonight a perpetual witness. We seek that we should so amend our ways that Thou canst give us a second year, a second decade, a second scroll of years. But until Thy holy Son comes from heaven, the light will shine from this place. Not only around the neighborhood but also to New Guinea and Peru and Brazil and Japan and to all, wherever men need to hear the gospel. O God, we pray Thee, help us that we may amend our ways and begin to be and do that for which we were created. Now we are looking to Thee for help, Lord; we expect Thee to bless us; we want Thee to do it. Amen.

Maintaining a
Vibrant Worship
Lifestyle

*And I John saw these things, and heard them. And when I had heard
and seen, I fell down to worship before the feet of the angel which
showed me these things. Then saith he unto me, See thou do it not:
for I am thy fellowservant, and of thy brethren the prophets, and of
them which keep the sayings of this book: worship God.*

Revelation 22:8-9

Throughout this series, I have maintained that worship is not
an event but a lifestyle. The more we treat worship as an event,
the more it becomes a caricature of God's intention, and is unacceptable to Him. To maintain a lifestyle of worship, we must
attend to it on a daily basis. If you regulate worship to a once-
a-week event, you really do not understand it, and it will take a
low priority in your life.

By nature, worship is not some performance we do, but a
Presence we experience. Unless in our worship we have experienced the Presence of God, it cannot rightly be called Christian

worship. I have pointed out that there can be worship apart from God, but such is not Christian worship. It is my contention that once we experience the actual Presence of God, we will lose all interest in cheap Christianity with all its bells and whistles vainly trying to compete with the world.

For worship to be a vital part of everyday life, it must be systematically and carefully nurtured.

Let me offer a few suggestions to help along the way. At this point, it is important to stay clear of all those sterile, mechanical regimens that think one size fits all. All of us are different, and although we are walking along the same path, we have different personalities. A few essentials need to be a part of our daily walk to maintain a vibrant life of worship. These are a few things that have helped me in my journey along the way with God.

Quiet

I put quietness first because unless we can find a place without distraction, the rest is undermined. We must withdraw from the world and find our repose in God. In such a frantic world as ours, it is almost impossible to find any quietness. Our world is riddled with noise of all kinds and intensity. Not only in the world, but increasingly the church itself echoes with noise and commotion. Finding a quiet corner to get away is a great challenge but well worth it.

When I first became a Christian, it was difficult to find a quiet place. Eventually I found refuge in a corner of our basement where I could focus on worship without interruption. Those were delightful times of fellowship with God and laid the foundation for not only my walk with God but also my ministry in the days to come.

I firmly believe it is important that we get still and wait on God. And it is best that we get alone, preferably with our Bible outspread before us. I usually have my *King James Bible*, but I do not think the version is that important. The important thing is to get alone with the Word of God. Then in the quietness of the moment, and as we draw near to God, we will begin to hear Him speak in our hearts. This is the most important part of our initial walk with God. To follow God arbitrarily is one thing, but I take great pleasure in the Scripture that says, "He that hath ears to hear, let him hear" what the Spirit sayeth (Luke 8:8). The saints of old always followed that voice. They got quiet enough to hear that "still, small voice of God" speaking to them.

For the average believer, the progression will be something like this: first, a sound as of a Presence walking in the garden; then a voice, more intelligible, but still far from clear. Then the happy moment when the Spirit begins to illuminate the Scriptures, and that which had been only a sound, or at best a voice, now becomes an intelligible word—as warm, intimate and clear as the word of a dear friend. Then will come life and light, and best of all, ability to see and rest in and embrace Jesus Christ as Savior and Lord and All.

The key here is to wait patiently and quietly on God. There is no need to rush. Noise is the enemy of the soul; and in our noise-enriched culture, it may take some doing, but the result is well worth the effort. Wait until He breaks through the tough exterior of your consciousness.

Cultivating quietness is a missing discipline in today's Christian church. There seems to be a wretched conspiracy in many churches to rob the saints of the quietness necessary to nurture their inner life, which is hid in Christ in God. The old saints would practice what they called "tarrying." They would get on their knees and tarry in God's presence until the light broke in their heart. Sometimes it took all night, but the wait was well worth it.

Scripture

All worship should begin with the Bible. This divine roadmap will lead us to God. It has been a neat trick of the devil to confuse us with a variety of translations. The Christian community is divided by which translation is the right one. I suggest that you settle this matter once for all in your own mind, no matter what it takes, and press on in spiritual growth and maturity. Then put the Bible in a prominent place in your daily life and allow nothing to interfere with reading it and meditating on it.

Our reading here should not be a marathon, but a slow, deliberate soaking in of its message. Bible reading calendars are no help here. There are times when one verse or even a phrase will strangely draw us. It would be impossible to go on until that Scripture has done its work in our heart. Do not faint here. Allow that Scripture to marinate in your mind and heart as long as it feeds your soul. God is speaking, and He deserves our utmost respect and attention. Often we regiment ourselves to a daily Bible reading schedule and hurry on in our reading to keep up. The importance of reading the Bible is not reading but fellowship with the Author. The proper reading of the Bible must be in the same Spirit that authored it.

I like to memorize portions of Scripture, especially the psalms of David. Charles Spurgeon used to say that we should read our Bibles until our blood became bibline. I like that. Memorizing the great passages of Scripture will go a long way in meditating on God, especially in the nighttime. "Thy Word have I hid in mine heart . . ." (Ps. 119:11) the psalmist said, and he knew something of delighting in the presence and fellowship of God.

Prayer

In your prayer life, quickly move beyond the idea of "getting things" from God. Prayer is not technical in the sense that if we go through the right motions, say the right words, automatically our prayer is answered. Our aim in prayer is not simply "getting our prayers answered." Here, we go beyond all that and luxuriate in the overwhelming presence of God. Prayer is not a monologue where we tell God what we think or want. Rather, it is a dialogue between two friends; an intimate fellowship that more often than not surpasses words. Words can be clumsy and grossly inadequate to express sufficiently how we feel. As the mystics and saints have encouraged, begin practicing the presence of God. This is not merely an exercise in imagination but the ecstatic joy of fellowship. Once you lose yourself in rapturous prayer, you will never go back to prayer by routine.

The key to prayer is simply praying. As we engage the God of the universe, our hearts are stretched upward in adoring wonder and admiration, resulting in spontaneous worship. Our heart always responds to that heavenly pull. This kind of praying is contagious and, thankfully, dangerous to spiritual status quo.

Hymns

I must confess that I am an ardent lover of hymns. In my library, I value a collection of old hymnals. Often, on the way to an appointment, I will grab one of these hymnals to read and meditate. After the Bible, the next most valuable book is a hymnal. But do not get one that is less than a hundred years old! Let any new Christian spend a year prayerfully meditating on the hymns of Watts and Wesley alone, and he will become a fine theologian. Then read a balanced diet of the Puritans and the Christian mystics, and the result will be more wonderful than you could dream.

The old hymnal is invaluable in my personal walk with God. This may be the most difficult. For a variety of reasons, many have tossed the hymnbook aside or at least have ignored it. It has been a successful ploy of the enemy to separate us from those lofty souls who reveled in the rarified atmosphere of God's presence. I suggest you find a hymnbook and learn how to use it. Perhaps one reason the hymnal has fallen out of favor with many is that we do not know how to read or sing a hymn. We are not taught in our churches the great hymns of the church; consequently, many Christians are the poorer, spiritually speaking.

Devotional Reading:
The Mystics and Saints

Apart from the Scriptures, which should be paramount in our daily walk with God, some devotional works of bygone saints can help us on our way. I am not thinking of those one-page daily devotionals popular with many people today. They may have some value for those just beginning their spiritual pilgrimage, but the growing Christian needs strong meat. If we are to mature in our Christian experience, we must have food to strengthen us for the journey.

In my search for God, I quite naturally was led to the Christian mystics. As a young Christian, I had never heard of them nor saw any of their books in the bookstore. A retired missionary thoughtfully placed into my hands one of these old Christian books and I was immediately in love. I discovered that these great saints were uncontrollably in love with God. My love and appreciation for these writers sprang out of my own heart's deep longing after and thirsting for God. These people knew God in a way that I did not, and I wanted to know what they knew about God and how they came to know it.

Certainly, in my admiration for these writers, I by no means endorsed everything they did or taught. I early learned that a hungry bee could get nectar out of any old flower and turn it into honey. For me, it was their utter devotion to God along with the ability to share their spiritual insights and observations that I valued. They assisted me in my walk with God as no other writers even of my day have. And, after all, that is all that really matters. I cannot place too much emphasis on the contemplation of divine things, which will result in the God-conscious life. These old mystics did just that for me.

Some have chided me about my affection for some of these old mystic friends of mine. I have learned to live above that. For me, I only require that a person must know God other than by hearsay. The intimacy of their relationship with God is all that truly matters. If a writer only has information to offer that he has obtained by research, I will pass on him. Give me the writer who has the passion and fire of God in his soul, which flows onto the page.

By "mystic," I simply mean that personal spiritual experience common to the saints of Bible times and well known to multitudes of persons in the postbiblical era. I am referring to the evangelical mystic who has been taught in the Christian Scriptures. He walks the high road of truth where walked of old prophets and apostles, and where down the centuries walked martyrs, reformers, Puritans, evangelists and missionaries of the cross. He differs from the ordinary orthodox Christian only because he experiences his faith down in the depths of his sentient being, while the other does not. He exists in a world of spiritual reality. He is quietly, deeply and sometimes almost ecstatically aware of the presence of God in his own nature and in the world around him. His religious experience is something elemental, as old as time and acquaintance with God by union with the eternal Son. It is to know that which passes knowledge.

Simplify Your Life

The average Christian's life is cluttered with all sorts of activities. We have more going on than we can keep up and still maintain our inner life with God. Some things need to be rooted out of our daily schedule in order to make room for that one essential thing in our life, the worship of God. Too many things in our life just suck the life out of us and are not essential to wholesome living. We find ourselves rushing through the devotional aspects of our life to give predominance to mere activities. Work without worship is totally unacceptable to God. It would be a good practice to go through your schedule once a month and find one thing to eliminate. Put it on the altar and see how God will respond. It would not be long until the most important thing in your life will be your personal worship of God.

Friendships

This I leave for last because it has the most potential danger. Your friends will either make or break your deeper walk with Christ. We must carefully choose our friends in this regard. Although it is not necessary to be rude, some friends will need to be marginalized to lessen the damage to our inner life. At times, we are thrown in with friends who are carnal in nature and frivolous in life. It is easy for our friends to distract us from our walk with Christ and from maintaining a vibrant life of worship. Often we will have to leave our friends behind in order to concentrate on our Friend.

Cultivate friendships with those who have made He who is the Friend of sinners their constant Companion.

These simple things will go a long way in maintaining a vibrant life of worship and praise. If what we believe does not make God more real to us, if it does not make us more Christlike in every aspect of our life, of what value is it? The maintaining of our worship is a responsibility we cannot shirk. It must be paramount in our daily life. The effect of all this is seen in, "But we all, with open face beholding as in a glass the glory of the Lord, are changed into the same image from glory to glory, even as by the Spirit of the Lord" (2 Cor. 3:18).

May God grant us a desire for God that supersedes all other desires.

Prayer

Dear heavenly Father, the world is very evil, times are waxing late and we are running out of time. Oh, God, lay hold of us. We pray that we may have eyes to see and ears to hear and hearts to understand. We pray that we may be saved from the routine and rut. We pray that we may have eyes inside and outside, anointed understanding. Help us, Lord, for Christ's sake. Amen.

Follow Tozer's new writings on Twitter at
http://twitter.com/TozerAW

A.W. TOZER

Compiled and Edited by James L. Snyder

THE
CRUCIFIED
LIFE

HOW TO LIVE OUT A DEEPER
CHRISTIAN EXPERIENCE

BETHANYHOUSE
a division of Baker Publishing Group
Minneapolis, Minnesota

CONTENTS

A DIFFERENT WAY OF LIVING

Some dates are so pivotal that they change the whole course of history. Unfortunately, many of those dates lie comfortably in the shadows of obscurity. One such date in the life of A. W. Tozer has eluded me.

As the story is told, Tozer, a pastor at the time, was visiting one of his favorite bookstores in downtown Chicago. As he was perusing the shelves of used books that were so familiar to him, he ran across an old book that he had never seen before. He purchased the book and took it home, and his life was never the same.

The name of the book was *Spiritual Counsel*, and its author, François Fénelon, struck a warm cord in Tozer's own heart. Although Tozer allowed others to borrow many books in his personal library, he never allowed this one particular book to leave his possession to the day he died. He talked about the book so much that people began to inquire about it. As far as Tozer could determine, the book was out of print, and no other copies were available. One man was so interested in the book that, though Tozer did not allow him to take it out of his library, he did allow him to come and type out chapter after chapter. Such was the prominence that Tozer gave to this book. Much to Tozer's delight, the book was eventually republished in an updated and expanded edition titled *Christian Perfection*.

When you read Fénelon's book, you soon recognize a heart-beat that was also shared by Tozer. No two people were more alike in the spiritual realm. In fact, Fénelon's work so inspired Tozer that if you listen carefully to his sermons, you can hear the words of François Fénelon peek through on many occasions. Tozer, of course, was familiar with the works of other great writes—A. B. Simpson, John Wesley and Andrew Murray to name a few—but something about François Fénelon stirred the depths of his heart and his passion for God.

Fénelon's book introduced Tozer to a whole line of Christian "mystics"—a word not highly acceptable in evangelistic circles during Tozer's time (or even during our own)—and he went on to introduce these mystics to the evangelical church of his time. Tozer was not so much interested in literature as he was in pursuing God, and if an author could open up his heart to more of God, he was interested in that person. As you read this book, you will find many of these old saints of God that stirred Tozer's imagination popping in and out, enriching the message that was so important to him.

During his younger years, Tozer was primarily an evangelist. Although he was also a pastor of a local church, he spent much of his time going around the country preaching in conferences and at churches and camp meetings. His primary message at the time was evangelistic. However, after he encountered François Fénelon, his message began to change. When we come to Tozer in this book, we are coming to a man who is aflame with the message of the crucified life.

The Crucified Life and Spiritual Perfection

Now, what did Tozer mean by the "crucified life"? This entire book is an answer to that question, but here we can simply say that it is the life Christ ransomed on the cross, redeemed from the judgment of sin, and made a worthy and acceptable sacrifice unto God. This represents a quality of life that is far above anything that is natural. It is altogether spiritual, which is a result of a dynamic inspiration from on high.

Another term that was not common among the evangelicals of Tozer's day was "spiritual perfection." This term came from François Fénelon, and it embodied the passion of Tozer's heart. Tozer was quick to point out that he wanted nothing whatsoever to do with anything that did not have biblical authority—and he also threw out anything that was extra-biblical. However, spiritual perfection was a term that Tozer found to be biblical, as Paul writes in Philippians 3:12: "Not as though I had already attained, either were already perfect: but I follow after, if that I may apprehend that for which also I am apprehended of Christ Jesus." This should be the great passion of the Christian's heart—to press forward unto what the apostle Paul called "perfection."

There were many things about the crucified life that interested Tozer. It was a life that was absolutely and irreconcilably incompatible with the world. It breathed the rarefied air of heaven while walking on earth. To the believer, it meant the absolute death of ego and the resurgence of Christ in his or her life. Emphatically, Tozer taught that Christ did not die on the cross just to save people from hell; rather, He died on the cross so that all could become one with Christ. That concept was so personally important to Tozer that anything that came between him and that unity with Christ had to be courageously dealt with and done away with, regardless of the cost.

The message of the crucified life was not a new concept. Tozer himself noted that all of the great Christians of the past wrote about this idea in some fashion. It was the unifying factor among a wide diversity of Christians down through the ages. The legacy of the church fathers, of the reformers, the re-vivalists, the Christian mystics and the hymnists all resonated on this one message. And while they might disagree on many points, in this one area there was a unique unity among them. The emphasis of the crucified life was to press forward—regard-less of the difficulties and in spite of the cost—to the state of spiritual perfection.

A Difficult Message

Tozer often confessed he would have preferred to simply talk about God all the time—about how wonderful God is and how wonderful it is to be on our way to heaven, enjoying the bless-ings of the Lord day by day. He would have preferred to preach such positive sermons. But the Spirit stirred him to keep press-ing the deep things of God. There was more to the Christian life than just being saved from the past and from one's sins. There was more to the Christian life than having a happy time on one's way to heaven.

Tozer saw the evangelical and fundamentalist churches of his day selling out to the world, just as the liberal churches did before them, and it disturbed him greatly. It bothered him to see these churches compromising with worldly values and slip-ping into the murky error of liberalism. It goaded him that the gospel churches were adopting worldly measures to build up church attendance, and he saw that many church leaders were using these things to promote themselves.

It was an era of what many called "easy believism." Simply put, the idea was that if you said you believed in Jesus, every-thing else would be all right. You did not have to change any-thing, for God loved you just the way you were. This kind of message stirred Dr. Tozer greatly. And Tozer was at his best when he was stirred.

It was for this reason that during the last years of his life, Tozer preached and wrote about the importance of living the crucified life. He felt an inward spiritual urging to sound the clarion call for the Church to return to the roots of the Christian message—the message of "Christ in you, the hope of glory" (Col. 1:27). Several times he said, "God did not call me to be a back scratcher," and anyone who heard him preach or read any of his editorials knew that was quite true. He was not interested in making people feel good about themselves; in fact, his agenda was quite the opposite. To Tozer, there was nothing good in man or even in the Christian—the only good was in Christ.

Tozer's goal was not to make attacks against a person, but he always sought to speak the truth as he saw it in love. As you might imagine, this did not always make him friends. One time, he told Dr. D. Martyn Lloyd-Jones of London that he had preached himself off every Bible conference in America. Of course, that was a bit exaggerated, because he was in demand at Bible conferences all across the country up until the time of his death. But some places did not invite him back. Regardless, he was tough and uncompromising on this issue because of what he felt was the seriousness of the condition of the evangelical church. He did not feel called of God to smooth ruffled feathers; rather, his calling was to ruffle some of those feathers.

Reverend Ray McAfee, a longtime associate pastor with Dr. A. W. Tozer, once told me the following story: Tozer was attending a holiness convention that was celebrating its fiftieth anniversary. He was the keynote speaker, and there were a number of preliminaries before he came to the pulpit. People were going around cutting other people's ties in half, there was impromptu singing along the lines of what we would call karaoke, and everybody was having a good old time celebrating the anniversary. McAfee could see Tozer tapping his right foot. The longer he sat there, the more he tapped his right foot. McAfee knew that Tozer was getting stirred.

When Tozer walked up to the pulpit, his first words were, "What's happened to you holiness people?" Then Tozer took them to the spiritual woodshed as they had never been taken before. Nothing was more serious to Tozer than the things of God. He had a sense of humor, but he did not consider the gathering of God's people to be a frivolous occasion but rather a time for worship and adoration of God. To Tozer, if you needed entertainment to get a crowd, it was not Christian.

The Challenge of the Crucified Life

This book is strong medicine for what Tozer considered a serious spiritual malady. The more serious the condition, the more radical the remedy; and for this reason, Tozer was willing to uncompromisingly confront people with the message of the crucified life.

It must be said that this message did not come without cost for Tozer. His friends and family often misunderstood him. He once wrote an editorial titled "The Saint Walks Alone," which he wrote from experience. It is easy to go along with the crowd, but the one who is committed to living the crucified life will always lean hard into the wind of opposition and misunderstanding.

Thus, living the crucified life is not an easy proposition—in fact, it will be the most challenging thing you will ever face. The cost is certainly high. The pathway is rough. The way forward is often lonely. But the rewards you will gain of knowing God in intimate fellowship will be well worth the journey.

Rev. James L. Snyder

PART I

. . . .

THE
FOUNDATION
OF THE
CRUCIFIED
LIFE

THE IMPORTANCE OF THE CRUCIFIED LIFE

Knowing this, that our old man is crucified with him, that the body of sin might be destroyed, that henceforth we should not serve sin.

ROMANS 6:6

Nothing weighs heavier on my heart than the subject of this study. If it were not such a crucial Bible teaching, one could ignore the controversies and go on to something else. However, such is not the case. The subject of the crucified life is vitally important to the health and growth of the Church.

The Church is not some impersonal abstract floating around in space. Rather, the Church is comprised of individuals who have trusted Jesus Christ as their Lord and Savior. The health of the Church is in direct proportion to the health of each individual Christian. If the Church is to grow and be healthy, the individual Christians comprising the Church must grow spiritually. Only a dynamically healthy Church can ever hope to fulfill the commission of Christ to "go ye into all the world, and preach the gospel" (Mark 16:15).

One important thing needs to be understood. Not all Christians are alike. Jesus said in Matthew 13:23:

But he that received seed into the good ground is he that heareth the word, and understandeth it; which also beareth fruit, and bringeth forth, some an hundredfold, some sixty, some thirty.

Too many of us are satisfied to be thirtyfold Christians. But the desire of our Lord is that we press on to become hundredfold Christians. The question then is, how are we to go on to this stage?

This is the focus of this book. I think it my duty to prod the thirtyfold and the sixtyfold Christians to press on to the ultimate Christian experience, being a hundredfold Christian. The path that accomplishes this is living the crucified life. I do not think it would be amiss to say that most Christian literature today is focused on the thirtyfold Christians. Some might venture out and address the sixtyfold Christians, but it is safe to say there are few who focus on hundredfold Christians. This book is dedicated to that very thing. I simply call it *The Crucified Life.*

With that being the case, it is incumbent upon me to define some elements I will use throughout this study. If I use one term and the reader understands it in a different way from the manner in which I am using it, then communication breaks down. So let me define some of the basic concepts that will be developed throughout this study.

The Crucified Life

I first need to establish what I mean when I use the phrase "the crucified life." A variety of phrases have been used since apostolic days to define the subject—phrases such as "the deeper life," "the higher life," "the wholly sanctified life," "the spirit-filled life," "the victorious Christian life," "the exchanged life." But after looking at some of the literature produced on this topic, none seems to be any deeper, higher, holier or more Spirit-filled than common run-of-the-mill Christianity. For some, the phrase seems to be merely a catchphrase.

Strange Inconsistency

What I mean by "the crucified life" is a life wholly given over to the Lord in absolute humility and obedience: a sacrifice pleasing to the Lord. The word "crucified" takes us back to what Christ did on the cross. The key verse for this is Galatians 2:20:

> I am crucified with Christ: nevertheless I live; yet not I, but Christ liveth in me: and the life which I now live in the flesh I live by the faith of the Son of God, who loved me, and gave himself for me.

From the natural standpoint, the crucified life is burdened with contradictions. The biggest contradiction, of course, is the phrase itself: "crucified life." If a life is truly crucified, it is dead and not alive. But how can a person be dead and alive at the same time? Being dead and yet alive is one of the strange inconsistencies of the life established for us by Jesus' dying on the cross. But oh, the blessedness of these seeming inconsistencies.

Scriptural Proof

This study does not advocate any kind of Christian experience not based squarely on the plain teachings of the Scripture. Everything taught in this study must square with the entire Word of God. Anybody can prove anything by piecing together isolated texts. What is the teaching of the entire Word of God? That is the question that must be considered. Too much of contemporary Christianity is borrowed from the philosophies of the world and even other religions—phrases and mottos that on the surface look great but are not rooted in Scripture or that mostly bolster one's self-image.

Whatever the teaching might be or whoever the teacher might be, we must strongly demand scriptural proof. If such proof cannot be presented, then the teaching must be rejected out of mind and out of hand. This may sound legalistic, but it is one of the absolutes that is part of the Christian experience. The Christian lives and dies by the Book.

I am not advocating in this study anything that cannot be proved by Scripture, and I do not mean just a verse here and there, but by the whole counsel of God. We believe in the whole Bible, not bits and pieces. The whole Bible supports the idea of progressing toward spiritual perfection in our Christian lives. Spiritual perfection is what the apostle Paul longed for and spoke about:

> Not as though I had already attained, either were already perfect: but I follow after, if that I may apprehend that for which also I am apprehended of Christ Jesus (Phil. 3:12).

The crucified life is a life absolutely committed to following after Christ Jesus. To be more like Him. To think like Him. To act like Him. To love like Him. The whole essence of spiritual perfection has everything to do with Jesus Christ. Not with rules and regulations. Not with how we dress or what we do or do not do. We are not to look like each other; rather, we are to look like Christ. We can get all caught up in the nuances of religion and miss the glorious joy of following after Christ. Whatever hinders us in our journey must be dealt a deathblow.

The Christian Mystics

Throughout this study will be quotes from some of the great Christian mystics going back to the days of the apostles. It is important to define what I mean by "mystic." This term has been much abused in the house of its friends. Perhaps it would be good to use another term for this, but every time something is renamed, it loses some of its original meaning. Therefore, without any regret or hesitation, I will stick with this old term.

I have found throughout my study that these old saints of God, the mystics, really knew God. "Mystic," then, refers to someone who has an intimate, a direct, relationship with God. In my pursuit of God, I want to know what they knew of God and how they came to know Him on such intimate grounds. (This is not to say I agree with everything they wrote, as I would not agree with everything anybody else would write.)

Back on the farm in Pennsylvania, we had an old apple tree. It was a gnarly, stark-looking tree. A casual glance at this tree might tempt a person to pass it up. Regardless of how terrible the tree looked, however, it produced some of the most delicious apples I have ever eaten. I endured the gnarly branches in order to enjoy the delicious fruit.

I feel the same way about some of these grand old mystics of the Church. They may look gnarly and austere, but they produced wonderful spiritual fruit. The fruit is what really matters, not the appearance. It matters not if the man wears a robe or a suit; it is the man that really counts. I am willing to overlook a lot if the writer genuinely knows God and "knows God other than by hearsay," as Thomas Carlyle used to say. Too many only repeat what they have heard from somebody who heard it from somebody else. It is refreshing to hear an original voice. Each of these mystics had that original voice.

The Church has always had this group of people—both men and women—who had such a hunger for God and a passion to know Him that everything else took second place. Many of them were harassed and tormented by the established Church.

Some even were martyred because of this uncontrollable passion for God. Many of them lived prior to the Reformation and had no idea what a protestant or even an evangelical was. For the most part, they were not interested in labels. They were only interested in pursuing God.

These men and women were not protestant, Catholic, fundamentalist or evangelical; they were simply Christians in hot pursuit of God. They had no banner to wave except Jehovah-Nissi. They had no honor to preserve apart from Jesus Christ. They gave witness to a life ablaze with love and adoration for God that nothing can extinguish. Not all the years since their death have been able to quench the fervor of their love for God.

Fortunately, for us, some of the great devotional literature of the Church that these men and women gave their lives to write has been preserved. In reading these great works, one is transported out of time and into the mystical wonder of pursuing God. It is as if time has no bearing between the author and the reader. It is hard to read such material for long without feeling the heartbeat of the author's passion. This, in my opinion, is what is missing among Christians today, especially in the evangelical church.

Pick up any hymnal, particularly an old one, and you will find many hymns by these great Christian mystics. Their pursuit of God is only matched by their desire to share the object of their love with any and all who will listen. Perhaps one of their quotes throughout this study will light a fire in your heart.

The *King James Version* Bible

To avoid confusion, I need to mention why I use the *King James Version* throughout this study. Although I have every Bible translation imaginable, I still place the *King James Version* at the top of the list of my Bibles to read. I certainly am not against other translations. In fact, I am usually the first one to buy the newest translation, but I give predominance to this version in my reading and study.

I know all the arguments against the *King James Version*, but answer me this: If it is as bad as some scholars tell us, why has God blessed it so much? More people have come into the kingdom of God through this blessed translation than any other. It has been translated into more languages than any other version; perhaps more than all the rest put together.

Does it not seem strange that the generation with the most advanced technology and the easiest-to-read Bible translations is the weakest generation of Christians in the history of our country? Church attendance has never been lower, and the Christian influence in our culture never weaker.

For so long we have heard the complaint that people do not read and study the Bible because the language is antiquated. Yet the generation who had only the *King James Version* was the generation that sparked revivals and missionary movements around the world. It just may be that the Bible translation was not the problem. It is my observation that the natural man does not understand spiritual principles. The problem has never been the translation. The problem has never been academic. The problem has always been spiritual.

One important point many fail to understand is that the Bible was never meant to replace God; rather, it was meant to lead us into the heart of God. Too many Christians stop with the text and never go on to experience the presence of God.

The "old" *King James Version* has been so mightily used of God that it deserves a place of honor in our reading and study. Even the most casual reflection on the past will reveal that the Spirit of God has used it to move upon men, opening up their hearts and minds to understand the Scriptures. It has always been "the Spirit itself beareth witness with our spirit, that we are the children of God" (Rom. 8:16).

I would recommend that you go to some secondhand bookstore and buy a used *King James* Bible. You might have to put down a few dollars, but it will be the best investment you have ever made. I know the "thees" and "thous" are rather cumbersome, but one of the most beautiful things about these words is that they slow you down when you read. Probably there is no greater offense in all of Christendom than speed-reading the Bible. The Bible must be read slowly and meditatively, allowing the Spirit of God to open up our understanding.

The Christian Hymnal

The last thing I want to define is "the Christian hymnal." My heart aches as I see this increasingly being neglected by congregations. The Christian hymnal is one of the great depositories of the Christian life and experience. The men and women behind these hymns were writing out of deep spiritual experiences. The poetry of some hymns may not be perfect. In fact, some may be very difficult to sing. Pushing the hymnal aside, however, is to forfeit one of the great spiritual treasures of the Christian Church. The hymnal connects us with our Christian heritage, a legacy that should not be denied to this generation of Christians. If we are going to press on to be hundredfold Christians, on to Christian perfection and the crucified life, we need this vital connection to the historic Church.

Show me the condition of your Bible and your hymnal and I will accurately predict the condition of your soul. Our souls need to be nurtured and cultivated, and nothing does that better than the Christian hymnal. I cannot imagine a Christian not spending quality time in the hymnal. Hardly a morning passes when I don't kneel down with an open Bible and a hymnal and sing comfortably off-key the great hymns of the Church.

I often counsel young Christians, after they have their Bible and their Bible reading established, to get a hymnal. If a young Christian would spend one year reading through and meditating on the hymns of Isaac Watts alone, he would have a better theological education than four years in Bible college and four years in seminary. Isaac Watts and others like him were able to put theology into their hymns. These hymn writers—both men and women—set their generation singing theology. And the theology of the heart bursts forth in melodious adoration and praise.

Pursuing the Crucified Life

Living the crucified life is a journey not for the faint at heart. The journey is rough and filled with dangers and difficulties, and it does not end until we see Christ. Yet though the journey may be difficult, the result of seeing Christ face to face is worth it all.

Face to Face
Carrie E. Breck (1855–1934)

Face to face with Christ my Savior,
Face to face—what will it be,
When with rapture I behold Him,
Jesus Christ, who died for me?

Face to face I shall behold Him,
Far beyond the starry sky;
Face to face in all His glory,
I shall see Him by and by!

Only faintly now I see Him,
With the darkened veil between;
But a blessed day is coming,
When His glory shall be seen.

What rejoicing in His presence,
When are banished grief and pain;
When the crooked ways are straightened,
And the dark things shall be plain!

Face to face! O blissful moment!
Face to face to see and know;
Face to face with my Redeemer,
Jesus Christ, who loves me so.

THE FOUNDATION OF THE CHRISTIAN EXPERIENCE

God, who at sundry times and in divers manners spake in time past unto the fathers by the prophets, hath in these last days spoken unto us by his Son, whom he hath appointed heir of all things, by whom also he made the worlds.

HEBREWS 1:1-2

An old Chinese proverb says the journey of 1,000 miles begins with the first step. If that first step is not taken, nothing else really matters. If you are not on the journey, talking about it does not matter. Many Christians talk about living the crucified life but nothing in their lives indicates they have even begun the journey.

Among the thirtyfold Christians, there is much joy that they have been saved but no anticipation of continuing on the journey toward spiritual perfection. They are so happy they are not what they used to be that they cannot see what God wants them to be.

Christianity has a glorious and victorious side that few Christians experience. If I have anything to say to the Church of Christ and evangelicals in the world, it is in this area of the victorious Christian life, this living the crucified life.

Our weakness is that we are not going on to know Christ in enriched intimacy and acquaintance; and, worse, we are not even talking about it. We rarely hear about it, and it does not get into our magazines, our books or any kind of media ministry and it is not found in our churches. What I am talking about is this yearning, this longing to know God in increasing measure. This yearning should push us forward to spiritual perfection.

I believe two basic reasons explain this. One has to do with Bible teaching on the deeper Christian experience: Most churches never get beyond the basic teaching of becoming a Christian. Even then, the teaching is quite watered-down and usually focuses on the fact that someday we are going to die and go to heaven. The other reason has to do with the cost. Many are not willing to pay the cost associated with the victorious Christian life. Erroneously, many are taught and believe that the Christian life is a free ride that eventually ends in heaven. After all, Jesus paid it all.

Throughout this study, I want to address these two factors.

What Is a Christian?

The first factor to address is simply, what is a Christian?

All kinds of definitions are floating around, but only those rooted in Scripture are valid. How many people think they are Christians because someone told them they were? Imagine going through life believing you are a Christian because someone told you that you were; then you die and find out you were not.

Quite simply put, a Christian is one who sustains a right relationship with Jesus Christ. A Christian enjoys a kind of union with Jesus Christ superseding all other relationships.

This is the generation of questions. Everybody seems to have his own question. Questions are important to ask, but it is more important to ask the right ones. A successful lawyer will win or lose a case simply by the questions he asks or does not ask. There is no end to questions, and we can be bogged down trying to answer each and every little one. Finding our way through the maze of questions today is an all-but-impossible ride.

I believe this whole thing can be boiled down to one important question that, if answered correctly, will solve all the other questions and make them irrelevant.

The Important Question

It was never in the mind of Peter to talk about the heroic example of our Lord. Christ's teachings were noble, and His example is well worth imitating. The New Testament centers the emphasis on Christ crucified and risen and presents Him as the last alternate object of faith. The important question to ask, then, is not just "what is a Christian?" but "what think ye of Christ?"

Today's evangelical church is abuzz with questions. A person can spend all his time trying to answer them. "What do you think of the Bible?" "What do you think of the Church?" And there are others we could note, but all these questions are completely out of date.

For example, the question, "What do you think of the Bible?" is outdated and has no meaning since the Bible was confirmed by the resurrection of Jesus Christ. Jesus Christ endorsed the Bible in its entirety.

The question, "What do you think of the Church?" has no meaning either. Nobody can ask that and be truly sincere about it because Christ said, "On this rock I will build my church and the gates of hell shall not prevail against it" (Matt. 16:18).

These questions, and many more like them, are inappropriate. So the question before us, and the question that really matters, is simply, what do you think of Christ? And what are you going to do with Christ? Every question we might ever have can be boiled down to the subject of Jesus Christ.

Everybody needs to answer this question of what we are going to do about this man whom God raised from the dead. Christ is the last word of God to humankind. It is written:

> God, who at sundry times and in divers manners spake in time past unto the fathers by the prophets, hath in these last days spoken unto us by his Son, whom he hath appointed heir of all things, by whom also he made the worlds (Heb. 1:1-2).

It is also written that "the Word was made flesh, and dwelt among us" (John 1:14). When the Word became flesh, God spoke. He spoke His Word in flesh, and the incarnated Christ is that Word. That sums up all that God would ever say to men. No new development in human psychology requires God to amend or edit what He has already said in Jesus Christ.

Our question then is about Christ Himself, and all other religious questions are reduced to, "what do you think of Christ and what are you going to do about Him?" Unless this is fully addressed, nothing else really matters.

Some pretend to have problems concerning this. Actually, they are in love with themselves and are blinded by egotism and self-love. I respectfully claim the right to doubt the sanity of those who are now saying, "I have problems about the Bible. I have problems about the Church. I have problems about morality." All these problems are reduced to one. God spake His eternal Word in Christ Jesus the Lord, so Christ has settled every question.

The question of honest seekers looking for proof of Christianity is bogus. God's raising His Son from the dead is the only proof, and that proof is infinitely capable of settling the mind of anyone who is concerned and who is sincere. So the question is not what proof is there of Christianity, because we are not dealing with Christianity. We are dealing with Christ. We are dealing with a man who became flesh, walked among men, gave His life for man and, to complete it, rose on the third day from the dead. The question is not what you think of Christianity but what you think of Christ and what you are going to do about Him.

Neither does the sincere man ask, "Is Christ who and what He claimed to be?" Some claim they have doubts and question whether Christ is who and what He claimed about Himself. There should be no question here at all, because the Scripture says Jesus was approved of God among men (see Acts 2:22). Great volumes of books have been written that would fill any building from the cellar to the roof trying to show that Jesus is what He claimed to be. The worshiping heart knows He is what He claimed to be because God sent the Holy Spirit to carry the confirmation to the conscience of man. It does not lie with evidence. History can offer no higher evidence than the fact that God raised Christ from the dead and set Him at His own right hand.

Jesus' Moral Teachings

The question of the sincere man is not, "How does Jesus compare with the teachings of the moral philosophers and the religions of the world?" Some present this question with an air of pretentious self-importance. This question is settled forever because the moral teachings of Jesus stand or fall with Him. Let any man take issue with Christ and he is done as far as being a Christian is concerned. No one can take issue with the Lord; no one can question the truth of the Truthful One; no one dare bring up the matter of whether or not Jesus is the Lord or whether His teachings are sound or whether He is approved of God. His moral teachings stand or fall with Him. Jesus Christ our Lord Himself is the object of our attention, not the teachings of Jesus.

The teachings of Jesus are dear to us, and through them it is possible to keep His commandments and prove we love Him. It is the person of Jesus that makes His teachings valid. God put the proof down on a spiritual level. It does not rest on reason but on conscience. If the resurrection of Christ were to rest on reason, then only the highly reasonable people could be converted. If the resurrection of Christ were to rest on man's ability to gather and weigh evidence, then the man trained in the gathering and evaluating of evidence might believe, but the simple-hearted man could never believe. The man who works with his hands and does not do much deep thinking would remain unconverted. With Christ it was just the opposite. The common people heard Him gladly.

A "Pricked" Heart

The appeal of Jesus Christ was always to the simple-hearted man who was troubled by his conscience. He brought a troubled and lacerated conscience to Christ. The conscience knew that Christ had risen and appeared to Peter and 500 brethren at once, and God had approved Him, confirmed Him, validated Him, marked Him, sealed Him and proved Him to be His Christ.

All kinds of people are converted, and not because they have the ability to weigh evidence. If salvation depended on my ability to know if a thing were true or not, or on my ability to know as a court of law whether it witnesses to the truth or not, then of course only lawyers and persons trained in the legal profession would have any possibility of salvation. But this truth of Christ rising from the dead leaps past all human reason, rises above it and goes straight to the conscience of every person so that as soon as a message is preached, everybody can know it immediately. They do not have to ask. They do not need to ask. In fact, it is an affront to ask. Jesus Christ is risen and has appeared to His disciples. God confirmed His resurrection, sent down the Holy Spirit, and now the Most High God Himself, maker of heaven and earth, has already rendered the verdict. God has sent His Spirit to carry the verdict to the conscience of man.

According to the testimony in Acts 2:37, the result of Peter's preaching was that men "were pricked in their hearts." The word "pricked" here simply means pierced lightly. Pierced lightly and yet so deep that the original Greek word had a qualifying and intensifying prefix on it. When the Scripture says they pierced the side of Jesus with the spear and found that He was already dead (see John 19:34), the word "pierced" is translated from one word. The original word used in Acts has a qualifying and intensifying prefix to it, indicating that the words of Peter went further into the hearts of the hearers then the spear of the soldier went into the side of Jesus. So the Holy Spirit carried the spear point of truth into the hearts of the people and they cried, "What shall we do?" (Acts 2:37). Peter had the answer for them immediately:

Repent, and be baptized every one of you in the name of Jesus Christ for the remission of sins, and ye shall receive the gift of the Holy Ghost.

Peter was saying, "You are to believe on the Lord Jesus Christ and then prove you believed by identifying yourself with Him in baptism. You are to identify yourself with Him in baptism and prove and show to the world that you believe in this One that has been raised from the dead." The people gladly received his word and were baptized, and that same day about 3,000 were added to the Church (see Acts 2:41). Facts and reason cannot have such an effect. I could argue with a man, I could reason with him, I could preach to him, and if I were capable of doing so with the oratory of Cicero or Demosthenes, when it was all over I could only convince his mind.

Our consciences can be awakened by the presence of Jesus having come out of the grave. Some people have been fooled into believing that it was the life of Jesus that saved us. No, He had to die. Some say it was at the death of Jesus that we were saved. No, He had to rise from the dead. All three acts had to be present before we could truly say we have a Savior we can trust. He had to live among men, holy and harmless, spotless and undefiled. He had to die for man and then rise on the third day, according to the Scripture. He did all three. What the Spirit of God carries back home to the heart the Holy Spirit impales on our consciences, and we cannot escape until we have done something about Jesus.

What Is the Cost?

The second factor to address is what is the cost of the crucified life. Yes, Jesus paid for our salvation, but there still is a cost we must each pay. The Christian life is not a free ride.

The "Do" Condition

What shall we do? Peter was never afraid of the word "do." Some in evangelical circles are afraid of the word "do." They all but infer that it is an improper word. But Peter was not afraid of that at all, because it is not the "do" of merit—it is the "do" of condition. What should I do that I may receive the benefits of the Lord Jesus Christ into my life? Peter said, "Believe on the Lord Jesus Christ and identify yourself with Him by baptism."

That is what we are supposed to do. That is what Easter means, and you cannot escape it. We may only celebrate it once a year, but it haunts us all year; and if in the providence of God you should die this year, it will haunt you to the grave and throughout eternity. For God has given His Son, Jesus Christ, to the world and said, "Believe on my Son":

> Whosoever believeth in him shall not perish . . . [and whosoever] believeth not is condemned already, because he hath not believed in the name of the only begotten son of God (John 3:16-18).

This is the "do" of condition. If Christ is alive, then you must *do* something about Him. If He is alive, then He is on your conscience until you have done something about it. And that He is alive is proven by the coming down of the Holy Ghost to carry the evidence straight to the conscience of man.

An Impaled Conscience

Thank God, He lives. Thank God, the fight is over. Thank God, the battle is won and the victory of life is ours. But until you have done something about it, it is on your conscience and will remain there until the ages have rolled away. He is on the conscience of millions who are doing nothing about it and trying to live a crucified life without facing it.

Others may try to do that, but I cannot. Christ died for me. He took my sins. God raised Him from the dead and sent the Holy Spirit to say, "This is my beloved Son . . . hear ye him" (Matt. 17:5).

So I must hear, I must listen, I must identify, I must admit, I must follow, I must devote, I must dedicate. I must follow the Lamb wherever He goes. He is on my conscience until I do. My conscience is impaled with the fact that He rose again in triumph of the resurrection and the confirmation of the saving grace for the whole human race.

Christianity rests upon one foundation: Jesus Christ. Before anyone can understand the depth of Christian experience and the dynamics of living the crucified life, this foundation needs to be established. No building can ever exceed the capacity of its foundation. The more important the building, the more important the foundation.

The right question to ask is simply, "who is Jesus Christ?" And closely following that is, "what am I going to do with Him?"

What Will You Do with Jesus?
A. B. Simpson (1843–1919)

Jesus is standing in Pilate's hall,
Friendless, forsaken, betrayed by all;
Hearken! what meaneth the sudden call?
What will you do with Jesus?

What will you do with Jesus?
Neutral you cannot be;
Some day your heart will be asking,
"What will He do with me?"

Jesus is standing on trial still,
You can be false to Him if you will,
You can be faithful through good or ill:
What will you do with Jesus?

Will you evade him as Pilate tried?
Or will you choose Him, whate'er betide?

Vainly you struggle from Him to hide:
What will you do with Jesus?

Will you, like Peter, your Lord deny?
Or will you scorn from His foes to fly,
Daring for Jesus to live or die?
What will you do with Jesus?

"Jesus, I give Thee my heart today!
Jesus, I'll follow Thee all the way,
Gladly obeying Thee!" will you say:
"This I will do with Jesus!"

3

THE RESURRECTION SIDE OF THE CROSS

If ye then be risen with Christ, seek those things which are above,
where Christ sitteth on the right hand of God. Set your affection on
things above, not on things on the earth. For ye are dead,
and your life is hid with Christ in God.

COLOSSIANS 3:1-3

The starting point of our journey is knowing who Jesus Christ really is. It is at this point we set our faith like a flint toward the heavenly Jerusalem. Our ultimate goal is to see Christ face to face. As with every other type of journey, so the journey of living the crucified life has many obstacles. If we rest upon our own strength, we fail. However, there is strength in Jesus Christ that makes the Christian journey successful.

Success in the Christian life is not automatic. The soul must be cultivated like a garden and the will must be sanctified and become Christian through and through. Heavenly treasures must be sought, and we must seek those things that are above and mortify the things that are below. This may not be written about much in the annals of the modern evangelical church, but it *is* written in the New Testament.

Too many are satisfied with the status quo and never press on to become hundredfold Christians. Satisfied with just "being," many do not go on to "doing." Our objective is to finish the race. Many begin, but few cross the finish line. What is the secret to pressing on? Where is the strength to be found to endure the race until the very end?

The Reason for Everything

Christ's triumph over death, the foundation and fountain of our faith, was everything to the early enraptured believers. Christ's rising from the dead was first an amazing thing, then it became a joyful wonder, and then a radiance of conviction supported by many infallible proofs, witnessed to by the Holy Ghost. This became to the first Christians the reason for everything.

The battle cry of those early Christians was "He is risen," and it became to them outright courage. In the first 200 years, hundreds of thousands of Christians died as martyrs. To those early Christians, Easter was not a holiday or even a holy day. It was not a day at all. It was an accomplished fact that lived with them all year long and became the reason for their daily conduct. "He lives," they said, "and we live. He was triumphant, and in Him we are triumphant. He is with us and leads us and we follow."

They turned their faces toward an altogether new life because Christ was raised from the dead. They did not celebrate His rising from the dead and then go back to their everyday lives and wait for another year to pull them up from out of the mire. They *lived* by the fact that Christ had risen from the dead and they had risen with Him.

"If ye then be risen with Christ . . ." That word "if" is not an "if" of uncertainty. The force of the word is "since ye are then risen with Christ." Paul declared in Romans 6:4, Ephesians 2:6-7 and elsewhere that when Christ rose from the dead, His people rose with Him. Mortality rose with Him. Spirituality rose with Him. And this rising from the dead was and is an accomplished fact.

The Treasures of Heaven

What does Paul mean when he talks about "those things which are above"? This is not some broad generalization as it may sound. They can be identified. We may draw a line down the middle of a page and over on the left-hand side put the things that are of the earth, and over on the right-hand side the things that are of heaven. The things that are of earth belong to sight, reason and our senses. The things that are in heaven belong to faith, trust and confidence in God.

Over on the left-hand side, we put pleasures of the earth, and over on the right-hand side, we put delight in the Lord. On the left we put treasures of the earth; on the right we put treasures "where neither moth nor rust doth corrupt, and where thieves do not break through nor steal" (Matt. 6:20). On the left, we put reputation among men and our desire to stand well with men; on the right we put our desire to stand high with God. Over on the left we put a rich dwelling place; over on the right we put a mansion above. On the left, we put a desire to walk with the best company here below; on the right we put a desire to walk with God here below. On the left, we put following man's philosophy, and on the right, following God's revelations. On the left, cultivating the flesh; on the right, living for the Spirit. On the left, to live for a time; on the right, to live for eternity.

By contrast, we see how different we are as Christians. We are to be so different from the world, so completely different. Go down the left-hand side and you will have sight, reason and senses; they give you the pleasures of the earth that make you want the treasures of the earth. They want you to want a good reputation among men and a rich dwelling place here. They make you want to walk with the best company and follow man's philosophy.

The things that are of God make our faith, trust and confidence in God and make us delight in the Lord and value the treasures that are above. They want us to stand high with God in a mansion in heaven, to walk with God below and follow God's revelation, and to live for the soul and for eternity.

A Church Different from the World

Paul writes to Christians to address a great mistake that we are always making. We must know better, but we are always confusing the world with the Church and trying to get the world to do what we have difficulty getting Christians to do. We are always preaching sermons, writing articles and singing hymns trying to equate our country and our modern civilization—or any civilization—with Christianity. It cannot be done.

The Christian Church is something apart. It is not black or white or red or yellow. The Christian Church is not for Canadians or Americans or Germans or British or Japanese. The Christian Church is a new creation born of the Holy Ghost out of the stuff of Christ's wounded side, and it is another race altogether. It is a people, or a race, held above this present race, and we are to be different from the world because we are risen with Christ. "Seek those things that are above and set your will—set your mind—on the things that are above where Christ sits on the right hand of God." That is the heart and truth.

The Scriptures teach us that Christ is out of the grave, alive for evermore and constantly present for those who have faith. He gathers with His people wherever they meet, anytime they meet—even in a cave, hiding from persecution. It may be a mule barn or it may be a cathedral, but wherever the people of God gather, there is God in the midst of them. They minister to the Lord and pray. So the Church of Christ lives because Christ lives, and it does not depend on seasons of the year. Christ is out of the grave and will never be back in that grave again. Death has no more dominion over Him. Therefore, because He is risen from the grave, we too are to be risen with Him and to seek those things that are above.

Certain imperatives are set before us because Christ is risen, and every holy voice from heaven above cries and exhorts that we should perform these commands and live with them. The Scriptures say "seek" and "set." "Seek . . . and set your affections on things above" and put off the old ways, forgive everybody in the world and dedicate your time to Him.

Too often, we give God only the tired remnants of our time. If Jesus Christ had given us only the remnant of His time, we would all be on our way to that darkness that knows no morning. Christ gave us not the tattered leftovers of His time; He gave us all the time He had. But some of us give Him only the leftovers of our money and of our talents and never give our time fully to the Lord Jesus Christ who gave us all. Because He gave all, we have what we have; and He calls us "as he is, so are we in this world" (1 John 4:17).

Cultivation of a Religious Mind

As an example, we ought to have Christian minds. Our difficulty is that we have a secular mind and a religious mind. With the secular mind, we do most everything that we do, and then we have a little private party for what we call the religious minds. With our religious mind we try to serve the Lord the best we can. It does not work that way. The Christian should not have any secular mind at all. If you are a Christian, you should "seek the things that are above"—there should be no worldly mind in you.

Some might ask, "How can I pursue my studies? How can I do my housework? How can I carry on my business?" You carry on your business, do your housework and pursue your studies by making them a part of an offering to God as certainly as the money you put in the offering plate or anything else you give openly and publicly to God.

Living the crucified life precludes this divided life. A life that is partly secular, partly spiritual, partly of this world and partly of the world above is not what the New Testament teaches at all. As Christians, we can turn some of the most hopeless jobs into wonderful spiritual prayer meetings, if we will simply turn them over to God.

Nicolas Herman, who was commonly known as Brother Lawrence, was a simple dishwasher in the institution where he lived. He said he did those dishes for the glory of God. When he was through with his humble work, he would fall down flat on the floor and worship God. Whatever he was told to do, he did it for the glory of God. He testified, "I wouldn't as much as pick up a straw from the floor, but I did it for the glory of God."

One saint praised God every time he drank a glass of water. He did not make a production out of it, but in his heart, he thanked God. Every time I leave my house, I look to God, expecting Him to bless me and keep me on my way. Every time I am flying in the air, I expect Him to keep me there, land me safely and bring me back. If He wants me in heaven more than He wants me on earth, then He will answer no to that prayer and it will be all over—but I will be with Him over there. In the meantime, while He wants me here, I will thank Him every hour and every day for everything.

Let us do away with our secular and worldly minds and cultivate sanctified minds. We have to do worldly jobs, but if we do them with sanctified minds, they no longer are worldly but are as much a part of our offering to God as anything else we give to Him.

Behavior Like an Awkward Goose

Christ is risen, and we have risen with Him and sit at the right hand of the Father with Him in spirit—and one of these days with a human body. In the meantime, we're to act as if we are up there in heaven, but a little bit different. A farm boy comes to the city and acts different because he belongs on the farm. The city boy goes to the country and acts different because he belongs in the city. The man who has not been on a farm walks around gingerly, trying to keep out of the mud and keep his shoes from being soiled. He is acting like a city man on the farm. As Christians, we ought to act that way.

In a manner of speaking, we belong up there. Our culture belongs up there. Our thinking belongs up there. Everything belongs up there. Of course, when you are down here, people recognize you and say, "Well, that fellow belongs in heaven." I know a lot of people that belong in heaven. I suppose one of the ugliest things in all of the world is a goose walking around on the earth. But one of the most graceful sights in the skies is a wild goose with its wings spread on its way south or north. I suppose we act awkward here because we belong up there.

Those of you who work in big offices surrounded by people who are not Christians cannot easily fit into the conversation when break time comes. You act awkwardly, and you are worried and ashamed and wonder why. It is because you belong to God. You have another spirit; you know another language, and you speak this world's language with an accent.

When others mention religion, they talk about it with an accent. They belong to the earth; you belong to God in the skies and, of course, they do not agree. They think you walk awkwardly down here, but they have not seen you with your wings spread yet. Wait until the time comes when the children of God spread their wings and soar away to meet Him in glory. Then they will see how graceful they are. While on earth, of course, they do not think we are.

Jewels on This Earth

This matter of being hidden with Christ in God can be naturally divided quite into four segments. The first point, "your life." The second point, "is hid." The third point, "with Christ." Then the last point, "in God." Here are the jewels on the earth from the sky. Your faith is strengthened assurance, and here is the cure of all cures: "your life is hid with Christ in God."

The hope of the Church is that "when Christ, who is our life, shall appear, then shall ye also appear with him in glory" (Col. 3:4). That is the hope of the Church. Not all the details. We were too smart a generation ago when we thought we knew all the details. Everybody knew exactly everything that could be known about prophecy. It has gone the other way now. Everybody is afraid to talk about prophecy, because what we had been taught has been kicked out from under us and some of our views. No question, He will come and when He does come, you will be with Him in glory. Just as you were with Him when He died and with Him when He rose, you will be with Him when He comes in glory. In the meantime, you are supposed to act as you believe.

It's just like the new bride who must be separated for a little while from her bridegroom. She writes some letters and eagerly calls him long-distance. She wants to be with him. He is out there somewhere, trying to get a home together for them. She says, "I don't care about the house. I want to be with you." It is not the house with the trimmings and the furniture and all the rest that's important. She longs for *him*. So it is with Jesus Christ. We want Jesus Christ, and the glory will take care of itself.

The Glory of God

I have read the book of Revelation and the hymns of the church and have tried to learn what I can about the glory. Most of us do not know too much about heaven yet. We may be surprised by what we see there and what we call the glory. We cannot know any more than we do now until He comes, but we can know it with increasing intimacy. By knowing Him we will know the glory, because He *is* the glory of that place—the Lamb is the light there.

Living the crucified life begins on the resurrection side of the cross. Jesus is alive; therefore, we live. But it is not I. It is Christ all the way.

Christ the Lord Is Risen Today
Charles Wesley (1707–1788)

Christ the Lord is risen today, Alleluia!
Sons of men and angels say: Alleluia!
Raise your joys and triumphs high, Alleluia!
Sing, ye heavens, and earth reply: Alleluia!

Lives again our glorious King, Alleluia!
Where, O death, is now thy sting? Alleluia!
Dying once, He all doth save, Alleluia!
Where thy victory, O grave? Alleluia!

Love's redeeming work is done, Alleluia!
Fought the fight, the battle won, Alleluia!

Death in vain forbids Him rise, Alleluia!
Christ hath opened paradise, Alleluia!

Soar we now where Christ hath led, Alleluia!
Following our exalted Head, Alleluia!
Made like Him, like Him we rise, Alleluia!
Ours the cross, the grave, the skies, Alleluia!

Vain the stone, the watch, the seal, Alleluia!
Christ hath burst the gates of hell, Alleluia!
Death in vain forbids His rise, Alleluia!
Christ hath opened paradise, Alleluia!

4

THE LONELINESS OF THE CRUCIFIED LIFE

One thing have I desired of the LORD, that will I seek after;
that I may dwell in the house of the LORD all the days of my life,
to behold the beauty of the LORD, and to enquire in his temple.

PSALM 27:4

The man who wrote Psalm 27 was David. David sought after God because he knew that "they that seek the LORD shall not want any good thing" (Ps. 34:10). He said, "My soul thirsteth after thee, as a thirsty land" (Ps. 143:6). Further, David said, "Truly my soul waiteth upon God: from him cometh my salvation. . . . My soul, wait thou only upon God; for my expectation is from him" (Ps. 62:1-5). David also said, "O God, thou art my God; early will I seek thee: my soul thirsteth for thee, my flesh longeth for thee in a dry and thirsty land, where no water is" (Ps. 63:1). David continually says, "My soul followeth hard after thee: thy right hand doth upholdeth me" (Ps. 63:8).

That is the language of the man David. You will find this same tone going back to Abraham and reaching all the way through the Old Testament. Today we seek God and stop searching, whereas the early saints sought God, found Him and continued to seek more of Him.

Follow After and Love Deeply

Some great souls seem very unusual to us because of this tone in their lives. I do not set any of them on a pedestal, for they get their virtue where we get ours—from the Lord Jesus Christ. Their merit comes from the same fount as ours; and ours, the same as theirs. The apostle Paul said, "Not as though I had already attained, either were already perfect: but I follow after, if that I may apprehend that for which also I am apprehended of Christ Jesus" (Phil. 3:12).

This produced people like Saint Augustine and John Tauler, Thomas à Kempis, Richard Rolle, Bernard of Clairvaux, Bernard of Cluny, John of the Cross, Madame Guyon, François Fénelon and Henry Suso. These names may sound unfamiliar to some but they were associated with the "longing after" Christian crowd, those who cultivated the same tone in their hearts as David of old.

I could name names that might be more familiar: Samuel Rutherford, John Wesley, A. B. Simpson. A thirsting and a longing for the cool water *drove* these men and women. When they found Him, they sought Him again. What a tragedy it has been that in our time, we are taught to believe in Him and accept Him, and to seek Him no more.

This is where the evangelical church is today. What I am trying to do is encourage people to want to seek God. Any arrow toward the target must be going in the right direction. It is the direction and the motion that matters. If God is the direction and if you are moving toward God, then I am happy.

In the Old Testament is a book few people read. I hesitate to read it myself, because it is a little raw. Most people do not read it because they do not know what it means. I am referring to the Song of Solomon. One of the old mystics, Bernard of Clairvaux, started to write a series of sermons on the Song of Solomon (*Sermons on the Song of Songs*), but he had only finished preaching the first chapter at the time his death. So I suppose he finished it over in glory.

The Song of Solomon is the story of a girl deeply in love with a young shepherd. It is quite a wonderful love story indeed and has been understood so by the Church. One of Charles Wesley's hymns, "Thou Shepherd of Israel, and Mine," is based on this book:

Thou Shepherd of Israel, and mine,
The joy and desire of my heart,
For closer communion I pine,
I long to reside where thou art:
The pasture I languish to find
Where all, who their Shepherd obey,
Are fed, on thy bosom reclined,
And screened from the heat of the day.

Ah! show me that happiest place,
The place of thy people's abode,
Where saints in an ecstasy gaze,
And hang on a crucified God:
Thy love for a sinner declare,
Thy passion and death on the tree;
My spirit to Calvary bear,
To suffer and triumph with thee.

'Tis there, with the lambs of thy flock,
There only I covet to rest,
To lie at the foot of the rock,
Or rise to be hid in thy breast;
'Tis there I would always abide,
And never a moment depart,
Concealed in the cleft of thy side,
Eternally held in thy heart.

This great hymn talks about God without being flippant. Our mentality today, however, is an "I believe in Christ; now let's go have a soda" type of Christianity. The Church of Jesus Christ never runs on its head. The Church runs on its heart. The Holy Spirit never fills a man's head. The Holy Spirit fills his heart. The efforts today to "assist" Christianity with philosophy and science are going to get a cold frown from almighty God, and then He will let them go, little by little, their blind way into liberalism. Somewhere God will have Himself a people, and they will be those who continue to cry after Him whom they love.

This is no place for human ethics. The anonymous author of *The Cloud of Unknowing* wrote, "Of the shortness of this word, and how it may not be come to by curiosity of wit, nor by imagination. . . . Remember him by longing of God both tried to think their way through." In other words, it is not through your thinking or imagination that you will reach God. In all of this, there is an element of the unknown.

Futile Thinking

I will not settle for anything less than the deep divine addiction that we call God, and I will strive to live beyond the power of thought or visualization. The primary difficulty in the evangelical Church is that we have been trying to *think* our way into God. Nothing could be more futile and frustrating.

It is only through grace that you can have the fullness of the knowledge of God, but of God Himself can no man think. You cannot think around Him, equal to Him or up to Him. But that hunger for Him in your heart will reach out and search until it finds the object of His love, which is God Himself.

How then can we know God? How can we pierce the cloud of darkness and be smote with a sharp dart of longing love? It is the longing for God without any other motive than reaching God Himself. Many have come up short and are satisfied with the works of God and even theology. Certainly, thought is necessary and right, but it ultimately is powerless because the seeking goes beyond the realm of the intellect. You cannot get through to God with your head. William Cowper's hymn "The Light and Glory of the Word" reflects this:

> The Spirit breathes upon the Word,
> And brings the truth to sight;
> Precepts and promises afford
> A sanctifying light.
>
> A glory gilds the sacred page,
> Majestic like the sun:
> It gives a light to every age;
> It gives, but borrows none.
>
> The hand that gave it still supplies
> The gracious light and heat:
> His truths upon the nations rise;
> They rise, but never set.
>
> Let everlasting thanks be Thine
> For such a bright display
> As makes a world of darkness shine
> With beams of heavenly day.
>
> My soul rejoices to pursue
> The steps of Him I love,
> Till glory break upon my view
> In brighter worlds above.

A Mighty Infilling

Although it happened unintentionally, the Scriptures have become for some a substitute for God. The Bible has become a barrier between them and God. "We have our Bible," they say with a certain amount of pride, "and we need nothing more." Examine their lives and you may discover that the Bible has not really made an impact on their lifestyles. Remember, it is one thing to believe the Bible but something else altogether to allow the Bible, through the ministry of the Holy Spirit, to impact and change your life.

One problem some have is to believe that if they read it in the Bible, they have already experienced it. It is one thing to read about the new birth in the Bible and quite another thing to be born from above by the Spirit of the living God. It is one thing to read about being filled with the Holy Spirit and quite another thing to experience the mighty infilling of the Holy Spirit that radically changes our life to a life of adoring wonder and amazement at the things of God. Reading and experiencing are two quite different things.

Apart from the Holy Spirit breathing upon it, the Bible can be a useless thing, just another book of literature. It may be fine literature, but there is something infinitely more valuable than the Bible.

Appropriate the Promises

We might remember singing a little Sunday School chorus that says, "Every promise in the Book is mine." But we neglect to realize that it is one thing to believe a promise and quite another thing to appropriate it into our lives. It is like a man stumbling in the darkness of the night, not able to see his hand in front of his face. His companion asks, "How can you see in this darkness?"

"It's all right," the man might say, "I have a flashlight in my pocket." Simply having a flashlight in your pocket does not light your way until you pull it out and turn it on. Simply believing the Bible does no good until we pull those promises of God out of the Bible and by faith appropriate them into our lives.

One little saying that goes around in evangelical circles is "God said it, I believe it, and that settles it." The problem with that is that if you do not believe something to the extent that you appropriate it in your life, do you really believe it? The Bible exhorts us to "walk in the light." But the light has no value whatsoever unless we are walking in it.

Separate Yourself

Some Christians have come to the point where they have talked their way about as far as they can get. They will never get any further with their head, so they might as well put it to rest. It is the hungry heart that will finally penetrate the veil and encounter God, but this will be in the lonely recesses of the heart, far from things in the natural world. This is where God will meet us—far from the maddening crowd.

Study the Old Testament Tabernacle and you will get an idea of what I mean. The high priest had to go through various stages until he finally separated himself from the natural light and entered into the presence of Jehovah. In that presence was the supernatural illumination of God's presence.

With nothing to protect him but the blood offering and the assurance of God's promise, the priest stood there in the presence of that supernatural shining. He stood there alone. Nobody could accompany him into that shining place.

This is very hard for modern-day Christians to grasp. We live in an era of helps. At no other time in history have there been more helps with the Christian life than today. It is a strange oxymoron that the more Bible helps we have, the less spiritual power we exhibit. That's because these helps can only go so far.

The teacher can teach a student to read, but that is really as far as she can go. What that student reads is really up to him. The teacher can help him so far; then he is on his own. This is true throughout life. There are some things in life that must be done by ourselves. Nobody can help us. Nobody can assist us along the way. That is why there is a breakdown in evangelical circles today. We want to rely on each other. We want to exercise the "ministry of helps." We are nothing unless we have a crowd around us, not realizing that to penetrate into the very presence of God is a very lonely journey.

Although there may be many companions along the way as we live the crucified life, nobody can experience our experiences for us. Moreover, we cannot experience anybody else's experiences. It boils down to simply this: God and us. And when we come into His presence, we come by ourselves. Christian fellowship is wonderful, but there comes a time when even that becomes a hindrance. You will be alone even when a crowd surrounds you. Although there were 3,000 converted through Peter's preaching on the day of Pentecost, each was converted alone. When the Holy Ghost came at Pentecost, it did not set upon them en masse. It set upon them individually, and each went through the experience as if he were the only one present.

You probably want to help others, so do it as far as you can, but God wants you to press through to where there is no natural light to help you. You cannot lean on anything natural when you're in God's presence.

Make Up Your Own Mind

A man once wrote in an evangelical magazine, "I have accepted the doctrines of such and such a denomination." He had allowed somebody else to make up his mind for him. That is why millions of people are contented Catholics (or Methodists or Presbyterians), because somebody does their thinking for them. Somebody assures them, says a word of love and consolation, and has done all the thinking for them. Someone higher up has taken up all the responsibility. All they have to do is obey without question.

I do not mean to be unkind. I only say this is why certain religious denominations can hold their people and never say, "It is you and God." You have to find God "as the hart panteth after the water brooks" (Ps. 42:1). You have to seek God alone. I will help you with Scripture and do my best to help you, but when He meets you, it will be by yourself. You cannot take the authority of somebody else. Nobody can come and say, "All right, it's done. I hereby now as of today, at this hour, declare you are all right."

A young Christian earnestly seeking God once said to me, "I think you've got it." Thank God, I knew better, because that could have been the end of me. Our desire is for everyone to cry out to God and look in His direction with nothing but the naked intent of seeking God Himself. I want God and I want nothing more.

Some believe that "justified through His redemption" is simply a figure of speech. I believe that when Jesus Christ said, "He that receiveth me, receiveth him that sent me" (Matt. 10:40), He meant that *He* had received me. And I am not going to be shown up by some bright scholar who tells me that Jesus' words were some illustration drawn from a foreign court of law. Maybe the illustration or figure was drawn from there, but in back of that figure of speech, bolstering it, is the hard-core reality in my life and future and hope for that to be more than an illustration.

It is a glorious solid hard-core fact, hard on the rock of ages. For Jesus Christ removed all legal hindrances of why I should not to go to heaven. But I believe a holy God must run His universe according to His holy law. If He runs His kingdom according to His holy law, I don't care, because I have broken every one of His laws either in intent or on purpose. So justification must be somewhere. Redemption must be somewhere. Something has to be done legally to permit me to have God and for God to have me. And it *has* been done. Thank God, it has been done!

Believe God

There are times when all we can do is believe God and what He says. Believe Him in love. The author of *The Cloud of Unknowing* says, "God Himself can no man think. . . . He may well be loved, but not thought." Almighty God created the universe, and His presence overflows into immense degrees and can never be surrounded by that little thing we call our head, our intellect. He knows that all we can do is seek but never arrive at God.

Empty Yourself

One phenomenon of nature is that there is no such thing as a vacuum. It does not exist in nature, and neither does one exist in the spiritual world. As long as a vessel is filled with something, nothing else can come in. And here is where a spiritual law comes into play. As long as there is something in my life, God cannot fill it.

If I empty out half of my life, God can only fill half. And my spiritual life would be diluted with the things of the natural man. This seems to be the condition of many Christians today. They are willing to get rid of some things in their lives, and God comes and fills them as far as He can. But until they are willing to give up everything and put everything on the altar, as it were, God cannot fill their entire lives.

One of the strange things about God is that He will come in as far as we allow Him. I have often said that a Christian is as full of the Holy Spirit as he wants to be. We can beg to be filled with the Holy Spirit. We can talk about it, but until we are willing to empty ourselves, we will never have the fullness of the Holy Spirit in our lives. God will fill as much of us as we allow Him to fill.

As we create a sort of vacuum in our lives, we are in fact inviting the Holy Spirit to come rushing in. On the day of Pentecost, there was the sound "of a rushing mighty wind" (Acts 2:2). The reason for that was that those disciples stood before God, emptied of everything. They had room for nothing but God. And when they presented themselves as empty vessels before the Lord, He rushed mightily to fill them.

No matter what generation you look at or what century you study, you will discover a consistency in what the Holy Spirit is saying and doing. From the day of Pentecost on down to this present hour, there is only one thing on the Holy Spirit's mind: to fill the Church with His glorious presence. His message is simply, "Empty yourself, and I, the Holy Spirit, will come fill you to overflowing."

A Self-Deliverance

Some people might say, "Pastor, I would be a better Christian if I had a better pastor." I wish it could be so. But you know that would not be the case, because the better pastor you had, the more you would become a spiritual parasite and lean on him. Often the most spiritual people attend churches where the pastor cannot preach his way out of a wet paper bag. The reason is because they have no help from the pulpit, so they have to learn to lean on God. If you get too much help from the pulpit, you tend to become a parasite and lean on your pastor. I believe in the priesthood of believers.

Get delivered from yourself. When you are stuck so far down in the mud that only God can pull you out, it will be a sound that can be heard a block away. Stop thinking that you are somebody. Stop thinking that you can make it as a blessed theologian. You know just so much. As someone once said, "God by love may be known and we may be holy, but taught, never." Be careful not to try to enter into the deeper life by your wits or your imagination. Do not try to look to God by yourself and keep God in your own heart. I do not mean it is not all right to go to an altar to pray. That is another matter. I am talking about the loneliness of the soul that is cut out of the crowd.

Even as the woman pushed herself toward Jesus and was crushed in the crowds that were touching Him on every side, she continued to push forward and finally touched the hem of His clothes. He said, "Who touched me?" (Mark 5:31; Luke 8:45).

Jesus' disciples pointed out that He was crowded on every side, but Jesus said, "I didn't mean that. I meant who touched me in faith" (see Luke 8:46). The disciples were merely jostled. They were with Jesus, but they just got jostled. But the woman who was by herself, separate, pushed toward Him and was touched by Him in faith and love.

We need to have our hearts healed. We need to have God's anointing on our hearts. There is an old hymn by A. B. Simpson that attests to this fact:

Yes, there's balm, there is balm in Gilead;
There's a great Physician there!
Let us bring Him all our sickness,
Cast upon Him all our care.

The crucified life is a blessed but lonely life that no man can walk for someone else.

The Light and Glory of the Word
William Cowper (1731–1800)

The Spirit breathes upon the word,
And brings the truth to sight;
Precepts and promises afford
A sanctifying light.

A glory gilds the sacred page,
Majestic like the sun;
It gives a light to every age,
It gives, but borrows none.

The hand that gave it still supplies
The gracious light and heat;
His truths upon the nations rise,
They rise, but never set.

Let everlasting thanks be thine,
For such a bright display,
As makes a world of darkness shine
With beams of heavenly day.

My soul rejoices to pursue
The steps of Him I love,
Till glory break upon my view
In brighter worlds above.

PART II

. . . .

THE DYNAMICS OF THE CRUCIFIED LIFE

5

The Case for Going On into the Promised Land

Moses my servant is dead; now therefore arise,
go over this Jordan, thou, and all this people, unto the land
which I do give to them, even to the children of Israel.
Every place that the sole of your foot shall tread upon,
that have I given unto you, as I said unto Moses.

Joshua 1:2-3

You can always test the quality of religious teaching by the enthusiastic reception it receives from unsaved men. If the natural man receives it enthusiastically, it is not of the Spirit of God. Paul says plainly that the natural man cannot know spiritual things. To him, spiritual things are plain foolishness (see 1 Cor. 2:14).

There is a type of religious teaching understood, received by and perfectly logical to the natural man. But the natural man does not know that which is of the Spirit of God. He does not have the faculty to receive it.

The natural man is of this world. He may be in perfect health and have an IQ of 180. He may be as handsome as a Greek statue or, if a woman, a perfect example of fine womanhood. Or he might be a perfect example of the young American. The natural man, though he is in this state, is unblessed and out of grace.

Contrary to the natural man is the spiritual man. This is the Christian who is mature in his faith, who is led, taught and controlled by the Holy Spirit, and to whom the Spirit of God can speak.

Then there is the carnal man. The carnal man is the immature Christian. He is no longer a natural man, for he has been renewed by the grace of God and is in a state of grace, but he is not spiritual. He is halfway in between the two. He has been regenerated but is not advancing in his spiritual life. He is not influenced or led by the Holy Spirit but rather is controlled by his lower nature.

Of the three types, it is the spiritual man who is living the crucified life. He is indwelt, led, taught, influenced and controlled by the Holy Spirit.

Old Testament Prototypes

The Old Testament prototype of the natural man—those who are not in a state of grace—was Israel in Egypt. Four hundred years the Israelites had been in Egypt, and a major part of that time they had been in bondage to Pharaoh. Then came Moses who, through blood and atonement and power, led the children of Israel out of Egypt with the Red Sea closing between Israel and Egypt. That corresponded to the new birth.

Regeneration, or rebirth, makes the natural man a Christian, which takes him out of nature and puts him in a state of grace. Israel came out of Egypt and went across the sea, and the sea closed behind them and the enemy died. Israel for the first time in 400 years was a free nation, redeemed by blood and by power.

This is like the Christian who for all of his lifetime has been subject to bondages of various kinds—chains and shackles and manacles have been upon his spirit. Now, through the blood of the Lamb, the power of the Spirit, he is brought out of Egypt, and the Red Sea closes after him. We used to sing the hymn "I've Turned My Back upon the World" by Elisha A Hoffman:

I've turned my back upon the world
With all its idle pleasures,
And set my heart on better things,
On higher, holier treasures;
No more its glitter and its glare,
And vanity shall blind me;
I've crossed the separating line,
And left the world behind me.

These words describe exactly what happened to Israel in the land of Canaan. It was God's benevolent intention that the natural man in bondage in Egypt should come out of Egypt and make an 11-day journey to the holy land offered to Abraham by God in covenant. The holy land—variously called the Promised Land, the land of promise, and Canaan—was to be the homeland of Israel.

Israel was not only to be out of Egypt but also to be in the holy land, their spiritual homeland. God brought them out so that He might bring them in. This point has been lost in our teaching today. God brings us out, not that we may be out, but that we may be brought in.

God saves a criminal not so that he might tell about it once a year for the next 40 years but so that he might become a saint. God takes him out of his bondage that He might lead that person into the Promised Land. And the farther in the man goes, the less he will have to say about where he used to be. It is not the mark of spirituality when I talk at length about what I used to be. Israel wanted to forget what she used to be and remembered only occasionally to thank God for her deliverance.

Today, we magnify what we used to be and write books to tell the world about it. Paul said, "Those things ought not even to be mentioned among the people of God" (see Eph. 5:12). They are not even to be mentioned in conversation. God brought you out, but He does not leave you in limbo. He brought you out so that He might bring you in, and that was the will of God.

After God brought Israel out of Egypt, He showed them, after an 11-day march, the Promised Land. The enemy could have been driven out, and they could have had the holy land of promise God had given to them centuries before. They would not be stealing it. They would be occupying it as their proper possession. God, who owned it, had given it to Abraham and his seed after him. Abraham's seed had been driven out and into Egypt. God was now bringing Israel back to put them in the land. They were not to be usurpers—not to take the land—but to occupy the land, which was properly theirs by a gift of the One who owned it: God.

Metaphorically, God brought the Israelites out of sin so that He might bring them into the spiritual life. The Israelites' march was a God-blessed, God-hovered-over and Shekinah-enlightened journey straight through to the Holy Land. When they arrived in the land of promise from which Abraham had come centuries before, they were to be spiritual men. They represent an Old Testament prototype of the spiritual man.

The Natural Man

If you are a natural man, no matter how learned, how talented, how handsome or how desirable you are, you do not know a thing about God and you do not know a thing about the spiritual life. You do not have the faculties to know it.

If a man who is stone deaf sits reading while a Mozart Symphony is playing, you would not blame him because he would rather read than listen to the music. He does not have the ability to enjoy the music. The ability you have in you to listen to the symphony is dead in him.

Or if you were in an art gallery looking at paintings and there was a man completely blind sitting on the bench, you would not say, "Why is that Philistine just sitting there? Why doesn't he get up and look at the paintings?" He does not have the ability to look at paintings. The ability you have to look at paintings is dead in him.

No matter who you are or how learned or religious you are, if you have not been regenerated, renewed, made over, brought to the light by the quickening of the Holy Spirit, you cannot know God. You cannot know spiritual things at all; you can only know the history of spiritual things. Any enthusiasm you have for religion is but an illusion.

The Spiritual Man

Paul says that we Christians who are quickened to life—who are God's children, who are not in the state of nature anymore but in a state of grace—but who continue without progress year after year, wander spiritually instead of moving straight ahead. Sometimes we may get a little closer to Egypt than to the Holy Land; then we again get a little closer to the Holy Land; then back to Egypt. So we swing on our pendulum, back and forth, occasionally looking over the sea and remembering that we used to be slaves.

Then we go to a prayer meeting or some revival, put out our arms, and we move so close to the Holy Land that we can almost touch it. But we are not going to either place. We are not going back into the world, and we are not going to push on into the spiritual life. So back and forth we go, swinging between the old world we came from and the new world where we ought to be.

To continue without progress year after year is to develop a sort of chronic heart disease. Your heart becomes harder and harder as time passes. The best time to plunge into the deeper spiritual life is when you are a young Christian and have enthusiasm and can form deep-seated habits.

If I were to try to learn Japanese at my age, it would almost be hopeless. I could learn to read and write it. But I could never speak it well enough to be understood, because I have been around too long and my tongue and lips and palate have been too used to only having to form English words. All the little twists, turns and slurs of the English tongue fit my mouth. The older I get, the harder it is for me to learn a new language. However, a young person can pick it up and rattle it off in no time flat. The younger you are, the easier it is to learn and speak a new language because over time, habits have a tendency to harden you.

The Carnal Man

Now, what about the carnal man? The carnal man is the immature Christian who does not go on or advance. He is slowed in His spiritual development and is not influenced or controlled by the Holy Spirit but rather by his lower nature.

When Israel came to Kadesh-Barnea after marching a little while in the direction of the Promised Land, they stopped (see Num. 13–14). Moses said to them, in effect, "We're about to enter into the land that has been the object of your hope since God brought you out of Egypt."

Israel responded, "We're a little afraid. So send up 12 men to spy on the land." So Moses sent 12 men to examine the land and report back to determine whether they could take it or not. When the spies came back, all of them reported that it was an exceedingly good land. There was water there. To people in that country, water amounted to riches untold. It was more valuable than silver and gold and diamonds. So to report that this was an exceedingly good land in which there was much water was equivalent to saying that it was a sort of paradise.

They found grapes so large that it took two men to carry one branch between them. They found dates, which would have been our equivalent of sugar, candy, preserves, marmalade jelly and sodas. Everybody has his sweet tooth, and they had their dates. Figs and dates were probably the sweetest part of their diet. And there were pomegranates. Pomegranates are berries but are near enough to citrus fruit to have been classified as it. They are literally packed with vitamins. They would be well worth having.

Then there was milk and honey. When the Bible says "a land flowing with milk and honey," this is not careless language (Exod. 3:8). There were a great many bees in the land. There was so much honey that the trees could not hold it all, so it literally dripped down on great rocks. And there was abundant milk from sheep and goats. This land was so different from Egypt, the land they had come from only a little while before.

Now, after 10 of these 12 men came back and reported what the country was like, they nevertheless said, "We advise you not to go up into the land because although it is an exceedingly good land with lots of water, grapes, figs, pomegranates, milk and honey, the people are large and strong. There are giants there and their cities are great and walled up to heaven."

A land with brooks of water, grapes, figs, pomegranates, milk and honey does not sound to me as if it were being eaten up by its giant inhabitants. Besides that, the spies had not stayed long enough to watch the inhabitants eat up anything. The 10 men were simply frightened and filled with unbelief and advised against going on.

"Let's stay here in the wilderness," was their advice. "We're free of Egypt, thank God, and are not slaves anymore. We are in the wilderness, and while it isn't the best, we will settle for it rather than go up against those giants in that wonderful promised homeland."

Then Caleb and Joshua stepped to the head of the line and said to Moses, "We are ready to go in. Pay no attention to these pessimists. We can easily take the land, and there will be bread for us. The land belongs to us, our father's God gave it to us—gave it to Abraham, our father—and it's ours. Let's go take it."

Caleb and Joshua told of the rich advantages in the land and were unwilling to allow the large strong giants in the walled cities to keep them out.

All the teaching today about the Church being the perfect democracy and about how there should be no leaders is just plain poppycock with nothing in the Old or New Testaments to support it. Twelve leaders were sent to spy out the land, and the people were more or less dependent on what those leaders said. Just as you and I are similarly dependent in this democracy upon our leaders in Washington to a large extent. And in the Church of Christ, it is the same.

The people heard the unfavorable report of the 10 men; that is, the majority report. Caleb and Joshua gave the minority report, but they were only two. The people wept and fell down in front of their tent doors, wishing they had not come out of Egypt. They complained to Moses and said, "Would to God we were back in Egypt."

All the Israelites could see was walled cities and giants. They could not see grapes or goats with their great utters dripping with milk or trees drooling sweet honey down onto the grass. They could not see the rolling grasslands and the brooks and rivers. All they could see were the giants in the land. They forgot that God said, "Go up and I'll give it to you." So they said, "You'll kill our poor women. You'll kill our children."

This is always the unspiritual man's argument: "I've got to think about my family. I've got a family after all, brother, and God wants us to be wise, and I can't push this too far. I can't become too spiritual because I've got to think about my family. I can't subject my wife and children to difficulties. I can't lay burdens on them." Always pleasing their wives and family, such a man forgets that the best heritage a husband can leave his family is the memory that he was a good man. A spiritual woman also faces stumbling blocks. Her family may fight her with hot language, scold her with sarcastic speech, oppose her and make her feel like an idiot. However, a spiritual woman will walk quietly away, sadder but wiser, and will admit that the best heritage she can leave her family is that she was a good woman.

Had these Israelites only believed, they could have taken all their wives and families into the Holy Land within a few hours. They would have had all that land. Instead, for 40 years, they wandered in the desert. They had been so afraid that those wives and children were going to be killed if they went into that land that they ended up walking for 40 years, wandering round and round and round in the desert. Now swinging back near to Egypt where they had been, now a wide swing close to the Promised Land where they should be. Back again to Egypt where they were not, then around again, then by the loop again near to where they ought to be.

They wandered for 40 years until those children were grown to middle age and those women were dead. Forty years of it because the men had whimpered and said, "We can't go. It would cost us too much. We can't mistreat our families. We have to be with our families on Sunday nights and Wednesday nights and all during the missionary convention. We have to be with our families. We can't take a chance of our children becoming juvenile delinquents."

The best way for a husband to save his family from delinquency is to show them an example of a man who loves God uncompromisingly. A man who seeks to be spiritual, even though it costs him his blood. A man who doesn't listen to the devil's ruse: "You give more than you should to the Lord's work already, and if you seek to become a spiritual man, you will harm your family."

Israel wandered in the desert for 40 years by God's judgment. God said, "Doubtless ye shall not come into the land" (Num. 14:30). Their fear of death and their doubts and complaining displeased God because the people brought "a slander to the land" (Num. 14:36).

Every man who stands in the shadows and slanders the deeper spiritual life is slandering the sunshine. Every man who refuses to enter into the holy life is in the wilderness, slandering the homeland of the soul. For 40 years, Israel wandered aimlessly about. God was with them. He did not destroy them; rather, He let them die one at a time. Occasionally, He would punish them, but He did not destroy them as a nation.

Spiritual Failures

I refuse to be discouraged about anything, but it gives me a heavy heart to walk among Christians who have wandered for 40 long years in the wilderness, not going back to sin but not going on into the holy life. Wandering in an aimless circle, sometimes a little warmer, sometimes a little colder, sometimes a little holier and sometimes very unholy, but never going on. Habits have been acquired and are hard to break, and it makes it almost certain that they will live and die spiritual failures. To me this is a terrible thing.

A man decides to be a lawyer and spends years studying law and finally puts out his shingle. He soon finds something in his temperament that makes it impossible for him to make good as a lawyer. He is a complete failure. He is 50 years old, was admitted to the bar when he was 30, and 20 years later, he has not been able to make a living as a lawyer. As a lawyer, he is a failure.

A businessman buys a business and tries to operate it. He does everything that he knows how to do but just cannot make it go. Year after year the ledger shows red, and he is not making a profit. He borrows what he can, has a little spirit and a little hope, but that spirit and hope die and he goes broke. Finally, he sells out, hopelessly in debt, and is left a failure in the business world.

A woman is educated to be a teacher but just cannot get along with the other teachers. Something in her constitution or temperament will not allow her to get along with children or young people. So after being shuttled from one school to another, she finally gives up, goes somewhere and takes a job running a stapling machine. She just cannot teach and is a failure in the education world.

I have known ministers who thought they were called to preach. They prayed and studied and learned Greek and Hebrew, but somehow they just could not make the public want to listen to them. They just couldn't do it. They were failures in the congregational world.

It is possible to be a Christian and yet be a failure. This is the same as Israel in the desert, wandering around. The Israelites were God's people, protected and fed, but they were failures. They were not where God meant them to be. They compromised. They were halfway between where they used to be and where they ought to be. And that describes many of the Lord's people. They live and die spiritual failures.

I am glad God is good and kind. Failures can crawl into God's arms, relax and say, "Father, I made a mess of it. I'm a spiritual failure. I haven't been out doing evil things exactly, but here I am, Father, and I'm old and ready to go and I'm a failure."

Our kind and gracious heavenly Father will not say to that person, "Depart from me—I never knew you," because that person has believed and does believe in Jesus Christ. The individual has simply been a failure all of his life. He is ready for death and ready for heaven. I wonder if that is what Paul, the man of God, meant when he said:

> [No] other foundation can [any] man lay than that is laid, which is Jesus Christ. Now if any man build upon this foundation gold, silver, precious stones, wood, hay, stubble; every man's work shall be made manifest: for the day shall declare it, because it shall be revealed by fire; and the fire shall try every man's work of what sort it is. If any man's work abide which he hath built thereupon, he should receive a reward. If any man's work shall be burned, he shall suffer loss: but he himself shall be saved; yet so as by fire (1 Cor. 3:11-15).

I think that's what it means, all right. We ought to be the kind of Christian that cannot only save our souls but also save our lives. When Lot left Sodom, he had nothing but the garments on his back. Thank God, he got out. But how much better it would have been if he had said farewell at the gate and had camels loaded with his goods. He could have gone out with his head up, chin out, saying good riddance to old Sodom. How much better he could have marched away from there with his family. And when he settled in a new place, he could have had "an abundant entrance" (see 2 Pet. 1:11).

Thank God, *you* are going to make it. But do you want to make it in the way you have been acting lately? Wandering, roaming aimlessly? When there is a place where Jesus will pour "the oil of gladness" on our heads, a place sweeter than any other in the entire world, the blood-bought mercy seat (Ps. 45:7; Heb. 1:9)? It is the will of God that you should enter the holy of holies, live under the shadow of the mercy seat, and go out from there and always come back to be renewed and recharged and re-fed. It is the will of God that you live by the mercy seat, living a separated, clean, holy, sacrificial life—a life of continual spiritual difference. Wouldn't that be better than the way you are doing it now?

We're Marching to Zion
Isaac Watts (1674–1748)

Come, we that love the Lord,
And let our joys be known;
Join in a song with sweet accord,
Join in a song with sweet accord
And thus surround the throne,
And thus surround the throne.

We're marching to Zion,
Beautiful, beautiful Zion;
We're marching upward to Zion,
The beautiful city of God.

Let those refuse to sing
Who never knew our God;
But children of the heavenly King,
But children of the heavenly King
May speak their joys abroad,
May speak their joys abroad.

The hill of Zion yields
A thousand sacred sweets
Before we reach the heavenly fields,
Before we reach the heavenly fields,
Or walk the golden streets,
Or walk the golden streets.

Then let our songs abound,
And every tear be dry;
We're marching through Emmanuel's ground,
We're marching through Emmanuel's ground,
To fairer worlds on high,
To fairer worlds on high.

6

A Discontent with the Status Quo

For whosoever will save his life shall lose it; but whosoever shall lose his life for my sake and the gospel's, the same shall save it. For what shall it profit a man, if he shall gain the whole world, and lose his own soul? Or what shall a man give in exchange for his soul? Whosoever therefore shall be ashamed of me and of my words in this adulterous and sinful generation; of him also shall the Son of man be ashamed, when he cometh in the glory of his Father with the holy angels.

MARK 8:35-38

Following salvation, the Holy Spirit rises up early, encourages the new Christian forward and urges him to urge others to go forward. The idea of there being a better Christian life than most people know is neither a modern development nor a modern idea. It can be traced all the way back to the Old Testament and the experience of Israel.

The history of Israel is indeed an illustration of this truth. God led the Israelites out of Egypt miraculously, through the Red Sea, into the wilderness and on through and across the River Jordan into the Holy Land. All the way, Israel was led by a cloud during the day and a fiery pillar by night. The people drank water from a rock and their food was angels' food, which came down from above. The whole history of Israel is filled with one miracle right after another.

But it was not long before changes took place. These changes did not happen overnight but occurred gradually, over many years. Slowly but surely the Israelites moved from the center to the perimeter. They soon fell prey to externalism. Instead of being led by God day by day, they became content to live by rote. They did today what they had done yesterday because they did it the day before.

The Fire of Internalism

This is where the prophets of the Old Testament stepped in and called Israel back to the center, to following Jehovah.

It is the same with the Church today. God wants us to have content, but we are satisfied with mere words. When we can simply say words, we in a measure satisfy our consciences. We love form without worship, but God wants worship whether or not it has form.

Like Israel of old, the Church today is satisfied with words, ceremonies and forms. The words the prophets spoke to the Israelites are as true for us today: God wants us to have content, love and worship—internal spiritual reality of that inner fire of God.

Once this fire of internalism dies down, externalism begins developing. It is at this time that God sends prophets and holy seers to rebuke the hollow form of worship that is merely ritual and to plead for what we call the deeper life, or the crucified life. This Christian life is something deeper than the average life among Christians and is nearer to ideal New Testament Christianity, which should be the norm.

It is not difficult to see in the history of the Church a gradual shift toward externalism. Occasionally God bolsters His people with a mighty revival. He begins to pour out His power, and people are stirred and break away from externalism and the empty hollow rituals that are a big part of their worship. They break through to an experience with God that is above the norm and what they had known up to that point. Many of the great hymns of the Church have come out of these great moves of God.

The Mechanics of Institutionalism

As great and wonderful as these moves of God are, however, it does not take long to drift slowly back into externalism. Once externalism gets a good hold, institutionalism begins to take over. Then follows form, ceremony and tradition, and the church begins to celebrate what once was and those who once were. An external ceremony replaces the inner fire of the Holy Spirit.

The prophets of God objected to this. In the book of Malachi, there is one of the loveliest, tenderest little passages imaginable. It is the testimony of the prophet Malachi 400 years before the Maccabees and before Christ came. Malachi was the last prophet to appear to Israel to bring them the sacred word of God. Malachi rebuked and warned in every way he knew. He exhorted and urged the people who had drifted into externalism and were satisfied with the whirling machinery and the motion of the pieces and parts, but cared nothing about the beating heart of worship and the life within it. Here is Malachi's tender little testimony about a few of those whom we would say saw the deeper Christian life:

> Then they that feared the LORD spake often one to another: and the LORD hearkened, and heard it, and a book of remembrance was written before him for them that feared the LORD, and that thought upon his name. And they shall be mine, saith the LORD of hosts,

in that day when I make up my jewels; and I will spare them, as a man spareth his own son that serveth him. Then shall ye return, and discern between the righteous and the wicked, between him that serveth God and him that serveth him not (Mal. 3:16-18).

This company of people was not many, but they were the called. They feared the Lord and spoke often to each other, and the Lord was pleased, so Malachi wrote about them in the book. That was worship according to the Old Testament.

The Faltering of the New Testament Church

We then come over into the New Testament with all the wonders of the incarnation, the crucifixion, the resurrection of Christ and the pouring out of the Holy Spirit at Pentecost. The Church began as Israel before her had begun, in a blaze of life and power. The Church was known for its simplicity, along with faith, love, purity and worship.

But again, the inner fire was eventually reduced to the ashes of externalism. So, again, God sent His prophets. Saint Augustine met God in a marvelous and wonderful way. While living in the framework of the organized Church, Augustine knew God with trembling rapture and worship, and he wrote about it in his magnificent and justly famous books.

Then came Bernard of Cluny in the twelfth century. He dreamed that someday he might visit Rome, and after much effort and preparation, he succeeded in realizing his dream. He went to Rome and visited the very headquarters of the Church. There he saw what was going on. He saw the pomp and circumstance of the priests. He saw that form and ceremony, with very little true spirituality anywhere, even among those in high positions, had taken over. This so broke his heart that he went back to his little valley and hid himself away and wrote his famous "The Celestial Country," one of the most rapturous pieces of literature ever penned by any human being on this earth. It was a mighty cry of a man hungry after God, protesting against all the formality—and particularly against the corruption—he saw in the Church.

Saint Francis of Assisi came along also protesting this formality in the Church. I think most invariably his order grew out of a great revival in the heart of this man. He formed his order that he might give spiritual religion a chance to live again. He had no more than died and gone to sleep with his fathers when formality and externalism took over again. This has been the history of the Church down the years.

These men I have named rebuked and pleaded for a life that was real. God has always had His men to plead and earnestly long that they might be holy and might have within themselves what they knew the Bible taught.

The Appearance of the Protestant Church

So far, I have been giving examples from the Roman Church, but now let me come to the Protestant Church. I point out to you quite sadly, as I must, that this shift toward externalism is just as strong within the Protestant Church as it ever was in Israel or in the Church before Luther's time. The temptation to go outward toward words, traditions, forms, customs and habits is too much to resist. We carry on our backs whole loads of traditions that have no place in the work of God. Jesus taught, "In vain they do worship me, teaching for doctrines the commandments of men" (Matt. 15:9). If we can allow a word to stand for the deed, we will do the word and not do the deed.

Tarnished Stained-Glass Windows

Whenever I am in a city, I make time to visit some of the cathedrals and great religious centers, whether Catholic or Protestant. In one city, a man took me around and told me, "These windows that you see are exact replicas of a famous cathedral in Europe. The artist went to Europe, copied with exquisite precision the stained-glass windows of that famous cathedral and brought them back to this country. This is a perfect replica of such and such cathedral, all of these beautiful stained-glass windows."

Then he said something rather shocking. "I want to point out something to you. You notice here and there are what appear to be spots and splotches? Notice how down along the edge, close to the frame, there's a bit of discoloration?"

I noticed this and told him so. "These windows are hundreds of years old and have stood for centuries, as nations and kingdoms rose and fell, and they naturally got washed only by the rains. Now they've collected on themselves a certain tarnish and discoloration and the dust of the centuries. There were those who believed that the dust and discoloration actually improved and mellowed the windows and made them look better than they were before. So when the artist went over to copy them, they did not wash the windows nor did they try to copy the windows without the dirt. But they copied dirt and windows so that what we have here is not only the artistry and the stained-glass windows of the cathedral, but we have in addition, perfectly reproduced, the centuries-old dust that gathered on the windows."

Those windows are a perfect illustration of what happened with Israel, what happened with the Early Church of Christ, and what happened with every order that has ever been established and every new denomination that has ever been born out of an earnest desire to bring men to God. They become like those tarnished stained-glass windows. The dust of the centuries gets on them and becomes a part of their beliefs and part of their practices, so they are hardly able to tell which is of God and which is simply the accumulation of tarnish from the centuries.

That is exactly what we have done in our time. Do not imagine for a minute that we have been without our prophets and seers who have stood and warned us and tried to bring us back to God. God still has those who are not content with superficial worship. They are not all of one denomination, but they are discontent with surface religion. They long to recapture the true inwardness of the faith, and they insist upon reality. They do not want anything artificial; they want to know that whatever they have is real. They would rather it be small and real than large and unreal. "A living dog is better than a dead lion," as it is said in the Old Testament (Eccles. 9:4).

And so it is better to have a little church that is real than a big church that is artificial. It is better to have a simple religion that is real than to have a great ornate ceremony that is only hollow and empty.

New Testament Exclusivity
Unfortunately, there are those who want nothing apart from the New Testament. They live among God's people everywhere. I find them here and there in my travels and I believe there are some in almost every religious group. Remember this: You and I are brought to the Bible, which is our rock from which we drink our water. This is our manna. This is our blueprint upon which we build our cathedral. This is our guide through the desert in the wilderness. This is our all in all, and we want nothing else. The people that I'm talking about want nothing except what is in the New Testament.

81

The difficulty down the years, as a rule, was not that men taught wrong doctrine, but that they did not live up to the doctrine they taught. This did not become apparent until a reformer or a prophet came along to rebuke the Church for holding the doctrine without having the inward reality of it. When such men like John Wesley came along, they did not try to straighten out the Church or correct its doctrines. They insisted on a witness in the heart that the things being taught are real in us. We follow these reformers and prophets because they found reality in the Word of God for their own hearts and they wanted nothing outside of the Bible. They simply wanted what the Bible had for them.

These of which I speak had only one source of riches, and all those riches are in Christ. For them, Jesus Christ was enough. It was not Christ plus something else. Jesus Christ was their all in all, fully sufficient. Those who seek the deeper Christian life and those who want the riches that are in Christ Jesus the Lord seek no place, no wealth, no things, only Christ.

Coattail Riders

So many men these days are using religion as a source of wealth, fame, publicity or something else. They are using religion to get something for themselves. It is obvious that they are taking advantage of whatever happens to be current, riding the coattails of whatever new thing has come along. I have outlived innumerable sheaves of men who came along and tried to cash in on whatever was popular at the time.

While these men latched on to whatever was popular at the moment, I went right on preaching the gospel. I never preached to big crowds, at least not in my own church. But I preached a consistent Christ. This desire of wanting to get a following, to be well known, to get a reputation, is not for those who are living the crucified life. Those who walk and live the crucified life have no desire for these things and are willing to lose their reputations if they must in order to get on with God and go on to perfection. They seek no place, no wealth, no thing. Those who long after God will not turn their heads to be elected anywhere to anything. Only static Christians seek after high ecclesiastical positions. They want to be somebody before they die.

Occasionally I hear about some big shot in the eyes of the world who has died. Immediately I say to myself, *What now, brother? While you lived, you climbed the ladder of success, trampling other men down in the name of Christ and religion. Now you are dead. The worms will eat you; and your poor spotted, tarnished soul and you now face the Judge of all the earth. What now, man?*

The Crucified Life of God Seekers

Those living the crucified life do not seek place or wealth, fame or high positions. Rather, they want to know God and to be where Jesus is. Only to know Christ—that is all. Paul said, "Yea doubtless, and I count all things but loss for the excellency of the knowledge of Christ Jesus my Lord: for whom I have suffered the loss of all things, and do count them but dung, that I may win Christ" (Phil. 3:8).

The seekers after God are deeply dissatisfied with mere form. You cannot fool them with painted toys; they want content.

In *all* denominations everywhere, there are godly people seeking the face of Jesus. And kindness and charity lead me to say that I think some of them are over on the other side of the fence. For example, Thomas Merton was a seeker after God. I believe he was an example of those who have never left the ancient Roman Church and who know God and are seekers after God. I personally cannot see why they do not leave, but I believe there are a few other such people. So God has His people everywhere, known by the fact that they hate mere form. Even though they may go through with it, they have something within them that is bigger than all of that.

When Brother Lawrence (born Nicholas Herman), author of *The Practice of the Presence of God*, was in his monastery, he said:

I learned to pray to God all by myself. I just talked to God all the time, everything I was doing—washing dishes, traveling, whatever I was doing—I was talking to my heavenly Father. I developed such a sense of God's presence around about me that I never lost it for 40 years. I did not need their forms. They told me set times to pray, and I did it. I was obedient. I prayed at set times, but it did not mean a thing anymore than it did at any other time. I had learned the inner secret of fellowship with God myself. I'd already found God and I was in communion with God all the time.

Brother Lawrence did what he was told and smiled, but he said it did not mean anything.

The Progress of the Average Christian Today

The average Christian's progress today is not sufficient to satisfy the longings of the seekers after God. They want something better than that. The average Christian today does not make much spiritual progress at all. He is converted, joins the Church, and five years later he is right back where he started. Ten years later, he is still where he was or he has even slipped back a little. That is not satisfactory to those who seek and thirst and hunger after God. "As the hart panteth after the water brooks, so panteth my soul after thee, O God. My soul thirsteth for God, for the living God" (Ps. 42:1-2). That is the testimony of a seeker after God. He is not going to let somebody's slow snail's progress keep him back.

Such seekers after God are impatient with the substitutes being offered today. When you do not have anything real inside of you, you try to get something on the outside that suggests something real. It is a well-known fact that when the fire goes out in the furnace, they paint the outside to make it look as if the fire was still there.

Unfortunately, the Church is the same. And this even includes evangelical and so-called full-gospel churches. Something from its heart has been lost, so bangles and dangles are used on the outside in order to pretend there is something real on the inside. But you cannot fool seekers after God with this kind of thing. They know better.

What have we come to, that the people of God are not shocked enough by Calvary, a man dying on a cross on a hill outside Jerusalem? And not just a man, but the Godman, dying for the sins of the world? Why does this leave them dull and unmoved? The recent outburst of modern theatrics has now taken over Protestantism. What started in the beginning as a small seed has grown; the dragon's seed has grown more dragons. The seekers of God do not like what's happening, and the hungry-hearted saints of God do not want it, so they read with great eagerness the lives of holy men in the devotional books from centuries past. But where is the *doing*?

The Fellowship of Prophets

I wonder if you have ever read *Sermons on the Song of Songs* or *On Loving God* by Bernard of Clairvaux. Have you ever read *Dark Night of the Soul* by Saint John of the Cross? Or *The Scale of Perfection* or *The Goad of Love* by Walter Hilton? Or *The Amending of Life* by Richard Rolle? Or *The Life of the Servant* or *A Little Book of Eternal*

Wisdom by Henry Suso? Or the great sermons by John Tauler and Meister Eckert? What about *The Imitation of Christ* by Thomas à Kempis? Or *Introduction to the Devout Life* by Francis de Sales? Or *The Cloud of Unknowing* or *The Letters of Samuel Rutherford* or the works of William Law or the letters of François Fénelon or the journal of John Fox? What about the writings of Nikolaus von Zinzendorf and Andrew Murray and John Wesley and A. B. Simpson? These men rose like the prophets of Israel and did not change their doctrine; they just professed it against the hollow externalisms of the world. They sought to recapture again the glory that was in Jesus Christ the Lord, of worship and prayer and the desire to be holy.

The men I have named formed a sacred fellowship through the years. But I do not find them, by any means, in the mainstream of evangelicalism today. There are men in evangelicalism today who are just ordinary men with no longing after God. They grind out their sermons week after week, take little trips here and there, fish and play golf and fool around and then come back and preach. They go on and spend their lives that way. But you cannot speak with them for long because there is nothing of substance to talk about after you have done a little chitchat business.

Not all preachers are that way. There are some whom you can speak with for hours on end and talk about God and Christ. These people are practical and clean and coolheaded and have no sympathy with false doctrines, and they keep away from extremes of excitement and fanaticism. They just want to know God and want to be holy. They want to seek the face of Jesus until they are aglow with His light.

I have described these men and women because what I really want to know is whether I described you. It is not a matter of how deep you have come, but do you have your diving suit on?

It is not how far the arrow has sped, but has the arrow left the bow? It is not that you are perfect but that you thirst after perfection. Or is your religion social? Are you satisfied with the once-on-Sunday sort of religion?

God has given you the wind, the rain, a body to contain your wonderful soul. He has given you an amazing mind and many fine abilities. He sustains you, holds you up, keeps your heart beating and waits to receive you yonder. But do you toss Him a crumb, so God gets what is left behind? Does God get only the tattered bits of your time, yet you say you are a follower of the Lamb? Do not fool yourself. You are not if you don't go deeper into the crucified life.

Are you weary of externalism, and do you long after God? I long after God. This is not old age talking, and this is not the result of anything I have been reading, except the Bible. This has been growing in me through the years. The only gratifying thing I have apart from my communion with God is the knowledge that I am not alone in my journey. God has His people everywhere who are in revolt against pretense, textualism, externalism and tradition. They want to seek God for Himself, as He is in the Scriptures, as revealed by the Holy Spirit.

God has His people, but there aren't many of them. Are you one?

A Mighty Fortress Is Our God
Martin Luther (1483–1546)

A mighty fortress is our God, a bulwark never failing;
Our helper He, amid the flood of mortal ills prevailing:
For still our ancient foe doth seek to work us woe;
His craft and power are great, and, armed with cruel hate,
On earth is not his equal.

Did we in our own strength confide,
Our striving would be losing;
Were not the right Man on our side,
The Man of God's own choosing:
Dost ask who that may be? Christ Jesus, it is He;
Lord Sabaoth, His Name, from age to age the same,
And He must win the battle.

And though this world, with devils filled,
Should threaten to undo us,
We will not fear, for God hath willed
His truth to triumph through us:
The Prince of Darkness grim, we tremble not for him;
His rage we can endure, for lo, his doom is sure,
One little word shall fell him.

That word above all earthly powers,
No thanks to them, abideth;
The Spirit and the gifts are ours
Through Him who with us sideth:
Let goods and kindred go, this mortal life also;
The body they may kill: God's truth abideth still,
His kingdom is forever.

7

BREAKING THE STATIC CONDITION AND GOING ON

*Stand fast therefore in the liberty wherewith Christ hath made us free,
and be not entangled again with the yoke of bondage.*

GALATIANS 5:1

One of the great problems dating back to the Early Church was that of the static Christian. The static Christian is one who is slowed in his spiritual progress. This is a problem we need to face today in the Christian Church. The great challenge is how do we get such Christians interested in becoming more than the average run-of-the-mill type of believers we see everywhere. So many Christians are static or are becoming static in their Christian experience.

The apostle Paul said, "Ye did run well; who did hinder you that ye should not obey the truth?" (Gal. 5:7). So the spiritual progress is stunted, slowed and going nowhere—it is static. Along with this is a lack of moral dynamics, which every Christian ought to know. I believe, if we will listen, we will hear God speaking: "He that hath an ear, let him hear what the Spirit saith unto the churches" (Rev. 2:7). If we could hear what the Spirit is saying today, we would hear Him say:

Moses my servant is dead; now therefore arise, go over this Jordan, thou, and all this people, unto the land which I do give to them, even to the children of Israel. Every place that the sole of your foot shall tread upon, that have I given unto you, as I said unto Moses (Josh. 1:2-3).

I earnestly believe we will hear the Spirit of God say, "Let us go on to perfection." Let us go beyond repentance from past sins, let us get beyond forgiveness and cleansing, let us go beyond the impartation of divine life. Let us first be sure we get these things settled to the point of absolute assurance. No deeper life can exist until life has first been established. No progress can be made in the way until we are in the way. No growth can happen until there has been new birth. All the efforts toward a deeper life, the crucified life, will only bring disappointment unless we have settled the matters of repentance from dead works, the forgiveness of sins and the impartation of divine light and conversion.

I want to break down for you two rather important requirements of the crucified life. These two things will go a long way in breaking the static condition. First, living the crucified life involves completely forsaking the world. Second, the crucified life means turning fully to the Lord Jesus Christ. This is the emphasis of the Bible in both the Old and New Testaments and is the standard formula that has come down to us from the very early days of the Church. You will find it written into the great hymns of the Church and the great books of devotion down through the years. These two things are necessary for a Christian who wants to go on and break the static condition of his life and become a growing, moving, progressive, dynamic Christian.

Completely Forsake the World

It is entirely possible to be religious, go to church every Sunday and yet not to have forsaken the world at all. The proof is that you will find professed Christians wherever you will find non-Christians. I want to be as broad-minded and fair as I can about this. I suppose there are places where you will not find a man claiming to be Christian. I do not know whether criminals who habitually destroy those who are their rivals—taking them out and shooting them—I do not know whether you find any professed Christians among them or not. I do know, however, that when certain criminals have died—by the bullet or whatever means—they have been heard to mumble something about their faith in God, and I suppose they think they have been escorted into the kingdom of God. Some people, though, try very hard to get these bloody men into the kingdom of God, unsaved, unblessed, unshriven, unforgiven. Men who don't even have the time to say, "God have mercy on me as a sinner." People try to get them into heaven simply by performing a religious service or by saying the criminal was a member of some religion or another.

I remember a young man who was a murderer had been sentenced to die in the electric chair in the Cook County Jail. His death had been set for certain day, but the date was changed because the original date fell on a holiday of his religion. They did not want to put him to death on a holy day of his religion. So they changed the day of his death to honor his religious holiday.

So you will find Christians—or those who claim they are Christians—just about everywhere. There has never been a sport invented so violent and vicious that you will not find Christians sitting around watching it with a New Testament in their hip pocket. I do not think there is any worldly pleasure anywhere that you will not find a Christian partaking of it. It is possible to be religious and not forsake the world. It is possible to forsake the world in body yet never forsake it in spirit. It is possible to forsake the world externally and still be worldly inside. Yet nobody can be a Christian in the right sense of the word until he has forsaken the world.

Isolated Nuns

The situation among nuns has been exactly that—forsaking the world and fully turning to Christ—but not among them all. I do not say this because I am a Protestant but because I have read what they have had to say about themselves. Great Christian souls tried to reform nuns in the thirteenth century and get them to be in their inner life what they were in their external outer life. They were hidden away from the world and their bodies were dressed in a certain way in order to show that they were separated from the world. Yet some of these great souls declared that these very people who separated themselves from the world were worldlier than some of those who were not so separated.

Great devotional writers tried hard to rouse the Church of their day that the nuns should be inwardly what their profession showed them to be outwardly. One such writer was Walter Hilton, who lived 200 years before Luther was born, so he never heard of Protestantism or the Reformation. Yet this English Christian was so strong in his faith that he wrote a series of letters to the nuns of a certain convent and warned them of this very thing. That series of letters is called *The Scale of Perfection*. It is a most wonderful book.

The opening chapter of this book is devoted to this subject. Hilton challenges the sisters to live on the inside what they appear to be like on the outside. In essence, he says, "You have come out of the world and closed the door on yourself and put on a certain garb, which indicates you are separated from the world. Now look out that you do not take the world with you into the nunnery and be as worldly in there as you were out on the street. Remember that it is the forsaking of the world in your heart that makes you unworldly."

Hilton urgently warns that it is entirely possible to put on the garb of the nun, live in a nunnery and still be worldly inside. It is possible to be religious and not forsake the world, and it is possible to forsake the world in body but not in spirit. It is never possible, however, to forsake the world in spirit if it is not forsaken in practice.

Shaky Sanctification

It is necessary to mention this because some supposed broadminded Christians would do almost anything that anybody will do. I have noticed that all you have to do is add "for God" or "for Jesus" onto a thing and, lo and behold, that which the Church has repudiated and earnest Christians have for years forsaken suddenly becomes sanctified. "I'm doing it for God." "I'm doing it for Jesus."

If you just get those prepositional phrases in at the end, something that was not ever counted right by the Church down through the generations, it is now suddenly looked on as right. This attitude takes in almost everything that the world has ever done. I am expecting one of these days to hear about the Association of Christian Bartenders who are "doing it for Jesus." "Oh, we're not like the world. We're not serving up this poison just in our own name. Before we accepted Christ, we used to deal this out for our sakes and for the money we made out of it, but now we're doing it for Jesus." The situation has not gotten that far yet, but give it time—we are on the way. All we have to do is wait a little, and we will sanctify almost anything by saying we do it for Jesus.

I warn you that you cannot do anything for Jesus that Jesus would not do. You cannot do anything for God that God has forbidden and turned the canon of judgments against. The only thing I can do for God is that which is holy like God, and the only thing that I can do for Jesus is that which Jesus has allowed and permitted and commanded me to do. But to live like the world and say, "I'm separated from the world in spirit, and I don't have to separate from the world because I'm separated in spirit" is contradictory. I know where this idea came from. If you sniff a little, you know what you smell? Brimstone. Because that statement comes from hell and certainly belongs there and does not belong in the Church of Christ. It is never possible to forsake the world in your spirit and not forsake it in reality. Let me illustrate what I mean.

Some Biblical Examples

Look at Noah. God said to Noah, "I'm going to destroy the world. Make me an ark; make it out of gopher wood" (see Gen. 6:13-14). Noah obeyed.

Now just suppose I had preached on separation from the world and said to Noah, "Noah, don't you think you ought to get into the ark?"

"Why," Noah would say, "that's the old-fashioned idea. After all, what is the world?"

The modern Church cannot agree on what is meant by "the world." According to modern teaching, "I am separated from the world in my heart, but I am going to stay right down here on the ground and sleep under the bushes and eat off the tree and live like other people. But I won't be of the world because I'm separated in my heart."

What would have happened to Noah if he had had that attitude? Before long he would have been sending up bubbles when the fountains of the great deep broke, the rain came down and the flood covered the mountaintops. Noah's body would have floated and descended along with the rest. However, Noah knew that to forsake the world meant to forsake the world. The Bible says he went into the ark, and God closed the door (see Gen. 7:16).

Now look at Abraham. God said, "Abram, get thee out of thy country, and from thy kindred . . . unto a land that I will shew thee" (Gen. 12:1). Abraham could have said, "I've had a call from God to forsake my country and my people and go to another land. But I do not think I should take that literally. I think that means forsake in spirit, so I'm going to live right here in Ur of the Chaldeans, and I'm going to go into the Holy Land in spirit."

Ridiculous. Abraham had to get out of the country in fact, so he departed, with Lot and his family. He had to forsake one thing in order to enter into the other.

Take *Lot* as another example. Lot finally got to Sodom and became an official of the town. The angels came to him and said, "Escape for thy life; look not behind thee" (Gen. 19:17).

Lot could have said, "Let's have a panel discussion on 'escape for thy life, look not behind thee.' What does it mean?" While engaged in discussing and debating the issue, the fire would have fallen and destroyed Sodom and Lot along with the rest. But Lot knew that "escape for thy life" meant get out of Sodom and stay out, for fire is coming.

The Christian Community
When the Early Christians were told that the love of the world and the things of the world meant they did not love God, they did not hold discussions on what "the world" meant or how far they could go and still please God. They got out of the world; they separated themselves completely from everything that had

the world's spirit. The result was that they brought down the world's fury on their own heads.

The world that existed then still exists today. The great God Almighty either now or later will confirm the truth of it, but the world is no different now than it was when they crucified Jesus and martyred the first Christians. It is the same world. Adam is always Adam wherever you find him, and he never changes. The reason we get along with the world so well is that we have compromised our position and allowed it to dictate to us while we in turn are permitted to dictate very little to the world. The result is that very few of us are in any way embarrassed by the world.

What the Church needs to fear is becoming accepted in the community. Any church that the unsaved worldly community accepts is never a church full of the Holy Spirit. Any church that is full of the Holy Spirit, separated from the world and walking with God, will never be accepted by any worldly community. It will always be looked on as being somewhat out of the ordinary. The laws might be set to protect us, and civilization might be such that Christians will not be physically attacked, but crucified Christians will be looked on as being a little bit off-center from what is considered the norm.

Someone once suggested that every Christian should get into a spacesuit, zoom out of here and get as far away from the world as possible. I am not saying that at all. I *am* saying that there is a world that is not the world God means when He said, "Love not [forsake] the world." You need to work and live and drink and sleep and bathe and grow and beget your kind and bring your children up in the world God made. That is not the world I am referring to.

The world we are to forsake is the one that organizes and fills itself with unbelief. The world that passes to amuse itself and build itself upon doubts, unbelief and self-righteousness. Jesus was in the world but not of the world. There is no contradiction here in what I am saying. There is a distinction between that part of the world that is divinely given, where Christians plant, reap, sow, work and live in the world by following God's commandments. God meant it to be so, and that is not "worldliness." Worldliness is the pride of life and the desire for what the eye sees and the longing of the ambitious soul for position and all that which the world does because of the sin in it. This includes all that is the world that overflows into a thousand things the Church has traditionally rejected.

Turn Wholly to the Lord Jesus Christ

So, the first step is to forsake completely the world, which is all negative, and turn your back on it. In so doing, you turn wholly to the Lord Jesus Christ, which is all positive. It is impossible to have a positive without a negative. The battery in your automobile is both positive and negative. If it were 100 percent positive, it wouldn't work. And if it were 100 percent negative, it wouldn't work either. There must be a balance of both positive and negative.

There are those who want to preach all positives, but positives without negatives do not exist. There are also those who want to preach only negatives, a list of all the things you cannot do. But you cannot have love without hate. You cannot have light without darkness. The one follows the other.

If I am to wholly follow the Lord Jesus Christ, I must forsake everything that is contrary to Him. The following is contingent on the forsaking. The positive must be balanced by the negative.

It is this that defines living the crucified life, not the turning away. That is negative. You can forsake the world, quit gambling, quit drinking, quit smoking, quit living for the world, stop going to any of the worldly places of amusement, quit dancing, never do any of these things. You can quit all that is negative and has no power to impart any life of any kind. But these negatives are necessary before there can be the positive.

The positive is that you turn to Jesus Christ. That is what gives the power and authority and the deep satisfaction of "joy unspeakable and full of glory" (1 Pet. 1:8). The negative can never shine. The negative can never be musical. The negative can never be fragrant. A man can go live in a cave, leaving everything behind in utter disgust, like time in a vacuum. He can escape into the woods, live in a cave and still not have any power, any radiance of joy, any inward glory. It is only turning to Jesus Christ that does this. And the two can be done in one act. If I am facing north and God commands me to turn south, I can do that in one easy motion. So when God says to forsake the world and turn to Christ, that can be done in one motion, one free and easy act. My turning from the world *is* my turning to Christ. It does not always work that way, but it can.

Suppose someone who had great power decided to do something about the darkness. Suppose this someone had a lot of gremlins or angels or something at his command and said, "I'm tired of this darkness. I want you to wipe the heavens clean of darkness." Suppose he got a thousand or a million or 10 million gremlins (or some other kind of imaginary beings) with mops and the creatures mopped the heavens of all the darkness. It would still be dark. Just wait until the sun comes up. The coming up of the sun will do what all the mopping of the heavens can never do. Just wait for the sun, that's all.

Imagine a young man who will not drink soda pop because it is worldly. So he sits at a soda counter and is disturbed about a glass of soda in front of him and complains that he feels a little worldly. Well, he is simply an unhappy man. I have never seen a happy Christian yet who was the least bit conscious of or concerned about the world. Never.

I have also never seen a happy Christian yet who was not taken up with Jesus Christ the Lord. The sun comes up, and the darkness goes out. No creature in the universe can wipe the heavens clean of the darkness; only the sun can do that. When the sun peeks out in the morning, it parts the darkness and the clouds flee away and the shadows are no more.

So when we turn with all our hearts to Jesus Christ our Lord, we find the deeper life, the crucified life. We find in Him the power to mature and the satisfaction and "joy unspeakable and full of glory." When we turn our eyes to gaze on the Son of God and our hearts are taken up with His person, every instrument inside our musical hearts beats, and the music starts. Then the radiance breaks out and, as Peter said, "ye rejoice with joy unspeakable and full of glory."

This is what I mean by turning to the crucified life. These two acts can be done at once. Turn from the world and turn to Christ. And all the natural things like eating, drinking, buying, selling, marrying—all the things that God created to be done that are not of the spirit of the world but are natural and of God—will all be sanctified. They will become fuel for the fires of the altar of God. So the common things, things that we call secular, will no longer be secular to us. The mundane things will be mundane no more, but heavenly. The most common thing can be done for the glory of God when we have turned from the world and the world's ways and look into the full face of the Son of God. The sun will shine and not all the gremlins of hell can wipe the sunlight away.

Hell could send up a legion of gremlins to wipe away the sunshine, and they could desperately follow the sun around the earth and never succeed in keeping the sunshine away from the earth, because when the sun shines on the earth, there *will be* sunshine. So hell cannot destroy earth or disrupt the spiritual happiness of your gaze into the face of Jesus. We are as free as the Son of righteousness "with healing in his wings" (Mal. 4:2).

Will you turn from the world and turn fully to Christ? This will go a long way in breaking forever the condition of being a static Christian.

Fully Surrendered—Lord, I Would Be
Alfred C. Snead (1884–1961)

Fully surrendered—Lord, I would be,
Fully surrendered, dear Lord, to Thee.
All on the altar laid, surrender fully made,
Thou hast my ransom paid; I yield to Thee.

Fully surrendered—life, time, and all,
All Thou hast given me held at Thy call.
Speak but the word to me, gladly I'll follow Thee,
Now and eternally obey my Lord.

Fully surrendered—silver and gold,
His, who hath given me riches untold.
All, all belong to Thee, for Thou didst purchase me,
Thine evermore to be, Jesus, my Lord.

Fully surrendered—Lord, I am Thine;
Fully surrendered, Savior divine!
Live Thou Thy life in me; all fullness dwells in Thee;
Not I, but Christ in me, Christ all in all.

8

THE GREAT OBSTACLE TO LIVING THE CRUCIFIED LIFE

Trust in the LORD with all thine heart; and lean not unto thine own understanding. In all thy ways acknowledge him, and he shall direct thy paths.

PROVERBS 3:5-6

Paul was a man who knew what he believed and where he stood. He knew God and was confident with a great cosmic confidence, yet that same man was the most distrustful of himself. As great as Paul was, he did not trust himself.

Before man, Paul was as bold as a lion; but before God, Paul could not say too much against himself. When he was in front of God, Paul actually had no confidence in himself at all. His confidence with God was in reverse proportion to his confidence in himself. The amount of self-trust Paul had was as little as the trust he had in God was great.

What do I mean by "self-trust"? Simply, it is the respectability and self-assurance that comes through education. It is what you learn about yourself and what your friends tell you about yourself and all the best that you may give yourself. Self-trust is the last great obstacle to living the crucified life, which is why we mill around the deep river of God like animals around a waterhole, afraid to go in because the water may be too deep. We never quite get it.

I want to quote a little from a man who had a wonderful name: Lorenzo Scupoli (1530–1610). He was one of those strange Catholics who, during his lifetime, was considered more or less a heretic because of his evangelical leaning.

He wrote a book called *The Spiritual Combat*, which is a practical manual for living. Scupoli begins by teaching that the essence of life is continually fighting against our egoistic longings. Scupoli says the way to win the fight is to replace our desires for self-gratification with acts of charity and sacrifice. The one who does not do this loses and suffers eternity in hell. The one who does it, trusting not in his own strength but in God's power, triumphs and will be happy in heaven.

Scupoli analyzes several common, real-life situations and advises on how to cope with each of them to keep your conscience clear and to improve your virtue. Anyone who continues to act against God is the cause of all that is bad. All good comes from God, whose goodness is limitless. Scupoli wrote:

> So necessary is self-distrust in this conflict, that without it you will be unable, I say not to achieve the victory desired, but even to overcome the very least of your passions. Let this be well impressed upon your mind; for our corrupt nature too easily inclines us to a false estimate of ourselves; so that, being really nothing, we account ourselves to be something, and presume, without the slightest foundation, upon our own strength.
>
> This is a fault not easily discerned by us, but very displeasing in the sight of God. For He desires and loves to see in us a frank and true recognition of this most certain truth, that all the virtue and grace which is within us is derived from Him alone, Who is the fountain of all good, and that nothing good can proceed

from us, no, not even a thought which can find acceptance in His sight.[1]

Why is self-trust so wrong? Self-trust is wrong because it
robs God. God says, "Will a man rob God? Yet ye have robbed
me. But ye say, Wherein have we robbed thee? In tithes and offerings" (Mal. 3:8). We have robbed God and taken away from
Him what belongs to Him. Paul states that God is the fountain
of all, and nothing, not even good thoughts, can come from us
unless they come from God first (see Rom. 11:35-36). If you ignore the fact that God is the source of everything and make a
converted and sanctified self the source, it is just as bad as it
can be because final trust in God has been taken away. Self
judges God and man and holds God to be less than He is and
man to be more than he is. This is our trouble.

Study theology and learn about how God is the source and
fountain of all things. Learn about the attributes of God and
see if yet in your heart you still believe that God is less than He
is and you are more than you are. Think of the moon. If the
moon could talk like a man and have a personality, it could say
within itself, *I shine on the earth and every time I'm around, the earth
becomes beautiful.* If someone could respond to the moon, they
would say, "Listen, you don't do that by yourself. Don't you
know that you have been discovered and found out? You don't
shine at all. You are simply reflecting the sun's light, so it's
really the sun that shines."

Then self comes to the rescue of the moon. "You're letting
your light shine and you're doing a good job," it says. "When
you're not up, one whole side of the earth lies in darkness. But
when you come up, a side lights up and I can begin to see rows
of houses. You're doing a fine job." The moon would not say,
"The glory belongs to God, because it is only by the grace of

God that I'm like this." All the time the moon is thinking that he is shining.

When the moon is shining, it is only a reflection light from the sun. And if the moon really understood, he could boldly shine and talk about it, because he would know that he was not shining at all. Similarly, Paul knew that he did not have a thing of himself that was fit for heaven. He had only the grace of God in him. It was God and not him. He completely and radically distrusted himself. No man can really know himself; he is not capable of knowing how he feels.

Everybody thinks they know what they sound like until they hear themselves on a recording. One of the most humbling things that ever happened to me was when I had a sermon recorded. For the first time I heard the sound of my own voice, and that recording did not lie to me. Up to that time, I had been told I had a fine preaching voice. Then I heard myself, and nobody needs to talk to me about *that* anymore. I have listened to myself, and I know how I sound. No man knows the sound of his own voice until he hears it, and no man knows how weak he is until God exposes him and nobody wants to be exposed.

It is important that we understand how dangerous it is to trust our good habits and virtues. Only God can bring us to the point of understanding that our strength is indeed our weakness. Anything that we rely on or trust can be our undoing. We do not realize how weak we are until the Holy Spirit begins exposing these things to us.

Dealing with Self-Trust

The question I must pose is simply, how do we learn this self-distrust? Basically, God uses four different ways to deal with this matter. These are supported and confirmed by the devotional writers, the great hymnists and the Christian biographers.

They weave like a common thread through the lives of those who are committed to living the crucified life.

A Flash of Holy Inspiration in Your Soul

I believe the first and best way to deal with self-trust is for God to flash some holy inspiration into your soul and expose it. This has happened to many people. For example, it happened to Brother Lawrence. In *The Practice of the Presence of God,* he wrote that for 40 years he was never once out of the conscious presence of God: "When I took the cross and decided to obey Jesus and walk this holy way, I gathered that I would have to suffer a lot." Then he said something rather strange: "For some reason God never found me worthy of much suffering. He just let me continue to trust Him and I put all my self trust away and I have been trusting in God completely." Brother Lawrence was living the crucified life, believing Christ was in him, around him and near him. And he was praying all the time.

God flashed some holy inspiration into the heart of Lady Julian of Norwich, and because of the revelations she received, she knew instantly that she was no good and that Jesus Christ was everything. She stayed in that position until she died. I think this is probably the easiest way for us to get it—for the Lord to give us a sweet, sudden burst of holy inspiration within our hearts that shows us the real self. Of course, this is where our doctrine gets in our way. We can believe the whole counsel of God, and our life may still be plagued with pride to such an extent that it hides the face of God. It is such pride that prevents us from going forward in victory. This cannot be corrected by a lecture on correct doctrine. Rather, we need the Holy Spirit to tell us the true condition of our soul. We need Him to reveal to us how bad we really are and lead us out of our spiritual swamp.

God-Imposed Physical Discipline

Another way in which God deals with our self-trust is the physical realm. Many people have a hard time believing that God would actually bring physical harm to our bodies. Yet the Scriptures bear out the fact that physical pain is one of God's effective means of dealing with an undisciplined self.

The Old Testament is filled with examples of physical suffering imposed by God, but probably Job stands out above all the rest. A casual reading of Job's story may not get to the real problem that Job had. Certainly, he was a good man, and the Scriptures bear this out. The problem with Job was that he was a good man and he knew it. If you are good but you do not know it, then God can use you. However, if you know how good and great you are, you cease to be a vehicle through which God can send His blessing.

The only way God could get to the center of Job's problem was through physical pain. Sometimes this is the only way He can get our attention. God is not above using this method to deal with the problems of pride and self-trust. And the suffering God sends will sometimes not be curable by any medicine. Of course, the only cure for such a physical ailment is renouncing the self and humbling ourselves before God.

Nobody likes to talk about this sort of thing today. Everybody wants to hear happy, cheerful inspirational thoughts that make us feel good. This is why to get a crowd to come to church today, we need a cowbell, a musical saw or a talking horse to have some fun and a little bit of entertainment for those who are bored with the simple, plain word of God. Nobody wants to hear about physical discipline or pain. After all, we believe in healing.

Extreme Trials and Temptations

Another method God uses to develop distrust of ourselves is extreme trials and temptations. From listening to some preachers and reading some books, it is easy to conclude that once a person is born again, that is the end of it—no more trials or temptations. Those who believe in the infilling of the Holy Spirit have somehow also communicated the idea that this is the end of all Christian experience. But the Bible tells us that after Jesus was filled with the Spirit, He was driven into the wilderness for some severe temptations.

When a Christian faces a difficult or extreme trial or temptation, he is tempted to throw in the towel and say, "God, it's no use. I'm just no good. You obviously don't want me, so I'm finished." All the while he forgets that God wants to teach us through these trials and temptations that self-trust is dangerous and unreliable. At times, when something blows up in our face, we think it is all over instead of taking it as proof that we are not mature Christians. We need to take the blowup as proof that we are nearer to our forever home today than we were yesterday. We need to understand that our heavenly Father is letting these things happen to us to wean us away from trusting ourselves and to move us to lean exclusively on the Lord Jesus Christ.

Some have the idea that repentance is to be a drawn-out affair that includes beating yourself down. I think we need to start with repentance, but there comes a time when we need to just turn everything over to God and then not do it anymore. That is the best repentance in the world. If you did something last week you are ashamed of, feel conviction and condemnation about it, simply say, "I repent." Turn it over to the Lord, tell Him about it, and then do not do it anymore.

What is the purpose of these severe trials and temptations that sometimes cause you to fail? It is not to show you that you are not a true Christian. Rather, it is to show you that your conscience is tender and you are very near to God. The Lord is trying to teach you that last lesson so that you rid yourself of self-distrust. The closer you are to God, the more tender your conscience is before the Lord, and the more severe your trial and temptation may be. Some in the Church have lied to us by inferring that the Christian life is void of difficulty, problems and trials. The exact opposite is the truth.

The great characters of the Bible shed some light on the subject. Remember Jacob's temptation? Remember Peter's temptation? All throughout Scripture (and all of Church history), there are countless individuals who encountered great trials and temptations. Hebrews 11 tells about many of those heroes of faith—those who endured extreme trials and temptations in life.

Sometimes a trial comes along, and we run to the Bible, pull out a quote and say, "According to this Scripture right here, we got it." We have certain confidence in ourselves. We think we know exactly what is going on. The problem is that we do *not* know what is happening, and so God will deal with our self-trust.

God certainly knows our feelings. He knows we are so proud of the way we rightly divide the word of truth and that we can disjoint a text like a butcher getting a chicken ready for the barbecue. With words all carefully laid out and knowing just where to put your finger on this or just where to put your finger on that, you are too smart for God to bless you. You know too much. You can identify everything, but the dear heavenly Father knows you do not really know much at all. He lets things happen to you until you recognize that you do not know what is happening. Your friends do not know what is going on either. And when you go to somebody you feel you can trust, that person will not be able to help you either. That is actually good news.

It truly would be terrible if we had some holy Saint Francis to whom we all could go to find out where we were, what was happening to us and what life is all about. God loves us too much for that. He is trying to teach us to trust Him, not people—to lean on

Him, not on people. I have been so scared that people would start trusting in me and leaning on me. However, fear not! God pulls the crutches out from under me occasionally, just to see if He can trust me.

As a Christian, you know some of the means God uses to teach His people. As a Christian, you love God, but you are sick of all the nonsense in the world. You are sick of all the nonsense in the Church. Your heart is crying after God just as the doe yearns after the water brooks. Your heart and your flesh cry out for the living God. Yet in spite of all this, you still trust yourself. You testify that you love your Bible and that your time of prayer is precious, but still your tendency is to trust yourself.

This tendency is more difficult to deal with because we do not talk about this anymore. This teaching left the evangelical and fundamental church a generation ago. Nowadays when someone becomes a Christian, everybody slaps him on the back and says, "Glory to God, Brother, you are born again!"

Ah, but the Lord says, "That's only the beginning." The Scriptures teach that God will rejoice over us with joy and with singing. This is not a picture of an angry God. Rather, it is a picture of a loving Father who is everlastingly patient toward us, His children. God is not judging us. God only wants His children to grow and develop into full-fledged Christians. Sometimes in order to accomplish this, God must send us through severe and harsh trials and temptations. But the destination is Christian perfection in the person of the Lord Jesus Christ.

The Footprints of the Age-Old Saints

I would condense the fourth thing God uses in dealing with our self-trust into one simple thought: Look around for the saintly footprints where you are right now. You are not alone in this journey. Look around for footprints and find out who made those footprints. You will notice that the footprints are those of the great saints who lived in ages past.

I am not interested in any of the modern footprints. I am interested only in those footprints that have come to us down through the centuries. If you look around and see these footprints, you will find them all going in the same direction. You will find they follow the footprints of Jesus. They are all going in the same direction. Look carefully and you will see some of them backtracking a little occasionally, but you will also see that they found their way at last and went back to following after Jesus. They are all following Christ.

Trust God

Now, the absolutely cheerful and confident Christian can expect this very same thing. You want the Lord to do something for you, don't you? You want Him to come down on you with a wave of grace. As a congregation, we want to again see the Reformation or a revival coming down on us with power. We want to see power in our individual lives. We want the Holy Spirit to come on us and demonstrate His power. We want to see all of that, but we need to be careful that we're not trying to work it up on our own.

I do not intend to try to work up anything. You cannot climb Jacob's ladder without sweat, perspiration and hard work. The work of God is not dependent on any man's schedule. I rarely know where I am going in my life's journey, but after I have been there a year, I can look back and see that my path has been relatively straight. I go to God, write out my prayers, wait on Him and remind Him, but nothing seems to happen. I seem to be getting nowhere, and then suddenly things break around me. I look back and see that God has been leading my every step, and I did not even know it.

I did not know where I was going, but looking back, I can see where I have been. I do not think we should always look back, but at least we should be able to look back and see the terrain where God has led us—the valleys and plateaus He has brought us through because He loves us in spite of ourselves.

The more my trust rests in God, the less I trust myself. If we truly desire to live the crucified life, we must get rid of self-trust and trust only in God.

We Give Thee but Thine Own
William W. How (1823–1897)

We give thee but Thine own,
Whate'er the gift may be;
All that we have is Thine alone,
A trust, O Lord, from Thee.

May we Thy bounties thus
As stewards true receive,
And gladly, as Thou blessest us,
To Thee our firstfruits give.

O hearts are bruised and dead,
And homes are bare and cold,
And lambs for whom the Shepherd bled
Are straying from the fold.

To comfort and to bless,
To find a balm for woe,
To tend the lone and fatherless
Is angels' work below.

The captive to release,
To God the lost to bring,
To teach the way of life and peace
It is a Christ-like thing.

And we believe Thy Word,
Though dim our faith may be;
Whate'er for Thine we do, O Lord,
We do it unto Thee.

Note

1. Father Dom Lorenzo Scupoli, *The Spiritual Combat,* chapter 8. http://www.holyro mancatholicchurch.org/articles/SpiritualCombat.htm.

Part III

The Perils of the Crucified Life

9

THE CURRENCY OF THE CRUCIFIED LIFE

What things were gain to me, those I counted loss for Christ.
Yea doubtless, and I count all things but loss for the excellency of the
knowledge of Christ Jesus my Lord: for whom I have suffered the loss
of all things, and do count them but dung, that I may win Christ.

PHILIPPIANS 3:7-8

When God calls a man to follow Him, He calls that man to follow Him regardless of the cost. The enemy can do his worst, but if a man is in God's hands, no harm can come to him. Nobody asked what it would cost a person to become a great football player. Or what it would cost a person to become a successful attorney. Or what it would cost a person to become a successful businessman. Everybody knows that the more important something is, the higher the cost. What costs you little or nothing is worth exactly that much. The challenge before us is simply this: What are we willing to pay, sacrifice or surrender in order to advance in living the crucified life?

Church history and Christian biography are filled with examples of what people have been willing to pay to live the crucified life. The martyrs of the Church form a long and glorious line. From the standpoint of the natural world, this sort of life does not look glamorous. But when we look at it from God's point of view, it takes on an altogether different perspective. The first Christian martyr was Stephen, who died at the feet of Saul, who later became the great apostle Paul. I am quite sure that Stephen's death made a great impression upon the young Saul.

That there has been over the last half a century a steady decline in the spiritual quality of Christian religion in America, no informed person will attempt to deny. I am not speaking of liberalism or modernism but of that evangelical wing of Christianity to which I myself belong by theological conviction and personal choice. I believe the situation has become so serious that the earnest observer is forced to wonder whether our popular evangelical religion today is indeed the true faith of our fathers or simply some form of paganism thinly disguised with a veneer of Christianity to make it acceptable to those who want to call themselves Christian.

Turn to the church page of any city newspaper or leaf through some of the popular magazines today and what you find there will make you sick at heart. We have come to our present low state as the result of an almost fanatical emphasis on grace to the total exclusion of obedience, self-discipline, patience, personal holiness, cross carrying, discipleship and other such precious doctrines of the New Testament. These doctrines cannot be made to harmonize with the doctrine of grace as taught by most modern Church fathers. Certainly, though these teachings are not denied, they are either allowed to die from neglect or relegated to a footnote with so many explanations and interpretations as to make them ineffective.

The grace that amazed our fathers—that brought them to their knees in tears and trembling worship—has by deadly familiarity become so mundane that it scarcely affects us at all. That which was so wondrously precious to the Moravians and Methodists and their immediate spiritual descendents has become cheap to a generation of Christians devoted to their own pursuits and engrossed in their own pleasures.

Dietrich Bonhoeffer

In my mind, one man epitomizes what one must pay, or give up, for the crucified life. That man was Dietrich Bonhoeffer, who lived under the shadow of the mad nihilist Adolf Hitler.

Bonhoeffer was in his thirties when the Nazis came to power. He was a brilliant scholar, theologian and a leader in the confessional church in Germany, and his keen, perceptive mind told him that the political consequences of national socialism would be a bloody war for Germany and the world. His sensitive Christian heart recoiled from the unbelievable malignity of Hitler and his band of assassins. As a preacher of the gospel, Bonhoeffer went boldly to the airwaves and warned his nation of the inevitable consequences of a political system "which corrupted and grossly misled the nation that made the 'Fuhrer' its idol and God."[1]

As the war clouds formed over Europe, Bonhoeffer left Germany and carried on his work in England. It was not long before his Christian conscience would not allow him to be in a place of safety when his country was experiencing turmoil:

> "I shall have no right to participate in the reconstruction of Germany after the war," he said, "if I do not share the trials of this time with my people. . . . Christians in Germany will face the terrible alternative of either willing the defeat of their nation in order that Christian civilization may survive, or willing the victory of their nation and thereby destroying our civilization. I know which of these alternatives I must choose; but I cannot make this choice in security."[2]

After returning to Germany, Bonhoeffer worked for the confessional church and with the political underground. He was soon arrested by the infamous Gestapo and clapped into jail, along with other members of his family. From then on, he was shuttled to different prisons and to different concentration camps. During this time, he served his fellow prisoners by witnessing, praying, comforting and assisting in every way possible. Those who knew him at the time tell of his "calmness and self-control . . . even in the most terrible situations." He was, they said, "a giant before man . . . but a child before God."³

Bonhoeffer was the German Luther, a man of remarkable spiritual insight. He did all he could to preach Jesus Christ as the Savior of man and embraced what he called "costly grace." He said that we shouldn't try to get into heaven cheaply, for the grace of God would cost us everything we have. The grace of God is costly because it cost Christ His blood, and it will cost us everything—maybe even our lives.

At the beginning of the war, Bonhoeffer was engaged to a lovely young woman. His sister, father and other relatives were also still living at the time. The Nazis pulled the old totalitarian trick: "You better buckle down and shut up, because we've got your family as hostages. And if you don't do what we ask you to do, it's your family who will suffer." That was their technique, so they told Bonhoeffer, "You surrender and shut up about costly grace and freedom in the gospel of Jesus Christ. Stop warning against Hitler and the Nazis, or we will kill your family."

Those sorts of threats usually work, but the Nazis had never come up against a man like Dietrich Bonhoeffer. With a calmness and serenity that only Christ can give, Bonhoeffer replied, "My family belongs to God, and you'll never get me to surrender by threatening to kill my family."

Years before, Bonhoeffer had written, "When God calls a man, he bids him come and die."⁴ On April 9, 1945, at the Flossenbürg concentration camp, Bonhoeffer was called on to do just that. He refused to allow himself to be rescued, lest he endanger the lives of certain others, so "he went steadfastly on his way to be hanged, and died with admirable calmness and dignity."[5]

Too many of the German people had grown arrogant with national pride and dangerously bloated with temporary success. So God in His mercy sent His man—a seeing man—to the country of the blind. But the nation of blind men hanged their prophet, cremated his body and scattered his ashes. It was only shortly after this that the blind men themselves faced national humiliation and final collapse.

No doubt, the greatest contribution of Bonhoeffer's ministry is his book *The Cost of Discipleship*. Even before the war, this prophet saw clearly. He wrote, "Cheap grace is the deadly enemy of our Church. We are fighting today for costly grace."[6]

Only the knowledge that truth is universal and that mankind is very much the same the world over enables us to understand how this young Lutheran minister, examining German Christianity in the mid-1930s, could diagnose so skillfully the disease that threatens to destroy evangelicalism in America a generation later. What concerns me is that what Bonhoeffer said of conditions in Germany then is terribly, frighteningly true of American Christianity today. The parallel is alarming.

Worldly Legs

Why do God's people not bounce right out and start going, rising, mounting, soaring and climbing? Why do they have to be petted, cuddled, looked after, followed around and held up? The reason is that they never acquired spiritual legs under them and the face of God is turned away from them. That is, they think that is the case; the truth is that Christ made full atonement for us so there is nothing between a Christian and God. Christ's atonement was so perfect and complete that it turns all that is against us into something that is for us. It turned all our demerits into merits. It moved everything that was on the debit side of the ledger to the credit side of the ledger. Everything that was against us was moved over to our side. That is the wonder of the atonement in Jesus Christ.

So why is it that we take so long to rid ourselves of this veil of obscurity? Why do we take so long to push it aside, see the sun shining and make our way up to the peak of our faith?

It is not God's fault, because floundering is not God's will for us. God wills that His children should grow in grace and in the knowledge of Jesus Christ. He wills that we should go on to perfection. He wills that we should be holy. So why don't we strive to be holy? The major problem is that we like ourselves too much. We struggle to keep up a good front.

A Good Front

I've seen some pity-seekers come to the altar, but as a rule, I do not pity them because they are struggling. Some might say, "Look at that. Isn't that wonderful?" But I say, "You know why they are struggling? They are fighting God." That is never a good sight to see. They are trying to keep up a good front, they do not want to surrender, they do not want people to know how unimportant they are and how useless and how small. They do not want anyone to peek into the poverty of their hearts. So they struggle to keep up a good front.

Americans spend billions of dollars yearly just to keep up a good front. Tear the front down of the average person and you will find he is a poor tramp in his spirit, in his mind and in his heart. We try to hide that inward state, disguise our poverty and preserve our reputation to keep some authority for ourselves. We want to have a little authority in the world. We do not want to give it all up. But God wants to take all authority out of our hands and get us to the place where we have no authority left at all. He wants to take it all away, and He will never bless us until He has taken it all away. As long as you are in command, as long as you say, "Now listen, God, I'll tell you how to do this," you will only be a mediocre Christian, dull of hearing, attending camp meetings, churches and having all the means of grace at your disposal, but still getting nowhere.

We like to have a little glory for ourselves. We are willing to let God have most of it, but we want a commission, just a little bit for ourselves. We want to rescue part of ourselves from the cost.

I am inclined to think that some people were just born to be little. They never amount to much. If they go to heaven, it will be by the grace of God, and they will take nothing along—they will go empty-handed. They will get through by the mercy of God. That is the only way anybody gets through, but God wills that you should take with you riches, diamonds, pearls, silver and gold tried in the fire. He wills that you should have a harvest of souls. He wills that you should send your good works before you. He wills that you should be a productive, fruitful Christian.

Yet a great many Christians are not going to have a thing to show God. They are simply not willing to pay the price. The writer of Hebrews said, "Ye are dull of hearing" (Heb. 5:11). He could not talk to his readers the way he wanted to, because while they had time enough to grow and mature, they had not.

Self-Defense

The truth is that we must stop defending ourselves, always having our fists clenched a little bit. We had a dear old woman who used to help at the altar. When she saw somebody praying with his fist closed, she would say to him, "Now, open your fist, honey. To pray with your fist closed means you are hanging on to something. Let it go. Let it go. Open your hands for God. That's it."

Whatever holds you back is a veil between you and God, and it is made up of things that are just silly. You will never be more than a common Christian until you give up your own interest and cease defending yourself. Put yourself in the hands of God and let Him alone. Stop trying to help God.

I never had a tooth pulled without trying to help the dentist struggle with the labor. Whenever I travel in an airplane, I instinctively try to help the pilot by leaning to the left and then leaning to the right. We are just as silly as that when it comes to the things of God. We want to help God out. No. Give yourself to God. Turn yourself over to Him and say, "Father, I'm sick of being a common Christian. I am sick of this mediocrity, of being halfway to where I ought to be, of seeing other Christians happy when I am not. I am weary of the whole thing. I want to go on, and I want to know You."

One man had a great experience with God, one that blossomed and grew into an even more wondrous experience. He walked with God and became known as a man of God. People came to him and said, "Brother, you were known for a long time as just average and suddenly you're blessed all over. What happened to you?"

"Well," he said, "I don't rightly know, but here's what happened and how it happened. One day I appeared before God and said, 'God, I have something to say to You. Never as long as I live will I say anything in prayer that I don't mean.' And then from there I started out."

The Currency to Exchange

Most Christians are satisfied living their entire lives as common Christians. They never experience the richness of what it truly means to be a Christian. Without a deep insatiable hunger for the things of God, there is nothing within them prodding them to go forward to perfection. The condition of today's Christian Church is the result of too many common Christians in leadership roles. Once again, we need a great move of the Holy Spirit to break out of the spiritual rut and press on to spiritual perfection. That move needs to start with individual Christians who are willing to give all to God and live the crucified life.

But just what is the currency associated with living the crucified life? What exactly is the currency that must be used in this exchange? Let me enumerate several things that I think we need to exchange in order to move on in our journey through the crucified life.

Safety

One of the first things that we need to exchange is our safety. Those who insist on a safe environment are never going to move forward in their journey to the crucified life. Dietrich Bonheoffer did not have safety in his life. In order for him to do what God wanted him to do, he had to exchange his safety. If safety had been important to him, he never would have gone back to Germany and face what he knew he was going to face. If your safety is so precious that you must preserve it at all costs, you will be hindered on your journey along the crucified-life pathway. Your safety is the price you pay to move on to new spiritual vistas.

Convenience

Another aspect of our currency along this line is convenience. Nobody that I have ever read about ever found dying to be convenient. The journey along the crucified-life pathway will be paid for by "mountains" of inconvenience. Those who are willing to part with their convenience will progress toward being hundredfold Christians.

Fun

Perhaps there has never been a generation of Christians who were more in love with fun than the present one. But this is also part of the currency to pay for the journey to the crucified life. None of the marchers in the Church found it to be fun. The great reformers of the church sacrificed fun in order to do what God had before them. It comes down to this: Hang on to your fun or exchange it for progress toward spiritual perfection.

Popularity

Many today are trying to make Christianity popular by marketing it as if it were a product on a store shelf. Nowhere in my reading of history have I ever discovered that what was popular with the crowd was right. In most instances, in order to move ahead, most great men and women of God had to lean against the wind of popularity. The cost for their advancement was their popularity.

Worldly Success

One more thing I might mention that must be exchanged on this journey is worldly success. Are you willing to exchange your success in business, in sports, in your career, in order to move forward and achieve spiritual perfection?

If we look at success from the world's perspective, Jesus' ministry was a terrible failure. All the apostles failed as far as the world's criterion is concerned. The great martyrs of the Church were absolute failures. According to the criterion of the world's idea of success, William Tyndale, who died because of his work, was an absolute failure.

The man or woman who is willing to exchange and surrender all aspects of his or her success is the one who is going to go on with God. We are not living for this world but for the world to come. The economy we are bartering in is not of this world but of the world where Jesus Christ is preparing a place for us. We have the awesome privilege of exchanging worldly success for favor with our Father which art in heaven.

The crucified life is an expensive proposition. Whoever is willing to pay the price is the one who will go forward in absolute victory and joyous fellowship with Christ. Christ paid the price for our salvation; we now pay the price for our full identification with Him and our walk and pilgrimage toward spiritual perfection.

New Year 1945
Dietrich Bonhoeffer (1906–1945)

With every power for good to stay and guide me,
Comforted and inspired beyond all fear,
I'll live these days with You in thought beside me,
And pass, with You, into the coming year.

The old year still torments our hearts, unhastening:
The long days of our sorrow still endure.
Father, grant to the soul Thou hast been chastening
That Thou hast promised—the healing and the cure.

Should it be ours to drain the cup of grieving
Even to the dregs of pain, at Thy command,
We will not falter, thankfully receiving
All that is given by Thy loving hand.

But, should it be Thy will once more to release us
To life's enjoyment and its good sunshine,
That we've learned from sorrow shall increase us
And all our life be dedicate as Thine.

Today, let candles shed their radiant greeting:
Lo, on our darkness are they not Thy light,
Leading us haply to our longed-for meeting?
Thou canst illumine e'en our darkest night.

When now the silence deepens for our harkening,
Grant we may hear Thy children's voices raise
From all the unseen world around us darkening
Their universal paean, in Thy praise.

While all the powers of Good aid and attend us,
Boldly we'll face the future, be it what may.
At even, and at morn, God will befriend us,
And oh, most surely on each new year's day!

Notes
1. G. Leibholz, "Memoir," in Dietrich Bonhoeffer, *The Cost of Discipleship* (New York: Simon and Schuster, 1959), p. 16.
2. Dietrich Bonhoeffer, *The Cost of Discipleship* (New York: Simon and Schuster, 1959), pp. 17-18.
3. Leibholz, "Memoir," in Bonhoeffer, *The Cost of Discipleship*, p. 19.
4. Ibid., p. 11.
5. Ibid., p. 26.
6. Ibid., p. 43.

10

The Veils that Obscure God's Face

Brethren, I count not myself to have apprehended:
but this one thing I do, forgetting those things which are behind, and
reaching forth unto those things which are before, I press toward the
mark for the prize of the high calling of God in Christ Jesus.

PHILIPPIANS 3:13-14

The New Testament message, objectives and methods have been allowed to lie dormant. Acts done in the name of the Lordship of Jesus Christ are Lordship in name only. Replacing Christ's true Lordship, we have introduced our own message, our own objectives and our own methods for achieving those objectives, which are, in every case, not scriptural at all.

Is it heresy—does it constitute a radical mind—if you pray for God to cleanse the intent of your heart with the unspeakable gift of His grace? This, of course, is the great prayer by the author of *The Cloud of Unknowing:* "God . . . I beseech Thee so for to cleanse the intent of mine heart with the unspeakable gift of Thy grace, that I may perfectly love Thee, and worthily praise Thee."

To long to love God and worthily praise Him should mean more than the words you say. It should cost you everything. Is that heresy? Should a man be put in jail for that? Should he be ostracized for it in the light of our hymnody, in the light of our devotional books, in the light of Church history all the way back to Paul and in the light of the lives of all the saints? No, I do not think so.

The apostle Paul said that to gain Christ, he would have renounced this entire world (see Phil. 3:7-8). He wanted everyone to know Christ as a conscious experience, to use the modern phrasing, and to receive the kingdom of heaven. He said that he prayed all the time for Christ to dwell in the heart of every believer (see Eph. 3:17). He told the Corinthians, "Examine yourselves, whether ye be in the faith; prove your own selves. Know ye not your own selves, how that Jesus Christ is in you, except ye be reprobates?" (2 Cor. 13:5). He told the Romans, "Now if a man have not the Spirit of Christ, he is none of his" (Rom. 8:9). It is by the indwelling of Jesus that we receive the riches of God and see His smiling face.

Unfortunately, there has developed between the Christian and the face of God what I will call "veils of obscurity." These veils hide the precious riches of God from those of us who press on to perfection. The effect is that we can no longer see the smiling face of God.

Recognize the Veils

On a dark cloudy day, the brightness of the sun is obscured. The sun is still there, but our ability to benefit from the sun's rays is greatly reduced. So it is in the spiritual world. There are certain veils that come between us and God and have a similar effect. These veils are usually of our own making. We allow them to develop in our lives, and most of the time we are not even aware of the total impact they are having on us. Let me describe some of the veils that are the most troubling.

Pride and Stubbornness

No doubt the first and strongest of these veils are pride and stubbornness. Nothing is more Adamic in our lives than these. The root of both of these is an inflated opinion of our own selves. That which causes us the most problem is that which we honor the most.

One term often used in this regard is the word "ego." This one word conveys the root of all of our problems with ourselves, with our families, with our friends and certainly with our God. It is when we usurp God's rightful place that the trouble occurs. The reason we do that is because we think more highly of ourselves than anybody else, including God.

Even if we find ourselves to be wrong, stubbornness will prohibit us from acknowledging that fact, so we cannot press forward. The problem with pride and stubbornness is that they focus on us and obscure the face of God, the One who in all cases provides the solution for our problems. Pride and stubbornness distort the importance of God's authority in our lives.

Self-Will

Associated with pride and stubbornness is self-will. The dangerous aspect of this veil is that it is a very religious thing. In the natural world, self-will is a positive thing. But when it is brought into a church context, it can be devastating.

Self-will always usurps God's will. On the surface, it seems very nice, but just cross self-willed people and watch what happens. Let something challenge anyone's self-will, including our own, and see how nice it really is. Self-will distorts the smiling face of God and veils the fact that God's will has our best interest in mind for the long run. Self-will is only concerned about now.

Religious Ambition

Religious ambition is probably the most deceptive of all the veils. A person can be very religiously ambitious. We see this all the time. Unfortunately, religious ambition usually distorts the will of God.

It works something like this. Most people want their church to grow and be a mighty force for God in their community. And this is admirable. But along comes a religiously ambitious person who generates so much excitement among the people that they forget what their purpose in the community is all about. It is not bigness that God honors. In fact, most of the time huge crowds hinder what God really wants to do.

Some pastors are pushing their churches beyond the scope of divine authority. Some churches are more into politics. Some are more into the social concerns. For other churches, the great interest is education. All of these things are good but not one of them is part of the commission God gave the Church. Simply because a person cloaks something with religious terminology does not make that thing an approved work of God.

Religious ambition easily distorts and veils the approval of God upon a company of people.

Claims of Ownership

Here is where we get into a lot of difficulty. Whatever I claim for myself becomes a veil obscuring God from my view. What I do not absolutely surrender and give up to God comes between God and me. Some Christians believe that if they fast enough and pray about something long enough, God will change His mind about a certain thing. That has never been the case. Not all the fasting and prayer in the world can remove this veil.

Once I put everything on the altar and leave it there, the brightness of God's smiling face will be seen. I think after Abraham relinquished any claim he had on Isaac, he looked at the world in a very different fashion. What you hang on to will weigh you down and hinder you in your pursuit of spiritual perfection.

Fear

The father of fear is unbelief. Fear distorts the smiling aspect of God's face. Do I really believe that God has my best in mind? Or is there a bit of fear in my heart obscuring His good intentions? My circumstances are no indication of whether the smiling favor of God is upon me. Fear causes me to look around at my circumstances instead of up at the smiling face of God.

If the three Hebrew children in the fiery furnace had been more conscious of the fire around them than that God was with them, they might have felt discouraged. But they looked beyond the fire and saw the smiling face of God. They were so conscious of God and His favor on them that the Scriptures tell us that when they came out of the fire, not a hair on their bodies was singed and their clothes did not have the smell of smoke (see Dan. 3:27).

Money

Money is another great veil that obscures God's face from the believer. How easy it is to be entangled in a web of finances. This includes not only having a lot of money but also not having enough money. Solomon wisely said:

> Two things have I required of thee; deny me them not before I die: Remove far from me vanity and lies: give me neither poverty nor riches; feed me with food convenient for me: Lest I be full, and deny thee, and say, Who is the LORD? or lest I be poor, and steal, and take the name of my God in vain (Prov. 30:7-9).

The veil of money has never been about how much money you have but rather about how much money has you. For most of us, it does not take very much money to obscure the smiling face of God. Whatever gets between you and God is all that is needed.

Friendships

Friendship is the most difficult veil and the one that causes us the most grief. Our friendships can get between God and us. I am not thinking just of our friendships with unsaved people. My experience has been that following my conversion to Christ, my unsaved friends left me. What I am mainly thinking of are the friendships we have within the Church. Sometimes those friendships become more important to us than our relationship with God.

The problem here is that there is a great deal of pressure for us to adjust to one another. The common denominator is ourselves. We are called not to adjust ourselves to one another but to adjust ourselves to God. Nothing is more wonderful and encouraging than Christian fellowship, but when that fellowship begins to replace our fellowship with God—and that can easily happen—it becomes a veil of obscurity.

Our Social Position

For many of us, this is the hardest veil to take down. For the most part, we establish our identities by the positions we hold. These positions then determine our influence in the church and in the community. We do not have to hold a major position or a high-paying one. It may even be a position that you volunteer to do. The danger lurks in allowing our position to replace God's approval in our lives. Man's approval can distort God's approval.

Take Down the Veils

These veils are all aspects of life that on the surface seem innocent but certainly can become something that obscures the face of God. Some Christians get this. Some understand the truth of this and are doing something about it. But others will be like the Israelites. They will come up to Kadesh-Barnea once a week for years and then turn around and go back into the wilderness. Then they will wonder why there is so much sand in their shoes.

Simply put, they will not go on beyond Kadesh-Barnea. They will not advance to the Promised Land. Moving forward toward a crucified life will take some work and commitment on our part, and one of the things we need to do is to take down our veils of obscurity so that the sunshine of God's smiling face is upon us.

The face of God is always smiling, and not all the veils I mentioned or even the devil can stop Him from smiling in our direction. The devil can blow up a storm and put it between us and the face of God, but God is still smiling. Remember, God is waiting for you to move up to see His smile. We are the ones who put up the veils that obscure the view.

Have No Rivals to God

Our God is a jealous lover and suffers no rival. Whatever rival you construct becomes an obstruction between you and your God. I do not say that you are not joined to Him and that you are not justified by grace. I say that this wondrous divine illumination, this ability to perfectly love Him and worthily praise Him, becomes veiled. It gets choked out and smitten down, and for a generation now, it has not even been taught.

If you will take the veils down and put them under your feet, you will discover they hide all that bothers you. All that worries you will be gone, and there will be nothing but the clean sky above. Christ does not have to die again. No cross will ever need to be erected again. Nothing needs to be added to the atonement. The face of God continues to smile on His people; however, there is a cloud, a veil, hiding that face and that smile.

Don't Be Cheated

Some people say that backsliding is true of sinners but could never be true of Christian people. It may be true of the masses, but it is not true of us. But Christians nowadays have been taught that they can rush to get their little hearts beating and get a fuzzy warm feeling from the hillbilly songs and grand theatrics and all the rest that make up worship in many modern churches.

I don't blame them. But they have been cheated, and the religious leaders have lied to them and wronged them just as in the days of Jesus. Jesus walked among the leaders of His day with His eyes bright and His vision keen and He said to them, "Whatever they say and do may be theologically right, but don't be like them." The leaders responded by saying, "We will kill that man." And they did kill Him. But on the third day, He rose again. Then He sent down the Holy Spirit into this world, and He is yours and mine.

Create No Limits for the Holy Spirit

Do not let anybody tell you how much you can have of the Holy Spirit. Only God can tell you how much you can have of Him. False teachers tell you not to get excited and not to get fanatical, but don't listen to them.

The last generation has been led in evangelical and gospel-church circles. That which is now fundamentalism will become liberalism in a short time. We must have the Holy Spirit back in our churches. We have to have the face of God shining down and the candles of our souls burning bright. We must sense and feel and know the wondrous divine illumination of the One who said, "I am the light of the world" (John 8:12).

Does saying this make me a fanatic? If that is fanaticism, then oh, God, send us more fanaticism. Real fanaticism is when you go against the Scriptures and add things and misinterpret the Word of God. But there is not one line of the Word of God that has been misinterpreted by what I am saying here. It is all based on the doctrine of the faith—the faith of our fathers that is living still.

Stop Wandering

The question is, are you willing to take down the veils of pride and stubbornness, self-will, religious ambition, ownership claims, fear, money, friendships and societal position? Are you willing to tuck them away under your feet?

Perhaps you have been under these veils for a long time. You've tried to pray your way around them, but it does not work that way. You must put these veils under your feet and rise above them. You must put all these things that exist between you and the peace of God away and look into the sunlight. Then relax. There is nothing more you can do. Our God waits, optimistically wanting to help you. He is willing to do it; He is anxious to do it, in fact.

Don't sit back and let yourself become discouraged. You may have been to so many altars and have read so many books that you became confused. Take down the veils between you and God and bask in the sunshine of His everlasting smile. For until God's people put the veils under their feet, nothing will ever happen.

I Take, He Undertakes
A. B. Simpson (1843–1919)

I clasp the hand of Love divine,
I claim the gracious promise mine,
And add to His my countersign,
"I take"—"He undertakes."

I take Thee, blessed Lord,
I give myself to Thee,
And Thou, according to Thy word,
Dost undertake for me.

I take salvation full and free,
Through Him who gave His life for me,
He undertakes my all to be,
"I take"—"He undertakes."

I take Him as my holiness,
My spirit's spotless, heavenly dress,
I take the Lord, my righteousness,
"I take"—"He undertakes."

I take the promised Holy Ghost,
I take the power of Pentecost,
To fill me to the uttermost,
"I take"—"He undertakes."

I take Him for this mortal frame,
I take my healing through His Name,
And all His risen life I claim,
"I take"—"He undertakes."

I simply take Him at His word,
I praise Him that my prayer is heard,
And claim my answer from the Lord,
"I take"—"He undertakes."

11

THE STRANGE INGENUITY OF THE CHRISTIAN

I can do all things through Christ which strengtheneth me.

PHILIPPIANS 4:13

The objective before us is to know Christ. We are to learn of Him, to know the power of Christ's resurrection, to be conformed onto His death, to experience in us that which we have in Christ. In order to do that, we must "count all things but loss for the excellency of [this] knowledge."

Allow me to go out on a limb and state something that I have no way of knowing for sure; it's a shrewd guess based on knowing spiritual laws. This is, simply, that once a person begins this journey of living the crucified life, during the first phase of that journey he will experience some of the worst weeks of his life. It is at this point that many will get discouraged and turn back. Those who persevere will find that instead of breaking into the clear bright sunshine, just ahead of them are more discouragements, doubts and deceptions.

Instead of lifting you up, this kind of teaching will cast you down. But let me say this: Those who have been so discouraged—those who have bumped their foreheads on the ceiling or scraped their chins on the sidewalk—and have gone down in some kind of defeat are the very ones who are getting nearer to God. Those who are unaffected—those who can still be worldly and not mind it—have made the least progress. But those who have found things going against them—those who in their longing and yearning for the crucified life, those who wait for Jesus Christ to lead them and instead wonder if He is discouraging them—they probably don't realize that they are very close to the kingdom of God.

"Simply by Grace He May See"

I want to give you another little phrase: "Simply by grace he may see." Or, to put it in modern English, "Let those see who can see by the grace of God." Or, to put it in the language of the Bible, "He that hath ears to hear, let him hear" (Matt 11:15; Mark 4:9; Luke 8:8).

I differ a little from the anonymous author of *The Cloud of Unknowing*. If people could not see, he simply walked out on them. He said, in effect, "I don't want to see janglers and money lovers. I don't want them to even look at my book." He was rather hard-nosed about this point.

I am a little more broad-minded than that. I am going to say that God sifts out those who cannot see in order to lead on by grace those who can see. Remember, even though the number of Chosen People be as the sands of the sea, only a remnant will be saved (see Gen. 22:17; Ezek. 6:8). Although many may wax cold, there is always a remnant.

We read the life of Adoniram Judson and say, "God, I want You to do that to me." We read of D. L. Moody's life and say, "Lord, I want You to do for me what You did to Moody." We want to tell God how to do it, and at the same time we want to reserve a little bit of the glory and have some areas in our life uncrucified. What we really want is a technical crucifixion. We are very happy to listen to another exposition on the sixth chapter of Romans on how we are crucified with Christ, but few people in reality truly want it.

Until we put ourselves in the hands of God and let God do with us as He wills, we will be just what we are—mediocre Christians singing happy songs to keep from being completely blue and trying to keep up the best we can. And while we're doing this, we will not be making any progress toward a crucified life and will not know what it is to be one with Him experientially. Our hearts must be cleansed and our true intent must be to perpetually love Him and worthily praise Him. Then we may be filled with His Spirit and walk in victory.

You do not know what it means to look on God and then go away, letting Him have His way with your life. You are afraid of that. You hope He is all right, you believe He is all right, and you know that the Bible says, "God so loved"; but still you are afraid that if you leave your life in God's hands, something bad will happen.

"See who by grace may see." Let us sit around, get old and wait for the undertaker. Go to conferences year after year and get nothing out of them. Listen to sermons year after year without learning anything. Study the Bible year after year but not make any progress and be just barely able to keep our chins above the water. We are strangely ingenious in fixing our Christian lives so that we get a little glory out of it and get our own way instead of getting God's way.

François Fénelon made an interesting observation: "We are strangely ingenious in perpetually seeking our own interest; and what the world does nakedly and without shame, those who desire to be devoted to God do also, but in a refined manner." This would be humorous if it weren't true. Evidently, the man who could not invent anything *can* invent a way of seeking his own interests.

The Five Ingenious Ways of Christians

There seem to be five ways that we have fallen into this strange ingenuity. The first is by *seeking our own interests while pursuing spiritual interests under the guise of seeking God's interests.* Being self-serving is where the strange ingenuity of Christians begins. Under the guise and pretense of seeking God's interest, we have a sly way of serving our own interests. We have become very clever in this endeavor. But we are only fooling ourselves into thinking that we are "about our Father's business" when we are actually doing our own business.

A pastor may talk about building the church and going around doing kingdom work for the glory of God. He may be quite eloquent about this, but what he is actually doing is shamelessly promoting himself while saying, "I'm doing this for Jesus' sake." When it comes right down to it, it is really his work, his influence, his ambition. That is why he is really doing it.

Musicians can go about a music ministry under the guise of serving the Lord while the same time promoting themselves. There is a fine line between promotion of self and exaltation of Christ. That line sometimes becomes so faint that people do not really know which side of it they are on. While pretending to seek the interest of God, they fall prey to promoting themselves. We want God to have the glory, but at the same time we would like a little commission paid to us for all the work we do. After all, God is "using us for His glory"; and we *do* have to make a living.

A second way is by *talking about the cross and living in the shadow of the cross, but never actually surrendering to it.* I do not find many people talking about the cross these days. But the few that do mention the cross seem only to live in the shadow of that teaching. They never actually fully surrender to the cross as an instrument of death to self. We want to die on the cross, but at the last minute, we always seem to find a way to rescue ourselves.

Nothing is easier to talk about than dying on the cross and surrendering ourselves, but nothing is harder than actually doing it. Talk is cheap, but the walk is what really matters. Some Christians have painted the cross in broad romantic strokes. The fully surrendered life is glamorized and popularized, but it is rarely realized. We can talk ourselves up to the cross, but at the last minute we always seem to find a reason to back down.

A third way is by *begging for the Holy Spirit to fill us while at the same time rejecting Christ's work in us* and *keeping things well in our own hands*. I find that another strange ingenuity among Christians is in the area of the Holy Spirit. It would be difficult to find a Christian not interested in being filled with the Holy Spirit. Of course, a variety of definitions of this doctrine have been floating around for years and clouding the clear teaching of the Word of God. That put aside for the moment, every Christian *does* desire to be filled with the Holy Spirit. I even find some Christians who ask God to fill them with the Holy Spirit. The only problem is that when God begins to move upon them, they reject that move.

They want God to take full control of their lives, but at the same time, they want to keep everything within their own control. The Holy Spirit will never fill a man or a woman who refuses to give up and give over to Him all control of their entire lives. Keep one compartment of your life back from the Holy Spirit, and it grieves Him that He cannot go any further.

Again, there are romantic ideas floating around about the work of the Holy Spirit in the life of the believer. But I want to emphasize that the work of the Holy Spirit can sometimes be harsh and routine. Before a field can be planted, it has to be plowed, and the plowing is harsh and deep. Similarly, there are things in my life that need to be uprooted, and that is exactly what the Holy Spirit wants to do.

We, on the other hand, want to give our lives over to the Holy Spirit, but at the same time, we want to control what the Holy Spirit does in our lives. We want to sit in the control room. We want to issue the commands and the "Thus saith the Lord." I have long concluded that the Holy Spirit works alone in my heart and needs no help from me, other than me simply surrendering absolutely to Him.

A fourth way that we fall into this strange ingenuity is by *talking about the dark night of the soul but rejecting the darkness*. I have read articles and even books dealing with this old theme of "the dark night of the soul." It soon becomes apparent after reading a little bit that most of the authors have no idea what the dark night of the soul really is. And this is where the strange ingenuity of the Christian comes into play. We embrace the dark night of the soul and, at the same time, we reject the darkness.

The dark night of the soul is not something pleasant to go through and does not end with a fellowship supper after church on Sunday night. It is a grueling experience that requires an absolutely strict detachment from everything that you normally rely on so that you are left with only Christ.

The dark night of the soul separates those who are genuinely interested in following Christ from those who just have a curiosity about the "deep things of God." We surely want God to do His work in our lives, but we want the lights left on. We want God to do in our hearts and lives that which will bring Him honoring glory, but we want to know and understand every step that He takes in our lives.

Darkness speaks of not knowing. We want God to *do*, but we want Him to do what He does within the scope of our comprehension. The dark night of the soul, however, is work of the Holy Spirit that exceeds the ability of any man or woman to understand. When we come through the dark night of the soul, we do not know what has really happened to us, but we do know who has made it happen.

A final way is by *using religion to promote our personal interests and advancement.* This is another strange ingenuity of the Christian. It amazes me just how religious people can get. Even the person who has rejected God in Christ and the Church seems to have a strong religious backbone that keeps him steady. But this use of religion for self can also be seen within the Church, in those who have embraced Christ and walk in the light of His Word.

We want to be involved in the work of the Lord, but we want to also be *known* as that faithful servant of the Lord. We want to do God's work, but we want people to know that we are doing God's work. We are ingenious and dream up religious ideas that have no other function than to advance someone's career.

We are perfectly willing to be as religious as possible as long as we can promote ourselves. It may seem strange, maybe even almost humorous, but it is one of the most damning elements operating in the Church today. It is what is robbing this generation of Christians of the spirituality needed to advance the kingdom of God. Perhaps the strangest example of this ingenuity in today's Christianity is seen in the aspect of religious entertainment and personalities, which promote man at the expense of God.

The Cure at the Cross

The only cure for our worldliness is the cross. We cannot put ourselves on the cross. We cannot choose the cross on which we will be crucified. Fénelon speaks of the various kinds of crosses—gold, silver, brass, wood, paper. The one thing they all have in common is that they crucify. How the cross will be used in your life is at the discretion of the Holy Spirit.

If I were to choose my cross and the time of my crucifixion, I would always choose the lesser of two evils. But when the Holy Spirit chooses, He chooses both the time of the crucifixion and the cross upon which He will crucify us. Our responsibility is to yield to His wisdom and allow Him to do the work without any advice from us.

At the Cross I'll Abide
Isaiah Baltzell (1832–1893)

O Jesus, Savior, I long to rest,
Near the cross where Thou hast died;
For there is hope for the aching breast;
At the cross I will abide.

At the cross (At the cross) I'll abide, (I'll abide,)
At the cross (At the cross) I'll abide, (I'll abide,)
At the cross I'll abide,
There His blood is applied
At the cross I am satisfied.

My dying Jesus, my Savior, God,
Who hast borne my guilt and sin,
Now wash me, cleanse me with Thine own blood,
Ever keep me pure and clean.

O Jesus, Savior, now make me Thine,
Never let me stray from Thee;
Oh, wash me, cleanse me, for Thou art mine,
And Thy love is full and free.

The cleansing pow'r of Thy blood apply,
All my guilt and sin remove;
Oh, help me, while at Thy cross I lie,
Fill my soul with perfect love.

12

Allowing God to Be Himself

Not that I speak in respect of want: for I have learned,
in whatsoever state I am, therewith to be content.
Philippians 4:11

When God said, "Let us make man in our own image," He put an insurmountable gulf between men and every other creature. From God's point of view, man is the highest form of creation. (God also bestowed on man above all other creatures the ultimate honor of His Son, whom He sent in the form of a man.) Something in man responds to something in God, which is a mystical link that no other creature possesses. So in order to know and understand man, we must come to an intimate knowledge of God.

You can put a statue of a person in a park; you can write his name on the walls of famous buildings; you can give the Nobel Peace prize and every kind of prize you can think of to him. But when it has all been said and done, you cannot say anything more of that person than God gave him a certain kind of life, a certain group of habits and a certain environment to be raised in—all are from God. Even the angels, archangels and seraphims cannot say anything more than that about themselves.

Ultimately, though, no matter who we are, we are as poverty stricken as the rest of mankind because we are afraid to use our religious imagination and afraid to believe what the Bible teaches us. The Bible talks about angels, archangels, seraphims, cherubims, watchers, holy ones, principalities and powers. However, we insist on only people; that is all. We are afraid to rise and let our faith-filled imagination enjoy the wonder of the universe.

Man is not like all the other creatures in God's creation. Man fulfills a role that no other creature can fulfill. As long as each living creature stays in its own environment and lives the kind of life God gave it, that creature fulfills that purpose for which it was made.

The creatures on the earth, in the air and in the sea all live in perfect harmony within their own environment. Day by day, they fulfill the purpose for which they were created by simply being themselves in the environment that God put them. Man is the only creation that is out of his original environment.

Roadblocks to Knowing God

An old German theologian once said, "There is nothing in the universe so much like God than the human soul." Everything in the Bible rests upon this truth. God created man with a soul, and in that soul is the capacity to know God and fellowship with God unlike any other creation.

Part of our worship experience is to rise up in a Spirit-filled imagination, see through the eyes of faith and look on God in adoring wonder and amazement. With our feet firmly rooted in the Scriptures, we can rise to that mysterious height of spirituality and become so God conscious that we lose a sense of all other things. Oh, to be lost in the wonder that is God! That is our spiritual heritage. That is the fullness of our redemption in Jesus Christ.

We must accept that as part of our creation and not fear that if we believe it, somebody will charge us with believing that man is all right. Man is not all right. Man is a fallen creature. Man is like an automobile that left the highway at a curve and rolled down among the rocks. Man is not all right. Man is lost.

I often hear preachers talk about a poor, lost, damned soul. No, never call yourself damned. You are lost if you are not converted. You are lost, but you are not damned. That is another thing altogether.

God created man to know Him, and to know Him in a fuller degree than any other creature can know God. No other creature has Christ, and no other creature has the capacity to know God.

The angels have certain capacities. They are holy and obey God. The seraphim sit around the throne and know God, but they do not know God as man knows God. God meant for man to be higher than the angels, and He made him in such a way that, for a little while, he is lower than the angels so that He might raise him higher than the angels. When it is all over and we are known as we are known, we will rise higher in the hierarchy of God than the very angels themselves.

Man lost his way because of his sin. We read about this in Romans 1:21: "Because that, when they knew God, they glorified him not as God, neither were thankful; but became vain in their imaginations and their foolish heart was darkened." Man, by his sin, has lost his knowledge of God. He has the potentiality to know God in a way no other creature can, but he still does not know Him because his conduct is unworthy and his heart is filled with a huge emptiness.

This is the reason we have crises all the time. We have lost our way and flounder in a sea of uncertainty.

Not Seeking the God Who Exists

What is the matter with mankind? We have been created to know God, but because of sin we have become vain in our imaginations. We do not like to have God in our knowledge. We have replaced God with everything but God. We have created a God out of our own imaginations.

This is the state of unregenerate man, but what I want to know is why Christians know Christ and God so little. I understand why the unregenerate man flounders in uncertainty, but why is it that the one creation of God who was created in His image knows very little about his Creator?

I can boil it all down to one sentence: We do not allow God to be Himself. We have lost all sense of knowing God as He is, and consequently we try to make God out to be what He is not. Instead of accepting the fact that we were created in His image, we have deteriorated to the point of believing that God has been created in *our* image.

God is not like us. We, however, are like Him because we have been created in His image. Why then the disparity? Why then this all-but-insurmountable gulf between God and us?

My thoughts on this matter are not the result of my advancement in years. I thought this way when I was converted at 17. At that time, I certainly did not have it developed this far, but over time I went back to the roots of my being. I studied the truths of Christianity. That is the wonderful thing about learning about our God: You can go back to the ancient fountain of our belief and read it over and over again. And then you'll know God for yourself all over again—where Adam started, and back further to where the world began, and back beyond that to where the angels began, and back to that ancient glorious fountain we call the being of God. And in Jesus Christ, we go back there as well.

You cannot know God like you know the multiplication tables or Morse code. You can know almost anything. However, when Paul said, "That I may know him" (Phil. 3:10), he did not mean intellectually but experientially. This means that to know God personally, my spirit must touch His spirit and my heart must touch His heart. Then I will experience the conscious knowledge of God.

It is one thing to hear about this concept but another thing to have lived that concept. It is one thing to hear that there has been a planet suddenly discovered but quite another thing to live on that planet. I can claim that I can know as much about a place by reading about it as most people who will go there. But everybody who goes to a place and comes back is all smiles for having actually been there. If you have actually been there, you know it in a way you cannot know it if you just read about it in a book.

The best unregenerate man can do is know about God. He can study the heavens and see the handiwork of God. The vastness of the universe reveals the unlimited nature of God. A delicate little flower blooming in the spring reveals the tenderness of God. All about us are indications of what God is like. But nothing in nature enables us to enjoy the intimacy of fellowship with God.

We can think of His attributes and rejoice in His grace. But the unregenerate can only do it as an academic exercise. For the unbeliever, God can only be understood through the lens of the microscope. God can only be examined in the laboratory of science. But it is only in a heart quickened by the Holy Spirit that God can really be known.

Settling for Secondhand Knowledge

With all our education, we still do not know God Himself very well. We do not know what fellowship we can have with Him. We leave each other all the time. We get together for fellowship and religious activities and all the religious prompts and lean one on the other, and then we walk away. Jesus said that He had His work to do; He had His healings, opening and unstopping ears, and answering questions. But He also had a personal knowledge of God that was intimate, and He was always able to lean on God.

Modern Christians are so busy doing this and doing that, going here and going there, that they know God only by hearsay. We hear of this and that, but we never hear it said for ourselves. We too easily settle for substitutes rather than the real thing. Under these circumstances, the most we can expect to hear is the indistinguishable echo of God's voice.

Wanting Things Instead of God

Another reason why Christians know Christ and God so little is that we want things instead of God. We are more interested in the gift than the giver. God wants to give us Himself. God wants to impart Himself *with* His gift. Separated from God, the gift is dangerous.

Living with Sins

The thing that stands the most in our way to this intimacy with God is, simply put, sin. The short route to intimacy with God is forgiveness of sins. The importance of this one thing in the life of the believer is vastly underestimated. Sin is responsible for our problems. Sin is the reason we were given such Scriptures as 1 John 1:9: "If we confess our sins, he is faithful and just to forgive us our sins, and to cleanse us from all unrighteousness."

The question that we should be asking is, why does God forgive sin? He forgives sin because sin is the roadblock that stands between us and Him. If we are ever going to know God, the roadblock has to be removed. So God can forgive sin. Why does God pour out His Spirit on us? In order that the Spirit can come and show us the things of God. Why does God answer prayer? In order that in answering prayer He might unveil His own face to us.

Relying on the Bible as an End in Itself

Why has God given us the Scriptures? It is by reading the Scriptures that we might know God. But the Scriptures are not an end in themselves. We hear them talked about as though they were an end in themselves. No man can believe more in the verbal inspiration of the Scriptures as originally given than I do. But verbal inspiration or any other theory of inspiration that makes the Bible an end in itself is a dangerous thing. The purpose of the Bible is not to replace God; the purpose of the Bible is to lead us to God.

The Bible is *never* an end in itself. I pray that God will raise up somebody that is able to make the Orthodox Church, the Bible people, the fundamentalists, the evangelicals, see and understand this. Remember that God Himself said that He was "a jealous God" (Exod. 20:5). We do not want anything or anybody to even remotely take His place.

Pathways to Knowing God

The only Christians you want to listen to are the ones who give you more of a hunger for God. You cannot know all that God has, but you can know all that God has revealed in Christ to your soul, which is infinitely more than you now know. When the Church of Christ returns to teaching this—when it gets serious, stops fooling around and begins to preach God Himself and all of the gifts of God—God will come along with Himself. All the blessings of God will come along with God. We want the fullness of the Spirit to fill us, we want godly living, we want a love divine, we want all of that, but if we keep those things apart from God Himself, we have only found a rose with a thorn.

If you find God, then you find all these things in God. You now say, "I've accepted Christ," and that is very wonderful and good. Paul had been converted and was one of the world's great Christians, but he still wrote: "That I may know him, and the power of his resurrection, and the fellowship of his sufferings, and be made conformable unto his death" (Phil. 3:10).

Everybody wants to know what the deeper life is, what living the crucified life is all about. I almost avoid speaking about this topic anymore, because people talk about the crucified life and the deeper life, but nobody seems to want God. As I come further into the knowledge of the triune God, my heart moves further out into God and God moves further into me. To know God is to experience a deeper life in God. Anything that keeps me from knowing God is my enemy. And any gift that comes between Him and me is an enemy.

I do not believe in keys, per se, but if there ever were a key to unlock the mystery of living the crucified life, it is simply this: Allow God to be Himself. This may seem like a simple thing. But if it were, Christians would not need encouragement to press on to spiritual perfection.

Christians are infamous for trying to put God in a box. The God who fits in a box is not the God and Father of our Lord Jesus Christ. The God who fits in the box is the God who can be controlled by man and who is at the beck and call of man. But this is not the God of the Bible. The God of the Bible is an awesome and mighty force in this universe—the God who created the heavens and the earth and everything that is—and He cannot be put in a little box created by mere man.

When we insist on allowing God to be Himself, there comes within our inner being an explosion of reality regarding the person of Jesus Christ. Our understanding of Him goes beyond academics and into that marvelous world of personal intimacy.

Perhaps the ultimate truth here is that when we allow God to be Himself, we then—and only then—discover who and what we are as men and women. We are then well on our way to living crucified lives.

My Lord, How Full of Sweet Content
Madame Guyon (1647–1717)

My Lord, how full of sweet content;
I pass my years of banishment!
Where'er I dwell, I dwell with Thee,
In heaven, in earth, or on the sea.

To me remains nor place nor time;
My country is in every clime;
I can be calm and free from care
On any shore, since God is there.

While place we seek, or place we shun
The soul finds happiness in none;
But with a God to guide our way,
'Tis equal joy, to go or stay.

Could I be cast where Thou are not,
That were indeed a dreadful lot:
But regions none remote I call,
Secure of finding God in all.

PART IV

THE BLESSINGS OF THE CRUCIFIED LIFE

13

THE BEAUTY OF CONTRADICTIONS

I am crucified with Christ: nevertheless I live; yet not I, but Christ liveth in me: and the life which I now live in the flesh I live by the faith of the Son of God, who loved me, and gave himself for me.

GALATIANS 2:20

A casual reading of the Scriptures could bring one to the conclusion that there are contradictions in the Bible. The enemies of the Bible have worked overtime to bring all of these apparent contradictions to light. Perhaps of all the "contradictions" in the Bible, no other author of the New Testament has been accused of contradicting himself more often than the apostle Paul.

Take for example what the apostle Paul says in 2 Corinthians 12:10: "Therefore I take pleasure in infirmities, in reproaches, in necessities, in persecutions, in distresses for Christ's sake: for when I am weak, then am I strong." What could be more contradictory? Paul says that when he is weak, then he is strong. This is obviously a great contradiction. How can you be strong when you are weak? And how can you put the word "pleasure" in the same sentence as "infirmities," "reproaches," "necessities," "persecutions" and "distresses"? No man in his right mind would associate these things with each other.

That is exactly the point: Paul is not in his "right mind." He is actually operating and ministering through the mind of Christ. What makes sense in the human mind does not make sense in the spiritual mind. And what makes sense in the spiritual mind seems to be contradictory to the natural man's mind or even the mind of the carnal man.

Two Contradictory Schools of Thought

Contradictory elements can be found even among Christians today. Within the framework of Christendom are two contradictory schools of thought. I am not referring to Calvinism and Arminianism, nor am I thinking of liberalism and fundamentalism. I'm referring to the reason we think Jesus came into the world.

Jesus Came to Help Us

The one school of thought holds that the Lord Jesus Christ came into this world in order to help us. That is, to take us out of the conflicts and the twisted situations we get into during our lives. The thinking is that we are all right except for a few twists and turns here and there, which surely the Lord can straighten out. Man is basically good except for a few little mistakes now and then.

This thinking also holds that the purpose of Christianity is to make us better people. By being Christians, we can be more popular and successful out in the world. No matter what our business is, Christianity and the teachings of Jesus could make us successful in it. For example, if you are a nightclub singer in the cesspools of the world, God will help you be the best nightclub singer you could possibly be. If you are running a crooked business, why, the Lord will help you to be successful and popular at that as well.

Believing this line of thought takes all of the supposedly good things in Scripture and claims them for ourselves. God simply wants to make us a good man (or woman). Feelings of low self-esteem can be quickly eradicated by believing that in Jesus, we can be the best we can possibly be. No matter what our problem is, Christ can make it go away. Christianity, according to this school of thought, is a sort of deluxe edition of life and helps improve the all-important self-esteem issues that we might have. It helps us to feel better about ourselves, which is viewed as the ultimate goal of all religion.

This "feel-better" Christianity has fostered an entire new industry of religious self-help. All you need to have a bestseller these days is the claim that what you say will help people feel better about themselves. Christianity is simply a huge following of people who believe that the teachings of Jesus in the Scriptures can help their self-images, bolster their egos and make them happy and cheerful. Visit any bookstore and you will see shelves of books written to encourage this type of thinking about Christianity.

To people who believe Jesus came only to help them—and this is what causes my heart to ache—Jesus died on the cross and suffered such intense pain and agony just so average Christians could feel better about themselves. Entire ministries today are devoted to this sort of thing, which has morphed into Christian "entertainmentism."

Instead of preaching sermons that "stir up your pure minds by way of remembrance" (2 Pet. 3:1), we now must entertain the congregation with the latest forms of entertainment available. Today's evangelical church is filled with entertainment toys of all sorts: projectors, bands, lights, noise—everything to capture the attention of poor, immature, underdeveloped Christians. If it rattles, if it is frivolous, if it makes a person laugh, it is accepted in the Church today with open arms.

If some local church decides to put away all of these entertainment toys and focus on Bible preaching and teaching, the crowds are sure to find another church, one that will tickle their fancy. Discipleship has given way to building self-esteem.

It is not so much what you know as it is how you look and feel that is important. This form of Christianity is not rooted in biblical truth but in cultural relativity, the aggrandizement of materialism. But woe be to the church that is not relevant to the surrounding culture.

To be fair, the temptation is too great for some pastors, and they succumb to the whims of the flesh. As long as the entertainment is "clean," it must be all right. But in my mind, to substitute intense worship of God for carnal entertainment is to misunderstand completely what it means to be a Christian.

It goes without saying that this type of thinking about Christianity satisfies the flesh. As long as the flesh is respectable, it is accepted in the Church these days. If it draws a crowd, it must be okay. If the people want it, why not give it to them? After all, so the reasoning goes, whatever it takes to get them in is all right as long as we can share Jesus with them. But I wonder what Jesus they are sharing with this crowd who wants their flesh satisfied.

I must point out here that "self" has done many good things in this world. It has built hospitals, orphanages, fed the hungry and clothed the poor. Self has been busy doing many good works. But the problem with these good works is that self requires the glory for all of these things. Now, if that self is highly religious, it is willing to give God 99 percent of the glory, but it wants to retain at least 1 percent of the glory so that people know what a faithful servant of the Lord the self is. This goes against scriptural teaching that God desires all of the glory. He will not share any percentage of His glory with any man.

Jesus Came to Put an End to Self

The other school of thought among Christians is that Jesus Christ came to bring an end to self. Not educate it or polish it, but put an end to it. Not cultivate it, give it a love for Bach, Plato and da Vinci, but to bring an end to self. This position pronounces a death sentence on everything related to self, or the ego. The apostle Paul set the standard when he said, "Not I, but Christ" (Gal. 2:20). The "I" must be eliminated in its entirety for Christ to hold His rightful position in our lives.

I must counsel that any church majoring in this ministry will pay a heavy price. The crowds will not flock to such a ministry, because they are seeking something to satisfy the flesh. They want something frivolous to entertain them, fluff them up and make them feel good about themselves.

But I do not think this is necessarily a negative. Those who do come to such churches possess an insatiable appetite for God and desire above everything else to see Christ glorified in their lives. The glory of God always comes at the sacrifice of self. I would rather have a congregation of 25 who seek to honor God 100 percent and give Him all of the glory than to have a congregation of 2,500 burdened with the curse of "entertainmentism" where God will have to fight for a percentage of the glory. To have God lurking in the shadows of the church is to not have God in that church.

Too many people underestimate the power self has as a distraction and a deception and, ultimately, its power to compromise solid biblical Christianity. The whole burden of New Testament theology is that the old self-values are false, that wisdom of the self is questionable, and that the self's goodness does not exist at all. The old self must go, regardless of the cost. In the old self-life, there is nothing redeemable. No matter how much the old self is cleaned up, it still contains an irredeemable core of corruption.

The new man is in Christ, and from now on we must reckon ourselves to be dead to sin but alive to God in Jesus Christ. The question that presents itself is, how do we deal with the old self?

If it is all that the Scriptures claim it to be, what is to be done with it?

This is where we come to another apparent contradiction in the Scriptures. Galatians 2:20, the key verse for the crucified life, is Paul's testimony, a beautiful type of personal theology thrown into an epistle that is not so beautiful. (The Galatians were known for their backsliding.) In Galatians 2, the apostle placed a little diamond that, in my mind, is at the center of the entire epistle: "I am crucified with Christ: nevertheless I live; yet not I, but Christ liveth in me: and the life which I now live in the flesh I live by the faith of the Son of God, who loved me, and gave himself for me."

Notice that this little verse has a number of contradictions in it. Paul starts the verse, with "I am crucified." On the surface, this looks like a contradiction. We know that no one who has been crucified will live to tell about it. So either Paul had not been crucified and can talk about it, or he had been crucified, in which case he could not talk about it.

No one has ever said, "Doctor, call the undertaker because I have died." If he had not died and was in his right mind, he would not say he had died. And if he had died, he would not be able to tell the doctor anything. Yet here is the apostle Paul saying that he has been crucified, and that in itself is a contradiction.

"Nevertheless I live." I could grant that by some wonder a man could say, "I have been crucified," as though he were speaking from the next world back to this one. But then Paul contradicts himself by saying, "Nevertheless I live." If he had been crucified, how then could he live?

Paul goes on to contradict that and say, "Not I." Then, going on further, he says, "The life which I now live in the flesh (I who have been crucified yet am alive and yet am not alive). And yet not I, but Christ now lives in me. I live in the flesh by the faith of the Son of God who loved me and gave Himself up for me." Talk about contradictions!

I deliberately emphasized the contradictions in this verse not because I believe there are any basic contradictions, but because this verse cannot be passed over when read, as is so often done with the Lord's Prayer or the Twenty-third Psalm. Either the verse means something or it does not. If it means something, I want to know what it means. If it does not mean anything, I ought to find that out and ignore it from here on. I do believe it means something. And not only do I believe it means something, but I also believe that it can be made practical, workable and livable in this present world in the lives of each one of us.

The old "I" must be absolutely crucified. That is what Paul is talking about in Galatians 2:20. Nobody can die partially. Either a person is dead or he is alive. This is much like drinking a glass of water with poison in it. That glass does not have to be filled 100 percent with poison to kill you. Even if only 1 percent of the liquid in the glass is poison, it will do the trick. In fact, it is my opinion that if only 1 percent of the liquid is poison, the glass is the more dangerous because the poison is less obvious. A glass with 100 percent poison will kill you outright. A glass with 1 percent poison will kill you for sure, but your death will be slower and drawn out and more painful.

In our Christian experience, if there is still some small shred of the old "I," the danger is great. That little bit will destroy just as surely as if the entire self were poison.

This is what Paul is talking about. The old self must go in its entirety and the new must come in its entirety. The "I" of the old self is crucified. We are dead, yet we are alive as we have never been alive before. It is not our life but the life of our blessed Redeemer that permeates every essence of our being.

Through this crucifixion of self, the life of Christ *can* be made practical, workable and livable in this present world in the lives of Christians.

"Yet not I, but Christ lives in me" is the most important phrase in Galatians 2:20. It is Christ in me that makes all the difference in the world. And until the old "I" is done away with, the life of Christ cannot come. However, many Christians hang on to the old "I" in desperation. So fearful are they that they might lose something, they forget what Jesus taught: "For whosoever will save his life shall lose it: and whosoever will lose his life for my sake shall find it" (Matt. 16:25). Until we are willing to lose, we will never find what God has for us.

What a great Christianity we evangelicals have these days. The liberals criticize us, and I for one do not blame them. They have a right; they do not have anything better to do. What a bunch of unworthy people we evangelicals have become, daring to stand up on our feet and preach to an intelligent audience that the essence, the final purpose and the cause of Christ is to save us from hell. How stupid can we get and still claim to be followers of Christ?

The purpose of God is not to save us from hell; the purpose of God is to save us to make us like Christ and to make us like God. God will never be done with us until the day we see His face, when His name will be on our foreheads; and we shall be like Him because we shall see Him as He is.

What a cheap, across-the-counter commercial kind of Christianity that says, "I was in debt, and Jesus came and paid my debt." Sure, He did, but why emphasize that? "I was on my way to hell and Jesus stopped me and saved me." Sure, He did, but that is not the thing to emphasize. What we need to emphasize is that God has saved us to make us like His Son. His purpose is to catch us on our wild race to hell, turn us around because He knows us, bring judgment on the old self and then create a new self within us, which is Jesus Christ.

The Beauty of the Lord

The most beautiful verse in the Bible is found in Psalm 90:7: "Let the beauty of the LORD our God be upon us." How wonderful is the beauty of the Lord our God? The sharp contrast to the beauty of the Lord our God is the ugliness of I, myself. The anonymous writer of the *Theologia Germanica* said, "Nothing burns in hell but self-will." That would be the "my," "me," "I" and "mine" that are the fuel of hell.

In the great divine exchange, God offers to trade our old selves, which have brought us so many problems, for new selves, which are Christ. The apostle Paul says, "And the life which I now live in the flesh I live by the faith of the son of God, who loved me, and gave himself for me."

To arrive at this point is well worth the journey. The pain associated with the sacrifice of the old self is nothing compared to the joy of experiencing that afflatus from on high coming down and penetrating every aspect of our life. In the natural world, the crucified life may seem full of contradictions, because the old nature, the self-life, is completely out of step with God and contrary to His nature. But when we crucify the self, God will give us His beauty, His joy, His Son.

Not I, But Christ
Frances E. Bolton (d. 1926)

Not I, but Christ, be honored, loved, exalted,
Not I, but Christ, be seen be known, be heard;
Not I, but Christ, in every look and action,
Not I, but Christ, in every thought and word.

Oh, to be saved from myself, dear Lord!
Oh, to be lost in Thee!
Oh, that it might be no more I,
But Christ that lives in me!

Not I, but Christ, to gently soothe in sorrow,
Not I, but Christ, to wipe the falling tear;
Not I, but Christ, to lift the weary burden,
Not I, but Christ, to hush away all fear.

Christ, only Christ! no idle words e'er falling,
Christ, only Christ; no needless bustling sound;
Christ, only Christ; no self important bearing,
Christ, only Christ; no trace of "I" be found.

Not I, but Christ, my every need supplying,
Not I, but Christ, my strength and health to be;
Not I, but Christ, for body, soul, and spirit,
Christ, only Christ, here and eternally.

Christ, only Christ ere long will fill my vision;
Glory excelling soon, full soon I'll see
Christ, only Christ my every wish fulfilling
Christ, only Christ my all and all to be.

14

THE REFRESHMENT
OF A REVIVAL

Abide in me, and I in you. As the branch cannot bear fruit of itself,
except it abide in the vine; no more can ye, except ye abide in me.
JOHN 15:4

Perhaps the greatest result of living the crucified life is that periodically it brings us to places of great spiritual victory. Throughout history, these periods have been referred to as revivals. Nothing is more needed right now in the contemporary Church than a revival.

A revival can occur on one of three levels. It can occur on a personal level, when an individual is revived. It can occur on a church level, when the whole church comes under a new spiritual impetus. It can occur on a community level, when a church overflows and the spiritual impetus in the church extends into the community.

A solitary person can enter into revival and have a revitalization of his spiritual life; a surge of power and an infilling of grace that causes him to enter into an experience so wonderful that words cannot describe it. Yet it would not affect the church that he happens to be attending. Within pretty cold churches, there have been greatly revived individuals, yet those churches did not experience revival because the churches opposed, neglected or considered these revived people fanatics or extremists and basically froze them out.

An individual church may experience an awakening, and such a revival impacts all of the individuals in the congregation and might even increase the number of individuals attending the church. People are lifted up and refreshed, and out of the frozen streams the ice breaks and the water begins to flow. Yet it often fails to extend beyond the local church. Many local churches have awakenings and refreshings, but these revivals do not get beyond the church walls into the community.

Then there is such a thing as a community revival where the Word does get into the community, going from one church to another, from one neighborhood to another, until the whole city is revived.

A community revival can start with an individual, extend to the church and extend out to include the community, but it can never occur in the reverse order. It can never begin in the community, unless there has been a church that has been revived, and no churches have ever been revived until individuals in the church have been revived.

Personal Revival

What do I mean by a "personal" revival? The best way I can describe it is that it is like a sick man returning to abundant health. Suppose a man has a blood count that is so low he is hardly able to get out of bed and can only stay up an hour at a time. Then, suddenly, he gets to a place where he is able to do a hard day's work, play on a baseball team and do anything else he wants because he has been restored to abundant health. Or imagine a weak battery that will barely turn a car engine over. Once that battery is recharged, it is filled with power and a spark will fly out from it and start the engine. That is what it means to be revived as a Christian. It is a new, refreshing rush of power from God.

This not only can happen to the individual but also to a church. But it must first happen to individuals in that church. I want to make this very clear, because it is important that we think right about this. There is no abstract idea here. We like to pray, "Oh, Lord, fall on Thy Church." Somehow, we imagine an abstract church somewhere and the Holy Spirit comes down and fills the church without the individuals inside being affected. But the Holy Spirit can only fall on individuals. There is no such thing as a church being blessed without having the members of the church touched. We pray, "Lord, bless Thy abstract Church," and we imagine a church detached from individuals, some sort of ideal church for which Christ died. But God cannot pour His Spirit out on His church unless He first pours it on the individuals within the church. The Holy Spirit "sat upon each of them," and so He will sit upon each of us (Acts 2:3).

Every local church is only as good as the individual members are, not one bit better. If God had some IQ test whereby He could test our faith or He had some way of taking our spiritual pulse, then we might add up all our membership and get the average, and the Church would be whatever the average is. Always remember, though, that the average does not make up the Church, for the Church is composed of individuals.

The lone soul can be revived. I am glad to be able to tell you that. God can send waves of glory, a new quickening to the lone individual. As a solitary individual, whether anyone else in your church receives revival or not, you do not have to wait around and say, "I'd like to see our church blessed," and then hope that when it is blessed you will also be blessed. The church can never be blessed until you or other individuals in your church are blessed. Whether the church gets any further on out or backslides and turns liberal, you can be blessed as an individual, and not all the rest of us put together can prevent that. You alone can be blessed whether or not your pastor personally knows about it.

When I was about 18 years of age, God came on me in a wonderful way and did wonderful things for me, but my church did not approve of it. In fact, they as good as told me that I was a bit extreme and that the church would be better without my company. I was not thrown out; I was just invited not to belong, and I left and went to a Christian and Missionary Alliance church. Whether the church believes or not, you *can* have all that God has for you as an individual. Whether your wife or your husband or father or mother or friend will agree or not does not make a bit of difference. God always is ready to help the lone individual.

The history of the Old Testament is filled with stories of lone individuals—men and women—meeting God. The story of revivals throughout the ages has been the story of lone men meeting God, of going out and finding God all alone. Sometimes they went down to the church basement, sometimes to caves, sometimes out under trees, sometimes by haystacks, but they went alone to meet God, and then the revival went out from there. I say that you, personally, can be blessed and yet not have a revival in your church. If you are attending a church that is suffering a spiritual malaise, a low level of or even a dead spirituality, never lower yourself to match that level. Instead, say to yourself, *By the grace of God, I'm going to be what I should be regardless.*

How to Have a Personal Revival

The big question then is, how can we experience a personal revival? In order to see a fresh outpouring of the Holy Spirit in our lives, there are four things that must be set in order. The work of the Holy Spirit is not capricious; rather, there are some well-defined spiritual rules that govern His work in our lives.

Set Your Face Like Flint

First, if you are going to have a personal revival, you must "set [your] face like a flint" (Isa. 50:7). A plow that is going to be used on sod must have a sharp point. Likewise, if you want a personal revival, you have to have a hard-nose because of all of the schemes and tricks of the world. You must set your face like flint and say, "I go by the grace of God. I want all that the New Testament has for me."

Set Your Heart on Jesus

Second, you must set your heart on Jesus Christ. Wherever He takes you, go with Him. Whatever He takes you away from, listen to Him and follow what He says. Whomever you must ignore, move away from. If you want to be all that God wants you to be, set your face like flint and go straight to Jesus.

I will always thank God that the Bible includes the passage where the blind man said, "Jesus, thou Son of David, have mercy on me" (Mark 10:47). His disciples went out and said to the man, "Be quiet. This is not done in church. Just keep still." Instead of their words discouraging him, it fired him to cry out more, until Jesus turned around and said, "What do you want?"

"I want to be healed."

And Jesus said, "Okay, here's your healing." The man received his eyesight because he paid no attention to the "timekeepers and referees" who served only to keep people away from Jesus.

I recently looked again at John Bunyan's book *Pilgrim's Progress* and read a page or two, more or less for the style than anything else. But you cannot read Bunyan very long just for the style, because the story of Christian and how he got into trouble on his journey is so fascinating.

Early on, Christian says, "I find by this book [the Bible] that I am in great distress. I must leave my hometown of Destruction and journey to a heavenly home." So he plans to start out for that heavenly home. He is in terrible stress before he begins, and he finally breaks down before his children and says, "Oh, my dear wife and children, I've gotten into an awful condition. Just awful."

His family basically replies, "We know what's wrong with you. You're just tired." So they put him to bed, and the next morning he got up and they said to him, "How are you feeling, Father?"

"I didn't sleep a wink. I couldn't forget that we're living in the city of Destruction."

Bunyan says that when Christian's family found that they could not quiet and console him, when they could not pat him on the back and say, "Go back to sleep and sleep it off," they started being harsh toward him and derided him. Then, when he would not give up because of their scorn, they ignored him.

I thought as I read it, *First they soothe you, then they pat you on your back and hope you'll quiet down. After that, they use harsh words, accusing you of thinking you are better than other people. And when that doesn't work, they deride you and start making fun of you. And when that doesn't work, they ignore you.*

That is exactly how it happens when you set your heart on Jesus and seek personal revival. If you decide to seek a deeper relationship with God and meet Him on your own and have a refreshing from God to get rid of the old barnacles and the weights and hindrances and get back a new spirit within you, you will find that some people will say, "Well, you're just excited. You've just allowed that man Tozer to stir you up." John Bunyan said that when Christian was treated like that, he went to be by himself and pray.

Set Yourself Up for Examination

The third thing you must do in order to experience personal revival is expose your life to God's examination. The trouble is that we keep ourselves and cover our hearts. Scripture says, "He that covereth his sins shall not prosper: but whoso confesseth and forsaketh them shall have mercy" (Prov. 28:13). Out of habit, we cover ourselves and try to hide our sins. If you want revival, you must allow the Scriptures to be the Scriptures in your life.

Expose your whole life to Jesus Christ. Expose yourself in prayer. Expose yourself in Scriptures. Expose your heart in obedience. Expose it by confession and by restitution. "Restitution" is a forgotten word today that nobody uses anymore. But it *is* in the Bible. "Restitution" means to get straightened out with people. When you make restitution, you will be amazed at how wonderful you will feel.

Set for Yourself Holy Affirmations

The fourth thing you must do for personal revival is to make some holy affirmations. Several affirmations that I have had to make before God have significantly changed my walk as a Christian. Let me share them with you, and then you take it from there.

Declare before God never to own anything. I do not mean for you to get rid of anything that you can use. I mean you should get rid of that bunch of trash you have in your life. Too many Christians are a bunch of pack rats, gathering everything, going out and bringing everything they can. If you were to find a magpie nest, you would find a variety of things: a mirror, a coat hanger, a piece of glass, maybe a dime. The magpie cannot use those things; the bird just likes them, so it collects them. Similarly, because of a coveting spirit, many Christians collect all around them things that they really cannot use.

Keep in mind that if you feel you own something, it is actually dragging you down. Cut loose from the ownership of that item, and then God will let you have it. Cut loose from inside yourself, and God will let you have the thing on the outside of yourself. This has to do with your automobiles, property, clothes and everything you have collected throughout your life. Take everything and say that God has it. Do not imagine for a minute that if you give God 10 percent, you are okay and you can keep the remaining 90 percent. God must have 100 percent. Once you give it all to Him, then He will make sure you have enough to look after yourself and your family.

If there is anything you own that God cannot have, you never will have a revival. If there is anything that you own that God cannot have, you cannot have God. God has a right to command whatever He wants the moment He wants it. The moment God knows that He can have whatever you have anytime He wants it, then the Lord will probably let you keep it, and it will be a blessing for you instead of a curse. It will help lift you up instead of being an anchor to weigh you down.

Another affirmation that has been important to me is to never defend myself. This is a tough one, particularly for Americans. Through the years, I have taken a great many people to the twenty-third chapter of Exodus to teach them how to trust God and not worry about enemies. If you try to fight people, you will only get bloody and bruised, and you'll feel miserable. You will stay an immature Christian and never have a revival. But if you let God do your fighting for you, you will come out all right.

Another affirmation that has been important to me is to never defame a fellow Christian. By this, I mean never believe evil about him or speak an evil report about him. Remember your past and your own tendency to give in to temptation. I think sometimes the Spirit of God shuts Himself up tight and cannot come on us because we have defamed a brother or sister Christian. Such an evil report becomes a weapon in the devil's hand.

As a pastor and a member of an executive committee, I am forced under God that if I hear charges against a man's life, I am obligated to protect the Church of God from that man. But this does not mean that I will defame that man or any other man by believing gossip or by spreading it.

Another important affirmation is never to receive or accept any glory. Oh, how we love glory. We just want to take a little of it for ourselves. We sing songs attributing glory to God and giving Him all the glory, but sometimes we do not really mean it. We want God to get *most* of the glory, but we would like to reserve just a little bit for ourselves. After all, we believe we have earned it.

Why You Should Seek a Personal Revival

Do not wait for tragedy to drive you to God. Some Christians start to get cold in their hearts and then some tragedy strikes, either to themselves or to their families, and out of that grief they say, "Forgive me, God." They want to start over. But must it always be like that? Must we always wait around for God to chastise us? Must we always come to God with bleeding backs? Determine before God that you will not wait for tragedy to drive you to Him. Take your cross voluntarily.

Many years ago when I was a very young preacher, I preached in a town called Despard, West Virginia. It was commonly called Tinplate because a great tinplate factory was there, but it was also a coal-mining area. I and some others went into that area and had some gospel meetings. The meetings were not exactly what some people thought they should be, and some began to feel burdened by the fact that no revival was taking place. At the meeting one night was a tall, handsome, blond coal miner. He said to his wife, "You know, our people need God. They need God, and this thing isn't going well. Honey, if it's all right with you, I'm going to take tomorrow off and wait on God and pray and fast all day long. I want to wait on God for revival for this town."

Instead of going to work the next day, he got down on his knees and waited on God with an open Bible all day long. The next day he went back to his work on the tipple. (The tipple is where the cars carrying coal are emptied out.) He was working on that tipple and suddenly something went wrong. The car jumped the track, crashed and broke apart. The cars at this mine were old-fashioned wooden ones, and this one broke into splinters sharp as daggers, and one ripped through this man's thigh. It pierced an artery, and this 47-year-old man bled to death on the dirt floor.

Remember, the day before he had spent with God. That struck me as a message from heaven above, and I thought ever since, *Dear God, how wonderful it would be to spend my last day with Thee alone in prayer.*

Now, the coal miner could not take every day off to pray, for he had to work and support his family. But I think it was a wonderful thing that he was so near to God the day before he died. He had unburdened himself to God the night before. You cannot spend all day with God and not be ready to go to heaven the next day.

Do not ask me why God took the dear man away. I will never know that. God never has let me in on all His secret plans. I only know that in the course of things, the man could have died anywhere any day. But the Spirit of God urged him to spend a day in prayer for his own soul and for his church. Suppose he had been too cold to listen or had been too far away to hear? Suppose he had been like someone running on automatic, not listening for God's call? He would have died on the tipple the next day all right, but oh, what a difference.

Maybe God is calling you to do something extraordinary, something that does not appear on your calendar or agenda, something to revive your own soul. Maybe God is calling you to do something radical and extreme for your soul. I hope and pray that the world and the pleasures of it are not so great that you are unable to hear Him. The biggest thing in the world is not whether you live to be 100 years old; the biggest thing in the world is whether you can hear God speaking to you now. That is what counts.

Is God saying anything to you? You can have a revival whether anybody else ever gets one or not. There is no reason why you personally cannot set your face like flint and determine to go wherever Jesus takes you. When you find Him, you will find the floodgates of mercy. You will find fresh oil. You will find a wonderful new revival life for yourself.

Old-Time Power
Paul Rader (1878–1938)

We are gathered for Thy blessing,
We will wait upon our God;
We will trust in Him Who loved us,
And Who bought us with His blood.

Spirit, now melt and move
All of our hearts with love,
Breathe on us from above
With old time power.

We will glory in Thy power,
We will sing of wondrous grace;
In our midst, as Thou has promised,
Come, O come, and take Thy place.

Bring us low in prayer before Thee,
And with faith our souls inspire,
Till we claim, by faith, the promise
Of the Holy Ghost and fire.

15

THE EVERLASTING REWARDS OF LIVING THE CRUCIFIED LIFE

*Behold, how good and how pleasant it is for brethren
to dwell together in unity!*
PSALM 133:1

The worth of any journey can always be measured by the difficulties encountered along the way. The more difficult the journey, the more satisfying the destination. I have been thinking of the crucified life as a journey. It has a beginning, of course, but the end is never this side of glory. I am reminded of this thought in a hymn called "The King's Business":

> I am a stranger here within a foreign land;
> My home is far away upon a golden strand;
> Ambassador to be of realms beyond the sea,
> I'm here on business for my King.

Not many Christians consider themselves strangers "within a foreign land." But that is exactly what we are if we are Christians. If we have begun the journey and are living the crucified life, this world certainly is not our home. That is why we should never get too comfortable in this life.

Some people have been misinformed about the Christian life and living the crucified life. For some reason, they think that it is an easy path. They believe that God will take away all of their problems and difficulties and that they will be able to live their lives without any kind of distraction or disturbance. As everybody who has traveled this journey knows, such is not the case. If your journey is not cluttered with difficulties and hardships and burdens, you just might be on the wrong path.

It is impossible to read the Bible and not see that every man and woman of God faced some extreme difficulties and troubles. Church history is also filled with stories of the struggles that believers have had, even beyond what the martyrs of the Church faced. If the Christian life is as easy as some people believe, then why all this history of struggle and difficulty and martyrdom?

Types of Difficulties

Difficulties can fall into several categories. First, difficulties can be a distraction. By "distraction," I mean that they can knock us off our main course. Back on the farm in Pennsylvania, we plowed using a horse. In order for that horse not to be distracted, we had to put blinders on it. It was that easy for a horse to get distracted.

The difficulties that come our way can distract us from our true purpose before God. We can become so immersed in our difficulties that we see nothing else. We can forget the direction we are going. If you study the history of Israel, you will find that their whole journey was filled with distraction after distraction. They would get going in one direction and then something would happen to distract them and pull them either to the left or to the right.

Of course, the difficulties that come our way can make us feel discouraged. Many people have a hard time believing that a Christian could ever get discouraged. When a Christian has difficulties that bring him to a point of discouragement, he is tempted to believe that he hasn't really been born again. The truth of the matter is that the various difficulties that he faces has the potential of shrouding his good sense and clouding him with a good dose of discouragement.

It is quite sad to read or hear of a person who has started out well but somehow got distracted, and that this distraction caused him to stop dead in his tracks. The apostle Paul dealt with this among the Galatian Christians:

Are ye so foolish? having begun in the Spirit, are ye now made perfect by the flesh? (Gal. 3:3).

The Galatians had started out well, but something along the way had distracted them from their original purpose and brought them to a state of discouragement. They began to feel as though they had to fight their own battles. That is where we also get into trouble. Difficulties are a common aspect of life. But we should be encouraged by what Paul wrote to the Corinthians:

There hath no temptation taken you but such as is common to man: but God is faithful, who will not suffer you to be tempted above that ye are able; but will with the temptation also make a way to escape, that ye may be able to bear it (1 Cor. 10:13).

I think in this same regard that the worth of a person can always be measured by what happens when he is really facing trouble. It is a given that we will face difficulties and troubles. The pathway to living the crucified life has many obstacles, hindrances and dangers. So it is not that we have these difficulties; rather, it is how we handle those difficulties that really determines the quality of our relationship to God. If we give up, what does that say about our trust in God?

The Example of King David

Nobody had more difficulties and troubles than King David, as recorded in the Old Testament. I am sure that in some instances, he brought some difficulties and problems on himself. But for the most part, his difficulties and burdens were because of God's call on his life.

David recounts these difficulties in Psalm 57. This is a most extraordinary psalm because it gives us a glimpse into the very heart of this man. The quality of David's life is seen in how he faced his difficulty.

In Psalm 57, David confesses the overwhelming nature of his difficulties. In verse 1 he calls them "calamities." It is always good to recognize the problem that is facing you. How many times do people ignore a problem or don't really see the problem in front of them? Nothing is more dangerous than being faced with a problem or difficulty and ignoring it.

David did not ignore his "calamities." He recognized them for what they were. He did not try to explain them away, ignore them or blame someone else for them. That is often what we do when we experience calamities. For some reason, we believe that if we can blame someone else for our problems, the problems will go away. That just doesn't happen.

I do not think there was a cowardly bone in David's body. From the time he faced Goliath until his deathbed, David feared nothing but God. Imagine a teenage boy standing with five smooth stones, facing one of the greatest soldiers of his time. Goliath was a giant in many regards. He was not just big, but he was also a fighting machine. I think it is safe to say that Goliath never lost a battle. His fighting record was tremendous.

That is why the Philistines sent Goliath up in front of the whole Israeli army. They knew what he could do.

However, Goliath had never met David before. Goliath accused David of not knowing what he was doing. He accused him of not understanding what was really at stake. But David told Goliath that he was not coming against him in his own stead but in the name of Jehovah, the God of Israel. As long as David was on God's side, he had nothing whatsoever to fear.

David's encounter with Goliath set a standard for David for the rest of his life.

The Positive Side of Difficulties

There is a positive side to these severe problems and difficulties: Much can be learned by facing them. But we must remember that the enemy facing us, the one attacking us, can discern where we are spiritually and use that against us. Here is the strategy of the enemy. He knows our weak points and attacks them with all the viciousness of hell's fire. But here is what the devil does not know. The apostle Paul points it out for us:

> I take pleasure in infirmities, in reproaches, in necessities, in persecutions, in distresses for Christ's sake: for when I am weak, then am I strong (2 Cor. 12:10).

Those on the journey of living the crucified life know the spiritual dynamic of this statement. It is in our weakness that God manifests Himself so mightily. King David knew that his strength was not in himself but in God.

False Solutions for Our Difficulties

Just as there are many difficulties and problems that we face in our journey, so too there are many solutions. Books by the truckload offer us solutions to one or another of our difficulties and problems. For the most part, however, these books miss the mark.

One solution offered these days is to engage the enemy. When we feel the enemy attacking us, we need to dig in our heels and have a face-off with him. This is a display of spiritual machismo. We want to show the troublemaker, and anybody else who might be watching us, that we're nobody to be fooled with.

The only problem is that the devil will never face you directly. And I might as well say it: The devil does not fight fair. The devil uses rules that he makes up as he goes along. For a Christian to think that he can outguess the devil is probably the most dangerous thought he can harbor.

The devil loves us to engage him in battle. This is what he lives for. He knows that he cannot win, but he also knows that he can do some damage in the process. The entire agenda of the enemy can be boiled down to one objective: embarrass God through some of His children. The devil thought he could do that with Job in the Old Testament. But what the devil did not know was that God was in absolute control every step of the way.

Another solution that some Christians try is using Scripture to defy the enemy. But what these Christians do not realize is that the devil knows Scripture better than some theologians. The devil's heart is not filled with doubt but with hatred and jealousy. His hatred of God and jealousy of God blind him to the reality of God's Lordship.

For any Christian to use Scripture without the Spirit is like engaging in a battle with a paper sword. It is not the Word only that will turn back the devil; rather, it is the Word and the power. The devil can quote Scripture better than any seminary professor, but when the Word is under the direction of the Holy Spirit, it will always find its deadly mark.

The Two-Part Solution for Our Difficulties

When Daniel was thrown into the lions' den, he did nothing to defend himself. He did not try to engage the enemy. He did not try to defy his enemies by quoting Scripture. He simply left his situation in God's hands. This brings me to David's solution to his problems. In Psalm 57, David reveals the only solution to difficulties and problems and calamities. There are two parts to this solution.

Part One: Take Refuge in God

In Psalm 57:1, David says, "In the shadow of thy wings will I make my refuge, until these calamities be overpass." Instead of going out to fight his own battles, David took refuge in God. How tempting it might have been for him to show the enemy his strength and might. To show his enemy that he was not somebody to be messed with must have been a great temptation for a man like David. Instead of engaging the enemy, however, David took refuge in the shadow of God's wings.

What a blessed truth to understand that, in the middle of all of our difficulties and calamities, we have a refuge. Certainly, there is a time to go forth into battle and engage the enemy. But this should only be under the direct orders of the Captain of our salvation. Young David understood this as he faced Goliath.

> And all this assembly shall know that the Lord saveth not with sword and spear: for the battle is the Lord's, and he will give you into our hands (1 Sam. 17:47).

The battle is always the Lord's.

Part Two: Exalt God

The other aspect of David's solution is found in Psalm 57:5. David took refuge in God but, at the same time, he was giving God an opportunity to exalt Himself. "Be thou exalted, O God." This was David's passion. The only way God could be exalted was if he, David, would find his refuge in God.

David was not an opportunist. That is, he did not look for opportunities to exalt himself above the people he was ruling or even to exalt himself above his enemies. Be sure, he had plenty of opportunities along the way to do this.

Although David was not a perfect man, he had a perfect trust in God and not himself. This is where we get into trouble. Certainly, we trust God; but for some reason, we trust ourselves above God, just in case God does not come through. David was not like that. He put himself in such a position that if God did not come through, everything would be lost.

Again, take for example when David faced Goliath. Do you appreciate the great risk David took? I have often wondered why King Saul allowed David to go out there and face Goliath like that. If David had failed, Israel would have failed. The entire situation between Israel and the Philistines boiled down to a teenage boy by the name of David and his five smooth stones and sling. It is hard to imagine David standing in front of the giant. If God did not come through, everything would have been lost for him and the Israelites.

The Language of Heaven

It boils down to this: Are you willing to say, "Oh, Lord, exalt Yourself above me and all that I am—possessions, friends, comforts, pleasures, reputation, health and life—everything. Test me, Lord, and see whether I can really leave everything in Your hands. Bring my life into line so that I will not be fully myself, but fully in You, knowing the truth that I can take refuge in You."

If you have come this far, may I suggest one further step in your prayer: "Oh, Lord, set in motion a chain of circumstances that will bring me to the place where I can sincerely say, 'Be thou exalted above the heavens.'"

Have you ever wondered what language they speak in heaven? This is it. This is the language of heaven. They will come from the north and the south and east and the west. They will come from German, Spanish, Greek and Syrian speaking countries. They will come from all around the world and will never have to sit down and go through the process of learning a new language. In the kingdom of God, everyone will speak the same language of which the keynote will be: "Worthy is the Lamb that was slain to receive glory and power and wisdom and might and honor" (see Rev. 4:11). You will know heaven's language when you get there without having to study it—and you will not speak with an accent.

Allowing yourself to be put in such a position that God is exalted is the goal of living the crucified life. When you allow God to be exalted in your difficulties, you will be in the perfect position to smell the sweet fragrance of His presence.

All Hail the Power of Jesus' Name
Edward Perronet (1726–1792)

All hail the power of Jesus' name!
Let angels prostrate fall;
Bring forth the royal diadem,
And crown Him Lord of all;
Bring forth the royal diadem,
And crown Him Lord of all.

Ye chosen seed of Israel's race,
Ye ransomed from the fall,

Hail Him who saves you by His grace,
And crown Him Lord of all;
Hail Him who saves you by His grace,
And crown Him Lord of all.

Sinners, whose love can never forget
The wormwood and the gall,
Go spread your trophies at His feet,
And crown Him Lord of all;
Go spread your trophies at His feet,
And crown Him Lord of all.

Let every kindred, every tribe,
On this terrestrial ball,
To Him all majesty ascribe,
And crown Him Lord of all;
To Him all majesty ascribe,
And crown Him Lord of all.

O that with yonder sacred throng,
We at His feet may fall!
We'll join the everlasting song,
And crown Him Lord of all;
We'll join the everlasting song,
And crown Him Lord of all.

Crown him, ye morning stars of light,
Who fixed this earthly ball;
Now hail the strength of Israel's might,
And crown Him Lord of all,
Now hail the strength of Israel's might,
And crown Him Lord of all.

16

SPIRITUAL GUIDES FOR THE JOURNEY

And I will give you pastors according to mine heart, which shall feed you with knowledge and understanding.

JEREMIAH 3:15

The way of the crucified life can be precarious, making a spiritual guide all but indispensable. But it is important to have a guide who understands the way sufficiently and can give clear instructions on how to live the crucified life. The Church has no shortage of people who have advice to give. There is, however, a shortage of spiritual guides with the wisdom needed to navigate such precarious living. The question to be considered is, how do you recognize a true spiritual guide?

It is crucial that we watch out for the false guides. For every true guide there are a multitude of false ones. The use of false guides is a popular strategy of the enemy to destroy the work of God in a person's life. Some guides are obviously false and easily recognized as such because their teachings are completely off-the-wall. What I am concerned about, however, are those false guides who are close to the truth.

One of the first things that should catch our attention about a potential guide is his use of Scripture. The most dangerous spiritual guide is the person who is 95 percent true to the Scriptures. Remember, it is not the truth that hurts you; rather, it is the evil. The 95-percent truth is trumped by the 5 percent of evil. This our archenemy knows only too well.

The true spiritual guide embraces all of the Scriptures, while the false guide will avoid certain passages of Scripture. This is something only the well-taught Christian can fully recognize. Unfortunately, the problem today is that many Christians are not well versed in the teachings of Scripture.

Another sign that should concern us is the use of extra-scriptural material. Many of these false guides will begin with some Scripture and gradually move into some extra-scriptural material. It might be a book or series of essays or some poetry. What it is makes no difference. Everything must be tested by the Word of God, which is the final authority for the Christian. The place of the Bible in someone's teaching should clue us in to the genuineness of a spiritual guide.

One more sign of false spiritual guides is their undue emphasis upon themselves. When the teaching always focuses on the teacher, that is a clue that something is wrong. The true spiritual guide will focus all of the teaching on Jesus Christ and only on the Christ of the Bible.

True Spiritual Guides

Most of the true spiritual guides are what I refer to as "evangelical mystics." I know the terminology is not acceptable in many Christian circles, so let me explain a little of what I mean. By "evangelical mystic," I mean someone who has his feet firmly and irrevocably planted in the Scriptures. This is the absolute first qualification of true spiritual guides. They have accepted the Scriptures as their only rule for faith and practice and have put their faith and trust in the Lord Jesus Christ of the Bible. I do not need any suppositions mixed with airy speculations. I want to know that my spiritual guide is committed to the Word of God.

Diagnose the Inner Spiritual Life

There are several other aspects of these spiritual guides that are important. First, true spiritual guides are what I would call soul surgeons who possess the power to diagnose the inner spiritual life. Traveling down the crucified life pathway, we certainly are in need of a physician of the soul who can trace with great skill our heart's troubles. Spiritual diagnosis is very valuable in maintaining solid spiritual health. It is one thing to diagnose a problem and something else altogether to prescribe a cure based on Scripture and not on worldly wisdom.

The wisdom of this world has nothing to offer the heart cry of the soul infatuated with God. All of the feel-good therapy can in no way touch the inner reaches of the soul. We need a spiritual guide who knows God, knows the Word of God and understands human nature.

Practice the Inward Life

Effective spiritual guides will be apostles of the inward life without ever succumbing to being merely introspective. They probe the interior reaches of the soul so that they may turn the inner eye outward, focusing upon the person of Christ. Their goal is to lead the soul upward into the wonderment that is God.

Exude Fresh Spirituality

What makes these spiritual guides so refreshing is their spiritual originality. In reading some of their works, you will catch a sense of the freshness of the dew of God's presence upon them. They do not just write a collection of words to produce copy but powerful words that produce in the heart of the man who longs for God a fragrance of God's presence. In reading these works, we have a sense that we are encountering the words of a true seer, someone who knows whereof he speaks.

We are so accustomed these days to reading books written by authors who copied from other books ad nausea. Such books have the musty smell of mindless repetition and spiritual bankruptcy. When we come to the literature by these spiritual guides, we quickly sense the difference. There is no repetition of religious ideology here but rather a sacred revelation of the heart and mind of God based upon the sacred Scriptures.

Experience the Same Difficulties that We Have

The thing that makes true spiritual guides so genuine is the fact that they live real lives and encounter real difficulties. Many of them were martyrs for the cause of Christ and left behind proof of their incredible devotion to God. They knew what it meant to suffer hardship for the cause of Christ. They did not live in ivory towers sheltered from the harshness and bitterness of the world's opposition to true spirituality. Many of them found themselves in exile because of their commitment to the inner way. Their ways were not easy and strewn with roses, but there was a fragrance of God's presence, which for them made all the difference in the world.

Devoted Exclusively to God

True spiritual guides are men and women who are devoted to God exclusively. Their lives are not dependent on human reason, imagination and feeling. Nor are they caught up in talking eloquently about divine things and spewing glowing thoughts about God that are far removed from the average Christian. They have discovered the simplicity of fellowship and solitude with God.

Hate Evil

The mark of devotion these men and women have are a common horror of evil and sin. Nothing so stirs their rage as the evil around them, particularly the evil in the Church. Nothing so stirs their imagination as thoughts of God and His kingdom within. They cultivate within themselves a perpetual habit of listening to that sweet inner voice of His presence. Out of such inner experiences comes a radical determination to obey that voice, regardless of the cost.

The Literature of Past Spiritual Guides

The literature of these evangelical mystics and spiritual guides focuses on the worshiper rather than the student. Everything is prepared for those God-enamored people who seek God above all other things and who disdain the things of this world.

The poetry of these evangelical mystics soars into the heavens above with such rapturous joy and delightful harmony with the divine. Reading the poetry of these spiritual guides is to experience their passion for God. Often after reading such poetry, I lay the book down and sigh deeply within, satisfied with the wonderful truth that the writer was able to express my deepest feelings for God in language far better than my ability to compose.

Whether reading a book of essays or poems, one must keep in mind that it was never intended to be used in public. These works were meant to be read in the privacy of personal worship. Surrounded by the solitude of adoring wonder, these authors lift our hearts in joyous anticipation of the manifest presence of God.

With all of that said, however, I need to set forth some guidelines for reading some of these great books of spiritual devotion. Never come to one of these books as you would come to another type of literature. Too many people in their rush to finish the reading miss out on the quiet of experiencing the presence of God. Some of these books will take you places you've never been before spiritually.

Come with a Spirit of Longing

The first thing to keep in mind when reading one of these Christian devotional classics is to come with the spirit of longing. Those with a strong sense of curiosity need not read these books. There will be nothing to satiate their curiosity. These classics demand that the reader come with a strong desire to know God. Without that strong desire, the reader will quickly tire and grow bored with the book. Nothing is here for the frivolous of heart. Nothing is here to entertain the mature Christian. Everything here stirs up an insatiable desire to know God in the fullness of His revelation. When this is done, the whole inner life will be quickened and enriched by truth.

Come After Praying and Meditating on the Scriptures

Another recommendation would be in the area of prayer. Only come to such books after significant time in prayer and meditation on the Scriptures. Anyone who comes unprepared and hurriedly will miss the whole intent of these books. If our hearts are not prepared to receive, our time in these books will not be time well spent.

This is one of the major things wrong with today's Christian Church. In our hurry to keep up with the culture around us, we have reserved little time to quietly wait before God and meditate on His Word. The reader who prepares his heart and mind to receive will experience in these classics vistas of glorious revelation of God.

Have a Devotional Attitude

Another thing has to do with our attitude. It is very difficult to find time, let alone intention, to quietly wait before the Lord. But when we come to one of these great spiritual classics, we need to come with an attitude of devotion. This is hard for us as Americans. We rush here and there with an energy that can't last forever. Then we collapse in a heap of exhaustion.

To get the most out of these books, it is important for us to learn how to develop the disciplines of silence and meditation. The world is too much among us. We need to learn how to shake it off and worthily come into the presence of almighty God. I believe that humbling ourselves in silence before God will create within us a real spirit of expectation of what we really expect God to do in and through this book that we have before us. That is why I said earlier that these books are not for public reading. These books are for a person to get alone and read quietly, slowly and meditatively. Getting away from all distractions will go a long way in developing the discipline of concentration on the things of God.

Surrender and Consecrate Yourself

Before beginning to read one of these classics, it is important that you make sure you have surrendered and consecrated yourself to God. The spiritual guides begin where others leave off. The assumption from their point of view is that you are ready to go further into the deep things of God, that you are already starting to live the crucified life. So before you begin to read, spend time alone with God and get your heart in such a submissive and obedient position that God can begin speaking to you through the voices of these spiritual guides.

If there are large areas of your life that remain unsurrendered to Christ, the reading of these books will benefit you quite little. Get the surrendering done. These works are all intended to help the pilgrim along the way, but you must already be started along the correct path.

Be Earnest

Another important aspect is to come with a sense of earnestness. These writers assume that the readers are serious. They are not writing to satisfy the curiosity of those who have no earnest intention of putting into practice the teaching. These books are for the souls of those who thirst for God—and only God. The books will not entertain you. None of them were written with entertainment or amusement in mind.

I have read many of these books and I have never found any of them to be fun. Each one has taken me deeper or higher into the presence of God, and the way is not an easy one. It is not for the fainthearted. Rather, it is for those who want to know God and care not about the price. There is no "fun" in these books, but you can be sure there will be plenty of glory for those who pursue their teachings in earnest.

Read Slowly

Another point needs to be established here. I highly recommend that you never read more than one chapter in a day. It is impossible to hurry through these books and receive the full benefit that they possess. Slow down, meditate long and hard on each and every chapter, paragraph, sentence and, yes, even word. These books are to be studied, meditated on, marked up, prayed over and read as long as they continue to minister to the soul.

Assemble a Library

There are in Christian literature those books that can be read once and then forgotten. Sir Francis Bacon wrote, "Some books are to be tasted, others to be swallowed, and some few to be chewed and digested: that is, some books are to be read only in parts, others to be read, but not curiously, and some few to be read wholly, and with diligence and attention." These great Christian classics fall under the last category.

I highly recommend assembling a library of these books to be read and meditated on for the rest of your life. It seems highly improbable to me that anybody would ever outgrow the richness found in these volumes.

The journey is rough. The path we have to tread is one filled with danger and trouble in difficulties. Only a trustworthy guide can help us along the way and enable us with great victory to live the crucified life.

Hiding in Thee
William O. Cushing

O safe to the Rock that is higher than I,
My soul in its conflicts and sorrows would fly;
So sinful, so weary, Thine, Thine, would I be;
Thou blest "Rock of Ages," I'm hiding in Thee.

Hiding in Thee, hiding in Thee,
Thou blest "Rock of Ages,"
I'm hiding in Thee.

In the calm of the noontide, in sorrow's lone hour,
In times when temptation casts o'er me its power;
In the tempests of life, on its wide, heaving sea,
Thou blest "Rock of Ages," I'm hiding in Thee.

How oft in the conflict, when pressed by the foe,
I have fled to my refuge and breathed out my woe;
How often, when trials like sea billows roll,
Have I hidden in Thee, O Thou Rock of my soul.

THE PURPOSE OF THE REFINER'S FIRE IN THE CRUCIFIED LIFE

If it be so, our God whom we serve is able to deliver us from the burning fiery furnace, and he will deliver us out of thine hand, O king. But if not, be it known unto thee, O king, that we will not serve thy gods, nor worship the golden image which thou hast set up.

DANIEL 3:17-18

God has in His arsenal an infinite number of tools that He at His discretion employs to accomplish His perfect purpose in our life. Of course, the prevailing question is, what is God's purpose in our lives? The answer to that one question will open up a whole world of understanding concerning what God is doing in our circumstances.

Some have the idea that God's purpose is to make our lives more tolerable here on earth. That rather cheapens what Christ did on the cross. If all He wanted to do was make our lives tolerable, then He could have done it in a variety of other ways. God's supreme purpose for us is to make us like His Son, Jesus Christ. If we understand that everything happening to us is to make us more Christlike, it will solve a great deal of anxiety in our lives.

If, on the other hand, we have the idea that God's purpose is to make this life heaven on earth, then God has a lot of explaining to do. It is not happening. The way is rough, and the pathway is littered with all kinds of distractions and disturbances along the way.

Throughout this book, I have referred to the cross as an instrument to accomplish God's purpose, His ultimate purpose in our life. I now want to refer to another tool that goes along with this: the Refiner's Fire. Let me point out the difference between these two. The cross deals with our self-life; to put self on the cross and have it absolutely crucified under Christ. But the Refiner's Fire takes a different approach. The purpose of the Refiner's Fire is to burn away all the bondage imposed on us by the world.

When I talk about "the world," I am not referring to the mountains and valleys and the meadows and the forest. I am talking about the spirit of this world that is diametrically opposed to everything that God represents. The spirit of this world is supervised by none other than the enemy of our soul, even Satan himself, which the Scriptures refer to as the "prince of the power of the air" (Eph. 2:2). The apostle Paul also refers to him as the god of this world:

> In whom the god of this world hath blinded the minds of them which believe not, lest the light of the glorious gospel of Christ, who is the image of God, should shine unto them (2 Cor. 4:4).

Even as God the Father did not spare His own Son the pains and the sufferings of the cross, so too God will not spare us any pain in bringing us to that ultimate place of Christlike-ness. As the author of Hebrews states:

> For whom the Lord loveth he chasteneth, and scourgeth every son whom he receiveth. If ye endure chastening, God dealeth with you as with sons; for what son is he whom the father chasteneth not? (Heb. 12:6-7).

A casual perusal of the Scriptures will bring one to the con-clusion that God is never in a rut. For the most part, He rarely repeats Himself. There was only one Daniel in the lions' den; only once did three Hebrew children get cast into the fiery fur-nace; and God only appeared once in a burning bush to a man. God, in His infinite wisdom and at His complete discretion, deals with His people to bring them to His appointed place.

The Refiner's Fire is simply an instrument by which God ac-complishes His purposes in our lives. We are never to worship fire. Remember that Israel fell into idolatry by worshiping the brazen serpent that stopped the death angel. The brazen serpent was only to remind them of what God had done, but they be-came more enamored with the object than the God behind the object. We are to allow God to use whatever instrument or tool He chooses to accomplish His purpose. Again, that purpose is to bring us to a point of absolute Christlikeness, because it is through the Son that He is glorified.

To understand God and His nature is to understand that nothing impure can stand before Him. Therefore, in dealing with us as sons and daughters, we must meet His standard of purity. Nothing impure, nothing from this world, nothing con-trary to the nature and character of God can be left in our lives. Some aspects of our lives are so resistant to God's grace that it necessitates fire to burn it completely out of our lives.

Requirements of the Crucified Life

In Daniel 3, we read the story of the Babylonian king Nebuchadnezzar who had an image of gold made and ordered all of the people in his kingdom to bow down and worship it. When Shadrach, Meshach and Abednego—men who served the Lord—refused to bow to the image, the king had them thrown into a fiery furnace. The actions of these three Hebrew children reveal several aspects that are crucial to living the crucified life.

Obedience

First, Shadrach, Meshach and Abednego were obedient to the Lord. Obedience is a primary component of the Christian life. Note that their obedience did not require them to know why this situation was happening to them, nor did it require God to do everything according to their understanding. I am sure they had no idea of why all of a sudden the tables had been turned on them. They had been good servants of Nebuchadnezzar, and he had honored them by placing them in positions of authority. Now everything seemed to be going against them.

As you think of this story, keep in mind that their obedience to God was what got them in trouble in the first place. It was the door into the furnace. As I have previously mentioned, somewhere along the line Christians have developed the idea that if they obey God it will keep them out of trouble. Yet that is not the purpose of obedience. In looking at the lives of the men and women of the Old and New Testaments, and even throughout Church history, we find that it was obedience that often got them into difficulties.

I referred earlier to Dietrich Bonhoeffer. His obedience sent him straight to the gallows. He could have escaped, but it would have required him to compromise his relationship to God, which was something he would never have thought of doing.

True obedience is the refusal to compromise in any regard our relationship with God, regardless of the consequences.

Keep in mind that the god of this world does not mind if you believe in God. "Thou believest that there is one God; thou doest well: the devils also believe, and tremble" (Jas. 2:19). The devil believes in God, so you are on the same page as him. He does not even mind if you worship God, provided you also worship the gods of this world. As long as you believe in God as millions of Americans do today and do not make Him the number one exclusive priority in your life, the devil has no issue with you. The evangelical church today is following the course of the liberal movement and going down the same pathway of compromise. One compromise here, another compromise there, and soon there is very little, if any, difference between the so-called Christian and the man in the world.

True obedience, as illustrated in the story of the three Hebrew children, always brings us to a point of no return. This is where faith comes in. We do not have to understand what is happening in order to obey God. We do not need to know the outcome in order to obey God. As a matter of faith and trust, we obey God simply because He is God. This obedience brings us to a point of a personal resolution where we do not have to be delivered from our trouble.

Obedience is recognizing God's sovereignty and authority and submitting to it without question and without regard to consequence. We see this aspect of complete obedience in the lives of Shadrach, Meshach and Abednego when they said, "Our God whom we serve is able to deliver us from the burning fiery furnace . . . but if not, be it known unto thee, O king, that we will not serve thy gods, nor worship the golden image which thou hast set up" (Dan. 3:17-18). Their obedience did not depend on God rescuing them from a hard place. They knew He could, but if He did not rescue them, it had no bearing upon their absolute obedience to God.

Surrender

The three Hebrew children's absolute obedience to God brought them to a place of ultimate surrender to the situation at hand. We do not like to talk about this. We want to talk about God delivering us from hard places so we can say, "Glory to God, He rescued me." But surrender means nothing of the sort.

The essence of surrender is getting out of the way so that God can do what He wants to do. So often we are in a position that God cannot do His work. Then we stand around wondering why nothing is happening. Nothing is happening because we are standing obstinate to God in refusing to surrender to the situation at hand.

Nebuchadnezzar was kind enough to give the three Hebrew children an opportunity to reconsider their position. After all, the world's philosophy is that you have to give a little to get a little. He tried to make it easy for them. In the natural, they were in a position where their allegiance to Nebuchadnezzar would have gone a long way toward helping the people of Israel. It would only have cost them a little compromise here or there. That is how the world works, but it is not how it works in God's kingdom.

One thing the three Hebrew children understood was who was supreme ruler in this world. Nebuchadnezzar thought so highly of himself, but he posed no threat to these Jewish men whose allegiance and loyalty was to God alone. Some would have us believe that by surrendering to a situation we are exercising a cowardly act. The only person who would buy into that philosophy is one who does not know the ways of God. While it is true that there are times when we need to stand against a certain situation or problem—when repudiating the situation is the order of the day—we must never confuse that with an opportunity to surrender in such a way that we get out of God's way and allow Him to do in us what He wants to do through us.

The furnace represented the worst the world could do. In fact, Nebuchadnezzar was so angry with these Jewish men that he ordered the furnace turned up seven times hotter than before. Then he commanded these Jewish men to be bound and cast into the fiery furnace. As Shadrach, Meshach and Abednego surrendered to the flames of that furnace, they were stepping into God's arena.

I note with a great deal of satisfaction that Nebuchadnezzar's men, whose job it was to throw these Jewish men into the fiery furnace, were the only ones consumed by that fire. In fact, the only thing the flames consumed was Nebuchadnezzar's men and the Hebrew children's bonds. That which was of the world, Nebuchadnezzar and the bonds, were absolutely consumed by the flame of that furnace. But nothing of God's was ever harmed.

> And the princes, governors, and captains, and the king's counsellors, being gathered together, saw these men, upon whose bodies the fire had no power, nor was an hair of their head singed, neither were their coats changed, nor the smell of fire had passed on them (Dan. 3:27).

I do not see why the world has any attraction for anyone. Anybody who can read anything about history will understand that the world always destroys its own. Joshua understood this when he told the Israelites, "If it seem evil unto you to serve the LORD, choose you this day whom ye will serve; whether the gods which your fathers served that were on the other side of the flood, or the gods of the Amorites, in whose land ye dwell: but as for me and my house, we will serve the LORD" (Josh. 24:15). If you want to follow the god of this world, Joshua said, then go for it. But, as he testified with great confidence, he and his house would serve the Lord. He understood that the world always turns on its own.

Nebuchadnezzar's men were destroyed because the three Hebrew children obeyed God and surrendered to the furnace. How in the world can you defeat such men as these? How can you threaten them into submission? The flame had caused no damage to them at all. That was the astonishing thing as far as Nebuchadnezzar was concerned. That which he had designed to destroy God's men had backfired and only destroyed his men.

If only we could get this into our head. If only we could truly believe that God has an agenda in this world and that we are part of that agenda. Although the circumstances of our life are opportunities for God to defeat the world, the only thing standing in the way is the hesitant Christian demanding that God rescue him from any trouble. But it is trouble that enables God to get the glory.

The same flame that consumed the natural world and the bondage imposed by the world on the Christian is the same flame that purifies the Christian. The fire burns out the impurities and brings the gold to a state of purification. The more intense the flame, the purer the gold.

Revelation

Thus, if we desire to live the crucified life, we must completely submit in obedience to the Lord and surrender our lives to God's authority so that He can do His work. Once we are out of His way, He then has the opportunity to reveal Himself to us and to the world around us as in no other way. Often, the only way the world can see Christ is through revelation brought by the Christian's experience in the Refiner's Fire.

After Shadrach, Meshach and Abednego had been thrown into the flames, Nebuchadnezzar looked into that furnace and saw something he never expected to see. He thought these flames that he had built would consume the men. Instead, not only did he see them alive and unharmed, but he also saw a fourth man in the furnace.

> Then Nebuchadnezzar the king was astonished, and rose up in haste, and spake, and said unto his counsellors, Did not we cast three men bound into the midst of the fire? They answered and said unto the king, True, O king. He answered and said, Lo, I see four men loose, walking in the midst of the fire, and they have no hurt; and the form of the fourth is like the Son of God (Dan. 3:24-25).

Oh, see that fourth man in the flame! That is the revelation of God. What does it take to experience God in this way? It takes a furnace. It takes obedience to God and submitting to Him in absolute surrender. That is all.

The Joy of God's Presence

The fire in the furnace reveals Christ in the midst of His people, sharing their fellowship. The flame of Nebuchadnezzar's furnace did not overcome the fragrance of God's presence. Imagine the joy of those men in the flames. There is no joy comparable to that joy of being in a place where God joins you in sweet fellowship. Never in the marketplace. Never on the mountaintop. Remember Peter on the Mount of Transfiguration. He wanted to set up a couple of tents, forget the rest of the world and enjoy fellowship with God. But the value of the mountaintop experience is revealed in the valley below in which we must tread.

The revelation of God is the fruit of the flame. How many times have we missed the fragrance of God's presence because we resist the furnace and the tribulation and the suffering before us? We have it all worked out. We read a couple of verses of Scripture and say, "I believe." That settles it. We think we can then go on our merry way to heaven, whistling "When the Saints Come Marching In." We want to be coddled on our way to heaven and have an easy life. We want to make sure that we are going to go to heaven when we die, but in the meantime we want to enjoy the pleasures of the world.

There is no revelation of God in following that path. There is no experiencing the fragrance of God's presence. There is no burning of the bonds that the world has imposed upon us, setting us free to follow our Lord. Yes, we walk by faith. But occasionally there are some glorious moments in which God reveals Himself to us. I tell you, this is holy ground. This is an area of sacredness incomparable to anything else this side of glory.

Keep in mind that God has a vision for us beyond the furnace. The fires serve its purpose, burning away the bonds of the world and purifying our relationship with God, and then we move on. Shadrach, Meshach and Abednego walked out of that furnace. Imagine the testimony they would have the rest of their lives. They certainly were creatures out of the fire. They were men who had met God in the wondrous, glorious fashion incomparable to anything else in their lives. They were counted worthy to suffer for Christ.

If we are ever going to see God in the fullness of His manifestation, we must be like these men. We must obey Him implicitly and surrender in such a way that He can place us where He wants to place us in order to show us what He wants to show us. And what He does to us He will also do through us to confound the wisdom of the world, who cannot figure out what we are.

God's most delicate tools are reserved for His special children. For the Christian on the path of the crucified life, God will bring into his pathway the fiery furnace, the Refiner's Fire, and show that Christian how much He really loves him.

Nothing Between My Soul and the Savior
Charles Albert Tindley (1851–1933)

Nothing between my soul and the Savior,
Naught of this world's delusive dream;
I have renounced all sinful pleasure;
Jesus is mine, there's nothing between.

Nothing between my soul and the Savior,
So that His blessed face may be seen;
Nothing preventing the least of His favor,
Keep the way clear! Let nothing between.

Nothing between, like worldly pleasure;
Habits of life, though harmless they seem,
Must not my heart from Him e'er sever;
He is my all, there's nothing between.

Nothing between, like pride or station;
Self-life or friends shall not intervene;
Though it may cost me much tribulation,
I am resolved; there's nothing between.

Nothing between, e'en many hard trials,
Though the whole world against me convene;
Watching with prayer and much self-denial,
I'll triumph at last, with nothing between.

Follow Tozer's new writings on Twitter at
http://twitter.com/TozerAW

Books by A.W. Tozer

More Wisdom From A.W. Tozer

Compiled and Edited by James L. Snyder

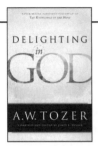

Never before published, this is the message A.W. Tozer intended to be the follow-up to his seminal work *The Knowledge of the Holy*. Drawn from his sermons, Tozer's teaching reveals how the attributes of God are a way to understand the essence of the Christian life—worship and service. Discover how to allow His character to be reflected in all that you do!

Delighting in God

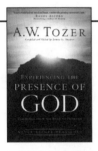

What does it mean to dwell in God's presence? How do you get there? This collection of Tozer's teachings on the book of Hebrews shows you the way. As you explore this epistle's sweeping grasp of history and the "hero stories" within, you'll be led to experience the presence of God.

Experiencing the Presence of God

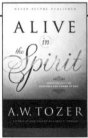

In this dynamic and biblical work, Tozer explores life in the Spirit. Though every Christian has the Holy Spirit, not every Christian is filled with the Spirit. You'll learn the difference and how, if we use the gifts of the Spirit with wisdom, the evangelical church can change the world.

Alive in the Spirit

BETHANYHOUSE

Also From A.W. Tozer

Compiled and Edited by James L. Snyder

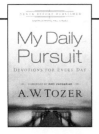

Let A.W. Tozer guide you in your pursuit of God with this 365-day devotional, full of never-before-published insights from a renowned servant of God. This book will challenge and inspire your heart and mind to truer worship, greater faith, deeper prayer, and more passion for Christ.

My Daily Pursuit

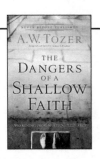

In this never-before-published compilation, A.W. Tozer warns believers in Christ against the great danger of spiritual lethargy. He calls us to awaken to the times in which we live and stand boldly against spiritual and moral slumber. Discover the spiritual change the Holy Spirit can bring to your life—and never grow weary in your pursuit of God!

The Dangers of a Shallow Faith

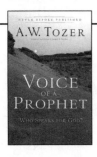

A.W. Tozer breaks down common misconceptions about who prophets are and what they do, revealing that their primary role today is—as it was in the Bible—to proclaim God's truth to believers, leaders, and the culture.

Voice of a Prophet

⬧ BETHANYHOUSE